Against Inequality

Against Inequality

The Practical and Ethical Case for Abolishing the Superrich

TOM MALLESON

OXFORD
UNIVERSITY PRESS

Oxford University Press is a department of the University of Oxford. It furthers
the University's objective of excellence in research, scholarship, and education
by publishing worldwide. Oxford is a registered trade mark of Oxford University
Press in the UK and certain other countries.

Published in the United States of America by Oxford University Press
198 Madison Avenue, New York, NY 10016, United States of America.

CIP data is on file at the Library of Congress

ISBN 978–0–19–767040–8 (pbk.)
ISBN 978–0–19–767039–2 (hbk.)

DOI: 10.1093/oso/9780197670392.001.0001

Paperback printed by Marquis, Canada
Hardback printed by Bridgeport National Bindery, Inc., United States of America

This book is dedicated to my mentor and friend Erik Olin Wright,
who is too soon returned to stardust.

Contents

Acknowledgments

Every book is a river of ideas formed by the confluence of hundreds of capillary streams representing the perspectives, knowledge, and wisdom of others. My debts to those who have helped me with this work are many and profound.

The original suggestion to write this book came from my PhD supervisor, mentor, and friend, Joe Carens. Though it turned out to be a much larger endeavor than either of us had originally intended, I am deeply grateful for the initial nudge.

The weaknesses and limitations of this book would've been far more substantial were it not for the generous feedback provided by a number of friends and colleagues. A sincere "Thank you!" to Reuven Avi-Yonah, Victoria Barnett, Fred Block, David Borman, David Calnitsky, Joe Carens, John Christman, Daniel Aldana Cohen, Steve D'Arcy, Bilge Erten, Marc Fleurbaey, David Gamage, John Grant, David Gray-Donald, Magnus Henrekson, Lane Kenworthy, Andres Knobel, Tammy Kovich, Chi Kwok, David Lizoain, Christopher Mastrocola, Gabe Oatley, Simon Pek, Sarah Perret, Seth Prins, Kavita Reddy, Ingrid Robeyns, Michael Rosen, Jakob Egholt Søgaard, David Wachsmuth, Bruce Waller, and Tingting Zhang. In particular I want to thank Kole Kilibarda for his immense efforts and penetrating insights; this book would not have been the same without him. Many thanks as well to Angela Chnapko and the team at Oxford University Press.

Neither this book nor any other life project would be possible without the understructure of care and support that undergirds my (and everyone's) life. In particular, I am deeply grateful to Leah Henderson, Rob Tarantino, Lindsey Levy, Sidney and Jules Tarantino, Sarah Malleson, Michael Rosen, LJ and Alex Malleson, and especially Roey Malleson. Thanks to Isabelle Ferreras, whose kindness, care, and unfailing support over the past few years have been incredible. Thanks also to my lovely partner, Mina Etezadi, for all the love and support and for letting me bore her to death about the importance of taxes.

Introduction

Elon Musk, the CEO of Tesla and the richest person in the world, currently possesses $270 billion dollars.[1] The median American worker would have to work for seven and a half million years to earn this much. To put the matter the other way round, the total amount of money that a typical American will earn in their whole life—after, say, 40 years of work—is the same as would be earned by Musk in just 14 minutes.[2] During the first six months of the COVID-19 pandemic, 250,000 Americans died and 20 million lost their jobs in the worst economic crisis since the Great Depression, yet the country's 614 billionaires saw their wealth actually increase by a third, from $2.95 trillion to almost $4 trillion (Manjoo 2020). Across the world, the richest eight individuals possess the same amount of wealth as half the entire planet—three and a half billion people (Oxfam 2017). Never across the entire expanse of human history has such a level of inequality been seen before.

In the rich, economically developed countries, the past 30 years have witnessed a general worsening of inequality. In some countries, such as Denmark and France, inequality has increased only a small amount, while elsewhere, such as the United States and the United Kingdom, it has exploded (Piketty 2014). In the Anglo-American countries, inequality is now at levels unseen for 100 years. In the United States, the Gini coefficient—i.e., the percentage of total income that would need to be redistributed to obtain complete equality—is 42% (the most equal countries in the world by this measure are Iceland and Slovenia, at about 26%, and the most unequal is South Africa, at 63%) (World Bank 2017). From 2010 to 2015, the richest 1% of the American population received (before tax) 20% of the country's income (Piketty 2020, 421). In 2015, the top 0.01% had an average income of $31.6 million, nearly 2,100 times more than a minimum-wage worker's average income (Pizzigati 2018, 32). According to economic historians, this inequality is worse than that of the Roman Empire—where at its height in the middle of the second century, the top 1% controlled 16% of total income (Scheidel and Friesen 2009, 81)—and also worse than in Russia in the years leading up to the world's first anticapitalist revolution (where the top

Against Inequality. Tom Malleson, Oxford University Press. © Oxford University Press 2023.
DOI: 10.1093/oso/9780197670392.003.0001

1% controlled roughly 18% [Novokmet, Piketty, and Zucman 2018, 213]). At a global level, the top 1% controls about 29% of total income (Milanovic 2016, 41).[3]

As stark as such inequalities of income are, inequalities of wealth are even worse. The top 1% of Americans own 40% of the country's wealth, whereas the bottom 40% own virtually nothing, at 0.2% (Piketty 2020, 422; Wolff 2010; see Figure I.1). Globally, the top 1% controls 46% of total wealth (Milanovic 2016, 41). By himself, Musk has a total net worth (in 2022) of $270 billion. This means that if he sits back, puts his feet up, and simply invests his fortune in the stock market, he will continue to earn (at a standard 5% return) roughly $13.5 billion every year. And this in a country where 550,000 people are homeless (US Department of Housing 2018).

Wrapping one's head around the scale of this inequality can be difficult. One useful illustration is that of the Income Parade.[4] Imagine that you are on the sidewalk watching a giant parade. Over the course of one hour the entire society will walk by, starting from the poorest and ending with the richest. Imagine also that each person's height is proportional to their income—the richer one is, the taller—so the median person in the very middle of the parade, with a median income of $36,000, will also be the median height (which for American adults is 5'6").

Now imagine that you are standing at the side of the parade. What would you see? For the first 12 minutes you would see only wave after wave of little people, all less than 2 feet tall. Not only is everyone very short, but at this stage the parade is dreadfully monotonous—with every minute that goes by people are barely getting any taller at all. After 30 minutes, the parade is now halfway over, and people are finally 5'6", and still things remain quite boring. After 40 minutes, the people are over 7 feet tall, and by 54 minutes they are 18 feet. At the very end of the parade, however, the giants appear. At 59 minutes and 24 seconds, we see the top 1%, who are 70 feet tall, the height of a seven-story building. And now with every instant that passes they are growing exponentially taller. In the last few microseconds we see the richest 0.001%—they are 1.4 miles tall, the equivalent of seven Eiffel Towers stacked on top of each other. Finally, Musk is an astounding 390 miles tall—his head reaches above the International Space Station.[5]

Another useful model for conceptualizing inequality is one I call the Parliament of Income. Imagine a House of Parliament consisting of 100 seats, where the seats are distributed according to income. In the United States, this would mean that the poorest third of the population have only 6 seats; the

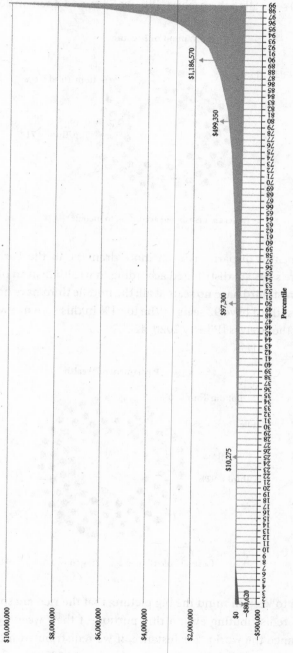

Figure I.1 The distribution of family wealth in the United States in 2016 (Urban Institute 2017).

middle third have 23 seats; and the richest third have 71 seats.[6] (The top 1% would have 20 seats all to themselves [Piketty, Saez, and Zucman 2018]).

Parliament of Income

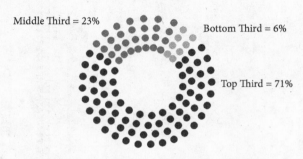

(seats are distributed according to income)

Once again, this disparity is even more dramatic in the Parliament of Wealth (where seats are distributed according to wealth instead of income). Here the poorest third have no seats at all; the middle third have only 8 seats; and the richest third have 92 seats.[7] (The top 1% in this scenario would have 40 seats all to themselves [Piketty 2020, 422]).

Parliament of Wealth

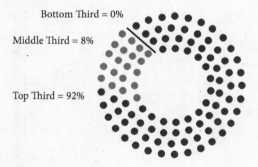

(seats are distributed according to wealth)

It is useful to keep in mind the big picture: that the rich are so extremely wealthy that redistributing even a tiny portion of their wealth could dramatically change the world. For instance, if we redistributed merely 2% of the wealth of the world's billionaires, thus leaving 99.99997% of the world's population completely untouched, we could entirely eliminate extreme poverty around the world.[8] Moreover, the billionaires would barely notice, as 2% is substantially less than they likely earn in a year, meaning this tax could be levied annually and their total wealth would actually continue to increase! In the United States, if we taxed only two individuals—Jeff Bezos and Bill Gates—at 2% of their wealth, it would be possible to completely eradicate American homelessness (again, their total wealth would not diminish).[9]

Furthermore, at least in the rich countries of the Global North, there is already so much wealth, workers and machines are already so productive, that it is entirely feasible for everyone to have all that they need from only a few hours of work. Consider the facts: if, miraculously, the United States were to transform itself tomorrow into a radically egalitarian country, spreading income and working hours evenly among the working population, then every adult could have the same median income that exists today, while benefiting from even better public services than exist in Sweden, plus a basic income, with each worker needing to work only three and a half hours per day![10] In pure material terms, our societies are already rich enough to provide the conditions for good and flourishing lives for all. In stark contrast to the long scope of history, when the deprivation that people suffered was the inevitable result of scarcity, the deprivation that exists today is fundamentally different because it exists side by side with abundance. Deprivation today is neither natural nor inevitable; it is manufactured, the result, ultimately, of political choice.

Clearly contemporary inequality is vast. The key question, however, is whether any of this matters. Is inequality truly a serious problem?[11] Many think not. Robert Nozick (1974) famously argued that inequality is completely justified when it is the result of free and voluntary transfers of property between consenting adults. Any attempt to establish egalitarian patterns of distribution is inherently tyrannical. Taxation, he wrote, is actually akin to slavery; it is "on a par with forced labor" (169). From a different direction, Greg Mankiw (2013) is the latest in a long line of thinkers to argue that inequality is morally appropriate because it simply reflects one's "just deserts."[12] "In the standard competitive labor market" he says, "a person's earnings equal the value of his or her marginal productivity" (30). The incomes of Steve Jobs, J. K. Rowling, and the One Percent are morally deserved, he argues, because they simply reflect the enormous contributions made to our welfare (21–22). Many prominent economists have amplified the notion that inequality is not an important area of concern. For instance, Nobel Prize winner Robert E. Lucas (2004) argues, "[O]f the tendencies that are harmful to sound economics, the most seductive, and in my opinion the most poisonous, is to focus on questions of distribution." Such ideas are of course the bread and butter of neoliberal and conservative politics, but they have also become prominent among middle-of-the-road politicians, as seen in President Bill Clinton's assertion "We do not resent people amassing their own wealth fairly won in a free enterprise system" (quoted in Pizzigati 2004, vii), and Peter Mandelson's (Tony Blair's cabinet minister) declaration "[We are] intensely relaxed about people getting filthy rich" (quoted in Pizzigati 2018, 12).

What motivates this belief that inequality is acceptable? Four major arguments are offered, two of which are practical, and two of which are ethical in nature. First and foremost is the Feasibility Argument: that it is simply not possible to significantly reduce inequality through the tax system—the rich will always be able to avoid taxation through loopholes, sending their money to tax havens, or emigrating. Raising taxes, according to this argument, is like squeezing one part of a giant balloon—the money will simply rush somewhere else. Only fools waste their time whistling against the wind in complaining about inevitability.

The second argument, which we will call the Cost Argument, is that even if it were possible to reduce inequality by raising taxes, doing so actually creates more costs than benefits because it incentivizes the rich to work less, save less, and invest less, leading to slowed economic growth, unemployment, and ultimately reduced prosperity for all—including the poor.

The third argument, the Merit Argument, is that people (particularly, rich people) morally deserve their income because it reflects their contribution to the economy, and thereby the well-being of others. Redistributive taxation therefore undermines one's just deserts.

The fourth and final argument is the Libertarian Argument, which holds that individuals rightly possess private property and often choose to voluntarily exchange it (e.g., in the market for other goods or services). Such exchanges typically generate inequality. But since they are the result of free exchange, it would be wrong to interfere. Taxation, in this account, amounts to governmental theft.

These arguments represent the four cornerstones of the justification of inequality. The primary goal of this book is to take such arguments seriously by analyzing each one in a careful and open-minded way.

The four arguments dovetail with a widely shared intuition that if there is a problem with the distribution of income and wealth in capitalist society, the core problem is not inequality but poverty. In philosophical writing, the doctrine that what matters is not inequality per se but poverty is referred to as "sufficientarianism."[13] In Harry Frankfurt's (1987, 21, emphasis added) words, "Economic equality is not, as such, of particular moral importance. With respect to the distribution of economic assets, what is important from the point of view of morality is not that everyone should have the same but that each should have enough. *If everyone had enough, it would be of no moral consequence whether some had more than others.*"

Conservatives frequently argue along analogous lines: if poverty is the problem, then the natural solution is economic growth. If poverty is what really matters, and the poor are getting richer (even slowly), then we can conclude that things are getting better overall; it becomes irrelevant if the rich are becoming far richer (e.g., Lucas 2004). The implication of such a perspective is that we can simply ignore the skyrocketing accumulations of the rich. In other words, to the extent that the focus is on poverty, questions about the legitimacy of the superrich—Is their income deserved? How does their wealth impact the rest of us?—simply fall off the radar. Such a conclusion is presumably deeply comforting to rich people.

On the other side of the debate, egalitarians strenuously disagree that inequality is unimportant. They typically view inequality as a distinct and independent problem that cannot be reduced to poverty.

The first and perhaps most important issue that egalitarians point to is that inequality risks undermining political democracy. The richer that elites become, the more they are able to use their wealth to lobby government; promote their favored politicians; hire armies of political activists; purchase newspapers, TV channels, and think tanks to amplify their views; and otherwise extend their political power (Gastil and Wright 2019). Not only does this undermine the foundational principle of democracy—equal influence over government; it creates a vicious cycle whereby economic power begets political power, which in turn can be used to shape the market in ways that allow rich people to become even richer, creating a spiral of mutually reinforcing power (Reich 2015).[14]

For one example, in the United States, where it is well-documented that the rich have come to have more and more disproportionate political influence (Gilens and Page 2014), it is noteworthy that the tax system has been significantly reworked to benefit them. Today the tax rate that is legally applied to capital income (i.e., income from capital assets like stocks, bonds, and real estate) is substantially lower than the tax rate paid by regular working people on their income. Indeed, in 2007 the average tax rate for the richest 400 households was only 16.6%, while it was 20.4% for taxpayers in general (Stiglitz 2012, 72). The billionaire Warren Buffett famously pays a lower tax rate than his secretary (ABC News 2012). An even graver concern is the ways in which the rich have been able to use their political clout to stymie desperately needed environmental regulations (minimizing carbon taxes, maintaining enormous fossil fuel subsidies, removing the United States from the Paris Accords, etc.). Economic inequality risks propelling democracy into plutocracy.

A second problem with inequality is that it arguably undermines the widely cherished ideal of equal opportunity. In unequal societies, children living on different sides of town, sometimes only a mile apart, grow up in effectively different worlds, with different possibilities and horizons of opportunities before them (Chetty, Hendren, Kline, Saez, et al. 2014). A superrich family may own multiple vacation homes scattered around the world, a private jet, indoor swimming pools, and employ cooks, cleaners, gardeners, private tutors, etc., while a poor family down the street may live in a dilapidated, rat-infested, crumbling apartment block with an empty fridge and lead in the water, shivering from an inability to pay the heating bill. Indeed, economists find a clear correlation between increased inequality and reduced social mobility: the greater a country's inequality, the less opportunity there is to advance (Andrews and Leigh 2009; Chetty, Hendren, Kline, and Saez 2014; Kearney and Levine 2014). Not only do the poor have fewer opportunities to live good lives, but they have less opportunity to live at all: if you happen to live in Englewood, a poor neighborhood in Chicago, your life expectancy will be an astonishing 30 years shorter than if you were lucky enough to live across town in the richer Streeterville (Lartey 2019).

As inequality worsens, so too does the amount of social friction. Eventually the very fabric of the community can start to tear. The bottom looks up with anger and resentment while the top looks down with contempt and mockery. In such conditions the cauldron of social life risks boiling over. Witness the riots in 2007 in the poor Parisian suburbs, as well as those on British highstreets in 2011. In both cases, poor, often racialized youth rioted, burned bus stops, broke store windows, and stole merchandise, such as expensive sneakers. Though there was undoubtedly a range of causes of these riots— racial ones in particular—the economic factors were clearly important too. When asked, the explanations given by the rioters were typically those of resentment of police brutality, feeling excluded from mainstream society, and the overarching frustration of being continually told by a materialistic society that the good life was the rich life, while simultaneously being denied any real possibility for achieving such riches (Abbas 2011; Equality Trust 2012; Phillips 2015). Countries with the most extreme inequality tend to have little "community" to speak of, if what we mean by community is neighbors sharing a similar lifeworld and interacting with trust and in peace; what they have instead is perpetual, simmering class conflict, which can at any moment violently explode. In South Africa, one of the most unequal countries in the world, the rich often live in gated communities, behind barbed wire, with patrolling security guards, leaving their homes only in bulletproof cars, frequently living in fear of armed robbery (Govender 2017). In Brazil, another extremely unequal country, so-called lightning kidnappings have become increasingly common, where rich people are kidnapped at gunpoint, taken to an ATM, drained of their cash, and then released (OSAC 2012).

We will see that there is extensive empirical evidence demonstrating that inequality tends to undermine social solidarity, making people less generous and less willing to help their neighbors, which not only worsens the quality of social life but also undermines the cohesion necessary for collectively funding a welfare state. Inequality also dampens civic engagement, fuels political corruption, worsens mental health, and increases a variety of crimes (including property crime and homicide; see Chapter 3).

For all of these reasons, egalitarians disagree that poverty is the only problem of economic distribution. Inequality matters too. Indeed, egalitarians view the conservative position as not merely incorrect in terms of the importance of inequality, but as deeply immoral in its apparent denigration of the foundational ideal of equal human worth. The basic egalitarian intuition is something like this: All human beings share the same fundamental parameters of existence—we are all born on this small planet in a remote corner of the Milky Way, living for a brief moment before perishing forever. Having one and only one life to live makes each life equally precious and entitled to equal concern. Each and every one of us has a life that matters. Therefore, all of us should have at least roughly similar access to the conditions necessary for living good and flourishing lives. To be denied such equal access is to be denied our birthright of equal worth. For egalitarians committed to this basic moral position, many of the conservative arguments about deservingness, merit, self-ownership, incentives, tax havens, and investment rates appear to be little more than rationalizations and subterfuge, because egalitarians simply cannot accept that the vast inequalities in life opportunities existing today are truly compatible with a belief in the equal moral worth of all.

Clearly the debates over inequality are fraught. Which side is right? That is a difficult and complex question with no easy answer. If this book, through careful examination of both sides of the argument, is able to advance our understanding of these issues by even a small amount, it will have been well worth the effort.

Let me lay my cards on the table. Although the moral issues are complicated, and some of the empirical data is difficult to interpret clearly, the balance of evidence leads me to conclude that the conservative justifications of inequality are, ultimately, unconvincing and should be rejected.

In its broadest form this book reaches two major conclusions. First, not only is it eminently feasible to reduce inequality, but the benefits of doing so outweigh the costs, likely by a lot. Practically all of the economic concerns with high taxation boil down to one thing: a worry about growth rates measured in terms of aggregate GDP. The need for never-ending economic growth is the siren song of our age. Yet I hope to convince the reader that such costs are overblown. On the one hand, the economic costs of imposing high levels of taxation are very unlikely to be catastrophic (due to the growth-promoting potential of redistributive public spending); on the other hand, the seriousness of the ecological crisis—the existential game-changing nature of the crisis—means that reduced growth of output is not obviously a bad thing, and may in fact be a good thing (at least for the rich countries, and at least to the extent that it can be disconnected from unemployment and economic insecurity).

The benefits of high taxes and inequality reduction are truly massive, and much more significant than is commonly appreciated. We will explore a number of important, though perhaps secondary benefits, such as reducing government debt and enhancing economic stability and employment (after all, the real danger of reduced growth is instability and unemployment, not reduced GDP per se). Beyond this, there are at least five areas of enormous benefit: meeting the urgent needs of the world's poorest, mitigating climate catastrophe, protecting democratic equality, reducing the threat of far-right populism and fascism, and expanding equal opportunity. Such benefits are difficult to overstate.

Furthermore, one of the major ideas of this book is that although the kind of reforms that we need to reduce inequality are substantial, they are perfectly feasible within the broad parameters of some kind of regulated capitalist system. No revolution is required. Even though I am personally sympathetic to the notion that the long-term goal should be to move beyond capitalism—by democratizing the economy and transforming the market system to be far more socially and ecologically just—investigating such changes would take us far beyond the scope of the present book.[15] My goal is much more modest: to try to persuade the reader that here and now, in the short to medium term, within the constraints of capitalism and without jumping into the unknown, much less inequality is perfectly feasible.

Granted, some anticapitalists will be frustrated with this approach. They will wonder, "If you recognize that capitalism is the root of the problem, why not focus on replacing it altogether with a better system?" My response is simply that the existing chasm between the world as it is and the world as I would want it to be is so great that no one book could ever investigate more than a tiny fragment of the needed change. We would require thousands of different kinds of books (and, perhaps even more important, other kinds of media), investigating all the myriad parts of the needed changes—the institutional, the empirical, the normative—focusing on different scales and different contexts and written to convince different audiences. At some point every author suffers the disappointment of realizing that writing for one audience immediately closes one off from others. But that is life. This book is aimed at a specific audience: university-educated residents of Anglo-American countries who are open to progressive ideas but are by no means radicals or revolutionaries. There are of course other vitally important audiences. But to reach them is the task of other books and other authors.

Hence Chapters 1 and 2 address the question of whether it is really possible to reduce inequality. The historical and comparative evidence from different countries provides us with relatively clear lessons about what works and what doesn't. Reducing inequality is indeed feasible; in many cases, we have good examples to emulate. (Although the focus is mainly on taxation, we look at a number of additional mechanisms that can also help to reduce inequality.) Chapter 3 examines the Cost Argument and ultimately concludes that the costs of significantly reducing inequality through high levels of taxation, though real, are, all things considered, far outweighed by the benefits.

The second major conclusion of this book is that, from a moral perspective, inequality at its current levels is indefensible. Not only should we reduce inequality substantially, but we should consider the bold step of setting maximum limits on income and wealth. In other words, it should be illegal to be a billionaire. Such people should not of course be physically harmed, but their excess wealth should be redistributed to those who need it far more. Chapters 4 and 5 investigate the Merit Argument, inquiring whether individuals morally deserve the income they receive in the market. Chapter 6 engages the Libertarian Argument by analyzing the issue of private property and whether the right to own, transfer, and exchange such property naturally justifies inequality.

The underlying ethical argument of this book is that people, and especially rich people, do not morally deserve their income because such income does not mainly derive from anything the individual does but is much more due to what I call the vast "understructure" of other people's prior labor. Beyond this, I will argue that we should also reconsider the standard assumption that individuals morally deserve rewards for their talents and efforts, because when we consider them closely we see that in fact talent and effort are themselves rooted in all kinds of luck, which some individuals happen to possess far more than others. The conclusion is that we should entirely abandon the commonplace notion that people deserve economic rewards because of the contribution they have made, since all of our abilities to contribute are always inextricably dependent on the fortune of genes and circumstance. This is indeed a radical conclusion as it flies against the common assumptions of most people. Yet I will try to persuade the reader that such a conclusion actually follows quite straightforwardly from a basic belief in fairness—that it's wrong for some people to have significantly better lives than others due to factors that are beyond their control.

Furthermore, this deep fact—that each of us is a unique product of random combinations of genes and social circumstance—is true about every single one of us. This uniqueness is one of the core respects in which all human beings are the same. All of us, equally, live finite and unique lives. That is the heart of what makes our lives equally precious and of equal moral value. And it's this equality of moral value—that your life matters and is just as important as mine—which explains why, ultimately, the economic things that each of us get in our lives (our income, public services, etc.) should be roughly equal (though of course not completely equal since different people, with diverse bodies and circumstances, will require different amounts of resources to achieve similar levels of flourishing). We should all get roughly the same amount because what really matters is not any empirical fact about what any of us are able to *do* (since that is arbitrary) but the moral fact of who we *are*: equal members of the human family. Another way to say this is that we should talk much less about what people "deserve" and much more about what they "need" to live good and flourishing lives.[16]

How much inequality is acceptable? The overarching argument of the book is that since people's talents, skills, and efforts are, at the end of the day, arbitrary from a moral point of view, their economic rewards should be largely equalized. All people, regardless of their skills or efforts, should be guaranteed the essential goods necessary to live a good and flourishing life, a position which I call Good Life Egalitarianism (GLE) (Malleson 2022). However, the goal should not be complete equality for at least two important reasons. The first is that different people with different bodies and circumstances will typically require somewhat different amounts of money and public services in order to equally flourish; e.g., a mobility-impaired person requires a wheelchair and an accessible bus system that an able-bodied person does not. Second, on practical grounds some level of income inequality is useful and necessary for providing incentives to make the market system work well (which is important for providing other things we have good reason to value, such as allocative efficiency, motivation to work hard and innovate, and increasing productivity allowing for increased well-being and leisure in the future).

For such reasons I argue in Chapter 7 that the goal should not be complete equality but a radical compression of inequality. The problem is not simply that the poor have too little, but that the rich have too much.[17] What is required, in other words, is limits to wealth. Leveling down is not the tyrannical policy that conservatives often imply, nor does leveling down in income or wealth necessarily imply leveling down in well-being—particularly for the rich; in many cases, it is ethical, sensible, and compassionate policy. I argue that the highest income one can earn should be limited to, say, 10 or 20 times the minimum wage (implying a maximum wage of $200,000 or $400,000 per year) and the maximum wealth that anyone is ever allowed to accumulate should be limited to roughly 200 or perhaps 400 times the median wealth (i.e., $20 million or $40 million). By the end of this book I hope to convince the reader that moving in this direction would provide huge social benefits at relatively low economic cost.

The idea that we need not just minimum but also *maximum* wages is unusual but not unheard of. Indeed, the idea stretches right back to the classical beginnings of Western thought; the wisdom of income limits seemed obvious to both Plato (who thought the ideal ratio between the richest and the poorest should be no more than 4:1) as well as Aristotle (who preferred a ratio of 5:1) (Pizzigati 2004). What should the threshold be? I must admit at the outset that any specific threshold will be somewhat arbitrary; there is no ideal ratio that makes perfect sense in all contexts. A threshold of 10:1 is no more sacrosanct than that of 5:1 or 15:1. Nevertheless, that does not obviate the importance of establishing *some* definite threshold. Notice that in other domains we necessarily and successfully impose many limits on human activities—speeding limits, minimum wages, campaign contribution limits, minimum age of consent—all of which are vitally important, even though the exact threshold chosen invariably remains somewhat arbitrary. We do not say that we must forgo establishing an age of consent because the choice of 18 years is somewhat arbitrary (Why not 17 or 19?), because we recognize that having *some* threshold is more important than being able to prove that there is a perfectly "right" one, which likely doesn't exist anyway. The argument is analogous for the case of maximum income and wealth. Although there will inevitably be strong disagreement as to what exactly the threshold should be, the importance of establishing *some* threshold is, I hope to show, compelling.

A central purpose of this book, therefore, is to insist on the importance of answering the following all too rare questions: What threshold for maximum income and wealth do *you* think is acceptable? Is a 10:1 income ratio compatible with democracy and social justice? What about 50:1? 100:1? 1,000:1? The reason such questions matter is that as inequality increases, the possibility of equal access to the good things in life, as well as the meaningfulness of our democracy, decreases. Presumably everyone would agree that a society in which the top 1% owned 100% of the income and wealth, and everyone else owned nothing would be unacceptable. Where, then, should we draw the line? A central goal of this book is to encourage lively conversation about what this threshold should ideally be. Such questions should be asked by each of us; they should be debated around the dinner table, in community meetings, on talk shows, and, of course, in the chambers of government.

The book is structured to start with the feasibility questions before moving on to the ethical questions. Philosophers will wonder why it is not the other way around. The answer is that most readers' main concern with egalitarianism is likely to be practical—that reducing inequality doesn't seem particularly feasible—so it makes sense to deal with this concern first. Moreover, the ethical chapters delve deeply into some of the complex philosophical debates, and since those debates may not be to everyone's taste, they are not forefronted.

Three chapters investigate the empirical economic evidence, and four engage in deep philosophical debates, yet despite the disparate literatures involved, I have tried to keep the writing as accessible as possible. As we shall see, the debates are sometimes intricate, but there is nothing overly technical or requiring extensive background study. Whether I have succeeded in illuminating the complex arguments while maintaining accessible language is, of course, for others to judge.

There are, of course, very many important topics that this book does not discuss. Every book inevitably brackets most of the world. In order to stay a reasonable length, this book will focus mainly on issues of inequality at a domestic level. There are, of course, vital issues of global inequality to explore, but they raise somewhat different questions (such as whether we require new global governance structures to engage in international taxation and redistribution and whether working-class people in rich countries could be persuaded to reduce their income in favor of much poorer people in other countries). Although I am sympathetic to many of the ideas and ideals of global egalitarianism, it would take us too far afield to fully engage those issues here. That said, the limits of what is possible for a specific country are often determined by global realities—due to things like tax havens—so even though our focus will be mainly on the domestic arena, we will discuss global issues as it is necessary to do so.

Finally, although this book focuses on economic inequality, that should absolutely not be taken to imply that this is the only or most important type of inequality that exists. There are numerous modalities of inequality in contemporary societies—based on race, gender, sexuality, ability, etc.—which are just as important and just as foundational to social life as economic inequality. Moreover, these different types of inequalities are often highly interrelated. Improving economic inequality would in many cases dramatically improve the lives of racialized people, women, queer people, trans people, individuals living with a disability, and others. We should never forget that those who are the poorest among us, and those who suffer the most from the harms of inequality, are not "poor people" tout court; they are poor precisely because they are racialized, gendered, disabled, and otherwise marginalized in various ways. In the United States, for instance, women working full time earn 81.8% of the wages of men working full time. Hispanic women earn only 62.2% of White men's median earnings, while Black women earn only 67.7% (Hegewisch and Williams-Baron 2018). Individuals living with a disability earn, on average, only $22,047 annually, a full $10,000 less than non-disabled people, and only 35.9% are employed (compared to the median employment level of 76.6%) (Kraus et al. 2018, 2–3).

Since current levels of economic inequality are highly racialized and gendered, economic justice issues are inherently issues of racial and gender justice too. Indeed, one of the most important ways to fight for racial or gender justice is to fight for economic justice. Doubtless, the most marginalized groups in society require a variety of different kinds of reforms to improve their quality of life—most of which are beyond the scope of this book. However, one of the most crucial things that they all require is being lifted from the bottom of the economic hierarchy and reducing the oppression from the top—and to those issues this book has much to say.

1

Is It Feasible to Reduce Inequality?

Income Tax and Market Regulations

Many people are sympathetic to the idea that inequality is too great and should be reduced. However, there is also widespread skepticism about whether it is possible to do so. These first chapters examine the two most common practical justifications of inequality. This chapter and Chapter 2 examine the idea that it's simply not feasible to reduce inequality; Chapter 3 examines the idea that even if it were possible, doing so would be a bad idea because the costs of redistributive taxation would outweigh the benefits.

Before beginning it will useful to clarify in our minds the major components of what generates inequality in the first place. Early in life, inequality is generated through different amounts of *inheritance*. Throughout one's working years, inequality can be compounded by *labor income*. Over time, inheritance, labor income, and capital income (i.e., income earned from the ownership of stocks, bonds, etc.) can further accumulate as stocks of *wealth*, which are typically reinvested and tend to accumulate ever further. Finally, all of these components will be impacted by the *tax and transfer system*.

Tackling inequality, therefore, will require addressing each of these major areas. Accordingly, this chapter proceeds by investigating the major tools available to us for reducing income inequality, in particular, income tax (on labor and on capital) and market regulations (particularly those that are crucial in the shaping of the labor market). In the next chapter we examine major tools for reducing wealth inequality: inheritance tax and wealth tax (as well as the related issue of tax havens). For each of these tools, we will ask how feasible it is for governments to use them in order to reduce inequality, always striving to steer clear of the twin dangers of naïve optimism ("It's easy to fix this!") on the one hand and apathetic cynicism ("Nothing can be done!") on the other. We will see that in some cases we already have good, concrete examples of what can be done. In other cases, we don't yet have good

Against Inequality. Tom Malleson, Oxford University Press. © Oxford University Press 2023.
DOI: 10.1093/oso/9780197670392.003.0002

examples, and so the task is to envision, carefully and cautiously, systems that would likely work (e.g., by learning lessons from unsuccessful examples).

The first section analyzes the possibility of high income taxes; the second analyzes the major labor market reforms that could reduce income inequality; and the third briefly describes a handful of other important tools for reducing inequality.

One important caveat is in order before beginning, which is that questions of feasibility have at least two main dimensions (Wright 2010). On the one hand there is the question of *achievability*—asking about the political and social forces arrayed for and against the proposal in question. On the other hand, there is the question of *viability*—asking whether the institutions, once successfully established, would actually work as intended. It is this second dimension of feasibility that concerns us here. The question of achievability is of course vital, but since it is inherently a context-specific question (what is achievable next year in, say, Sweden is very different from what is achievable in the United States), it is one that we must bracket here; whether progressives are powerful enough to get strong egalitarian policy passed by government will depend completely on the specific country and timeframe in question.

Reducing Inequality through Income Tax

Is it possible to reduce inequality through high, potentially very high, income taxes—with top rates of, say, 70, 80, 90, or even 100%? The first place to look for an answer is the historical record. History, of course, does not prove anything—past possibility is no guarantee of future viability, since times may have changed and things which worked at one point may no longer be possible. Nevertheless, nothing is more illuminating for expanding our sense of the feasible than seeing how other people did things in different times and places, which is why the study of history can be such a useful antidote to the dead weight of cynicism, awakening us to the immense malleability of human institutions and the vast scope of alternative possibilities.

Interestingly, even though the United States is widely seen today as the epicenter of low-tax neoliberalism, it was actually instrumental in inventing progressive taxation in the first place (Saez and Zucman 2019e). The United States was the first country in the world to introduce top marginal tax rates above 70%—first on income from 1919 to 1922, then on estates from 1937 to 1939 (Piketty 2014). In 1942, shortly after the attack on Pearl Harbor,

President Franklin Roosevelt actually called for a 100% marginal income tax rate, declaring, "In time of this grave national danger, when all excess income should go to win the war, no American citizen ought to have a net income, after he has paid his taxes, of more than $25,000" (quoted in Brownlee 2000, 57–58). In today's dollars this would represent a maximum income of roughly $385,000 (about 18.5 times the minimum wage[1]—a radical proposal indeed). Roosevelt didn't get his maximum wage, but he did get something close. During World War II, the top tax rate was raised to over 90%, reaching a high of 94% in 1944–1945. All told, for nearly half a century, 1932–1980, the top federal income tax rate in the United States was 81% (Piketty 2014).

Although these rates were very high, it is important to realize that there is a significant (and sometimes very sizable) difference between the *statutory* legal rate and the *effective* rate that individuals actually pay after all the various loopholes are exploited.[2] And, of course, it's the effective rate, not the statutory rate, that actually matters for reducing inequality. In the case of the United States, the loopholes have frequently been so large that the actual tax rate the rich were paying was substantially lower. For instance, in 1952 the top marginal rate on the richest 1% of households was 91%, whereas the effective rate was only 32.2%. By the 1960s the effective rate was about 25%, and it didn't change much in subsequent years (Brownlee 2000, 61). It has been estimated that in the mid-1960s millionaires were paying only 19% of their total income (Auten, Splinter, and Nelson 2016).

In other words, other than for a brief period during World War II, the United States has not had very high income taxes on the rich. That said, the United States may well be an outlier here. As Scheve and Stasavage (2016) show, in other rich countries the gap between effective and statutory rates are, in many cases, substantially smaller than in the United States.

Figure 1.1 shows that outside of the United States, the statutory tax rate often is a fairly good proxy for what the rich actually pay (they always pay less than the statutory rate, but often not drastically less). Many countries are indeed able to force the rich to pay their taxes.

Moreover, while the United States has never had very high effective *income* tax rates on the rich, it would be a mistake to conclude that it has never succeeded in taxing the rich aggressively. In fact, the United States did successfully implement high taxes on the wealthy at various points. For instance, throughout the 1960s and 1970s, total tax rates were indeed quite high, though this was mainly due to high rates on *corporate tax* as opposed to income tax. (The main difference between US tax rates in the 1960s and

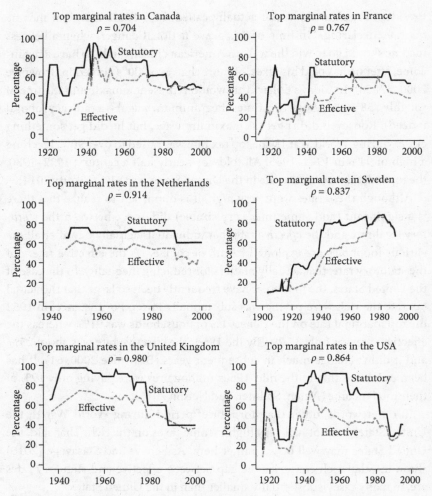

Figure 1.1 Top statutory and effective income tax rates on the top 0.01%; 0.05% for the Netherlands and United Kingdom (Scheve & Stasavage, 2016, 61).

today is mainly due not to a drop in individual tax rates but to the collapse in corporate rates [Saez and Zucman 2019e].) Moreover, when we look at taxes more broadly (combining income tax with poll taxes, estate taxes, and, most important, the corporate tax) we see that the total federal *effective* tax on the richest 0.01% in 1970 was a whopping 74.6% (Piketty and Saez 2007, 13). For every dollar a millionaire made, in other words, they paid 74.6 cents to the state. This is the important point: although infrequent, high taxes are not at all unprecedented, even in the United States.[3]

In the United Kingdom during the 1950s and 1960s the top marginal rate was 90%, while the effective rate (in 1970) for the top 0.05% was estimated to be 69.2% (Piketty and Saez 2007, 18). This is a very high rate indeed. To see this, recall that the highest marginal rate doesn't apply to all your income, but only to the top portion. To give a simplified example, if one has a total income of £300,000, and there is a 30% tax on the first £100,000, a 70% tax on the income £100,000–£200,000, and a 90% tax on the income £200,000–£300,000, the overall effective tax rate works out to 63%. In other words, the fact that the British effective rate was so high—69%—implies that rich people really were paying their taxes. The 90% statutory rate was working because, unlike in the United States, these high rates were not undermined by deductions and loopholes. Indeed, the effective rate of total taxes (income tax, estate tax, and payroll tax) on the top 0.05% in 1970 was a staggering 91.7% (Piketty and Saez 2007, 18).

Another good example of successful implementation of high levels of taxation is Denmark. The historical zenith of the marginal income tax rate in Denmark was almost 100% in 1967 (Atkinson and Søgaard 2013, 18). Still today, high taxes are common. For instance, the "participation tax rate," which is the effective average tax rate on labor force participation due to income taxes, payroll taxes, consumption taxes, and means-tested transfers, stands at an impressive 87% (Kleven 2014). More broadly, if we look at total taxation—i.e., the amount of total revenue that the government taxes from all sources—we see that Denmark (along with Sweden) has had the highest level of tax in the world over the past 40 years; total taxes peaked in 2014 at a massive 48.53% of GDP, meaning that the government, through all its taxes, successfully collects roughly half of the entire economic output of the country (OECD 2018b). Of course, these taxes do not all fall on the rich, but large amounts clearly do.

Overall, the income share of the Danish top 1% fell quite consistently from 1870 (when they received about 20% of the country's income, the same as what currently happens in the United States) to receiving only 6.4% in 2010 (see Figure 1.2; Atkinson and Søgaard 2013, 13). This is a powerful illustration of what is possible, and a compelling rebuttal to those who believe that intentional, planned inequality reduction is impossible (cf. Scheidel 2017).

Along with Denmark, arguably the best example of high taxation is that of Sweden. For 50 years, from the 1940s to the 1980s, the top statutory rate

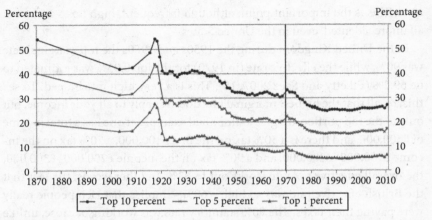

Figure 1.2 Top income shares in Denmark 1870–2010 (Atkinson and Søgaard 2013, 12). *Note*: The vertical line in 1970 indicates the change from family to individual taxation.

was over 70%. When one combines the income tax paid at the state and local level, plus social security contributions paid by employees, the top marginal tax rate reached 85% in the late 1970s (subsequently falling to about 55% by 2009 [Stenkula, Johansson, and Du Rietz 2014, 177]). As seen in Figure 1.1, Scheve and Stasavage (2016) estimate the effective income tax rate in the 1980s for the top 0.1% to be roughly 80%. Such rates helped Sweden attain, by the mid-1970s, the lowest level of inequality of any modern rich country that we have data for (Piketty 2014). For example, if you were a business owner in Sweden in the early 1970s, paying yourself a salary out of dividends, you would have been compelled to pay 52% corporate tax, in addition to 75% dividend tax (the same rate as was imposed on top labor income), plus an additional 1.2% wealth tax—all of which meant that your total business tax bill would add up to about 95% of profits (Henrekson 2017). In terms of total taxation by the government, Sweden holds the record for the highest level of overall taxation that the rich countries have ever seen, at 49.48% of GDP in 1987 (OECD 2018b).[4]

Over the past 30 years, tax rates have dropped in many places with the spread of neoliberal ideas and the increasing mobility of businesses putting downward pressure on corporate tax rates. Yet even today there are still good examples of high tax rates. Looking at the top effective marginal rate (i.e., the total tax paid on the last dollar earned by a high-income worker, which Fritzon and Lundberg calculate by combining all social security contributions, payroll taxes, consumption taxes, and income taxes), the authors find that the highest contemporary rate in the world is Sweden's, at 76%. Four other countries have rates above 70%: Slovenia, Belgium, Portugal, and Finland. By contrast, the UK rate is 59%, 55% in Canada, and 47% in the United States (Fritzon and Lundberg 2019, 11).

In sum, implementing very high taxes on the rich is entirely possible. Historically, we have seen instances of very high marginal income tax rates—even above 90%. Moreover, the evidence shows that these rates have been real—the rich actually pay them. (Even in the United States, high rates existed for many years, once we combine all forms of taxation.) Moreover, as numerous authors have documented, these high rates really have successfully reduced overall inequality (Atkinson and Søgaard 2013; Clark and Lawson 2008; Hungerford 2012; Piketty and Saez 2007; Piketty, Saez, and Stantcheva 2014). To take just one of the many examples, Clark and Lawson (2008) demonstrate that a 10-percentage-point increase in top marginal tax rates concretely results in a 4-point reduction in the Gini coefficient. (A 4-point difference is roughly the difference between the inequality that exists in the United Kingdom and that in Austria.)

These historical facts should reassure us that it is indeed possible to tax the rich in order to reduce inequality. Of course, such evidence can only be suggestive. The fact that high taxes were possible in the past does not guarantee that they are possible now. For instance, one might worry that the mobility of capital or new avoidance techniques are now so sophisticated that high tax rates have become impossible. Is that the case?

The two most prominent obstacles to successfully imposing income taxes on the rich are avoidance and emigration. Let us analyze these issues in turn.

Avoidance and Evasion

The basic lesson from the past 30 years of tax research is that tax changes have a clear and unambiguous impact on *avoidance*[5] but an unclear and ambiguous impact on *real effects* (such as effort, amount of hours worked, and level of private investment [Diamond and Saez 2011; Goolsbee 2000; Meghir & Phillips 2008; Saez, Slemrod, and Giertz 2012]). So while it is unclear whether, or to what extent, the wealthy respond to high taxes by actually working less or investing less (we analyze the existing evidence in Chapter 3), there is no doubt that they clearly do try to avoid and evade taxes: they try to find loopholes, they arrange their affairs so that their income comes in a form which is taxed less, they shift the timing of when their income is realized—in short, they do whatever they can to reduce their tax payments as much as possible (Auten, Splinter, and Nelson 2016). Indeed, in many cases, the loopholes are so large, and the evasion opportunities so straightforward, that the rich can easily avoid paying a lot of tax. Hence the billionaire Leona Helmsley's famously candid declaration, "We don't pay taxes. Only the little people pay taxes" (quoted in Sweeney 2015, 6).

What enables tax avoidance and evasion? There are three main factors.[6]

The first is the extent of third-party reporting, meaning the extent to which one's income is directly reported to the tax authorities by a third party, such as an employer, a bank, or a financial institution. It is widely known that tax enforcement is excellent whenever third-party reporting is in place. And conversely, when there is no third-party reporting (e.g., in the case of self-employed earnings or small cash payments), tax evasion will typically be endemic. In the United States, for instance, a tax compliance study by the Internal Revenue Service (IRS) in 2012 found that the evasion rate for personal income is 56% when there is "little or no" information reporting, yet it is less than 5% when there is substantial third-party reporting (Kleven, Kreiner, and Saez 2016). Kleven et al. (2011) find similar results for Denmark.

The upshot is that there tends to be little tax evasion for working-class and middle-class people because their income comes almost entirely from their employers, who automatically report such income. (The exception is the self-employed, where avoidance is much more common.) The rich, on the other hand, frequently acquire their income from a variety of different sources. The portion of their income that comes from salaried employment, say, as upper management in a firm, will be third-party-reported and so not evaded. But other parts of their income may come from a variety of other sources, such as interest payments, dividends, and appreciation on mutual funds and derivatives, which may not be subject to rigorous third-party reporting, allowing greater scope for tax evasion.

So the first step in preventing avoidance is instituting rigorous third-party reporting for all income. This already exists for most people—those whom Helmsley calls the "little people"—but it needs to be extended to other types of income, for instance, by having banks and money managers compelled by law to report the income of their clients directly to the tax authorities. There would clearly be significant political opposition to this from the rich, but there is nothing technically difficult about doing so, since essentially all that is involved is the forwarding of income statements (which banks and money managers already possess) to the tax authorities. Indeed, the financial data that we require already exists: financial institutions already have electronic records of all their transactions, and wealthy individuals already receive regular income statements. All that is needed is mandated, regular forwarding of this information to the public authorities.

The second key factor is the breadth of the tax base (i.e., the extent of income and other assets that are subject to taxation). The more exemptions, loopholes, and deductions there are, the smaller the tax base. For instance, if one type of income (e.g., stock dividends) is taxed at a lower level than other kinds of income (e.g., salary), then upper managers and CEOs will do their best to rearrange their income so that they get paid more in dividends and less in salary, and hence pay less tax overall. Such income shifting is very common among the rich. In the contemporary United States, the top federal income tax rate is 37%. In reality, however, most rich individuals pay far less than that. The main reason why is that wealthy people typically own a lot of capital, and the tax rate on capital income (such as capital gains, dividends, selling a business) is 23.8%, significantly lower than the tax rate on labor income (Hemel 2019). This is why Warren Buffett pays a lower rate than his secretary. This is a bizarre fact about the American system that is worth emphasizing: people who earn their money from *laboring* pay a significantly higher tax rate (almost double) than people who earn their money from *investing*. This is perhaps the most important loophole to shut. In order to be able to raise income tax rates to high levels, rich people need to be prevented from avoiding tax by simply shifting their income into other sources. To accomplish this, the essential tax principle needs to be that *all types of income—in particular, income on capital—must be taxed at the same (or at least roughly similar) levels.*[7]

There is nothing impossible about doing this. For instance, the Tax Reform Act of 1969 raised rates on capital gains to bring them closer to ordinary rates. And again in 1986, the major tax reform closed many of the prevalent loopholes and eliminated the previously existing gap between tax rates on capital and those on labor income (Auten, Splinter, and Nelson 2016). A number of other countries have adopted this principle of taxing all income at the same rate. For instance, the 2018 IMF report for Denmark finds that "the combined rate on dividends, including the CIT [corporate income tax] paid before distribution, reaches 54.8 percent, which is very close to the top rate on labor income" (64). And look again at the case of Sweden in Figure 1.1: from roughly 1970 to 1990 the effective rate was *nearly identical* to the statutory rate—and this at extremely high levels, up to 80%—demonstrating that it is entirely possible to close loopholes and deductions if the political will exists to do so.

The third factor which determines the scope of tax avoidance is the extent of enforcement. In many jurisdictions, there is simply not enough effort expended to investigate rich people's tax claims, and the penalties for defrauding the tax system are far too weak to motivate compliance. In the United States, for example, the IRS is frequently unable to investigate the tax compliance of the rich because of insufficient resources. In 2017, the IRS had only 9,510 auditors—down from over 14,000 in 2010. Indeed, the last time the IRS had fewer than 10,000 auditors was in the mid-1950s. In 2017 the IRS audited only 4.4% of returns with income of $1 million or higher, less than half the audit rate from a decade prior (Sarin and Summers 2019).

Reducing this aspect of avoidance is quite straightforward: simply increase the resources of the tax collectors. Instead of the meager 4.4% of rich people being audited, I would advocate increasing this to 20%, so that every rich person knows that they will be audited roughly once every five years.[8] That would be effective deterrence; if rich people knew that they wouldn't get away with evasion, they would surely attempt to do far less of it. Taking a step back, it's remarkable to recall that in no other area do we allow widespread criminal activity to continue simply because we can't be bothered to hire sufficient numbers of police officers. Of course, hiring more auditors will cost more money, but the Congressional Budget Office estimates that spending an additional $20 billion on enforcement in the next decade would bring in $55 billion in additional tax revenues, and these estimates don't even include the indirect deterrent effects of greater enforcement, which the Treasury Department has estimated are three times higher. Indeed, it has been estimated that every extra hour spent auditing someone who earns more than $1 million a year generates an extra $1,000 in revenue (Sarin and Summers 2019). In other words, hiring more auditors pays for itself. In their study of Norway, Alstadsæter, Johannesen, and Zucman (2018) found that by increasing its enforcement effort, the Norwegian government successfully reduced tax evasion and raised tax revenue by 30% (a rise which was sustained over time). Their conclusion is that "cracking down on evasion by the wealthy can be an effective way to raise tax revenue, increase tax progressivity, and ultimately reduce inequality" (3).

The other aspect of the enforcement problem is that tax fraud is often dealt with by little more than a slap on the wrist. In 2018 there were only 517 convictions for tax fraud in the entire United States; that represents a minuscule 0.03% of rich households (i.e., households in the top 1%). We don't know the proportion of rich families that are engaging in tax fraud, but it is likely to be orders of magnitude higher than this. For instance, in Norway, in exchange for amnesty, fully 11% of the richest individuals in the country voluntarily declared they were engaged in tax fraud (Alstadsæter, Johannesen, and Zucman 2018). This suggests that the current US system is dramatically failing to catch those who are stealing from the public purse. Moreover, only 68% of convictions led to prison, and the average sentence was 17 months. Forty-four percent of offenders were White and 36% were Black (USSC 2019c). Compare this to more conventional low-level robbery, where 58% of offenders are Black and only 24% are White; 99% of these offenders were sentenced to prison, and the average prison sentence was 107 months—six times longer (USSC 2019b). And as if that wasn't egregious enough, note that the median loss for tax fraud was $309,000, whereas it was only $2,100 for robbery. In other words, even though tax fraud is simply a different kind of robbery (stealing from the public), and even though it involves much larger amounts of money than conventional robbery, it is punished far less, likely because it is the wealthy who are committing the crimes as opposed to suffering from them. The disparity is similar for the "crime" of selling marijuana, a drug which scientists say is mostly harmless (Nutt et al. 2007). Here 91% of offenders were sentenced to prison, with an average sentence of 29 months, which is a sentence 40% longer than for tax fraud (USSC 2019a). Even more dramatically, the American Civil Liberties Union (ACLU 2013) has found that more than 3,200 people across the country are actually serving life sentences without parole for nonviolent offenses. Of those prisoners, 80% are behind bars for drug-related convictions; 65% are African American, while only 18% are White—evidence of what the ACLU calls "staggering racial disparity." The crimes that led to life sentences include stealing gas from a truck, shoplifting, possessing a crack pipe, facilitating a $10 sale of marijuana, and attempting to cash a stolen check (6, 21). There is thus an astounding asymmetry in how the US judicial system currently treats tax fraud compared to other nonviolent crimes (particularly those committed by poor and racialized people). A Black man stealing a chocolate bar risks being thrown in jail, while a White man stealing a million dollars from the state through sophisticated tax fraud is more likely to be given only a stern warning (if not a job offer from PricewaterhouseCoopers).

Opponents of taxes on the rich often discuss avoidance and evasion as if they are perfectly reasonable behaviors. For instance, Aaron Wudrick (2019) opposes taxing the rich on the insouciant grounds that, "[w]hen the wealthy leave a jurisdiction, they're not paying any taxes there anymore. Trying to squeeze a little more comes with the risk of getting nothing." Likewise, Chris Edwards argues, "Wealth taxes encouraged avoidance, evasion, and capital flight" (2019, 1). Such cavalier sentiments are extremely common, but note the implication: that it's the attempt to levy a tax that is the problem, not the criminal act of evasion itself, which is portrayed as natural and inevitable. In contrast, imagine if one were to say "Anti-theft laws simply encourage theft to be committed underground and in other jurisdictions." Clearly such a position would be absurd. It is not the laws that are the problem, but the underlying unethical activity.

In my view, society should be clear and forthright that tax evasion is a serious, morally reprehensible crime. As will be argued in later chapters, what tax evasion really represents is direct robbery from the community—the result of which is to deprive people, particularly poor people, of their right to hospital beds, clean classrooms, and affordable homes. Tax theft should be seen not only as a serious crime but as a *more serious* crime than petty theft, personal drug use, or other such nonviolent infractions—and so should have more serious consequences. Instead of locking up poor Black men for smoking marijuana and letting billionaires simply pay a meaningless fine for facilitating mass tax evasion, it would be more sensible for the severity of consequences to be reversed. What exactly should be done to tax evaders? That is a difficult question. Some jurisdictions will presumably wish to use jail as their main source of punishment and deterrence for those convicted of large-scale tax fraud on the grounds that few things are as likely to concentrate the mind of billionaires and their accountants as the prospect of being dragged out of their office in handcuffs. In my judgment a less carceral approach would be preferable; this might involve the perpetrator having their personal wealth confiscated, having their professional employment licenses revoked, perhaps being declared legally bankrupt, and being required to perform several years of community service. (Such an approach would have as its aim not hurting or punishing, but deterring and disincentivizing, as well as repairing some of the damage done.)[9] Each jurisdiction will have to decide for itself how best to deal with tax criminals, but the basic moral principle is clear: tax evasion is a worse crime—more dangerous and more damaging—than petty theft or personal drug use, and so should be treated as such.

Another important point is that prosecutions for tax evasion should be levied not only against the principal evader; there should also be significant consequences for those who helped to facilitate the evasion, such as the accountants, bankers, and money managers—as well as strong legal protections for whistleblowers. The general principle of tax enforcement should be to penalize the *facilitators* as well as the principals.[10] This is vitally important because it's the existence of the massive estate planning industry that allows widespread evasion to happen in the first place. In particular, the "Big Four" accounting firms constitute an important part of what has been called the "wealth defense industry" (Ajdacic, Heemskerk, and Garcia-Bernardo 2021; Winters 2017);[11] a crackdown on their tax evasion activities is crucial.

In sum, it is clear that evasion is a real obstacle to raising taxes on the rich. If a progressive government were to raise income taxes to high levels, but make no other kinds of policy change, we would undoubtedly see massive avoidance and evasion and, subsequently, much less reduction of inequality than hoped for. That said, we have a clear understanding of how to effectively prevent large-scale avoidance if we so choose: implement extensive third-party reporting, broaden the tax base by closing loopholes, and increase enforcement efforts. Indeed, this is not merely theoretical; the evidence shows that when these things are done, it is entirely possible to raise taxes to high levels in the real world. The Scandinavian countries are good examples (Kleven 2014). For instance, experts have noted that Denmark is able to successfully implement such high taxes on the rich because of these elements: it has strong enforcement through wide third-party reporting—about 95% of all income is third-party-reported, where tax evasion is virtually zero; it also has a broad base, with limited loopholes and deductions (Kleven and Schultz 2014). As a result, the overall evasion rate is extremely low—only 2.2% of income (Kleven et al. 2011). Likewise, the examples of the high effective tax rates in the United States during World War II, the United Kingdom in the 1960s, and Sweden in the 1970s provide strong evidence that, when the political will exists to do so, it is entirely possible to tighten the tax system to significantly prevent evasion. The bottom line is that reducing inequality requires raising taxes *and simultaneously* reducing avoidance opportunities. It is not feasible to do the former without the latter. Yet this is not unrealistic, as an electorate willing to support high taxes would presumably have no hesitation about simultaneously reducing avoidance, which is, after all, a less controversial policy.

Emigration

Although avoidance is the most important obstacle to collecting high rates of income tax, another important issue is emigration. The worry here is that the rich will flee their home country to live where the tax rates are lower. And indeed, the rich have always threatened this. For instance, in 1894 Ward McAllister, a wealthy New Yorker, threatened that if Congress were to levy a 2% (!) income tax, it would drive "rich men to go abroad and live" (Pizzigati 2004, 495). Sometimes the rich really do leave; famous cases include those of Gérard Depardieu, Björn Borg, and Michael Schumacher, all of whom quit their home countries in order to pay less tax (Buch-Hansen and Koch 2019).

These headline cases aside, is emigration a genuine worry? Theoretically, there are strong motives on both sides. On the one hand, emigrating may result in lower taxes and so significantly increase one's wealth. On the other hand, there are serious costs: it is difficult to remove one's fixed assets without paying tax; there is often cultural pressure to avoid looking like a social pariah; and importantly, for most it is a very unhappy choice to abandon one's home, where one has family, friends, community, and years of intimate connection. Moreover, although rich people typically don't love high taxes, they often do want to live in a society where high taxes are paid—so that their neighborhoods are safe, the schools are good, the infrastructure is solid, and there are high levels of social trust and low levels of civil discontent.

The empirical evidence is also mixed. Young and Varner (2011) find no evidence that American millionaires leave their state to avoid the imposition of "millionaire taxes" (even though that is a far easier thing to do than leaving one's country). Pizzigati (2018) points out that even among billionaires—those who presumably have the most extreme incentive to emigrate—only 13% reside outside their nation of birth, and of those, only a third left for a tax haven.

On the other hand, Akcigit, Baslandze, and Stantcheva (2016) find that top tax rates do significantly impact the location of "superstar inventors." They find that a 10% decrease in top tax rates translates into a 26% increase in foreign superstar inventors. Likewise, Moretti and Wilson (2017) find that tax rates exert a significant effect on the geographical location of star scientists.

That said, it is hard to gauge the relevance of the Young and Varner (2011) and Moretti and Wilson (2017) studies for our purposes because the tax rates in question are much lower than the ones we are envisioning here, so there might be *more* of an effect than the studies suggest; then again, it is presumably much easier to move out of state than leave the country, suggesting that there might be less of an effect than the studies imply.

Probably the most powerful evidence comes from two studies by Henrik Kleven and collaborators. Kleven, Landais, and Saez (2013) studied the location decisions of wealthy soccer players and found a large effect of tax rates. Similarly, Kleven et al. (2014) found large effects of high-income foreign workers moving to Denmark in response to a specific tax cut. They concluded that "the scheme had a very large effect on the number of highly paid foreigners in Denmark" and that "incentives to offer tax havens for highly skilled workers are likely to generate tax competition across European countries. This will require international coordination and the design of rules regulating such special schemes" (336, 376). However, the authors also point out that while higher taxes do discourage high-income foreigners from moving to Denmark, they largely do not encourage Danish natives to leave— which is important for overall tax capacity, since it's the native population that pays the overwhelming share of tax revenue.

In sum, the weight of the evidence does seem to suggest that, without any preventative measures, a country which introduced very high income taxes would likely suffer from significant emigration of the rich.

What, then, are some practical policies that could help to reduce the risk of emigration? Three stand out. First, countries should emulate the kind of law which already exists in the United States, where the IRS levies an income tax on the worldwide net income of its citizens, regardless of where they currently reside (Avi-Yonah 2013; Westin 2013). This means that rich individuals cannot escape US taxes by setting up shop or investing in a foreign country.[12] With such a policy in place, individuals could escape taxation only by renouncing their citizenship. Needless to say, that is quite a serious thing to do, as it means that they forfeit their right to live and work in their home country, lose the right to visit friends and family without a visa, and give up diplomatic protections. Nevertheless, some rich people may desire to do this, so a second important policy would be to impose a significant exit tax on those renouncing their citizenship (at least for those with substantial wealth). This too is eminently feasible, as seen by the example of Section 877A of the Internal Revenue code, which imposes an exit tax on rich expatriates, so that any wealthy US citizen who moves abroad and renounces citizenship is subject to a 30% income tax on the unrealized gains of all their assets (as if they had sold all their property before expatriation [Westin 2013]).

The basic goal of such policies should be to prevent people from leaving with significant resources. If anyone desires to emigrate, they should be free to do so, but they should not be able to take with them large amounts of what I will argue later is really the community's wealth. Finally, legal policy is not the only tool that can be useful here. A third policy that government and progressive people can attempt to use is moral suasion. Progressives can and should argue that millionaires who flee the country do so in order to enrich themselves at the expense of the community that helped create their wealth in the first place—and so rightly face public censure and criticism.

In sum, high levels of taxation would likely produce significant pressure to emigrate. Nevertheless, implementing a couple of complementary legislative policies (such as taxing worldwide income and imposing a stiff exit tax) would likely prevent emigration of the rich en masse.

Labor Market Reforms

Although the bulk of this book focuses on taxation as the major tool for reducing inequality, this is obviously not the only tool that matters. In the rest of this chapter we briefly look at some other important ones.

A central driver of economic inequality is, of course, the widely different incomes that people earn in the labor market. The explosion of economic inequality in the United States over the past 30 years has been driven by strong divergences in the income of different classes.[13] The rich have seen their incomes explode (from increasingly exorbitant CEO salaries, among other causes), while the poor and middle classes have seen their income stagnate or decline as trade union membership and real minimum wages have fallen. Over the years these income differentials have built up, leading to ever greater inequalities of total wealth (Piketty 2014; Reich 2015; Stiglitz 2012).

So far we have been discussing the feasibility of reducing inequality through redistributive taxation. But it's important to realize that *predistribution*—the amount of money that one is able to earn from working or owning property—matters just as much for total inequality as does *redistribution*. The predistribution of income—i.e., the differentials in earnings among different people—is determined by the ways that markets are shaped and regulated. Neoliberals tend to portray income as being determined by the neutral forces of supply and demand (e.g., Mankiw 2013). But this is wrong. As we will see in Chapter 4, markets are always politically shaped in certain ways, ways that radically influence the kind and extent of supply and demand that exist, and thereby radically alter one's resultant income. In other words, income is not determined by supply and demand in a neutral way, but is determined by the politically shaped bargaining power of individuals in contexts where politically-shaped-supply meets politically-shaped-demand. Reich (2015, 83) puts it this way: the fundamental reason for rising inequality is not globalization or tax cuts, but that unequal rules have been "baked into the building blocks of the 'free market' itself." The bottom line is that by shaping and regulating markets differently, it is possible to significantly alter the income received by different groups as well as the overarching levels of inequality (Ackerman, Alsott, and Parijs 2006; Atkinson 2015; Baker 2011, 2016).

What are the most important tools for reducing predistributive inequality? In the following subsection we focus on a few of the most important labor market reforms, then we look at several additional reforms to market systems more generally.

Unions

Unions deserve pride of place in any account of inequality reduction. The spread of neoliberalism over the past several decades has seen a steady decline in unionization. From 1980 to 2008 every OECD country other than Spain saw their union membership fall. By the end of the 20th century, UK union membership was at its lowest level in 60 years. In the United States, private sector unionization in 2019 was at only 6.2% (BLS 2020). Indeed, de-unionization has been extensive in every part of the world (with the exception of southern Africa [Pontusson 2013; Standing 2002]). Many places have also witnessed a significant erosion of union rights and powers. According to Britain's Trade Union Congress, "UK trade unions members have fewer rights to take industrial action than in 1906 when the current system of industrial action was introduced. Those participating in lawful industrial action remain vulnerable to dismissal and victimization" (Atkinson 2015, 94).

The decline of union strength has played a central role in worsening inequality (Farber et al. 2021). As Pontusson (2005, 61) points out, changes in union density reliably predict wage inequality trends more generally.[14] Koeniger, Leonardi, and Nunziata (2007) concur, showing that union density is highly, and statistically significantly, associated with inequality.[15] Likewise, Obadić, Šimurina, and Sonora (2014, 135) find that falling union membership in Europe from 2000 to 2011 is associated with an increase in inequality. Figure 1.3 shows that American inequality is remarkably correlated with the rise and fall of union membership rates over the past century.

Consider the fact that 50 years ago, when General Motors was the biggest employer in the United States, the typical GM worker earned the equivalent in today's dollars of $35 per hour. Fast-forward 50 years, and the largest employer is Walmart, with an average hourly wage of only $16.40 (Thomas 2021). This difference is not due to smaller profits—Walmart is immensely profitable. (Shareholders of giant firms are doing just as well today as in earlier decades, and likely better.) Of course, these companies operate in different industries; nevertheless, an important source of the differences in wages is the fact that GM workers had a strong union behind them, whereas Walmart workers do not. For another example, consider the fact that if you work at McDonald's in the United States you will make roughly $8.90 per hour, but if you perform the exact same job in Denmark, you will make $20 per hour (Alderman and Greenhouse 2014). Once again, the main difference is that the Danish workers are unionized. It is true that the Danish Big Mac costs more, but only slightly (35 cents more than in the United States

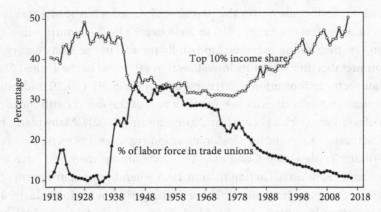

Figure 1.3 Changes in trade union strength and inequality in the United States, 1918–2008. Reproduced from Wilkinson and Pickett (2018, Figure 9.3). The original data comes from Gordon and Eisenbrey (2012).

[Reich 2015]). So while the cost of living is more in Denmark—a Big Mac costs roughly 10% more—the wages of McDonald's workers are 125% higher. In other words, the main difference is that Danish corporations earn less while workers earn more, due to the increased bargaining strength that workers have from being part of a union. It is facts like these which have motivated some observers to describe the decline in unions as the "counter revolution of our time" (Henry Phelps-Brown qtd in Standing 2002, 56).

Beyond their role in bread-and-butter issues of wages and benefits, unions are central to the struggle for a more just and egalitarian society. Pontusson (2011, 101) sees strong unions as a fundamental, if not *the* fundamental "institutional prerequisite for successful social democracy." Not only are unions directly useful in reducing inequality through collective bargaining, but just as significant, they provide the infrastructure and backbone of many social movements pushing for further change. Strong unions lead to strong social movements and social democratic parties, which in turn can lead to more political power, which can then lead to further progressive changes, such as a pro-union environment, creating a virtuous cycle. Even in the United States, unions play a profound role in furthering progressive policy; for instance, in recent years unions have been instrumental in pushing through the Affordable Care Act (even though the vast majority of union members already had health insurance), in efforts to raise the minimum wage, and in drives to increase paid family leave, paid sick days, and more (Baker 2016). We should therefore conceptualize reforms to encourage unions as a kind of *accelerative reform*—i.e., reforms which not only marginally improve things in themselves but are catalytic in fostering further reform. It is hard to overstate the fundamental importance of unions, not just for inequality reduction but for economic justice and democracy more generally.[16]

The relative strength or weakness of unions is of course not a natural phenomenon, but is significantly influenced by the rules and regulations of the labor market: how easy it is to join, what rights unionized workers have, how easy it is to strike, how easy it is to acquire new members, and so on. During earlier periods of classical liberalism, business owners and the rich were often successful in rendering unions completely illegal, such as the Combination Laws of 1799 and 1800 in Britain. As late as 1936 (*Carter v. Carter Coal Company*), the court majority in the United States was still ruling that collective bargaining was "an intolerable and unconstitutional interference with personal liberty and private property" (Reich 2015, 12). Even when not illegal, union activity has typically been heavily restricted by the state; from the dawn of industrial capitalism to World War II there has been a long history in every Western country of union activity being directly and openly attacked by the police and the army—infamous examples include the Ludlow Massacre (1914) and the Battle of Blair Mountain (1921) in the United States, the Winnipeg General Strike in Canada (1919), the Ådalen shootings in Sweden (1931), and the Battle of Orgreave in the United Kingdom in 1984.

In the contemporary American context, unions are weakened by a number of important regulations. Many states are "right to work" states, meaning that employees of a unionized firm cannot be compelled to join the union or pay dues, even if they benefit from the union collectively bargaining on their behalf. This has the effect of letting workers free-ride on union activity, thereby undermining the incentive for new individuals to join the union. In many states, rampant anti-union intimidation is common, and though technically illegal such regulations are often not enforced. In fact, a major way that union rights are undermined is by underfunding the enforcement agencies; for instance, if an employer summarily fires all the workers who are engaged in a union organizing drive (as occurs not infrequently),[17] such actions are formally illegal under the National Labor Relations Act. However, since Congress cut the funding necessary for enforcing the act in 1980, there has been a large backlog of cases. If it takes a year or more for a case of labor intimidation to come to the National Labor Relations Board, those workers who had the formal right to be reinstated will of course be long gone, leaving the employer safe from unionization (Reich 2015). Another important legal restriction is that which limits the kind of strikes that unions are allowed to engage in. For instance, in the United States it is illegal for unions to engage in intermittent strikes, "work-to-rule" (or slowdown) strikes, sit-down strikes, or secondary boycotts (in which workers show solidarity for the strike of other workers).

Facilitating high union membership and powerful unions requires, by contrast, a supportive legislative framework, which we know from the comparative evidence is entirely plausible. For instance, even though the Canadian and American economy and culture share many similarities, Canada's total unionization rate has dropped only a few percentage points since the 1970s, remaining at almost 30%, roughly three times the American rate. The difference is explained in large part by the fact that Canada has been significantly more union-friendly over the past four decades, making it easier for unorganized workers to join unions and for unions to secure contracts for their members (Baker 2016).[18] More broadly, a number of countries successfully achieved high union membership in various periods throughout the 20th century. The Nordic countries in particular have long maintained very high levels of union density. For instance, in the mid-1980s, union membership in Finland, Denmark, and Sweden was a remarkable 85%, 95%, and 96%, respectively (Blanchflower and Freeman 1992, 59). Even today, after significant attempts by conservative government to usher in neoliberal reform, Sweden retains a union membership of 66% (in 2017), and Iceland's has grown to 92% (in 2018 [OECD 2019b]).

Policies aimed at strengthening unions should focus on two basic dimensions: aiming to ease the formation of new unions with new membership, and enhancing the bargaining powers of existing unions. The former includes policies such as instituting a simple, easy process for the legal creation of a new union (such as a straightforward "card check" procedure, whereby a new union becomes legally certified as soon as it signs up a sufficient proportion of the proposed bargaining unit, usually about 55%, with no election necessary [Riddell 2004]); broad interpretation of who is legally considered an "employee" (to prevent employers from claiming that its workers are independent contractors); replacing "right to work" rules with automatic enrollment rules, with the right to opt out (so that by default workers pay dues and don't free-ride); and guaranteeing union representatives the right to communicate freely with workers. All of these policies need to be vigorously protected from employer coercion. Policies to promote the bargaining power of unions include expanding the range of issues on which companies are legally obliged to consult their unions; increasing the kinds of collective action that are legally allowed, such as solidarity actions; and fostering the creation of business organizations to facilitate sector- or industry-wide collective bargaining, as well as integrating labor organizations into the construction of national economic policy. Moreover, many labor specialists advocate a movement toward sectoral bargaining (aimed at covering whole industries, instead of decentralized bargaining in individual firms), such as has recently been advocated by the UK Labour Party (McGaughey 2017).[19]

Full Employment

It is well-known that full employment (meaning a situation where virtually everyone who wants a job can find one) significantly reduces inequality.

While all classes of employees benefit from employment, the poorest typically work the fewest number of hours and have the most precarious jobs, and are therefore the ones who benefit most from full employment. For example, during the period of high employment in 1996–2000, the poorest fifth of workers saw their annual hours increase by 17%, compared to the richest fifth, whose hours increased only 1% (Baker and Bernstein 2013). Indeed, over the past four decades, the only time American workers in the middle and bottom of the wage distribution saw consistent gains in real wages was during this period of low unemployment (Baker 2016). Larry Bartels (2004) has shown that since World War II, poorer people (e.g., those in the 20th percentile) have seen four times more income growth under Democratic presidents than Republican ones—a difference which he attributes mainly to the different levels of employment stimulated by different governments. Recall also that Black people consistently have double the unemployment rate of White people (Baker 2016). Women also have consistently lower employment rates (Moyser 2017). Therefore, improving employment rates serves to bolster gender and racial justice as well as economic justice. To take one specific example, in 2010, in the immediate aftermath of the Great Recession, the White unemployment rate peaked at 9.2%, while the unemployment rate for Black teens was a catastrophic 49%. It is hard to think of *any* social policy in the universe of policy possibilities that would be likely to have a more dramatic impact on the future lives of such Black teens than those which would help them to secure steady jobs (Baker 2016).

For such reasons Atkinson (2015) has argued that just as rich countries typically have a specific inflation target, they should also institute a specific unemployment target. In other words, he advocates that government should actively use the traditional Keynesian tools of fiscal and monetary policy (primarily increasing government spending and lowering interest rates) to increase aggregate demand in the economy and thereby increase employment levels as much as sustainably possible (recognizing, of course, that employment stimulation must be balanced with inflationary concerns as well as debt concerns).

In addition to the importance of increasing employment in general, I would also point to the usefulness of increasing *public sector* employment. This too is a kind of accelerative reform because the more people who are employed by the public sector means the more people who rely on taxation to pay their salaries—which helps to shift the balance of power in society away from a pro-business low-tax orientation toward a pro-caring-state high-tax orientation.[20] A good model in this regard is that of the Nordic countries, which have created huge numbers of public sector jobs, largely for women in caring professions (such as teaching and child care). This not only increases good-quality employment (thereby reducing inequality); it also helps to make child care more accessible, which frees women from such responsibilities, allowing them to enter the labor market as equals, reducing inequality even further (Kleven 2014; Pontusson 2011).

Quality, Accessible Education

One of the most obvious and important tools for reducing inequality is increasing access to quality educational opportunities. It is no coincidence that children born to the highest-income families in the United States in 1984 were 74.5 percentage points more likely to attend college than those from the lowest-income families (Chetty, Hendren, Kline, Saez, et al. 2014, 1). So an important policy goal for progressive governments is to make university cheap, if not free. That said, probably the most important intervention in this domain is early childhood education. Esping-Andersen (2002, 30) writes, "[A]ll available evidence indicates that (early) childhood is the critical point at which people's life courses are shaped. Remedial policies once people have reached adulthood are unlikely to be effective unless these adults started out with sufficient cognitive and social skills. A social investment strategy directed at children must be a centrepiece of any policy for social inclusion."

The Nordic experience suggests that educational equality and economic equality are closely linked. Nordic countries spend the highest percentage of GDP on public education in the OECD (e.g., in 2016 the United States spent 3.2% of its GDP on public education, 47% less than Denmark, which spent 4.7% of GDP), and this translates into not only high performance but more equal levels of performance. In terms of literacy, Nordic countries have the highest mean scores and also the most compressed distributions of test scores (Pontusson 2011, 97). This is in stark contrast to the United States, where some students perform excellently while others perform terribly (due in large part to the massive differences in school funding, which often falls along racial lines). For instance, in 1999, the average score of 17-year-old Black students in mathematics was 283.3, almost identical to the average score of 13-year-old White students (283.1); in reading, Black students perform even worse (Barry 2005, 58).

Minimum Wages

Another useful tool for reducing inequality is the minimum wage. In the United States, the federal minimum wage was among the highest in the world in the 1950s and 1960s (reaching a high in 1968 of more than $10 per hour in 2019 dollars). But it has eroded dramatically since then, now sitting at only $7.20 per hour, basically a poverty wage, equivalent to only 45% of the median income. Indeed, from its peak in 1968, the minimum wage has dropped 30%, which is quite astonishing for a country that is both at peace and economically growing (Piketty 2020, 531). Minimum wages are not simply an issue of inequality; they can be a matter of life or death, as poverty can lead to despair and even suicide. In their powerful study, Dow et al. (2019) estimate that raising the minimum wage and the earned-income tax credit by 10% each would prevent about 1,230 suicides every year. In contrast to the United States, the minimum wage in France has risen steadily over the years (see Figure 1.4). It is now worth about 60% of the median income (Atkinson 2015).

There are, of course, limits to how high the minimum wage can be raised before leading to increased unemployment (which will occur if labor costs exceed worker productivity). But the best work on the subject indicates that there is often significantly more room here than is commonly supposed, because higher pay can actually increase productivity via increased motivation and loyalty (Card and Krueger 1993; Schmitt 2013).

CEO Pay

At the other end of the spectrum from minimum wages is the salary of those at the top, particularly CEO pay. Here too there is nothing natural about wage levels. Like other labor market outcomes, CEO pay reflects the rules, regulations, and norms of the particular market in question. In the United States, CEO pay has skyrocketed in recent years, with a terrible impact on inequality. In the 1960s, a CEO earned roughly 20 times as much as a typical worker. That ratio rose slightly to 23:1 by the early 1970s, 58:1 by the end

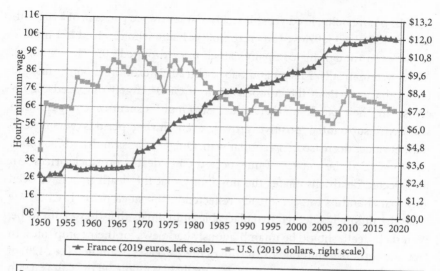

Interpretation. Converted into 2019 purchasing power, the federal minimum wage increased from 4,25$ per hour in 1950 to 7,25$ in 2019 in the U.S., while the national minimum wage (Smig in 1950 and then Smic beginning in 1970) rose from 2,23€ per hour in 1950 to 10,03€ in 2019. Both scales are based upon purchasing power parity (1,2$ for 1€ in 2019). **Sources and series:** see piketty.pse.ens.fr/ideology.

Figure 1.4 Minimum wage in France and the United States, 1950–2019 (Piketty 2020, 531).

of the 1980s, 120:1 by 1995, 376:1 at the peak of the stock bubble in 2000, down to 276:1 by 2015, and jumped back up to 351:1 in 2020 (Baker 2016, 132; Mishel and Kandra 2021). The idea that such pay oscillation reflects an oscillation of real productivity stretches credulity. Overall, between the years 1978 and 2013, CEO pay increased by 937%, whereas pay of the typical worker grew only 10.2% (Reich 2015, 97). Moreover, given that CEO pay has not exploded in many other countries (Piketty, Saez, and Stantcheva 2014), if we are to believe that pay genuinely reflects performance, we must therefore believe that since the 1990s American CEOs have suddenly become vastly more productive than all the other CEOs across the globe.

Not only has CEO pay skyrocketed; it has also become increasingly delinked from real corporate performance. Particularly egregious examples of this phenomenon include the cases of Martin Sullivan, who received $47 million when he left AIG even though the company's share price had dropped 98% on his watch and American taxpayers had to pay $180 billion to keep the firm afloat; Thomas Freston, who was CEO of Viacom for only nine months before being fired yet still received a severance package of $101 million; and Michael Jeffries of Abercrombie & Fitch, who received $72 million in pay even though his company's stock price dropped 70% (Reich 2015). More systematically, Mishel and Sabadish (2013) examined 350 firms and found that growth in the compensation of CEOs largely outpaced the increase in their stock market value. Strikingly, executive compensation witnessed substantial positive growth even during periods when stock market values decreased. In a similar vein, Quigley, Crossland, and Campbell (2017) studied the impact of unexpected CEO deaths on stock prices. An unexpected death eliminates the possibility that the death may have been anticipated and its impact already reflected in the stock price. If CEOs are truly the uniquely talented, irreplaceable individuals that they claim to be, then their death should be unambiguously bad news for their companies. In fact, the authors found that in 100 out of the 240 cases examined (i.e., 42% of the time), the price of company stock actually *rose* following the CEO's death (947). Though none of these pieces of evidence is completely conclusive,[21] they are at the very least hard to square with the idea that CEO salaries are a reflection of executive worth.

There is a lively ongoing academic debate as to why exactly CEO pay has increased so dramatically in the United States. Commentators point to a number of factors. First, CEO pay has increasingly included incentive bonuses in the form of stock options. The result is that if you are, say, an Exxon executive, and the price of oil suddenly increases for some reason, you will become instantly and massively richer (Baker 2006). The second and more fundamental reason has to do with corporate governance structure. American corporate governance rules allow managers to exert significant influence over who sits on corporate compensation boards, meaning that they have significant leeway to essentially write their own paychecks (Bebchuk, Fried, and Walker 2002; Stiglitz 2012). The board of directors (who have the formal power to cut CEO pay) usually have very cushy jobs, receiving high salaries for sitting on these corporate boards, typically over $100,000 for short hours, and are often friendly with the CEO, and so have no incentive to rock the boat (Baker, Bivens, and Schieder 2019). Moreover, although shareholders do have an incentive to restrain corporate pay (since they are the ones who will benefit from reduced corporate costs), they face a collective action problem in that it is hard to coordinate large numbers of disparate shareholders to act in unison, especially when it's so easy to simply sell one's shares and walk away if one is really unhappy.[22] Perhaps the deepest root of the problem is that other stakeholders of the corporation, such as workers, are systematically excluded from exerting any influence over executive compensation; rather than workers or the community at large having any influence, compensation is set by what are essentially old boys' clubs on the basis of "peer group" compensation with CEOs in other companies, even in completely different industries, leading to a never-ending spiral of upward pay as compensation boards constantly try to match the rising CEO salaries elsewhere (Clifford 2017).

A third important factor is the decline of high tax rates. Piketty, Saez, and Stantcheva (2014) point out that CEO pay is highly correlated with top tax rates (even when controlling for firm and CEO characteristics); see Figure 1.5. When taxes are high (as they used to be in the United States and United Kingdom, and still are today in parts of Europe), executive pay is more modest, likely because top executives have little interest in fighting for them and boards of directors have little incentive to offer them, given that 80–90% of any raise would go straight to the government (Piketty 2020). When top tax rates drop, however, the incentive structure completely changes, and top executives find themselves with strong incentives to push for salary increases any way they can.

What, then, are sensible policies for reducing wages at the top? One approach would be to increase tax penalties for companies where the ratio of CEO-to-worker pay passes a certain threshold. For instance, the recently proposed CEO Accountability and Responsibility Act (2021) would increase the corporate tax rate on American corporations whose CEOs are paid more than 100 times the median pay of all employees. Although this is clearly moving in the right direction, such policies by themselves are unlikely to reduce CEO pay unless they are complemented with changes to corporate governance structure. One possibility here would be for the government to implement "say-on-pay" legislation, giving shareholders a right to vote every few years to accept or reject the pay package of top executives.[23] Most fundamentally, the long-term goal needs to be to empower other stakeholders, particularly workers, to acquire influence in corporate governance. For instance, Pischke, Hallock, and DiNardo (2000) show that a 10% increase in unionization reduces the pay of CEOs by 2.5% or more. Additionally, probably the most straightforward and effective mechanism for restraining CEO pay is simply to reintroduce high tax rates on total CEO income (including on stock options and other forms of payment).

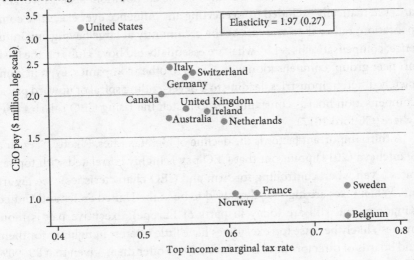

Panel A. Average CEO compensation

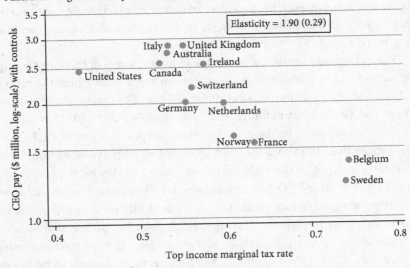

Panel B. Average CEO compensation with controls

Figure 1.5 International CEO pay and top tax rates (Piketty, Saez, and Stantcheva 2014, 264).

Other Tools for Reducing Inequality

Beyond the labor market there are a number of other kinds of market interventions and regulations that could play an important role in feasibly reducing inequality. Though this is not the place for any kind of comprehensive investigation, we would be remiss to not at least mention a handful of the most important such tools.[24]

Reducing Monopolies

A monopoly is a situation in which there is only one seller of a product, meaning that the seller can continue to raise their prices without much fear of consumers leaving since they have nowhere else to go. In this way monopolies drive up profits, particularly benefiting wealthy corporate shareholders while harming average consumers, with the overall impact of worsening inequality. Indeed, many of the firms that are the most profitable today are those that benefit from monopolies, such as tech companies like Microsoft and Google, with monopolies in the form of copyrights, and pharmaceutical companies like Pfizer, with monopolies in the form of patents.[25]

It is an open question as to how prevalent monopoly and oligopoly (i.e., industries with only several sellers) truly are in contemporary economies, but evidence indicates that their prevalence is significant. Foster, McChesney, and Jonna (2011, 8) claim that "economic concentration is greater today than it has ever been," pointing to the fact that the Global 500 (the biggest 500 firms in the world) controlled about 40% of the entire world's GDP by 2008. Along similar lines, Reich (2015, 30) shows that between 1978 and 2011 the rate at which new businesses formed in the United States fell by half, which he attributes to monopoly conditions making it harder for new businesses to enter the sector (see also Hirst and Bebchuk 2019).

A key issue here is the way that society chooses to incentivize innovation, particularly vis-à-vis copyrights and patents. For instance, Baker (2011) points out that US consumers spend close to $300 billion per year on prescription drugs that would sell for roughly $30 billion—10 times less—in a competitive market. It is true, of course, that creating the drugs in the first place costs a lot of money, but the goal for progressive policy in this regard should be to separate payment for *researching* the drug from payment for *accessing* the drug. Baker points out that if payment for research were made independent of payment for the drug, then drugs could be sold on the market without patent monopolies, just as generic drugs are today, massively reducing their cost. There are a number of alternative possibilities for funding research without relying on the monopolistic, inequality-generating nature of the patent and copyright system. One such possibility is a prize system, whereby the government could offer financial prizes for important research (Baker 2011, 2016; Stiglitz 2007); another would be to simply enhance direct public funding, whereby the state provides grants for promising research projects via some kind of independent scientific body, like the National Institutes of Health in the United States or the Natural Sciences and Engineering Research Council in Canada (Mazzucato 2013). The point is not that such systems are unquestionably superior; rather, the income generated by monopoly is not natural but set by very contingent political choices, and so we should experiment with ways to reduce it, without overly harming incentives for innovation.

Housing Support

In many cases, the housing market is a significant driver of worsening levels of inequality (Arundel 2017; Fuller, Johnston, and Regan 2020; Rognlie 2016; though see also Di 2005). The main reason for this is that even though homeownership is more widespread than wealth ownership in general, it is still quite unequal. In the United States, for instance, the top 1% own 9% of housing assets, the top 10% hold 40%, while the bottom 50% hold only 12% (Cho and Francis 2011). This means that if house prices increase, the effect will be to disproportionately increase the assets of the already wealthy, thus skewing inequality ever further.[26] Cities like Vancouver, San Francisco, and London have seen a particularly dramatic version of this dynamic in recent years, whereby those lucky enough to own homes have seen their wealth skyrocket.[27] A number of important consequences follow from rising property prices. Many people, particularly young people, find themselves essentially locked out of the housing market altogether (hence "generation rent"). The rising property prices put pressure on rental prices too, causing an affordable housing crisis, and with it the risk of evictions, homelessness, and the resulting traumas.[28] And society as a whole becomes more of a "rentier society," whereby wealth accumulates faster to those lucky enough to own property (such as houses or investments) rather than those who earn their income from labor (Fuller, Johnston, and Regan 2020; Piketty 2014). For example, owning a house in London currently brings the average homeowner the same income (from increasing property value) in two days as the average worker will earn from five days of actually working (Chakrabortty 2016).

Given this, it seems sensible that the first goal of an egalitarian housing policy would be to reduce the massive and arbitrary windfalls that are accumulating to wealthy homeowners. An important aim here is to reduce the extent to which housing is treated as an investment asset (whereby wealthy people and corporations buy multiple properties that are not lived in, flip properties, and purchase cheap properties that they let sit vacant waiting for price rises, etc.). The more that housing becomes a commodity to invest in and speculate on, the more its availability will become contingent on market ebbs and flows, wreaking havoc on those who require regular stable housing not as an investment opportunity but as a shelter and a home.[29] Possible tools here include levying penalties on owners of vacant houses,[30] taxing foreign home buyers, increasing property taxes (particularly on second homes or "mansions"), and making such taxes more steeply progressive. Indeed, since the major reason that house prices increase so much has nothing to do with the individual homeowner but much to do with the luck of living in a thriving community (that is safe and has good schools, a vibrant economy, etc. [Albouy and Zabek 2016]), it makes sense for the community to tax away significant amounts of the gains accruing to homeowners so that they can be shared out more equitably.

The second goal of an egalitarian housing policy is to help poor and low-income people accumulate wealth. How can housing policy facilitate this? The standard approach in Anglo-American countries has been to help broaden homeownership to more and more people. One important example of the feasibility of this is the US government mortgage supports for middle-income White people in the middle of the century. Congress introduced several federal policies and programs to institutionalize the long-term, fixed-rate, fully amortizing mortgage, insuring lenders against financial loss and subsidizing homeowners for billions of dollars through the mortgage interest tax deduction (Chappell 2017). Remarkably, the Federal Housing Administration has funded more than half of all first-time homebuyer mortgages in the past 80 years (Blumenthal and McGinty 2015).[31]

There are, however, serious downsides to this approach. Perhaps the biggest problem is that it does nothing to help the poor who cannot afford to purchase a house, even with government support. Another problem is that state subsidization of homeownership feeds into the demand for private housing, pushing up house prices and so potentially worsening overall wealth inequality. A third problem is that it reinforces the commodification of housing, which again puts low-income people at risk because it turns a fundamental need—a secure shelter—into an asset for wealthy people to speculate on. A fourth problem is that housing is, generally speaking, a poor choice as a vehicle for wealth accumulation. Having all your wealth tied up in one place (your house) is a bad investment decision, since it is illiquid and nondiversified. Moreover, people tend to live near their jobs, meaning that a recession in a region can simultaneously destroy both one's income and one's housing equity (as the Great Recession showed with devastating clarity).[32] As Di, Yang, and Liu (2003) point out, investing in financial assets like stocks and bonds reliably outperforms returns from housing, which is why the rich don't invest nearly as much of their wealth in housing as do the middle class. Last, it may well be that the promotion of widespread property ownership spurs conservative values, such as NIMBYism, the stigmatization of poor renters as a second-class out-group, and a belief in "independence" with corollary anti-welfare-state preferences (Gregory 2016; McCabe 2016).

The other path is that of increasing the stock of high-quality, publicly owned, rental housing, ensuring housing as a basic human right so that everyone, including the poor, has guaranteed shelter—what some call a "public option for housing" (Cohen et al. 2019). Most countries have social housing to some extent, though investments in it have significantly declined over the past few decades (and usually fall far short of demand). Austria (particularly Vienna) and Denmark are instructive examples, with 38% of housing in Vienna being social housing, and 22% in Denmark (Hearne 2017; Scanlon, Whitehead, and Arrigoitia 2014).[33] In Denmark, for example, social housing is not seen as second-tier housing, but is often the housing of choice for middle-class people too. It accommodates one million people in more than 8,500 units, owned by 550 nonprofit housing associations, with roles for tenants in management ("tenant democracy") and funding from the state via the Danish Housing Investment Bank (Hearne 2017). In the American context, Gowan and Cooper (2018) argue in a similar vein that the US federal government should financially support local governments to build large numbers of affordable, mixed-income, publicly owned, rental housing. The hope is that public ownership will allow increasing land value to benefit the public coffers in general, not simply wealthy property owners, and mixed-income housing will reduce the concentration of poverty, helping to foster class and racial integration.

Universal Child Care

Some of the poorest members of society are women, and particularly single mothers (Esping-Andersen 2002). There are obvious reasons why this is so. Women do the overwhelming bulk of unpaid caregiving and household labor,[34] which puts them at a significant disadvantage in the labor market compared to men. For this reason, feminists have long advocated for universal child care. Such a policy would not only improve gender equality; it would also help to reduce economic inequality by improving the economic position of those at the bottom of the income hierarchy.

This is eminently feasible. Nordic countries have long provided universally accessible child care, as does Quebec. Though the gross costs are large, the net costs are often much more modest because child care enables women to work more, which means they pay more tax. One optimistic study actually finds the total cost of Quebec's child care program to be zero, given the increased tax revenues (Fortin, Godbout, and St-Cerny 2012). A more cautious study from the United Kingdom estimates that providing high-quality universal child care would cost £27.9 billion per year (which is roughly 1.5% of GDP [De Henau 2015]). In any case, the evidence is clear that provision of universal child care really does work in reducing gender inequality (Fortin, Godbout, and St-Cerny 2012; Hegewisch 2009; Vermeylen et al. 2008). It is no surprise that the countries in the world with the lowest gender pay gap are the Nordic countries, which also have the strongest policies of universal child care (WEF 2018).

Basic Income

In addition to taxing the rich, the most straightforward way to reduce inequality is to enhance the amount of resources in the hands of the poor. A Basic Income is one potentially powerful mechanism for achieving this.[35] A Basic Income, formulated as a negative income tax, works though the tax system so that high earners pay taxes as usual, whereas low-income people would actually receive money from the government (hence a "negative income tax"). The lower one's market income, the larger the Basic Income one would receive.

Although Basic Income is becoming increasingly popular, it has not yet been implemented at a national level anywhere, though there have been a number of pilot projects over the years (Widerquist 2013). There are several major attractions of a Basic Income. It would abolish the current means-testing system of welfare, which is widely recognized across the political spectrum as being deeply dysfunctional, in part because of its humiliating and stigmatizing aspects and in part because it creates an "employment trap," since getting a job means losing your benefits, thus disincentivizing employment. A negative income tax, on the other hand, would not be stigmatizing (since large numbers of people would automatically receive it as part of the regular tax process), and it abolishes the employment trap since the amount one receives does not disappear altogether if one gets a job, but slowly reduces as one's earnings increase, so that at every level of income one would always earn more by working more. If set at a sufficiently generous level, a Basic Income would dramatically reduce poverty and inequality. For instance, Widerquist (2017) estimates that in the United States a Basic Income of 2.95% of GDP would provide $12,000 to each unemployed person, plus $6,000 per child; the employed would also receive a benefit in inverse proportion to their income. In total, fully 129 million people (40.2% of the entire population) would receive some benefit from the scheme, the average size of which would be $4,100. A major strength of Basic Income is that it enhances economic security. This is important because the insecurity and instability of contemporary neoliberal capitalism are two of its worst features. Providing everyone with a guaranteed floor, so that one knew that one's essential needs would always be met, no matter what, could be life-changing: it would provide people more freedom to say no to domineering bosses or abusive partners;[36] it would allow people to quit their jobs to go back to school or retrain in a different field; it would allow entrepreneurs to take more risks; it would likely reduce stress and improve mental health; and it would provide increased freedom for everyone to be able to focus more on the aspects of life most meaningful to them.

The impact of a Basic Income on inequality would of course depend entirely on its level. For instance, Widerquist (2017) estimates that a Basic Income set at $12,000 per unemployed individual (plus $6,000 per child), costing 2.95% of GDP, would reduce the official poverty rate in the United States from 13.5% of the population to approximately zero, lifting 43 million people (including 14.5 million children) out of poverty. To the extent that the costs of the program are paid for by taxes on the rich, such a program would dramatically reduce inequality.

A major obstacle to implementing a Basic Income is the cost.[37] Widerquist's (2017) estimate is 2.95% of GDP. The Canadian government estimates the cost of a national Basic Income to be $76 billion, or 4.3% of GDP (set at 75% of Statistics Canada's low-income threshold of $16,989, minus 50% of any earned income for individuals, and $24,027 for couples minus 50% of any combined earned income [PBO 2018]). These costs are substantial and clearly represent a significant impediment to realizing the program. But from the perspective of inequality reduction, the cost is not entirely a problem, as long as it is paid for out of progressive taxation. Basic Income, in other words, could be a powerful complement to enhanced taxation, reducing inequality downward from the top and upward from the bottom simultaneously.

Democratizing the Firm

Given how central corporations are to modern economic life, it is not surprising that the way they are governed has profound implications for the level of inequality across society. Corporations tend to generate inequality through two basic mechanisms. On the one hand, they generate *labor income inequality* due to the vastly different bargaining power between workers and top executives. (As mentioned previously, American CEOs earn, on average, roughly 350 times a typical worker's salary [Mishel and Kandra 2021].) On the other hand, corporations generate *ownership inequality* because modern firms are structured in such a way as to vest ownership rights of the firm's profits to shareholders. Workers get a wage, but no ownership rights to any of the profits. Because of this, capital is owned very unevenly across the economy: half of all households own zero stock, while the richest 10% own over 80% of all financial assets (Blasi, Freeman, and Kruse 2013, 12).

For these reasons, a major if not fundamental avenue for tempering inequality is seeking ways to democratize the firm. Other than unionization, which we've already discussed, probably the three most common models for democratizing firms are Employee Share Ownership Plans (ESOPs), code-termination, and worker cooperatives.

ESOPs are an American legal mechanism for increasing worker ownership (Kruse, Freeman, and Blasi 2010). The basic idea is that ESOP legislation provides companies with tax breaks to incentivize the selling of ownership shares to internal workers, paid for out of company profits (which often occurs when the initial founders wish to retire and prefer not to abandon the firm to a competitor). ESOPs have long enjoyed broad bipartisan support, which has helped them grow significantly.[38] Today there are over 10,000 ESOPs, representing 10 million workers and almost a trillion dollars of market value. Of these, roughly 3,000 are either majority-held or 100% owned by the employees (Blasi, Freeman, and Kruse 2013, 164).

Codetermination (or *Mitbestimmung* in German) is the practice of giving workers the ability to elect a certain portion of the governing boards of large firms (usually one-third, though up to half in large German enterprises). This practice is best known in Germany, where it has been firmly established since 1976, though it also exists in a number of other European countries, such as Austria, the Netherlands, and the Scandinavian countries (Addison 2009; Jäger, Noy, and Schoefer 2021; McGaughey 2016). Although codetermination has never existed in the Anglo-American countries, it has gained more attention in recent years than perhaps ever before. Jeremy Corbyn in the United Kingdom, as well as Elizabeth Warren and Bernie Sanders in the United States, developed prominent codetermination legislation as central parts of their economic policy platforms in their respective bids for prime minister and president.[39]

The appeal of codetermination is obvious. Since workers are typically far poorer than CEOs and upper management, they will have more desire to compress wages at the top and raise them at the bottom (hence reducing inequality). It also stands to reason that they will have more desire than shareholders to see their firm actually pay its fair share of taxes (not evade them via tax havens or other loopholes) since poorer workers will typically benefit more from the public services that such taxes provide than will rich shareholders (again reducing inequality). Although there is some evidence supporting this latter claim,[40] caution is required here as the bulk of the evidence finds only small effects of inequality reduction from codetermination (see the review of the evidence from Jäger, Noy, and Schoefer 2021).[41] This is likely due to the fact that as it is most commonly practiced, codetermination gives workers only a minority of seats on the board, meaning they never have the power to actually overrule management.[42] For this reason, the recent proposal from Isabelle Ferreras (2017; Ferreras, Malleson, and Rogers, forthcoming) for the "bicameral firm," whereby large firms would be governed by two chambers—one representing workers and one representing shareholders—where each has equal veto power over the other, would likely be an important improvement over traditional codetermination in this regard.

More radical are worker cooperatives, firms that are collectively owned by the workers themselves and governed on the basis of "one worker, one vote" (Dow 2003; Rothschild and Whitt 1986; Zamagni and Zamagni 2010). In small co-ops workers might make collective decisions in a participatory fashion; in large ones, they necessarily elect their own management or choose their own governing board. The best-known example is the Mondragon Corporation in the Basque region of Spain, a conglomerate that includes (as of 2017) 98 worker co-ops (as well as many noncooperative firms), with over 80,000 employees, and total resources of about €25 billion (in 2014).[43]

In addition to fixing a major fault in capitalist economies—that workers are systematically disenfranchised from having a voice at their place of work[44]—worker-co-ops could also play a significant role in reducing inequality. As democratic organizations, worker co-ops are free to set their internal pay ratios at any level they choose, but it is noteworthy that they tend to have much more egalitarian pay schedules than conventional firms; most worker co-ops restrict the ratio of top-to-bottom pay to roughly 3:1 (compared to the 300:1 in US corporations [Malleson 2014a]). This means that if worker co-ops spread significantly across the US economy, they would compress inequality by a factor of approximately 100. Moreover, worker co-ops do not only dramatically improve wage labor equality; they also radically improve capital ownership equality, since all members of the co-op (not just a minority at the top) are legally co-owners, and so receive a share of the profits. Hence the more that co-ops spread, the more regular workers become joint owners of the economy, receiving a regular stream of income from capital ownership.

The major limitation of worker cooperatives is that they are currently very rare, representing fewer than 1% of firms in most economies. In the United States, for instance, there are only 465 co-ops out of 6,100,000 employing firms, i.e., 0.0076%.[45] Yet such rarity is not inevitable. In the Emilia Romagna region of northern Italy, for example, 13% of the economy is controlled by worker co-ops. The empirical evidence demonstrates that once set up, co-ops operate just as efficiently and productively as similar-size conventional capitalist firms (see Malleson 2014a for a compilation of the evidence). The chief obstacle to their flourishing, in other words, is not internal inefficiency but the rarity with which they are set up in the first place (Dow 2003). This means that governments wishing to foster the expansion of worker co-ops would need to facilitate the formation of new ones, for instance, by extending financial support to new cooperative ventures, such as a cooperative bank, providing a clear legal framework, and establishing educational resources (such as cooperative business management programs in universities).

Summary

By way of a summary, consider the remarkable image in Figure 1.6.

Two things are striking. First, as seen on the right side of the image, inequality in the United States has exploded in recent years as the income of the richest has skyrocketed. However, just as important, the left side of the image shows that from 1946 to 1980, while income after taxes was growing for everyone, it was growing significantly faster for the poor than the rich, meaning that overall, inequality was falling. This was due to a number of factors: higher taxes, stronger unions, higher minimum wages, less capital mobility, and so on. But the fact remains that even in the extremely "free market" United States, and not overly long ago, the reduction of inequality was perfectly feasible. That is an important lesson for the future.

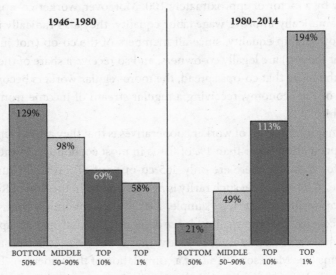

Figure 1.6 Income growth over time in the United States. Image from @ ProgressForThePeople; data from Piketty, Saez, and Zucman (2018, 578).

2

Is It Feasible to Reduce Inequality?

Wealth Taxes and Tax Havens

Reducing Inequality Through Wealth Taxation

Although all the tools we looked at in the previous chapter are important for reducing inequality broadly speaking—say, between the bottom 20% and the top 20%—it is doubtful that by themselves they are sufficient to deal with the thorniest problem of all: the wealth of the superrich. Warren Buffett, for example, paid only $1.8 million in federal income taxes in 2015, representing approximately 0.003% of his total wealth (Hemel 2019). Generally speaking, the superrich have incomes of many millions of dollars every year, which means that even at very high rates of income tax, their overall wealth will still increase year in, year out. For example, even if Jeff Bezos were forced to pay a 90% effective income tax, he would still accumulate 800 million *more* dollars every single year,[1] far more than he is ever likely to consume. As long as one's income after tax is greater than what is consumed (as is likely for the superrich), one will continue to grow ever richer, widening inequality ever further. And this is true even with income tax rates at far higher levels than those which currently exist. The key point is that even an inconceivable 100% effective income tax would only reduce the great fortunes of the superrich at an extremely slow pace. For example, assuming a 100% effective income tax, and that Elon Musk spends $100 million every year, it would still take 2,700 years to reduce his total wealth to normal levels. This is the primary reason why relying on income tax is insufficient to reduce inequality at the very top. To meaningfully reduce inequality, we require a wealth tax.[2]

A second, and related, rationale for taxing wealth (as opposed to income alone) is that what really matters for inequality in terms of opportunities, the impact on democracy, health and well-being, etc. is not the *flow of income* per se but the total amount of assets—i.e., the *stock of wealth*—that some people have compared to others, since this represents the true financial power (or lack thereof) at one's disposal. While the top 1% control 20% of US

Against Inequality. Tom Malleson, Oxford University Press. © Oxford University Press 2023.
DOI: 10.1093/oso/9780197670392.003.0003

income, they control 40% of total wealth (Piketty 2020). Incredibly, the top 0.1% control roughly the same amount of wealth as the bottom 90% of the entire population (Saez and Zucman 2019c). This means that focusing on income misses the deeper reality of what is at stake. As Brian Thompson notes, "While the income gap provides a huge hurdle to equality, the wealth gap presents a mountain" (quoted in Strand and Mirkay 2020, 282).

A third rationale for a wealth tax flows from Piketty's (2014) influential work demonstrating that wealth frequently accumulates in capitalism because owners of capital tend to receive higher levels of return than the rate at which the economy as a whole is growing. This dynamic means that, if left unchecked, capitalism will tend to concentrate wealth at ever higher levels, transforming society more and more into an owner-dominated rentier society. According to Forbes, from 1987 to 2007 the world's largest fortunes grew at 6–7% per year (corrected for inflation). This is three to four times faster than average wealth and roughly five times faster than average income. If such a trend continues unabated, eventually the billionaires, financiers, real estate magnates, and oil princes will come to own practically everything (Piketty 2020, 685). This implies that we require wealth taxes above 5% simply to stabilize the current concentration of wealth; actually reducing inequality will require higher levels still.

A final rationale for a wealth tax is that it is a useful instrument for accessing the wealth that is often hidden from more conventional taxes, such as when rich people stash their income in the corporate form (e.g., as corporate stock) in order to avoid paying income tax or dividend tax. For instance, Larry Ellison reportedly owns $17 billion in Oracle Corporation stock, yet he paid himself an annual wage of only $1 so as to avoid income tax. (He pays for his consumption by borrowing from the bank against this stock ownership [Gamage 2015].) Elites commonly avoid income tax by being paid in stock, and avoid capital gains tax by not selling their stock, instead simply borrowing against their stock ownership. (This saves them money because the interest they have to pay on their loans is typically much less than either regular income tax or capital gains tax.) A wealth tax can get at this hidden-away wealth in a way that income taxes cannot. Moreover, given that globalization has made it easier for corporations to move, all countries face significant downward pressure on their corporate tax rates to prevent corporations fleeing to greener pastures. So egalitarians who wish to find ways to impose high taxes on the rich will be forced to impose them largely on immobile sources like labor, land, consumption, etc. That's a good strategy, but it will have the undesirable side effect of rich people shifting their money into the corporate form to avoid such taxes. The wealth tax is thus a fundamental backstop on taxation of the rich because it provides a way of accessing the wealth stored in corporations, which would otherwise be beyond the public's reach, without relying solely on (the likely limited) corporate income tax.

In this chapter we focus on two plausible tools for taxing wealth: a wealth tax and an inheritance tax. We also examine the difficult issue of tax havens.

Reducing Inequality through a Wealth Tax

Although income taxes are familiar and well-known, wealth taxes are much less so. A wealth tax is an annual tax applied to one's net global wealth (i.e., all assets minus debts) above an exemption threshold. A number of European countries have implemented wealth taxes over the years. In the 1990s, 12 countries had a wealth tax, though by 2022 this had dropped to only 3 (Norway, Spain, and Switzerland). Although the European experience is useful and instructive in many ways, we will see that these taxes have typically been designed in ways that are far from optimal. The European wealth taxes have tended to share the same basic features. They mostly have quite low thresholds. (For instance, Austria, Germany, the Netherlands, Norway, Spain, Sweden, and Switzerland all have or had thresholds of less than €200,000, in equivalent 2019 euros [Kapeller, Leitch, and Wildauer 2021, 8].) Such wealth taxes are therefore not simply a tax on the rich but fall on many middle-class people as well. The rate of tax is also generally quite low—typically around 1%. (The highest top rate is in certain regions of Spain at 3.75%, though this is limited by the fact that Spain also places a cap on the total payable tax.)[3] They all allow significant (and, as we will see, often very problematic) exemptions for various types of wealth. As a result of the low rates and broad exemptions, the wealth taxes typically raise only small amounts of total revenue. In most countries they raise roughly 0.2% of GDP. The one exception is Switzerland, which raises several times more, at 1.08% of GDP (Scheuer and Slemrod 2021, 212).

Indeed, to date, the practical experience of wealth taxes has been disappointing. This is because wealth taxes commonly face a number of significant obstacles. One obstacle is liquidity, but probably the three biggest are widespread undervaluation, large-scale avoidance through loopholes and deductions, and high levels of evasion (or "capital flight") to tax havens.[4] Is it possible to overcome these obstacles to implement an effective wealth tax that really does reduce inequality? Let us investigate.

Liquidity

The issue here is that if the wealth tax threshold is too low (e.g., a million dollars or less), then individuals who have a small income but sizable fixed, illiquid, assets worth this much—such as if one owns a small business or a home in a city with a booming real estate market—will be unable to pay the wealth tax out of their income and so will be forced to sell their major asset. In the political debate over the wealth tax in France, opponents continually brought up the example of a retired fisherman who had a small pension (€1,000 per month) but a house that was worth €3 million because it was located in a place that over the years had become a fancy resort; he was thus unable to pay the wealth tax (Boadway and Pestieau 2018). Though effective as political rhetoric, it must be pointed out that such examples are misleading as they are extremely rare (Loutzenhiser and Mann 2021). One option for dealing with such situations is to allow exemptions for people's businesses or houses, but the problem with this route is that it opens the floodgates to all kinds of gaming (as taxpayers rush to shift their wealth into these kinds of asset in order to avoid the wealth tax). A much better option would be to simply set the threshold somewhat higher. As Loutzenhiser and Mann (2021) point out, if a wealth tax were implemented in the United Kingdom, a low tax threshold of £250,000 at a rate of 2.5% would mean that 1.75 million adults would be at risk of liquidity problems, whereas if the threshold were set higher, at, say, £5 million with a tax rate of 0.2%, only 10,000 adults would be. With a high threshold, there will still be some people who face liquidity problems (perhaps because they've invested all their assets in illiquid bonds or in holiday homes), but for such people, being required to sell an occasional asset to pay the tax is hardly a problem because by definition they are asset-rich (we need not be too worried about rich people having to sell an occasional asset to pay their tax); moreover, such wealthy people will likely have access to credit that they could always use to pay their tax, even if most of their assets are illiquid (Saez and Zucman 2019b).

Valuation

A major concern with the feasibility of a wealth tax is valuation. Is it really possible to accurately measure the total wealth of a rich individual—their houses, boats, cars, jewelry, artwork, stocks, bonds, derivatives, pension funds, life insurance schemes, etc.—and do so every single year for each and every rich individual? Clearly this is no easy task, and critics are right to point to the real difficulties here. A particularly thorny aspect of the problem is the difficulty in measuring hard-to-value types of wealth. For instance, Kamin (2015) points out that 49% of the assets of rich people (the top 1%) are not easily valued. They own houses that have been owned for many years and so may have a very different value than their original purchase price; likewise, family businesses that are not traded on the stock market do not have an obvious value; similarly, jewelry and precious art—such as important paintings—may be difficult to value in the abstract without actually going through the process of putting them up for sale. The other dimension of the problem is the sheer volume of things to be measured—all the cars, boats, jewels, homes, stocks, bonds, and so on. Given the magnitude of items involved, governments have typically relied on self-reporting of wealth for calculating taxes, with subsequent audits of small numbers of random people. The problem with this approach, of course, is that self-assessment typically leads to massive undervaluation (as tax appraisers hired by rich individuals unsurprisingly tend to significantly undervalue the wealth of the person who has employed them). This problem is compounded to the extent that wealthy people can typically expect to be audited only very rarely or never at all. The more lax the official monitoring, the stronger the temptation to undervalue one's assets.

Given these problems, it is tempting to dismiss the wealth tax as simply infeasible. However, a number of countries have successfully implemented a wealth tax, coming up with a number of practical (if imperfect) solutions to valuing all kinds of assets (Chamberlain 2020; Daly, Hughson, and Loutzenhiser 2021). In fact, modern societies possess more than enough tools to make a wealth tax work effectively. The basic solution is to use third-party reporting, not self-assessment, as much as possible; for the remaining assets, we can use modern techniques of prospective and retrospective valuation, combined with increasing enforcement (hiring more auditors and creating stiffer penalties for fraud).

As Saez and Zucman (2019b) point out, the key to successful modern income taxation is third-party information reporting, so that tax authorities receive information directly from third parties (such as employers and financial institutions). The same principle should be followed for the wealth tax. In other words, financial institutions should be required to provide the tax authorities with annual information on as many assets as possible (such as interest-bearing assets, publicly listed stocks, assets indirectly held through mutual funds, pension funds, real estate, vehicles, mortgages, loans, and other debts), the general principle being that all assets should be priced at their current market value. Having a system of widespread third-party reporting would go a substantial way toward making a wealth tax effective. After all, it is well-known that third-party reporting leads to high levels of valuation accuracy and minimal avoidance (Hochguertel and Ohlsson 2012). For instance, the study that found the highest levels of evasion of the wealth tax (Brülhart et al. 2019a) is from Switzerland, where the government relies on citizens to self-report their wealth. It seems reasonable to suspect that if details of Swiss wealth were automatically transmitted from the banks to tax authorities there would be far less evasion.[5]

Now it is of course true that not all wealth can be easily subject to third-party reporting. But most can. Saez and Zucman (2019d) estimate that fully 80% of the wealth of the top 0.1% wealthiest families is in the form of assets that are regularly traded, such as publicly traded stock, bonds, and real estate, and so have a clear market price: "Among the 15 richest persons [in the United States], 12 of them—representing 83% of the wealth of this group—are large shareholders of corporate giants Amazon, Microsoft, Berkshire Hathaway, Facebook, Oracle, Google, Walmart, and Las Vegas Sands, whose stock is publicly traded and thus has a well-defined market value. For them, avoiding the wealth tax is impossible. How could Jeff Bezos pretend that his wealth in Amazon stock is worth only a fraction of its observable market value?"

For assets that cannot be subject to third-party reporting, a plausible solution is to use modern accounting techniques of formulaic prospective and retrospective valuation (Gamage 2019). In prospective valuation, the future value of an asset is estimated by starting with the purchase price and then applying a standard formula to estimate the future price (perhaps based on the economy-wide normal rate of return). With this information, tax authorities can estimate the tax that should be paid by working forward from the initial purchase price of an asset. Retrospective valuation means that when an asset is sold its earlier value is retrospectively calculated by applying a standard formula in reverse; in this way retrospective valuation can be used to calculate the tax that should have been paid in each year based on working backward from the sale price. With this information, the tax authorities can reconcile any mistakes in taxation. If the tax that should have been paid exceeds what was actually paid, the taxpayer is simply charged the difference (plus interest), and if the tax paid exceeds what should have been paid, the taxpayer is refunded the difference (plus interest). Gamage (2019) points out that the combined use of formulaic prospective and retrospective valuation would allow the tax authorities to vastly reduce the amount of audits and assessments performed by actual humans, dramatically simplifying the system.

Wealth tax skeptics, like Kamin (2015), suggest that there are two particularly important concentrations of wealth which are difficult to value: those of real estate and closely held businesses. Yet valuing real estate is not particularly difficult since it is already widely done (often by municipalities for calculating property tax). Of course, there will inevitably be disputes as to its accuracy, but this could presumably be improved by the use of prospective and retrospective valuation, as well as the use of modern data-based web technologies like Zillow, which provide estimates of the value of most real estate based on a range of publicly available information, such as data on the sales of comparable houses. Such information could easily be systematically reported to tax authorities (Shakow 2016).

For large privately-held companies (such as Uber), the financial sector already routinely values such companies; they are listed on secondary markets, and their stock transactions are centrally registered. The IRS (or other tax authorities) could simply mandate that financial institutions report their valuations of private businesses to them. For valuing small businesses, a number of workable practices have been developed around the world. For instance, Switzerland estimates the value of small private businesses by using simple formulas based on the book value of the assets and multiples of the profits (Eckert and Aebi 2020; Saez and Zucman 2019b).

None of this is to claim that there will be no difficulties or complexities. There will undoubtedly remain some hard cases, for instance, small private businesses with multiple owners that have different amounts of equity, works of art,[6] and personal effects. Yet even here the basic principles are straightforward. First, extend third-party reporting protocols across ever wider swathes of the economy. Second, apply standardized formulas based on prospective valuation (reconciled with retrospective valuation at a later date). Third, hire as many professional auditors as needed and make the penalties for fraud more severe. (Since we are talking about taxing the assets of the superrich, there is very little downside in hiring many more auditors, since each new auditor will likely return more money than they cost to hire.) Fourth, allow exemptions for small assets (such as jewelry or personal effects worth less than, say, $5,000) in order to keep the job of tax auditors manageable. Fifth, keep the tax exemption threshold high, so that the total number of claimants is low (e.g., the top 5% or 1% of the population only). Sixth, it may also be useful to apply tax rates within "bands." This would mean that everyone in lower tax bands—such as between $2 million and $4 million or between $5 million and $10 million—would pay exactly the same tax rate, regardless of how much money they make within the band. The advantage of this is that it makes valuation quite a bit simpler—individuals don't need to prove their exact wealth, only which general band they fall into. The caveat is that banding wouldn't be appropriate high up the wealth scale, since it would make no sense to tax someone who possesses $100 million the same as someone who has $100 billion; nevertheless, at low rates, banding may help to accommodate the inherent imprecision of valuation and thereby reduce the scope for disputes (Daly, Hughson, and Loutzenhiser 2021).

How burdensome is it for taxpayers to pay for all the accounting to comply with the wealth tax? Estimates range quite widely, from a German estimate of 0.6–3.6% of the wealth tax due (Bach, Beznoska, and Steiner 2014) to 19% in the United States (Leiserson 2020). The most comprehensive and up-to-date study is from Burgherr (2021), who examines the international evidence as well as the experience of the United Kingdom in administering comparable taxes (such as the inheritance tax). He estimates that the cost of complying with a well-designed wealth tax for taxpayers is 0.1% of taxable wealth; in other words, assuming a 1% wealth tax, taxpayer costs would represent roughly 10% of the total tax being paid.

In sum, valuation is a real obstacle to the implementation of a wealth tax, and it is unlikely to ever be solved perfectly. Nevertheless, it does seem possible to do well enough; that at least is the conclusion of tax experts who actually work in the field (Troup, Barnett, and Bullock 2020; see also Daly, Hughson, and Loutzenhiser 2021). Indeed, if the practice of reconciliation of taxes is widely used (based on retrospective accounting from when an asset is eventually sold) so that taxpayers receive rebates for any significant miscalculations, it seems difficult to argue that they are hard done by, or that temporary inaccuracies of valuation really matter.

Avoidance and Evasion

Beyond valuation, the most serious concern with the viability of a wealth tax is whether it will simply be avoided and evaded en masse. As Slemrod (2007) points out, the history of taxation is also the history of ingenious attempts to evade it—from third-century Romans burying their jewelry to evade the luxury tax to 18th-century English homeowners bricking off their fireplaces to escape the notice of the hearth tax collector. The European experience with wealth taxes has in fact shown avoidance to be a significant problem. According to the OECD's (2018a) comparative study on wealth taxes, the most common forms of avoidance are using tax shelters (such as trusts in order to hide ownership), hiding assets abroad in tax havens, and, most important, taking advantage of a range of loopholes and deductions. For example, in some cases business assets have been exempted due to worries about stifling investment and entrepreneurship; in every case pension assets have been exempted due to concerns about harming retirees; artwork and antiques have been exempted due to difficulties in valuation and worries about breaking up collections; forest lands have been exempted for environmental reasons; nonprofit organizations have been exempted; the French wealth tax exempted stocks of wine and brandy; the Norwegian wealth tax provided large exceptions for primary residences; the Spanish wealth tax exempts life insurance policies, and so on (Edwards 2019; Perret 2021). Such exemptions are deadly to the efficacy of the wealth tax because they provide extreme incentives for taxpayers to shift their wealth into such assets, causing the tax base to shrivel and tax revenues to dry up. This is why a number of countries gave up on wealth taxes altogether, and the ones that maintain the tax raise very little; recall that even though the Spanish wealth tax is quite radical (its top rate is 3.75% of one's wealth), the massive loopholes mean that it actually accomplishes very little, raising only 0.18% of GDP (Scheuer and Slemrod 2021).

Exemptions are therefore deeply problematic for two reasons. First, they lead to widespread gaming of the system, so that the rich end up avoiding paying the taxes (defeating the fundamental purpose of the wealth tax). For example, the rich in Norway are able to shift their assets into luxurious primary residences, which are exempted at 75% of their true market value; the rich in Spain are able to shift their assets into certain types of business shares, which are tax-exempt. Second, exemptions make the wealth tax unfair and often regressive because the moderately wealthy are in many cases less able to avoid the tax than the extremely wealthy. For instance, in Sweden, a common objection to the wealth tax (which played a significant role in its demise) was that exemptions on business equity made it easier for very rich individuals who owned large firms to avoid the tax than it was for middle-class people, who were stuck paying it (Perret 2021).

An essential principle of a workable wealth tax, therefore, is that there must be no (or very few) exemptions so that the tax base remains broad. One particularly vexing issue here is whether there should be any deductions offered for businesses. In Spain, for example, the government introduced an exemption to the wealth tax on the shares of owner-managers who were substantially involved in the management of their business (in order to not harm investment and business growth). Yet studying this exemption, Alvaredo and Saez (2009) found that it progressively and substantially eroded the wealth tax, as wealthy business owners reorganized their activities to take advantage of this exemption. Indeed, they found that the share of the exempted stock as a proportion of all closely held business stock exploded from 15% to 77%. This is a difficult issue because there is a hard trade-off here: on the one hand, business deductions will likely lead to widespread avoidance; on the other hand, there are good reasons for wanting some kinds of exemptions for business because we want to allow firms (particularly young businesses) to grow and create future jobs and wealth for future tax revenues.

Another difficult issue is pensions. All European wealth taxes have exempted pensions on the grounds of not wanting to threaten retirement income and because it was widely seen as inappropriate to tax individuals on the basis of wealth which is not in their present control. On the other hand, pensions can constitute a large share of one's wealth, and so exempting them shrinks the tax base (Perret 2021). In my judgment, as long as the tax threshold is high, it would seem best to include pensions in the valuation of the assets of the rich.[7]

Wealthy people also commonly use trusts and foundations to obscure their wealth. One solution adopted in some countries is to treat trusts as "see-through" entities, meaning they are obliged to identify the settlor and beneficiaries to the tax authorities. Formulaic rules can then be applied to divide the assets between them. That said, this is not a perfect solution as it can open the door to other types of avoidance (Perret 2021; Saez and Zucman 2019b).

Another common form of avoidance is emigration. While internal migration to avoid a wealth tax appears quite common, emigrating out of one's home country seems to be much less so (Advani and Tarrant 2021). We discussed this issue in the previous chapter. Here we need only add that there are good policy options for minimizing emigration to avoid wealth taxes. One option is for a tax "tail," meaning that individuals who leave are still charged the wealth tax for a set period of years after departure. This option has been used by India and Germany and is similar to the Spanish model (Chamberlain 2020). Another option is an exit tax, which could be levied on the total value of one's estate, perhaps at a one-off high rate in order to discourage this kind of avoidance. In Chapter 4, I will argue that practically all of one's wealth (especially for the very rich) is due not to individual achievement but the vast "understructure" of cooperative and historical labor, composing the myriad social, cultural, and institutional infrastructures provided by other people. If this is correct, then it is entirely appropriate for a country to prevent rich individuals from running away with large amounts of wealth that was really coproduced by the society at large.

What does the empirical evidence say about the scale of avoidance of wealth taxes? The most pessimistic study is from Switzerland by Brülhart et al. (2019a), who find very large avoidance: a 1% increase in the wealth tax lowers the amount of wealth that rich individuals declare by 12.6% after one year and 43.2% after five years. Duran-Cabré, Esteller-Moré, and Mas-Montserrat (2019) find in Spain a 15.34% reduction after one year and a 32.44% reduction after four years. Zoutman (2018) in the Netherlands finds an 11.6% reduction in one year and 13.8% reduction after four years. More optimistically, Jakobsen et al. (2020) in Denmark find an 8.9% reduction for the moderately wealthy and an 11.3% reduction for the very wealthy after eight years. Agrawal, Foremny, and Martinez-Toledano (2020) in Spain find a 5.8–8.6% reduction after four years. Seim (2017) studies Sweden, and Ring (2021) studies Norway, and both find very low levels of tax avoidance: a 1% increase in the wealth tax lowers reported wealth by only 0.09–0.27% and 0.054%, respectively.

The most comprehensive study of wealth tax avoidance comes from Advani and Tarrant (2021). They argue that these wide differences are due in part to different methodologies,[8] in part to different time horizons, and in part to differences in design. In terms of design, three issues are crucial: third-party reporting, exemptions, and whether the tax is imposed by a central state authority or decentralized regions. Switzerland and Spain have little or no third-party reporting (whereas it is extensive in Denmark).[9] Likewise, Spain has much wider exemptions than Denmark. And Spain and Switzerland both organize their wealth taxes by region, which means that some regions have substantially higher taxes than others, leading to substantial migration (since it's much easier to migrate to a nearby city than to leave one's home country). With these factors in mind, the Swiss case looks very different. Brülhart et al. (2019a) estimate that the lack of third-party reporting could explain as much as 50% of the avoidance, and that internal migration accounts for roughly 34% of the response (Brülhart et al. 2019b). Hence, implementing relatively straightforward design fixes, such as instituting third-party reporting and a centralized tax system could reduce avoidance from 43% to just 6.9%. Even if only half of the reporting response could be shut down, this would bring the tax avoidance response down to 17.7% (Advani and Tarrant 2021, 533). In sum, a careful analysis of the cross-country evidence suggests that "a well-designed wealth tax, which covers all assets and makes extensive use of third-party reporting, could achieve an elasticity in the region of 7–17 after a period of four to eight years, depending on assumptions made about the size of international migration responses. This implies that a 1 per cent wealth tax could reduce the tax base by 7–17 percent" (534). This is still substantial evasion, but it is not disastrous.[10] After all, the "tax gap"—that is, the difference between what the richest 1% of Americans is supposed to pay, compared to what they actually pay—in terms of income tax is a massive 28% (Sarin 2021). Yet no one concludes from this that the income tax is unworkable. Indeed, the sensible conclusion is the opposite: enforcement should be tightened and collection methods improved. Similarly with the wealth tax: as technology improves, making third-party reporting easier, and global coordination on tax evasion increases (which, as we discuss below, is already slowly happening), it is entirely possible that the level of avoidance reported here could be reduced in the future.

How much would it cost a government to administer and enforce the wealth tax? As Burgherr (2021) documents, the estimates vary widely: from 2.07% of wealth tax revenue in France to 14% in Ireland and 1.0–2.3% in Switzerland. German estimates are controversial, ranging from as low as 0.12–1.4% to as high as 20%. Burgherr's conclusion is that the "overall evidence suggests a central estimate for the administrative costs of a modern wealth tax for the tax authority of about 0.05 per cent of taxable wealth" (693).

How much of the wealth tax revenue is spent on administration depends on the tax rate. A wealth tax of 1% of wealth would imply administration costs of 5% of wealth tax revenue, while a rate of 2% would imply administrative costs of 2.5%. In sum, the best evidence to date suggests that the total administrative costs for government should be small and entirely manageable.

Learning from the European Experience

The European experience with wealth taxes has demonstrated a number of potential problems. The most salient critiques are the following.

1. The wealth taxes raise only small amounts of revenue, usually less than 1% of GDP.

Although this is true, it is not necessarily a problem. It depends entirely on the goal. If the goal is to *raise substantial revenues* to fund public programs for all, then indeed a wealth tax is unlikely to be a good tool (though even here it depends on how high the tax rate is set; a radical wealth tax with high top rates could raise substantial sums [e.g., see the estimates in Kapeller, Leitch, and Wildauer 2021]). But if the goal is to *reduce inequality* by taxing the very rich and excluding everyone else, then we should not expect to raise large amounts of revenue, nor is this a problem. (Even 1% or 2% of GDP taken entirely from the rich would reduce inequality substantially, particularly given that it would be reapplied every year.)

2. Most wealth taxes have low thresholds, which means the middle class must pay (leading to resentment), and significant numbers of people face liquidity problems.

This is true. A better designed wealth tax should raise the threshold to exclude everyone but the rich.

3. It's impossible to accurately value large amounts of wealth, particularly of the rich.

In fact, as we've seen, modern techniques do allow for most assets to be valued quite easily, and countries have developed a number of workable (though admittedly imperfect) practices for dealing with the hard-to-value cases. Moreover, just as developed countries have generally improved their capacity to collect other kinds of taxes over the years, it seems likely that administrative capacity in this regard should improve in time too (Troup, Barnett, and Bullock 2020).

4. The European wealth taxes allowed all kinds of exemptions and deductions, which led to widespread avoidance and sometimes regressiveness (as the rich were often better able to avoid the tax than the middle class), all of which contribute to an overarching sense of unfairness.

This too is a real problem. Exemptions are deadly to a well-functioning wealth tax. A well-designed tax would have as few exemptions as possible.

5. There will inevitably be mass avoidance through exemptions and mass evasion through tax havens.

While avoidance is a real issue, and one that is not likely ever to be perfectly resolved, we have seen that it can be significantly mitigated by good design (in particular, rigorous third-party reporting, strong enforcement, and centralization). And as we discuss below, much can also be done to mitigate the dangers of tax havens.

6. Wealth taxes will deter investment and entrepreneurship.

This is a major (perhaps *the* major) critique of high taxes. We discuss it in depth in the next chapter, where we will see that the bulk of the evidence suggests that it is in fact not likely to be a major problem (the basic reason being that even if taxes do discourage some investment and entrepreneurship, *spending* the tax revenues can also encourage new investment and entrepreneurship elsewhere).

Despite these critiques, two important points should be kept in mind. First, although a number of these critiques of the European experience are entirely valid and fair, what they point to (at least for the most part) is design flaws—thresholds that are too low, lack of third-party reporting, overly broad exemptions, insufficient enforcement, and so on. So the sensible conclusion is not that wealth taxes are inherently infeasible (they're not), but rather that

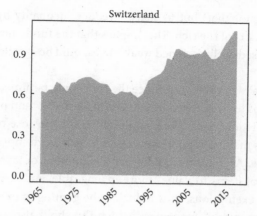

Figure 2.1 Individual net wealth tax revenues as share of GDP (Perret 2021, 543).

their design should be improved. Second, it's important to recognize that even with all of these problems, the European wealth taxes still basically worked. They could have functioned a lot better, clearly, but it's not as if they simply failed or collapsed. While some places did experience declining revenues, a number of countries (France, the Netherlands, Norway, Spain, Switzerland) saw stable revenues for decades. Consider the case of Switzerland. Even though this country has had perhaps the worst experience of any in terms of avoidance (due to the decentralization of the wealth tax encouraging migration, and the lack of third-party reporting combined with historic bank secrecy facilitating broad evasion), plus all the usual difficulties of valuation, still the Swiss wealth tax remains highly popular and has been able to generate stable and even increasing amounts of revenue for over 50 years (see Figure 2.1).

Nevertheless, it's clear that, generally speaking, the European wealth taxes have not worked as well as many hoped. The six issues listed above led many countries to give up on the wealth tax. But as Perret (2021) persuasively argues, there is good reason to believe that the next generation of better designed wealth taxes can and will perform significantly better.

Ingredients of a Viable Wealth Tax

In my view, the next generation of wealth taxes should be designed with one clear goal in mind: not to raise large amounts of revenue per se (income taxes are better for that) but to sharply reduce inequality by targeting the accumulated assets of the rich. This implies that the fundamental features of an evidence-based, well-designed wealth tax should be as follows.

1) Institute a high threshold. Since the tax should be aimed at the top 5%, or perhaps top 1%, it should exclude at least 95%, and perhaps 99%, of the population. Such a threshold makes the purpose of the tax clear, as well as making it politically easier to galvanize support and harder to oppose. A high threshold keeps the number of taxpayers (and the number of items to value) more manageable, and it avoids the need for most exemptions, thus reducing the gaming of even the most sophisticated money managers. A high threshold also avoids problems of liquidity or harming young businesses. (For instance, if a threshold of $5 million with deductions for small business turns out to cause too much gaming by rich people, then the threshold could be raised, say, to $10 million, but with the removal of all business exemptions.) A high threshold also changes the nature of avoidance and evasion, making it less something that "everyone does" and more clearly something immoral which only a small number of wealthy people are doing.

2) Set progressive rates, with higher rates for the superrich. Recall that rich people typically earn at least 5% per year on their assets, so the top rate needs to be at least this high, if not higher, if it is to accomplish the goal of actually reducing the mountains of wealth controlled by the superrich.

3) The tax base should be as broad as possible, minimizing the existence of deductions or exemptions, since every exemption opens the door to gaming and manipulation. One plausible exemption is for personal effects (say, those of less than $5,000) so as to reduce the total number of items that must be evaluated. There are also difficult choices to make in terms of exempting pensions and perhaps also small business assets, though as the OECD (2018a) warns, real care must be taken here.[11]

4) Implement extensive use of third-party (not voluntary) reporting on as wide a base of assets as possible.

5) Enhance enforcement: more auditors, stronger penalties, an exit or tail tax to discourage expatriation, as well as crackdowns on tax havens and the money managers who facilitate them (which we discuss next).

6) Establish formulaic prospective and retrospective evaluation, with reconciliation, for the remaining assets that are not third-party-reported.

Even with all of this we should not expect the wealth tax to work perfectly. In particular, there will still undoubtedly be some evasion. But that by itself should not discourage us from implementing such a tax. After all, the IRS estimates that roughly 16% of income tax in the United States is avoided every year (Cassidy 2019). Yet that is hardly a reason for scrapping it; if anything, it is a reason to try harder to tighten its enforcement. The same reasoning applies to a wealth tax.

One good model is the proposal from Kapeller, Leitch, and Wildauer (2021) for a European-wide wealth tax. Their "strongly progressive" model would apply a wealth tax of 2% to those with more than €2 million in wealth (so 99% of households would be exempt). The rate would increase to 3% beyond €5 million (i.e., the richest 0.3% of households), 5% beyond €10 million (the richest 0.1% of households), 7% beyond €50 million (the richest 0.01% of households), 8% beyond €100 million (the richest 0.005% households), and 10% on net assets beyond €500 million (the richest 0.001%, or 1,200 households). Even with a relatively pessimistic assumption of "strong evasion," the authors estimate that this tax would raise 2.6% of GDP (or 5.6% of total European government revenue of the EU22), substantially reducing inequality.[12]

A final important model of an effective, feasible wealth tax is that proposed by US presidential candidate Bernie Sanders (designed by tax experts Emmanuel Saez and Gabriel Zucman 2019a). Sanders's proposal was for a wealth tax on American households with a net worth of at least $32 million—the top 0.1% of richest Americans. (In other words, 99.9% of Americans would be untouched by the tax.) The wealth tax would kick in at 1% and rise steadily to a maximum of 8% for wealth over $10 billion. The wealth tax would apply to a comprehensive base with no exemptions whatsoever. It would be enforced through systematic third-party reporting and audits. There would be a significant increase in the enforcement budget of the IRS (including an audit of 30% of wealth tax returns for those in the 1% bracket and a 100% audit rate for all billionaires), as well as a preventative exit tax of 40% on the net worth of all assets under $1 billion, and 60% for assets over $1 billion, on any US citizen who renounces their citizenship in order to avoid the tax. Last, the tax would "include enhancements to the international tax enforcement and anti–money laundering regime including the strengthening of the Foreign Account Tax Compliance Act [FATCA]" (Sanders 2019).[13] (We will discuss the FATCA more below.)

Should a tax like these be implemented in the future, it would undoubt-edly face some difficulties at the margins in terms of valuation, and there will always remain some levels of persistent avoidance (for instance, it's in-evitable that the tax authorities will miss the occasional Rembrandt [Avi-Yonah 2019].) Nevertheless, if designed according to the principles outlined above, it seems likely that it would be largely effective.

Tax Havens

There is no generally agreed-upon definition of a "tax haven," but it is usu-ally understood to mean a place—usually, but not always, outside of one's country—where one can hide money to avoid taxes. Tax havens are primarily used by wealthy individuals and even more so by large corporations.

How do they work? For individuals, the most common strategy is that a rich person, call him Joe, instructs his lawyer to set up a shell company (i.e., a company that doesn't actually perform any real business) in a tax haven, call it "X Company," in the Cayman Islands, where there is very low cor-porate tax.[14] Joe, who lives in a large American city, then goes down to his local branch of a Swiss bank and opens a bank account for X Company in Switzerland. Joe then "purchases" services, such as consulting services, from X Company in Cayman. (These are fake purchases, as X Company doesn't actually do anything.) He pays for these services by sending money from his real bank account in the United States to the newly created X Company ac-count in Switzerland (which he secretly controls). The end result is that Joe has successfully transferred money from a known legitimate bank account to a secret, hidden account; thus at the end of the year, when he comes to pay taxes, his income and wealth will appear that much smaller, and his tax obli-gation will be correspondingly smaller too (Zucman 2015).

A useful way to understand the issue with tax havens is that they create two fundamental obstacles for tax collectors. One problem is *opaqueness*. Tax havens make it very difficult for a country to know how much income individuals (and corporations) are earning, the various sources of income, where genuine eco-nomic activity is taking place, etc. The related problem is that of *income siphoning*, meaning that individuals (and corporations) hide their income by splitting it into different portions in different places, so that the tax authorities have no idea of the big picture, no understanding of an individual's or corporation's total global income, making it impossible to tax actors comprehensively.

How significant a problem is this? Economists have long discussed the precise scale and scope of tax evasion through tax havens. The consensus is that it is very significant indeed. Alstadsæter, Johannesen, and Zucman (2019) find that at least 14% of the richest Scandinavian households were evading taxes on the eve of the financial crisis of 2008–2009, and stunningly, that the top 0.01% evade a massive 25% of their tax liability in tax havens. Likewise, wealthy Spanish taxpayers who chose to disclose offshore assets during the 2012 tax amnesty were found to be hiding an average of 30% of their net worth (Mas Montserrat and Mas Montserrat, cited in Advani and Tarrant 2021). In other words, tax evasion is absolutely rampant at the top. The most commonly cited estimate of the total scale of money hidden in tax havens comes from Zucman (2015, 3), who postulates that at least 8% of global wealth is held in tax havens. He cites this as a minimum, estimating that the true figure might well be in the range of 10–11% (45). This is a big deal: tax fraud is costing governments billions and billions of dollars (in 2021, tax fraud cost governments roughly $483 billion in lost revenue [GATJ, PSI, and TJN 2021]).

Zucman (2015), Shaxson (2011), and other specialists (e.g., Pogge and Mehta 2016) have long pointed out that tax havens are pernicious. They contribute significantly to inequality as the rich use them to avoid paying their taxes, and the falling tax revenue leads governments to shift taxes away from the rich (who can avoid them) toward the middle class and poor (who cannot). Tax havens lead to a loss of public revenue, which is a problem for all countries but particularly devastating for very poor countries.[15] Tax havens also undermine democracy, since they prevent the populace from being able to choose for themselves the level of taxation they wish to impose and the amount of redistribution they wish to achieve (Dietsch 2015). In addition, tax havens undermine human rights because they facilitate the activities of terrorists, gangsters, drug traffickers, and money-launderers.

Relatedly, a major problem with tax havens is that they make it very difficult for countries to impose comprehensive sanctions on criminals, oligarchs, or belligerent states. This problem was made excruciatingly visible during the Russian invasion of Ukraine in 2022. Within a day or two of the beginning of the invasion, practically the entire world was united in its condemnation of Russian violence, but what could be done? The West would not respond militarily for fear of escalation against a nuclear power. This left financial sanctions as the best nonviolent tool for pressuring the Russian regime. Indeed, the West did impose a range of sanctions; however, their ability to impose sanctions quickly and effectively against Russian elites was significantly hamstrung because of the existence of tax havens hiding and protecting their wealth (Piketty 2022; TJN 2022). If the Western countries had previously shut down tax havens (and mandated comprehensive sharing of information about who owns what assets), they would have had much stronger tools at their disposal to immediately freeze the assets of Russia's ruling class. That could well have stopped the war much earlier and saved many lives. The bottom line is that the essential nonviolent tool for states to impose pressure on rogue individuals or war-mongering states is financial sanctions, yet such sanctions will be far less effective as long as tax havens exist. Ultimately war criminals have much less to fear as long as tax havens exist.

Tax havens also undermine the rule of law. As Sweeney (2015) points out, tax evasion is probably the largest area of ongoing, well-known corruption remaining in the West. Tax havens also corrupt market economies by giving a competitive edge to large multinational companies—which often have extensive tax avoidance practices—over smaller companies, for reasons that have nothing to do with productivity or innovation. For all these reasons Shaxson (2018, 107) rightly describes tax havens as "a cancer on the global economy."

There is no secret as to why tax havens are as widespread as they are. Contemporary states engage in very little systematic monitoring and registering of the wealth that exists in the world, and without accurate information about the existence of wealth, taxing it becomes impossible—if you don't know about it, you can't tax it. Moreover, there are very minor penalties and punishments for countries that set themselves up as tax havens. Since havens are lucrative, they will clearly not stop without the threat of real sanctions. Likewise, there are typically only minor penalties or punishments for the individuals who conceal their wealth or the money managers—and wealth concealment industry more broadly—that facilitate tax evasion. (If both rich people and their bankers knew that they faced not a slap on the wrist but actual jail time, being arrested in front of their colleagues and dragged off in handcuffs, or having their assets seized and declared bankrupt, surely the prevalence of tax fraud would drop significantly.)

The key question, of course, is whether it is actually possible to close, or at least substantially reduce, tax havens. Given the global dimension of the problem (that shutting down one haven by itself won't necessarily help if another one somewhere else can just open up), as well as the fact that havens exist because they further the interests of many of the world's most powerful people, it is easy to feel pessimistic about the possibility of reducing tax havens. As Shaxson (2018, 103) admits, "no magic bullet can solve this vast political and economic conundrum. Any serious effort to do so would run headlong into some of the world's most powerful interests."

What, then, should be done? Since the fundamental problems are opacity and income siphoning, any genuine solution must get to the heart of these issues. Three areas of reform therefore seem vital. First, reforms should provide automatic exchange of information between tax authorities in different countries. Second, banks should be required to register the names of the actual human beings who ultimately control the assets in question; so-called beneficial ownership registration is necessary for a country to know who actually owns the country's assets, since it is common for the real owners to hide behind various trusts or shell corporations (Knobel 2019a). Third, reforms should tax citizens on the total amount of their global income (with tax credits for taxes paid in other countries to avoid double taxation).

Given the global nature of the problem, it is useful to think about the possibilities of reform on two levels: first, reforms that individual countries could enact unilaterally and therefore are simpler to implement and feasible over a shorter term; second, reforms that require global (or at least multilateral) coordination and therefore are more ambitious and medium term in nature.

There are a number of things that countries could do unilaterally to crack down on havens. We've already mentioned a couple of the most obvious lines of defense: increase penalties for tax fraud and increase the resources of the tax authorities to perform more numerous and extensive audits. (Recall Alstadsæter, Johannesen, and Zucman's 2018 estimate that enforcement efforts encouraging the disclosure of offshore assets in Norway resulted in a 30% increase in taxes paid.) In particular, all public officials should be required to disclose every penny of their wealth (from both domestic and offshore sources). For them more than anyone else, tax fraud should lead to criminal prosecutions (Dietsch 2015). Individual states also can and should require beneficial ownership registration. It would be useful for governments to collect and publish the information about asset ownership in the country. Having transparency about who owns what is vital for a democratic society to have actual oversight over how its economy is functioning. With this information NGOs, social movements, and political parties can hold their government accountable by asking what is being done with this information to crack down on tax evasion, money laundering, terrorist financing, and so on.[16]

Another important action is to increasingly regulate the banks and big accounting firms, while simultaneously providing stronger protection for whistleblowers (Alstadsæter, Johannesen, and Zucman 2019; Henry 2016). For example, when Bradley Birkenfeld, a former employee at the Swiss bank UBS, revealed that the bank's representatives were knowingly helping Americans to commit tax fraud, the American government took the rare action of actually taking the bank to court, so for the first time bankers faced the actual prospect of losing their jobs or even going to jail. This threat of real sanctions worked: in March 2009 UBS agreed to reveal to the IRS the identities of 4,450 clients, believed to be the most egregious of the tax evaders. The importance of this case was that it demonstrated to all that the banking secrecy of foreign tax havens was no longer impenetrable but could be effectively challenged through the courts (Johannesen et al. 2018). In Shaxson's (2018, 106) words, "Little focuses the minds of bankers and accountants like the threat of jail or the loss of a license to operate in a big economy."

More generally, it's important to realize that countries can always choose to levy taxes on the "residence" of asset owners, as opposed to the "source" of economic activity. A rich individual can always avoid paying taxes based on the "source" of their income by simply moving their income to a tax haven. However, if you tax based on "residency," then rich individuals have to pay tax on their total income, regardless of whether that income is domestic or international. In other words, resident taxation is, in general, the better approach because it allows for deep economic integration without undermining the tax base (Genschel and Schwarz 2011). The caveat is that resident taxation requires sharing information with other countries (since it will only work if other countries report to you how much your residents are earning in their country). The only way for a rich person to escape residence taxation is to give up their residence. But that is costly both in financial terms (particularly if there is an exit or tail tax) as well as in personal and emotional terms (of leaving one's home).

Perhaps the most important avenue that countries can unilaterally pursue is legislation to force foreign banks operating in the country to automatically exchange their data with the tax authorities. In the United States before 2014, it was very easy for rich people to set up accounts in the Cayman Islands, Switzerland, or the Bahamas, knowing that they would be beyond the reach of the IRS. But that significantly changed in 2014 with the passage of the Foreign Account Tax Compliance Act, which compels foreign financial institutions to identify the accounts held by US citizens and report the details to the IRS. There are two crucial design elements of FATCA. First, it imposes *automatic* exchange of data. (There doesn't have to be any formal request or prior suspicion.) The second and probably most crucial feature of the legislation is that it has real teeth: if foreign banks fail to report such information, they face significant fines (a 30% tax on all the dividends and interest income paid to them by the United States). FATCA appears to be quite successful: most of the world's tax havens have agreed to cooperate and now routinely pass information to the IRS.[17] According to Lily Batchelder, prior chief tax counsel to the US Senate's Finance Committee, FATCA has "dramatically improved our ability to uncover hidden, offshore accounts" (quoted in Cassidy 2019). However, it is still too early to know how effective it is in compelling tax compliance for very rich individuals with sophisticated avoidance capabilities (Johannesen et al. 2018).

As important as such reforms are, we will never get rid of the system of tax havens without serious international coordination (because shutting down one haven can always lead to another one springing up somewhere else). It is important to emphasize that only 10 years ago such international cooperation was widely seen as utopian. However, there has been dramatic improvement in this area such that the global landscape of tax evasion has been significantly reformed and is continuing to be so. The OECD has set up two important systems through the Common Reporting Standard for combating tax havens: the Exchange of Information upon Request, which allows signatories to request information on specific people, and the Automatic Exchange of Information (AEOI). The AEOI is similar to FATCA in that it allows for automatic exchange of information between signatory countries. Participating jurisdictions send and receive pre-agreed information each year, without having to send a specific request. The AEOI is an important milestone in the fight against tax havens; it means that bank secrecy, which existed for decades and was the heart of tax evasion, no longer exists to the same degree. For instance, it is no longer possible for, say, a Canadian citizen to simply open a secret bank account in Switzerland, because every year the Swiss banks now automatically share their information on their Canadian clients to the Canadian government. These systems are relatively new and still developing, but at the time of writing, 97 countries (including those in the EU, Russia, China, and many of the most prominent tax havens, such as Bermuda, the Cayman Islands, the Bahamas, and Switzerland) have all signed on, enabling tax authorities to obtain data on 84 million financial accounts, covering total assets of €10 trillion (Perret 2021). This is a very encouraging development.

Indeed, preliminary evidence of the effects of the AEOI is encouraging. For instance, after Switzerland committed to automatically exchanging information in 2015, compliance increased dramatically: the amount of assets voluntarily disclosed in the canton of Zurich almost doubled, jumping from 3 billion Swiss francs during 2012–2015 to roughly 5 billion during 2016–2019 (Eckert and Aebi 2020; for additional evidence, see O'Reilly, Ramirez, and Stemmer 2019).

Nevertheless, there are some important limitations. The United States has refused to participate (so even though it requests information from other countries through FATCA, it has refused to reciprocate in providing automatic exchange of information). Moreover, not every country is participating.[18] So a rich Canadian can avoid the CRS by hiding their money in a tax haven that is not part of the system. Another loophole is that the information exchanged is financial—so other forms of assets (real estate, cash, gold) are not included. In addition, the information exchanged often does not identify the ultimate owner, which allows for sophisticated legal maneuvering to allow evaders to continue to evade. So there are clearly improvements that need to be made (Noked 2018).

The bottom line, however, is that the most common forms of tax evasion—such as opening a secret account in Switzerland—are now impossible. More sophisticated forms of evasion still do exist, and we do not yet have data on the extent to which the AEOI has reduced total tax evasion.

The most comprehensive (and ambitious) proposals for eradicating tax havens call for setting up some sort of global tax registry to coordinate tax matters (Knobel 2019b; Tanzi 2016; Zucman 2015).[19] For instance, Zucman proposes the creation of a worldwide register of all financial wealth, recording who owns all the stocks and bonds in the world. Central depositories for global trade of stocks and bonds already exist; the problem is that they are not truly global (they are national or sometimes regional), and they are run by private companies (such as the Depository Trust Company in the United States and Euroclear and Clearstream in Europe). Zucman proposes that governments take control of these central depositories, gradually unifying them into a single global financial register, which will then automatically share information with national tax authorities.[20] Possessing this information would allow tax authorities to confirm whether or not their citizens are in fact disclosing all of their assets. The problem with this proposal, of course, is that getting all the countries of the world to join such a scheme would be quite a feat, to say the least. It is perhaps somewhat more plausible to envision the EU and/or the United States starting something like this (likely motivated by the desire to root out money laundering and terrorist financing just as much as tax evasion). And since the vast majority of private wealth ends up in these financial centers (though money is often hidden in the Global South, almost all of it ends up being invested in the Global North), obtaining a registry in these regions would be a significant blow to tax evasion around the world.

Corporate Taxation

We have been discussing the use of tax havens by wealthy individuals. But in fact the largest players using havens are actually corporations. Indeed, many of the largest companies across the globe are currently getting away with tax fraud on a gigantic scale. Apple, the richest company in the world, made profits of $305 billion between 2008 and 2015 but paid a foreign tax rate of only 5.8% (ITEP 2017). In the single year of 2018, Amazon made $11.2 billion in profit yet paid not a penny of US federal income tax—they actually received a tax rebate (Gardner 2019)! In fact, 55 of the largest corporations in the United States paid zero taxes in 2020, despite collective profits of $40 billion (Gardner and Wamhoff 2021). Recall, by contrast, that the average American worker pays a 22% effective income tax rate. Overall, the US Government Accountability Office estimates that 83 of the country's 100 largest companies have subsidiaries in tax havens (Shaxson 2011, 8).

One of the most important macroeconomic phenomena in the world over the past 30 years has been the collapse of corporate taxes, due in large part to "tax competition," that is, the pressure that each country feels to lower its own taxes in order to attract foreign investment and prevent their corporations fleeing to lower-tax jurisdictions. The facts here are startling. Between 1981 and 2017, the average statutory corporate tax rate in the OECD has fallen by almost half, from 42% to 23% (see Figure 2.2).

So although we have mainly discussed the wealth of rich individuals, individual wealth and corporate wealth are in practice tightly interwoven. When corporations pay less tax—either because of reduced rates or because they

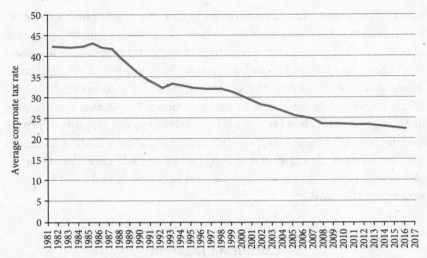

Figure 2.2 Average OECD statutory corporate tax rate (Clausing 2018, 38).

use tax havens—it is ultimately their wealthy individual shareholders who reap the rewards.[21] The use of the corporate form—particularly the offshore shell company—is one way, if not the main way, that rich people hide their income from the tax collector.

How have states reacted to tax competition driving down corporate tax rates? A common response has been to broaden the tax base, mainly by shifting taxes away from mobile sources (like corporations) toward immobile ones (such as new income or consumption taxes). Moreover, the new taxes on immobile sources are often regressive taxes, meaning that they fell on poorer people more than richer. This shift away from taxes on the rich, toward more taxes on poor and middle-class people, has generated increased inequality overall. In Dietsch's (2015, 48) words, "OECD countries have bought fiscal stability in terms of revenue at the cost of a less redistributive system."

For example, in Brazil between 1985 and 1997 the top personal income tax rate fell from 60% to 25%, and the tax on corporate profit fell from 50% to 15%, whereas the lowest rate increased from 0 to 15%. From 1995 to 2001, the employee income tax rate rose by 14% and social security contributions by 75%, while taxes on profits were reduced by 8%. Today 70% of Brazil's tax revenue comes from indirect taxes such as value-added taxes, which are often regressive (Dietsch 2015, 49–50). A similar phenomenon has occurred in the United States: since the 1950s, corporate taxes have plummeted, from providing a third of all government tax revenue in the 1950s to less than a tenth today. This loss of revenue has been compensated by a significant increase in taxes on workers in the form of new payroll taxes. Moreover, as the gap between corporate taxes and income taxes has grown, the rich have converted more of their income and wealth into corporate forms, the result of which has been to drive down the effective tax rates on the wealthy (Shaxson and Christensen 2016).

It is important to realize that cuts to corporate taxes are not only detrimental to equality, but they also damage democracy. This is because a major way that society is able to exert democratic control over corporations is by using the tax system to incentivize or disincentivize various behaviors. If a community wishes to encourage companies to, for instance, hire a more racially diverse staff, or more individuals with a disability, encourage more unionization, pollute less, pay CEOs less, or promote more women into upper management, then a basic tool at its disposal is to offer tax subsidies or threaten tax penalties in order to motivate the desired behavior. The problem is that the lower corporate taxes are cut, the less leverage a government has to wield this democratic tool. Lower corporate taxes mean reduced ability for democratic control over the economy.

Corporate tax evasion works somewhat differently than individual evasion. The most common method involves corporations setting up shell companies in order to claim that their production happens in low-tax jurisdictions. Take the case of the banana company Chiquita (this example comes from Shaxson 2011). The actual production process involves growing a banana in, say, Honduras, which is then transported to Canada and eaten by a consumer there. So Chiquita should pay taxes in Honduras and Canada—the places where it is performing real business. However, to avoid taxes, Chiquita will do something like this: it will set up several subsidiaries, call them Fake Banana 1 located in the Cayman Islands, Fake Banana 2 located in Switzerland, and Fake Banana 3 located in the Bahamas. Chiquita then sells the bananas picked in Honduras to its subsidiary Fake Banana 1, which then resells them to Fake Banana 2, and then on to Fake Banana 3, before finally arriving in Canada. Now the actual bananas are not traveling to these places; all that is moving is the legal ownership of them. The purpose of all this paperwork is that Chiquita pays taxes based on the size of its profits, and they can now declare that they made zero profits in Honduras and zero profits in Canada; in fact, all their profits were made in Cayman, Switzerland, and

Bahamas—lo and behold, places with very low corporate tax rates. In this way, Chiquita can avoid paying practically any tax. This is not an unrealistic example. In 2006, the *Guardian* newspaper found that the three biggest banana companies operating in the United Kingdom were making hundreds of millions of pounds yet paying only 0.031% tax. This is a tax rate which is roughly 1,000 times less than regular working people pay.[22]

What can be done about such tax evasion? Recall again that the fundamental problems are opacity (no one knows exactly where corporations are operating or how much money they're making [Kleinbard 2016]) and income siphoning (multinationals siphoning funds into various subsidiaries to avoid taxes on their total global profits). Given this, there are four reforms that would fundamentally fix the problem: country-by-country reporting, formulary apportionment, global minimums, and, if necessary, a shift to immobile but progressive tax bases.

The basic solution to opacity is country-by-country reporting. This is an accounting practice requiring companies to publish how much profit and cost they incur in each and every country in which they operate (instead of publishing total profits and costs as a grouped sum). This transparency allows tax authorities to see where genuine business activity is occurring rather than where profits are simply being shifted around to avoid taxes (TJN 2020).

The basic solution to the income siphoning problem is to treat multinational firms not as collections of separate entities but as the single unitary enterprise they in fact truly are. Probably the most comprehensive proposal for doing so is unitary taxation with formulary apportionment.[23] The idea here is that the total income of a multinational is calculated by country-by-country reporting, and then using a standardized formula to divide that income among the different countries in which the firm engages in real business. The formula needs to be carefully devised in a way that makes it hard to manipulate. For instance, it could be based predominantly on sales, since firms cannot easily manipulate where their consumers are located (Zucman 2015). (The classic formula is the Massachusetts apportionment, which allocates profit on the basis of an equal weighting of company sales, employees, and fixed assets.) After the profits are divided among countries, each country is then free to tax their portion of the profits at whatever rate it chooses. For example, suppose Amazon makes $10 billion profits in a year, and 50% of its sales, payroll, and assets are in the United States; then $5 billion would be taxable at whatever rate the United States decides to levy (Murphy 2016). With this system in place multinationals would no longer be able to shift income to low-tax jurisdictions (without actually shifting their real business there).

Formulary apportionment already exists in the United States between its states and in Canada between its provinces (though it stops "at the water's edge," meaning that domestic firms do not need to include their foreign activity). The process is straightforward: the profits of US firms are calculated at a national level, then attributed to the various states using a standardized formula that is hard to manipulate, leaving each state free to charge any percent tax it chooses. So we know that such a system can work. What does not yet exist is formulary apportionment of international profits. An individual country could unilaterally adopt this practice, requiring each company to provide a breakdown of their global profits, country by country, applying a formulary apportioning calculation, and then taxing their share of the multinational's profit (with a complementary system of tax credits to firms paying taxes elsewhere to avoid double taxation). But as always, the more that such a system could be coordinated internationally, the better, as that would vastly reduce evasion possibilities and help to iron out the inevitable complexities (Shaxson 2018). Total global cooperation would not be required. Zucman (2015) estimates that if either the United States or Europe (and ideally both) implemented such a system, it would substantially reduce corporate tax evasion.[24]

A third important reform is to implement a global minimum corporate tax rate to stop the race to the bottom. It will of course be difficult to get everyone to go along, but the large economies are the ones that matter most, and they have strong incentive to do so. (Large economies like France and Germany have no incentive to indefinitely allow their corporations to relocate to Luxembourg.) It's worth pointing out that the fundamental problem here is the divide between those who want to minimize their tax obligations (the owners of capital) and those who benefit from higher taxes (regular working people). Hence an important avenue for dealing with tax evasion is to find ways to give regular working people more say over how their employers operate. If workers had enhanced say on corporate boards, they may well be less inclined to evade taxes and would definitely be opposed to shutting down their own place of work so that their jobs could be shipped overseas (Vitols 2021).

Fourth and finally, to the extent that companies are successfully avoiding taxes, countries can protect themselves by broadening the tax base by shifting taxation toward more immobile factors: labor, consumption, inheritance, and land. The crucial thing to recognize is that although this kind of shift has typically been regressive (e.g., replacing progressive corporate taxes with regressive payroll taxes, which increases inequality), there is absolutely no reason why this has to be the case. It's entirely possible to tax labor, consumption, inheritance, and land *progressively*, such as through progressive income taxes, luxury taxes on consumption, and high rates of property tax for expensive houses or second homes. Unless rich people are actually willing to emigrate, most of their resources are going to be immobile, and so available to be progressively taxed.

A recurring theme in the literature on taxation is the importance of taxing the income and wealth of the rich *comprehensively*. If just one portion of their income or wealth is taxed, while other portions are left untaxed, or taxed at much lower rates, then wealthy individuals will simply shift their portfolios around to avoid paying taxes. Taxation works only if the base is broad. This means that, as much as possible, taxes on the rich must be significant not only on labor and capital income but also on corporate profits (which of course will ultimately become income for the shareholders). The difficulty is that international tax competition poses a risk for any one country seeking to unilaterally raise its corporate taxes as it risks corporations fleeing to lower tax jurisdictions. Now it may well be the case that this risk is overblown, since many corporations simply can't move (for instance, because they provide services to local consumers)[25] or because, all things considered, they don't want to move because the high taxes provide things that are actually more valuable to them, such as social stability, highly educated, healthy workers and an efficient, well-developed infrastructure.[26]

Nevertheless, it is reasonable to assume that individual countries (particularly smaller ones) will not want to raise their corporate tax rates significantly higher than their neighbors'. What, then, can a progressive government do to maintain comprehensively high tax rates? The best policy would probably be to keep corporate taxes as high as possible without going too much higher than their neighbors'. Such taxes should be complemented with higher rates of progressive taxation on immobile sources. Having a gap between these tax rates will mean that some income will inevitably be shifted into the corporate form, but that is not the end of the world. If more cash is being stored inside the corporation (and can't be shifted out without paying high taxes), then firms will have more incentive to invest, which is good for the broader economy.[27] Moreover, it is not a fatal obstacle to our ability to tax the rich if they store a portion of their wealth inside corporations, since such wealth can still be accessed via the wealth tax. Therefore, rich people will be able to avoid paying tax on their corporate wealth only by avoiding the wealth tax, which, as we saw, would require permanently leaving the country and paying a punitive exit tax.

To come full circle, recall that imposing a wealth tax will inevitably lead to some avoidance and evasion. However, a common method of evasion that happens today, in the absence of a wealth tax, is that billionaires like Elon Musk and Larry Ellison stash their wealth inside corporations (e.g., as stock) and thereby avoid paying income tax. Imposing a wealth tax would get at much of this wealth (since the value of these stocks is widely known, and Musk and Ellison can hardly hide the fact that they own their companies). The bottom line is that while a wealth tax would lead to some avoidance, it could also play a vital role in reducing some of the avoidance that is already happening.

How realistic are the kinds of reform we have been discussing? Five or 10 years ago they would have seemed extremely optimistic and their implementation a long way off. But things have changed dramatically in the past few years. What once seemed utopian is no longer so. Perhaps the biggest change is in public consciousness. The regular explosion of shocking tax scandals (LuxLeaks in 2014, Panama Papers in 2016, Paradise Papers in 2017, Pandora Papers in 2021, the Credit Suisse leak in 2022, and so on), as well as the increasingly obvious way that truly scary and dangerous people (terrorists, money-launderers, drug lords, war criminals) rely on tax havens, have made them increasingly unpopular.

As mentioned above, in 2014 the OECD initiated an international system of automatic exchange of information, which currently includes 97 countries, 84 million financial accounts, and €10 trillion in assets.

A true milestone was reached in 2021, when the G7 (the 7 richest countries in the world) agreed to impose a global minimum corporate tax rate of 15% (Islam 2021). Encouragingly, the agreement also introduces an element of unitary taxation with formulary apportionment (though only for a small part of the profits of 100 or so multinationals). Among the 130 countries that have signed on are the prominent havens Bermuda and the Cayman Islands and the major powers India and China. This is a big deal: it is the first time in all of history that a global minimum corporate tax rate will exist. Indeed, the French finance minister Bruno Le Maire called it "the most important international tax agreement in a century" (CBC 2021).[28]

In 2021 the EU Parliament took the important step of making it mandatory for multinational corporations to publish country-by-country reporting data (though to date they must publish information on only the European countries in which they operate). This breaks an important taboo over publishing such data in the public realm. The US House of Representatives has gone even further, passing a bill requiring multinationals to disclose information on *every country* in which they operate (though at the time of writing it remains unclear whether such legislation will pass the Senate [Parkin 2021]).

In sum, the goal for egalitarians in this domain should be to raise corporate taxes as close to income tax levels as possible (so as to prevent tax shifting). To the extent that corporate taxes must be significantly lower than income taxes to prevent capital flight (and it's worth repeating that it is not guaranteed that higher taxes will automatically lead to this), then governments should shift to progressive taxes on immobile sources, and in particular should impose a wealth tax to access the wealth that rich people stash inside the corporate form. Additionally, individual shareholders should be taxed on their capital income based on their residency (not the source of their income). To prevent avoidance and evasion through tax havens there should be enhanced legal enforcement, including regular audits, automatic information sharing between countries, and comprehensive beneficial ownership registration. Corporate taxes should be levied by an apportioning formula based on country-by-country reporting and backstopped by a global minimum tax rate.

Reducing Inequality through Inheritance Tax

Hugh Grosvenor, the Duke of Westminster, inherited £9 billion at the age of 25, becoming the world's richest person under 30. With extensive real estate holdings, he is said to own "half of London" (SkyNews 2016). Not only is such inheritance an obvious affront to democratic norms; it is also a major source of inequality. According to Piketty (2014, 402), in the United States in 2010, inheritance accounted for roughly 66% of the total wealth of all individuals. This means that inheritance tax has an important role to play in reducing the transmission of large fortunes. Inheritance taxes today are quite widespread: 17 OECD nations, including the United States, impose them in some form. That said, they typically collect only small amounts of revenue; none of them collects more than 1% of GDP. (Belgium and France collect the most, at 0.7% and 0.6% of GDP, respectively.) On average, joint gift and inheritance taxes make up only 0.1% of GDP, compared to total tax revenues, which are more than 34% (Drometer et al. 2018). In part that is an indication of the low rates that are commonly imposed, but it's important to keep in mind that inheritance tax is never likely to raise large amounts of revenue because it touches only a small fraction of the population (those who die each year), and it applies to only a fraction of that fraction (the rich). This means that the purpose of the inheritance tax (like the wealth tax) is somewhat different than taxes: the purpose is not to raise substantial revenue per se but to reduce the concentration of wealth at the top—not to fund the welfare state but to reduce inequality.

As with income tax, the large number of countries that have implemented inheritance taxes give us significant real-world evidence about what works and what does not.

Let us look first at when and why inheritance taxes fail. The United States is a good example of a broken (or, one might more aptly say, a "fixed") system. Successive Republican governments have created numerous loopholes and deduction opportunities to such an extent that the tax is now widely considered "voluntary," given how easy it is to avoid. The statutory rate is reasonably high—currently at 40%—but thanks to the loopholes, the effective rate is closer to 17%. There is also very little enforcement. For instance, in 1975 the IRS audited fully 65% of the largest 29,000 estate tax returns filed the year before; by 2018, they were auditing only 8.6% of the 34,000 returns. All in all, the estate tax collects very little. In 2017, for instance, the revenue collected from wealthy individuals who died in 2016 was only $20 billion. That represents a mere 0.13% of the $15 trillion net worth that the top 0.1% wealthiest families owned in 2016. Indeed, in 2013 only 0.14% of all estates— a couple thousand families—paid any estate tax at all. In other words, as it is currently constituted, the US estate tax does virtually nothing to reduce overall inequality (Reich 2015; Saez and Zucman 2019b, 2019d). That said, the main lesson to learn from the US case is not that an inheritance tax can't work—it has worked better in the past—but that such systems can quite easily be broken. For the most part, the US inheritance tax is now intentionally designed to not overly bother the rich.

On the other hand, there is significant evidence around the world showing that inheritance tax systems can have an impact on the transmission of wealth at the top. Ishi (1980) shows that in Japan, the inheritance tax played an important role in inequality reduction, reducing the Gini coefficient by roughly 14% throughout the 1970s. In Sweden in the 1970s, the inheritance and gift taxes, combined with the capital gains tax, meant that the deceased owner of a large firm would be required to pay almost 80% of the value of the estate (Henrekson 2017).[29] In their groundbreaking work, Scheve and Stasavage (2016) show that a number of countries have successfully implemented high levels of inheritance tax over the years. For instance, in 1975 the United Kingdom had a top rate of 75%, Sweden had a top rate of 65%, and in 1950 Japan had a top rate of 90% (112).

Based on the comparative evidence on inheritance taxes, there are three main obstacles to the tax working well. The primary issue is the prevalence of exemptions and deduction opportunities. These come in different forms; in the United States major deductions exist for charities, trusts, and foundations, as well as the step-up basis that applies to capital gains. Kopczuk (2013) points out that tax deductions for charitable contributions are the second largest deduction (after the marital deduction) used by estate taxpayers and the largest one for unmarried taxpayers. Trusts and foundations are another major way that individuals hide their money. For instance, Hugh Grosvenor was able to inherit £9 billion with only minimal inheritance tax because the family wealth is held in a trust (Garside 2016). Setting up a trust allows rich individuals to remain the beneficial owners of the assets while simultaneously shrouding the assets in secrecy. For instance, if I stash several million dollars away as shares in a newly formed trust, the company will be listed under the name of the trustee (my lawyer), not me, and my lawyer will have the right (through legal confidentiality) not to mention me, even though I remain for all intents and purposes the effective owner (Shaxson 2011). As mentioned in Chapter 1 (footnote 7), step-up basis is a particularly egregious loophole that allows capital gains unrealized at death (typically in the form of closely held stocks in private businesses) to be excluded from taxation. This means that wealthy individuals can avoid paying capital gains taxes while alive, and then pass their wealth on to heirs who, due to this loophole, do not have to pay the tax either.

A second issue with inheritance taxes is that the rates are often too low. Since the whole point of such taxes is to mitigate extreme wealth at the top, they will only be effective at high rates.

A third issue is that if the tax threshold is too low, there may be risks of destroying family businesses. The image of the family farm that upon death must be sold off because the children cannot afford the inheritance tax has been one of the most successful rallying cries in galvanizing opposition to the inheritance tax. However, while this is a logical possibility, it shouldn't be overstated. Neither the American Farm Bureau nor the *New York Times* has been able to identify a single instance of this ever occurring (Batchelder 2016).

Given these issues, what do tax experts recommend for instituting an inheritance tax as effectively as possible?

First, the system should be as simple as possible, with few loopholes or deductions, ideally none. Of course, some states may wish to maintain deductions for charitable giving, but even this is a controversial matter. Instead of offering tax deductions in the hope that benevolent rich people will solve the problems of the world, I suspect that a far better approach—more democratic, more accountable, and more effective—would be to deliberate as a society about the areas we wish to spend money on domestically (or donate to internationally), and then collectively raise the money to do so through fair and progressive taxation—including on inheritances. (We discuss this issue more in Chapter 7.) Trusts, foundations, and other intermediaries should be heavily regulated. Sensible policy here would be to force trusts to declare who the ultimate owners of their assets are so that the market value of such assets can be included in the relevant individuals' tax returns (OECD 2018a; Saez and Zucman 2019b).

Second, the rate of the inheritance tax should be progressive, high, and kick in at a relatively high threshold. In terms of thresholds, there is an inevitable trade-off. The lower the threshold, the more money states can raise. But low thresholds lead to the risk that families who are not particularly rich will be forced to sell their family home or family business. This creates immense political pressure for deductions and exemptions, which then open the floodgates to all kinds of gaming and avoidance. Raising the threshold mitigates that problem (as we need not shed any tears if wealthy children are forced to sell their family mansion or luxury yacht). But it also means that fewer people will be required to pay the tax, reducing the total revenues collected. Since inheritance tax is levied only once in a person's life, it is not likely to raise significant revenues, so it is better to see it not as the primary tool for raising large amounts of revenue for redistribution (income taxes are better for that purpose) but rather as a tool for reducing great fortunes and limiting the transmission of class privilege. Keeping the threshold at a high level, but with very high top rates (allowing no exemptions), would serve that purpose well.

Third, many scholars advocate framing the tax as an *inheritance tax* (where the recipient of the inheritance and gifts pays the tax) as opposed to an *estate tax* (where the donor pays the tax). The major advantage of an inheritance tax system is that it discourages passing on large amounts of wealth to one person. Since the recipients have to pay a progressive tax on the income they receive, less total tax will be paid if donors give smaller amounts to more people (or to people who have received fewer gifts and bequests from others) instead of larger amounts to fewer people, which is exactly what you want if the goal is to reduce inequality and break up family dynasties. Politically, an inheritance tax may also be an easier sell to the public, as it is harder to cast it as a "death tax," and harder to argue that the children (or other recipients) who have to pay the tax are genuinely harmed, as that would require arguing that they have the right to start life as millionaires in positions of social superiority to their neighbors.

Tony Atkinson (2015) persuasively argues that the ideal inheritance tax should take the form of a lifetime capital receipts tax: everyone would have a threshold for the total amount of gifts and bequests they can receive in a lifetime tax free. (Transfers between spouses or partners would not be taxed.) Above that point, taxes would kick in progressively. This would allow every citizen to receive a lifetime of gifts up to, say, $250,000 tax free.[30] But any gifts beyond this point would be increasingly taxed. (I would advocate for extremely high top rates: 90% or even higher for vast fortunes.) Such a policy would allow for generous family support, while at the same time markedly reducing inequality. After all, giving a generous gift to a loved one is one thing; passing on a lifetime of class privilege, not to mention social power over one's neighbors, is quite another.

Summary

This and the previous chapter have analyzed a number of potential tools for reducing inequality. Is it feasible to do so? Overall, the general answer must be yes: each tool can effectively reduce inequality, at least somewhat. That said, the possibility of an instrument functioning is far different from a guarantee that it will function well. None of the tools we have examined work flawlessly, and all require careful design to overcome common problems and obstacles.

Income tax can reduce inequality, but only if there is extensive third-party reporting; a broad tax base with limited exemptions and loopholes, particularly to ensure that capital income is taxed at rates similar to labor income;

and increased enforcement efforts, including policies to tax global income and impose an exit tax on those wishing to expatriate. Even with these complementary policies, there will inevitably be some avoidance, some evasion, and some emigration. Nevertheless, with careful design, such problems should be quite manageable.

We have also seen a number of predistributive labor market regulations for reducing inequality. Unions are an important tool here, though their ability to reduce inequality will depend on their ability to acquire new members and the scope of their bargaining rights. Full-employment policies can reduce inequality, though they must be balanced with concern for price stability. Likewise, educational opportunity can reduce inequality, particularly if it is accessible, of high quality, and targeted at young children. Increased minimum wages can also be effective, though this must be balanced with employment concerns (particularly if wages outstrip the productivity of low-wage workers by too great a margin). Limiting the pay of upper managers and CEOs is also likely to be an effective policy.

Other important tools for reducing inequality include breaking up monopolies (e.g., creating alternative incentive systems that rely less on patent and copyright monopolies); increasing taxes on the accumulating housing wealth of the rich; providing universal child care; introducing an income guarantee, such as a Basic Income; and, over a longer term but perhaps most fundamentally, expanding workplace democracy.

Yet although income taxes and predistributive reforms are vital, they are inadequate for dealing with the superrich. For them, the only way to make fundamental inroads is to tax the stock of wealth—hence the need for an inheritance tax, a real estate tax, or, ideally, a comprehensive wealth tax.

Since we have less real-world experience of successful versions of the wealth tax than we do for the other policies, the analysis is unavoidably somewhat more speculative. Nevertheless, we have seen that there are good reasons to believe that an effective wealth tax could work well as long as it is designed cautiously and carefully. Perhaps unsurprisingly, the main required features are largely the same as those required for successful income and inheritance taxes. That should reassure us. Given that we know it's possible to have effective income and inheritance taxes, we should feel at least moderately confident that a successful wealth tax, which faces similar obstacles, could be designed too. (To put the matter another way: those who think that a wealth tax is impossible must explain why it is not impossible to have a successful inheritance tax.) An effective wealth tax would require a high threshold, progressive rates (with high rates for the superrich in particular), a broad tax base with minimal exemptions and deductions, the extensive use of third-party reporting, enhanced enforcement, and formulaic prospective and retrospective evaluation, with reconciliation, for the remaining assets that are not third-party reported. Like all taxes, a wealth tax would work much better if it were part of a broader ecology of anti-tax-avoidance policies, such as increased enforcement not just of perpetrators but of facilitators (bankers and accountants). Reducing tax evasion requires measures to reduce opacity (in particular, the deepening and broadening of the existing OECD system of automatic exchange of information and expansion of public registries of beneficial ownership) as well as measures to tax entities on their global income—for individuals this means taxation based on residency, and for corporations it means moving toward a system of country-by-country reporting with formulary apportionment—multilaterally if possible, unilaterally if necessary.

Ultimately, the wealth tax is a major policy tool with great promise for an egalitarian future; it offers the same kind of progressive possibility for the 21st century as the income tax (which fundamentally built the welfare state) was able to do for the 20th.

Inheritance tax can work effectively too, but only when loopholes are closed, rates are raised (especially for the very rich), and thresholds are kept relatively high (so that new exemptions are not required for liquidity problems). Ideally, inheritance taxes should take the form of an income tax on the lifetime receipt of bequests and gifts.

In sum, we should be cautiously optimistic that inequality reduction is indeed workable. Governments wishing to reduce inequality have myriad tools at their disposal, and most of these tools have extensive histories and proven track records. The more that a country can make use of these tools, and use them well, the more that inequality will be reduced. Ultimately, the biggest obstacle is not technical know-how or design. We know, broadly speaking, how to reduce inequality. The most significant obstacle is political will—in particular, the resistance of the wealthy and the powerful who have much to lose financially (even if they have much to gain in their humanity). As is often the case, the fundamental obstacle is not technical feasibility but class power.

3

Should We Aim for High Taxes and Low Inequality?

Weighing Costs and Benefits

In unequal societies like the United States today, the richest people often pay very low rates of tax. In 2007, Jeff Bezos paid no federal income tax (even though his net worth was $190 billion, and the stock value of his company, Amazon, had doubled that year). Likewise, he paid no income tax in 2011, though he claimed a $4,000 tax credit for his kids. Similarly, Elon Musk paid not a penny in income taxes in 2018 (Walker 2021). Should we force the rich to pay more?

It is often thought that even if it is possible to reduce inequality by raising taxes to high levels, we should not do so, since the costs—in terms of reduced incentives, investment, productivity, and resultant slower economic growth—are far more significant than any benefits which redistribution might bring. This chapter investigates whether this is true. We begin by comparing the *economic* costs with the benefits of high redistributive taxes. We will then consider the *social* costs and benefits. Finally, we will consider the whole package in order to weigh the total costs versus the total benefits. The overarching question is whether higher taxes and lower inequality are good overall. Of course, it's possible to reduce inequality in various ways, but in this chapter our focus will be on reducing inequality by way of high taxes.

The background assumptions are these: we are imagining a contemporary, rich, neoliberal country (the United States, United Kingdom, Ireland, Canada, Australia, New Zealand) which could follow two distinct paths. On the one path, we imagine that the country stays on its present course, with low taxes and high levels of inequality. On the other path, we imagine the country radically changing direction, veering toward equality by gradually but continually ramping up its tax rates over the years. We will assume that this society gradually increases taxes on most people, and in particular

Against Inequality. Tom Malleson, Oxford University Press. © Oxford University Press 2023.
DOI: 10.1093/oso/9780197670392.003.0004

increases taxes on the rich (say the top 1% or 5%) to a very high level. We assume further that the tax revenues are spent on standard public programs, such as public services and infrastructure. Of course, any really existing egalitarian society would undoubtedly want to implement a number of predistributive measures in addition to taxation, but to keep the thought experiment as simple as possible, we will bracket those issues. Furthermore, we assume that in this society, popular assumptions have shifted sufficiently such that the majority of the population desires less inequality, hence they are willing to vote for progressive governments, though they are also sensitive to economic costs. (In other words, their progressivism has limits; they will not tolerate economic disaster.) We also assume that although most of the population prefer more equality, they do not always act in their day-to-day lives in ways that are entirely ethically consistent with such preferences, meaning that they may be tempted to take advantage of tax loopholes or other such things, at least as long as it is easy and relatively risk-free to do so. In addition, we assume that the rich and business owners possess similar kinds of profit-maximizing incentives as they do today. In terms of government law and policy, we assume that a progressive government that has a mandate to significantly reduce inequality through taxation also has a mandate to implement a number of complementary anti-avoidance reforms. So we assume that the major components identified in the previous two chapters have been implemented: the tax base has been broadened (there is widespread third-party reporting; loopholes and deductions have been removed; there is a relatively similar rate of taxation on capital income as labor income); there are high thresholds for wealth taxes; there are significantly resources devoted to enforcement; there are taxes on foreign income, exit taxes, and crackdowns on tax havens. The assumption is not that any of these policies work perfectly, but that all in all the tax system works more or less satisfactorily.

An investigation of this kind that aims to compare an existing state of affairs with a counterfactual always faces a very real danger, which is that we end up comparing a real society (warts and all) with an ideal one. In such comparisons, the ideal will always triumph. Such a comparison would be biased from the start and convince no one. To guard against this, we should strive to be as balanced and fair as possible in evaluating costs and benefits. In particular, when estimates about the costs or benefits of a practice are unclear—as they often are—I will err on the side of being conservative and cautious in the evaluation.

Economic Costs and Benefits

Reduced Incentives to Work

The first question to consider is whether high taxes will lead rich people to put in less effort or hours of work. From a purely theoretical perspective, the answer is not at all clear. On the one hand, the "substitution" effect implies that taxes reduce the reward for working, suggesting people will work less. Indeed, it seems undeniable that at the extreme of a 100% effective tax, with people receiving nothing in return for their labor, most people would not work. On the other hand, the "income" effect implies that a reduced income means that people can't afford to consume as many goods, which may motivate them to work harder to compensate. For instance, those who have specific monetary goals that they are working toward—buying a house, saving up for a new car, etc.—may well choose to work more after a tax rise in order to reach their goals.

It also seems clear that work effort is not driven solely by income but also involves nonfinancial factors such as status, power, the intrinsic pleasure of work, satisfaction from providing a useful service to others,[1] workplace norms of what is expected, and so on. Consider those lucky few in contemporary society who love their job (such as tenured professors like myself who get paid to spend their time reading and teaching). If I were guaranteed basic material security—a home, ample food, healthcare, child care, a pension— and a modest disposable income for small pleasures, I would happily work at a 100% effective tax rate.

Indeed, one of the noteworthy aspects of employment in contemporary capitalism is that the workers at the top of the hierarchy—such as doctors, managers, business owners, executives—enjoy jobs that not only pay the most but also tend to provide the most nonmonetary rewards in being the most meaningful, exciting, influential, or intrinsically rewarding. That does not mean that workers in these jobs would work for free, but it does mean that a tax rise may make little difference in terms of the hours or effort they exert at work. For many at the top of the economic hierarchy, the drive to work hard is surely just as much about status as money per se. The CEOs, Wall Street bankers, and star athletes who are working 60 hours per week are doing so not simply for the money but also for the status, respect, and prestige they receive for being at the top (as well as following the norms of what people around them are doing).

Another important psychological factor is that many of the rich are driven by a desire to win the competition—to end up with more than others, to be the "best." Now whatever one may think of the moral tenor of such an ethic (hopefully an egalitarian society would reduce it somewhat), it is one that can coexist with a highly progressive tax regime. The male executive who is driven solely by the desire to be in the top 1% will still be in the top 1% after everyone pays their taxes—it's just that he'll be less rich in absolute terms. But since such people will still be very well off, even with very high taxes (keep in mind that even a 99% marginal tax rate means 99% on the top portion of their income, not 99% overall), such people who are primarily motivated by their relative position vis-à-vis their neighbors will not likely be particularly discouraged by high taxes.[2]

The last point is that to the extent that any of the rich become socialists and accept the ethical arguments of the kind outlined in this book (likely very few, alas), their perspective will not be that taxes represent the government stealing that which is "mine," but rather that taxes are a correction of the market's immoral distribution (see Chapters 4–6). So they will no longer see taxes as the taking of a natural, preexisting income, but will instead see post-taxation income as their slice of the cooperatively-produced pie. The psychological evaluation is thus no longer "Look how much the government is taking from me!" but rather, "My labor is rewarded with a slice of the pie that we, my compatriots (and forebears) and I, have collectively baked, and it's a slice that allows me to live very comfortably." We can always hope that at least some of the elites embrace an egalitarian project. Nevertheless, the success of egalitarianism will clearly rely more on whether it is possible to generate broadly held egalitarian norms across the bulk of the population rather than whether it's possible to persuade the elites.

All this is to say that on a purely theoretical plane, the result of high taxes on work effort is unclear. What does the empirical evidence suggest? Unfortunately, most of the existing evidence is on the impact of taxes on regular working people. There is wide consensus in the literature that higher taxes on such people have only small impacts on labor supply; there are very small effects for men, and somewhat higher ones for women, particularly single mothers (Meghir and Phillips 2008). Meghir and Phillips describe the consensus in the literature that "male hours of work are almost completely irresponsive to changes in work incentives" (46). Although this conclusion is fascinating—and very different from the common refrain in much popular discussion—it is only marginally relevant for us, since we are interested in the impact of taxes on the rich (and at much higher levels than is common in the empirical literature). What is the impact of this likely to be?

Probably the study that directly addresses this question best is from Moffitt and Wilhelm (2000), who studied the 1986 US Tax Reform Act, which dramatically reduced top tax rates, from 50% to 33%. They found that the significant change in tax rates had virtually no impact on labor response (measured in hours of work). They concluded that there is "essentially no evidence" that rich individuals change their hours of work in response to tax rates (221). In their systematic review of the evidence, Meghir and Phillips (2008, 3) concur: "For highly educated and wealthy men, taxes do not affect whether they work or not and how many hours they put in a week or even a year." Diamond and Saez's (2011, 172) conclusion is the same: "[N]o compelling study to date has shown substantial responses along the real economic responses margin among top earners." In another review of the evidence, Saez, Slemrod, and Giertz conclude that while the rich do respond to taxes by shifting the timing of their transactions (e.g., in anticipation of changes to tax laws) and by taking advantage of various loopholes, it is not true that taxes actually lead to changes in work effort: "[W]hile there is compelling U.S. evidence of strong behavioral responses to taxation at the upper end of the distribution around the main tax reform episodes since 1980, in all cases those responses fall in the first two tiers of the Slemrod . . . hierarchy—timing and avoidance. *In contrast, there is no compelling evidence to date of real economic responses to tax rates (the bottom tier in Slemrod's hierarchy) at the top of the income distribution*" (2012, 42, emphasis added).[3] Additional indirect evidence comes from the fact that Japanese CEOs have long had substantially higher marginal tax rates, and typically earn less than a fifth of their US counterparts, and yet they work just as many hours as American CEOs, if not more (Ramsay 2005). More generally, Piketty, Saez, and Stantcheva (2014) investigated the question of what the optimal level of tax would be if the goal were simply to maximize government revenue (taking into account the likely behavioral responses of the rich); their answer is that the top rate is a staggering 83%, far far higher than anything that currently exists.

However, even given all this evidence, we should still be cautious in our conclusions, since we do not yet possess studies examining changes to the labor supply for the rich when a wealthy country introduces very high taxes. Although the extant evidence is suggestive, it is not conclusive.

Then again, even if the existing evidence is wrong, and high taxes on the rich *do* dramatically reduce labor supply, one may still wonder if that would make a meaningful difference for the economy as a whole. After all, we are imagining that the very high tax rates apply specifically to the richest people (the top 1% or 5%), whereas the majority of economic actors are much less affected. Now one might believe that the top 1% are the most productive and brilliant members of the economy, so that any reduction of *their* effort will constitute a serious loss. But that is a mistaken view of what the economy really is. As we will discuss in more detail in the next chapter, economic output is the result not of the effort of individual geniuses but rather of the immense efforts of the collective labor of the "understructure." What really matters for economic development is the slow, cumulative buildup of productivity on the basis of increasing capital stock, knowledge, and technology (Abramovitz, 1993), which itself depends on the relatively smooth functioning of a market system, intertwined with a legal and political system, itself intertwined with a cultural system and a care infrastructure, all of which are underpinned by the ecological systems that make human life possible. Even geniuses are just the tips of broad social icebergs. They may be eye-catching, but we should not overestimate their economic importance.

To see this, think of a simple economy where all the villagers are growing corn on separate plots of land, but with similar tools and technologies. The top 1% most productive farmers will grow somewhat more than others, but what matters most for overall economic production is not how much corn is grown by the 1%, but how much is grown by the 99%. It is the total product that matters for the well-being of society as a whole—and the production of any individual matters very little for that. Even in the area of technological or scientific breakthroughs, it is wrong to think of these as due to individual genius (Alperovitz and Daly 2008). Even if an individual comes up with a decisive breakthrough, they are only able to do so on the basis of the immense work that others have done—all the prior scientific understanding, as well as the mountain of more mundane labor and care work that has kept the scientist alive, fed, and nurtured, the lights on, the water clean, and so on. And given that the vast majority of scientists, engineers, academics, and garage tinkerers are not part of the 1%, the higher taxes we are discussing would not overly impact them, so there is little reason to fear that their productivity would collapse.[4]

The issue of labor supply applies to wealth taxes as well as income taxes. In terms of the wealth tax, there is little evidence of much effect (Advani and Tarrant 2021). Brülhart et al. (2019a) find no evidence of reduced labor due to wealth taxation in Switzerland, nor does Seim (2017) find any significant effect in Sweden. In contrast, Ring (2021) identifies a small positive effect in Norway. What about the inheritance tax—will this reduce the incentive to work throughout one's life? Though this is logically plausible, there is very little empirical evidence to show that it actually happens (Batchelder 2009). Interestingly, there may actually be a stronger effect in the opposite direction: by reducing the unearned wealth of recipients, an inheritance tax can actually increase work incentives. Along similar lines, Holtz-Eakin, Joulfaian, and Rosen (1993) find that those who receive an inheritance tend to work *less* than those who don't; for instance, a single person who inherits $150,000 is roughly four times more likely to leave the labor force than a person who inherits under $25,000. Likewise, Brown, Coile, and Weisbenner (2010) find that receiving an inheritance increases the probability of retirement.

The final point is that even if taxes do lead to work reduction, this might actually be a good thing. From an economic perspective, if the total demand in the economy remains the same, but taxes lead to a reduction in the supply of labor from top earners, this would presumably result in the opening up of new employment opportunities at the top of the ladder (and since these are generally highly attractive jobs, this would be a positive source of new employment). For instance, if new taxes led to doctors across the board deciding they would prefer to work only half-time, this would create job openings for twice as many doctors (surely a boon for society at large). Beyond this, work-time reduction has the potential to bring a number of other important social benefits, such as fostering greater gender equality and ecological sustainability, which we discuss further below.

In sum, we cannot be entirely confident of the impact high taxes would have on labor supply of the rich. The most reasonable, and cautious, expectation is that there may be some reductions in work, but this would likely be quite minimal.

Investment, Innovation, and Productivity

High taxes may well impose significant costs in terms of reduced private investment. On the other hand, if tax revenues are spent on public investment, they may lead to significant boosts in economic productivity. This is an important point to keep in mind. From the perspective of an individual or a corporation, a tax will always feel like a cost and a burden, but for the country as a whole, a tax is better thought of not as a cost but as an *internal transfer*

(Shaxson and Christensen 2016). So to get a clear picture of the total impact of high taxes we need to consider both sides of the transfer: the costs occurring in one place versus the benefits occurring in another. Let us look first at potential costs.

Perhaps the most serious worry about high taxes is that they will lead to reduced private investment, and thereby slow economic growth. There are several mechanisms by which this might occur. Higher taxes might lead business owners to reduce investment (because they might no longer be able to afford the cost of investing, or they might doubt that the expected posttax profits are worth the effort), taxes might discourage entrepreneurs from starting new businesses in the first place, or taxes might distort price signals so that people no longer work in areas where they are most productive.

What does the evidence say? There is indeed some empirical evidence to suggest that taxes do influence investment decisions. In one important study, Carroll et al. (1998) found that a 5 percentage point increase in marginal income tax rates reduces the proportion of entrepreneurs who make new capital investments by 10.4% and decreases mean investment expenditures by 9.9%. Likewise, Vartia (2008) finds that corporate taxes have a negative effect on productivity. However, the evidence does not appear to be particularly robust. In his analysis of top tax rates since 1945, Hungerford (2012) finds, in contrast, that there is actually no statistically significant relationship between top tax rates (on income or capital gains) and rates of investment or productivity.

In terms of the effect of wealth taxes, the empirical evidence suggests that savings and investment responses are small (Brülhart et al. 2019a; Seim 2017), possibly even positive in some contexts (Duran-Cabré, Esteller-Moré, and Mas-Montserrat 2019; Ring 2021). Indeed, if the wealth tax allows business assets to be partially exempted (so as not to deter investment), it is likely that the rich will increase their assets stored here (since moving assets into low-taxed businesses from high-taxed sources like vacation homes will save them money), potentially stimulating investment and expanding employment. This appears to have happened in Norway, where Bjørneby, Markussen, and Røed (2020) find that far from killing jobs, the Norwegian wealth tax actually led to *increases* in investment and employment.

In terms of entrepreneurship, Hurst and Lusardi (2004) point out that most new businesses in the United States start very small and with low amounts of capital; therefore they would not be impacted by the taxes that we're discussing. For instance, of those households not owning a business in

1989 but owning one in 1994, 61% had less than $5,000 in business equity in 1994, and over 75% had less than $25,000 in business equity. Only 8% of new business owners had business equity greater than $100,000 (340). Overall, the authors find that while it's true that the rich do start proportionally more businesses, the vast majority of new businesses do not require a lot of money (and so presumably would be unaffected by high taxes on the rich). More generally, Vartia (2008) finds that high income taxes reduce entrepreneurial activity. In their review, Clingingsmith and Shane (2015) find some evidence that taxes reduce entrepreneurial activity, but also a lot of ambiguity. Most recently, Darnihamedani et al. (2018) were unable to find any clear relationship between income taxes and innovative entrepreneurship. Interestingly, a number of studies have found that inheritance of a family business reduces firm performance, implying that a robust inheritance tax could actually improve general economic productivity (Bloom and Van Reenen 2007; Pérez-González 2006; Villalonga and Amit 2006; though see also Molly, Laveren, and Deloof 2010). In sum, the jury is still out on this issue.

In terms of labor-market productivity, some worry that high taxes will lead to distortions, on the grounds that certain high-skilled individuals will refuse to do various jobs at a reduced income. The idea here is that in an idealized market system, the most productive workers are supposed to be lured to the most productive businesses paying the highest salaries, whereas in an egalitarian society, the most productive would no longer receive such rewards and so might prefer to work at a less productive business, making second-best use of their talents, resulting in some inefficiencies. For example, in an unequal society, a highly talented individual may agree to take a very stressful job which requires frequent flying around the world and constantly having high-pressured meetings, but agrees to do so because it pays $1 million per year. However, they might refuse to do such a job for, say, $300,000, preferring instead to take a more comfortable management job closer to home to spend more time with their family. Such a scenario is conceivable, though I doubt very common. How much would this be an issue for the overall productivity of the economy? It is hard to know. Presumably jobs that offer an imagined societal maximum of $300,000 will still be able to attract very talented individuals. Moreover, what is presumably most important for long-term productivity is not finding the one perfect person for the job—that does not exist in most cases—but rather finding someone who is well-suited for it and who over time is able to learn, improve, innovate, rest, take breaks, and stay energized and excited. That seems entirely possible in a high-tax regime.[5]

Relatedly, it is sometimes thought that high taxes mean that individuals will be less inclined to invest in their capabilities (which economists disturbingly call "human capital"). The idea is that many people will no longer bother going to university or medical school or doing a PhD if they do not think it is possible to earn millions of dollars at the end of it. That strikes me as highly unlikely. Even with very high taxes, investing in one's education is still likely to pay off, so pursuing higher education will remain a smart, sensible route to better pay and employment opportunities. After all, many of the jobs that require higher education—doctors, lawyers, architects—would still pay more than the majority of other jobs, even with high taxes. Moreover, many professional jobs are prestigious and so desirable on nonmonetary grounds. Having the opportunity to attend university—spending one's time reading, thinking, meeting new people—is often deeply enjoyable, and in many respects more of a privilege than a burden. The idea that would-be engineers or scientists will say to themselves, "If I can't become superrich, then I will not bother going to university; I will forsake the learning, friendships, expanding horizons of education, and I will forsake the likelihood of a greater income at the end and a substantially greater lifetime income, opting instead to become a truck driver right away," is pretty hard to believe. If anything, I suspect that the truth is closer to the opposite: that if there were higher taxes, and so more accessible educational opportunities, a higher proportion of the population would actually choose to go to university, thereby boosting society's total "human capital."

A sensible and cautious conclusion would be that high taxes may well lead to moderate economic costs, perhaps from reduced entrepreneurship but more likely via reduced private investment of firms.

That said, it is vital to recognize that this is only half the picture: higher taxes may also lead to enhanced *public investment*, which can benefit the economy in numerous ways. Even if taxes do harm one goose's ability to lay golden eggs, they may also provide new grass to feed other geese so that they begin laying golden eggs of their own.

The first potential benefit of higher taxes is via enhanced investment in infrastructure—better quality roads, bridges, electricity grids, high-speed internet connections, etc. According to the International Monetary Fund, well-designed public infrastructure investment raises output in both the short and long term (Abiad et al. 2014).[6] Public investment is particularly vital for long-term infrastructure investments, such as in a green energy grid or high-speed public transit across the country, since private investors are unlikely to undertake such investments, even if they are profitable, because the payoff is far in the future.

A second important benefit of high taxes is the possibility of more generous investment in science and technology. It is well-known that a fundamental basis of economic growth is society's level of knowledge and technology (Alperovitz and Daly 2008).[7] In Stiglitz's (2019, 183) words, "the true source of a country's wealth—and therefore increases in productivity and living standards—is knowledge, learning, and advances in science and technology." The important point is that there is good reason to believe that an egalitarian high-tax society would perform better on this score than an inegalitarian low-tax society. One reason is that the knowledge produced through research and development, as well as the basic sciences, is a public good; as with all public goods (which are goods that people can easily benefit from without paying for), the market will tend to chronically undersupply them. For instance, 77 out of the 88 most important innovations that happened between 1971 and 2006 (according to *R&D Magazine*'s annual awards), or 88%, were fully dependent on federal research support (Block and Keller 2009). Likewise, a massive 97–99% of the research funding for the Oxford-AstraZeneca COVID-19 vaccine came from public and charitable sources (Cross et al. 2021). It stands to reason, therefore, that more public investment would lead to more innovation. Moreover, when private firms do produce knowledge, they will invariably try to keep it secret—as well as lobbying to extend their copyright and patent monopolies as much as possible—thereby stifling further innovation. Mazzucato (2013) has demonstrated that major, paradigm-shifting innovation typically requires a long time horizon, as well as large, risky investments. For such reasons, the private sector generally performs this function far worse than a risk-taking entrepreneurial state. After all, what the private sector really wants is not long-term risks but short-term sure things: "most of the radical, revolutionary innovations that have fuelled the dynamics of capitalism—from railroads to the Internet, to modern-day nanotechnology and pharmaceuticals—trace the most courageous, early and capital-intensive 'entrepreneurial' investments back to the State" (3). For all of these reasons, an egalitarian society that generously funded public research leading to open-access knowledge would likely perform significantly better on this score.

A third economic benefit of high taxes is the possibility for enhanced investment in education and human capabilities. Ha-Joon Chang (2007), among others, points out that a person's economic productivity comes down to two fundamental components: *incentives* to work hard and the *capabilities* to work productively. Neoliberal, inegalitarian societies tend to focus on the first (by reducing welfare protections, stripping back workplace protections, and undermining unions, so that workers are more motivated because they're terrified); however, such societies often perform poorly in terms of the second crucial ingredient. Think of the tremendous losses in "human capital"—all those potential Ramanujans and Einsteins that never came to be because they were born into deprived Black or Brown neighborhoods in Baltimore, the Parisian suburbs, or Indigenous reservations in Canada, or poor White neighborhoods in rural Mississippi or the Appalachians, attending terrible rundown schools and dead-end jobs which stifled their potential and extinguished their capacity for brilliance. It is hard to believe that an egalitarian society in which the money of the superrich is not spent on yachts, personal jets, and vacation homes, but is instead invested in excellent, state-of-the-art education for everyone, including poor, previously marginalized children, would not perform significantly better in terms of developing general capabilities. And this is not mere speculation. As we saw in Chapter 1, the evidence bears this out. The more egalitarian Nordic societies spend significantly more on public education than the neoliberal countries, producing better educational outcomes, which leads, other things equal, to more productive citizens (Pontusson 2005; see also Piketty 2020, ch. 11).[8] The point here is worth emphasizing and generalizing: whenever one hears the common objection that high taxes will be detrimental to the economy, it is useful to remember that such objections typically focus on the impacts *on the rich*. Yet we must always counterbalance this by asking about the impacts of redistributive policy *on the poor*.

A fourth potential benefit from high taxes is that redistributive spending increases aggregate demand, and thereby increases employment. Whereas wealthy people tend to save 15–25% of their income (the superrich save much more, practically all of their wealth), those at the bottom usually spend 100% of their money. So redistributing some of this money to the poor will cause more of it to be spent, increasing total demand, thereby stimulating businesses to create more jobs to satisfy the demand (Stiglitz 2012). The venture capitalist Nick Hanauer puts it this way: "I earn 1,000 times the median wage, but I do not buy 1,000 times as much stuff. My family owns three cars, not 3,000" (quoted in Pizzigati 2018, 88).

A fifth point is that just as a portion of tax revenues will not be spent on productivity-enhancing things, it's also true that a significant portion of the assets of the rich is used wastefully from the perspective of the broader economy. This is particularly true for the ownership of mansions, yachts, jewelry, and fancy cars. The more that such low-productivity assets are taxed away to be invested instead in high-return investments such as infrastructure or education, the better for the economy as a whole. Indeed, it's informative to reflect on the fact that one of the major reasons why the rich countries became rich in the first place—for instance, comparing South America to North America—is that in South America the economic surplus was siphoned off by the elites and colonizers to be consumed as mansions and palaces, often in Europe, whereas in North America colonialism followed a different (though just as violent) path, whereby a significant amount of the economic surplus was not simply consumed by the rich but was reinvested into local productive activity, eventually leading to substantial economic growth (Chang 2002; Galeano 1973).

Before concluding this section, let me mention a final, and more speculative, potential benefit from high taxes, which is that a society with more taxes and public spending may actually stimulate *more* entrepreneurship. The simple Maslovian logic here is that a society with more taxes will likely have increased economic security (from enhanced public spending on healthcare, child care, education, pensions, etc.); enhanced security can free people from being so consumed by the necessity of making ends meet that they become increasingly able to experiment and take greater risks, leading to enhanced innovation (Maslow 1943).[9] It strikes me as eminently plausible that for every Atlas who shrugs from high taxes, a dozen new Atlases, previously crushed by insecurity and hopelessness, will find themselves able to leap into the unknown, taking risks and innovating.

Taken together, these six arguments provide good reason for suspecting that high taxes can produce significant benefits to economic production, provided of course that they are spent in effective, productivity-enhancing ways. Hence, the belief of Alan Greenspan (prior chair of the US Federal Reserve) that "[a]ll taxes are a drag on economic growth. It's only a question of degree" (quoted in Frank 2000, 491) is spectacularly myopic.

In sum, high taxes may induce moderate economic costs; on the other hand, public spending can lead to significant economic benefits. The net result is not clear. But it seems doubtful that high taxes would lead to any major reductions in growth (presuming of course that a good portion of the taxes truly are invested into productivity-enhancing venues and not wasted or embezzled by a corrupt state). The best available evidence that we have to get a grip on the big-picture net results of costs and benefits is that which examines total economic growth in relation to total taxation levels. We examine this evidence in detail below, but the upshot is that the bulk of the evidence finds no significant correlation between high taxes and diminished growth. (If anything, there is a slightly positive relationship between taxes and growth.)

Other Potential Issues Related to High Taxes

Before examining the big picture issue of tax rates and total economic growth, there are at least two other important economic consequences that flow from high taxes which we should take note of. The first is the issue of debt. Typically, low-tax countries do not have the revenue to pay for many of the public services that their population demands. Hence borrowing money—accumulating debt—is a common way for governments to provide services without increasing the tax burden (at least in the short term). The problem with this approach is that as debt accumulates, so too do the interest payments on the debt. And this means that over time, more taxpayer money must be spent on the interest payments servicing the debt. Yet since tax revenues come from the people at large—poor and middle-class people pay tax too, particularly consumption taxes—whereas government debt is overwhelmingly sold to rich people,[10] what interest payments on the debt really represent is a transfer of resources from regular working-class citizens to the rich. As Piketty (2014, 566) explains, "debt often becomes a backhanded form of redistribution of wealth from the poor to the rich, from people with modest savings to those with the means to lend to the government (who as a general rule ought to be paying taxes rather than lending)." A society with high rates of taxation could more easily reduce its debt and so suffer less of this kind of upward redistribution.

The second issue is more speculative but also potentially very important. This is the issue of economic stability. It is well-known that over its history, capitalism has been shaken and battered by periodic, disastrous recessions. Before World War II these recessions often culminated in full-blown depressions, with devastating results (massive unemployment, breadlines, suicide, not to mention the emergence of fascist populism). Since World War II, recessions have continued to occur regularly, but happily they have been significantly less deep and severe.

This reduction in the severity of recessions marks a vast improvement in society's general well-being. But it is not completely clear why this mitigation has occurred. Perhaps the most plausible explanation is that the key change from pre– to post–World War II was the marked difference in overall levels of taxation and corresponding social spending, which exploded during these years (see the top image of Figure 3.1). Across the OECD, it was World War II, more than anything else, that really brought welfare states into existence by way of new tax rates that were extremely high compared to prewar levels (Scheve and Stasavage 2016). This matters because, in addition to the military spending, the increased taxes were largely spent on social services (pensions,

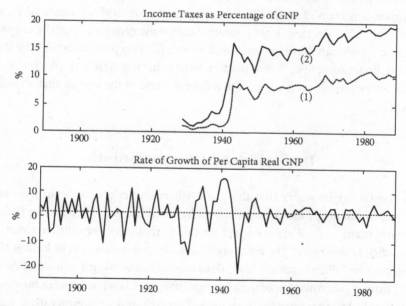

Figure 3.1 Taxes as a share of GNP (top) and growth of real GNP per capita (bottom) (Gale and Samwick 2016, 31). In the top graph, line 1 consists of federal, state, and local individual income taxes; line 2 includes social security and retirement taxes as well as federal corporate taxes. In the bottom graph, notice that the oscillation of GNP growth (and particularly the severity of downturns) has become much more muted after World War II.

healthcare, welfare, unemployment insurance, disability insurance, etc.), and this spending tends to be strongly countercyclical, meaning that in times of recession, government spending on such things automatically increases. This is why social spending is often referred to as an "automatic stabilizer." In times of recession, when the private sector is collectively cutting its spending, increased government spending stimulates the economy and leads to more jobs (or at least reduces unemployment). Social spending (from high taxes) thus provides a double whammy: it increases countercyclical spending, which leads to softer downturns, and since this spending is not just generalized spending but is targeted to welfare services that people need, particularly in times of recession, such spending doubly cushions the blow.

If this line of reasoning is correct, it would seem logical to expect that a society with significantly higher taxes than is common today would for similar reasons have more robust automatic stabilization, and hence somewhat more employment security. That would be a major advance indeed, in part because recessions are so dangerous to the general well-being, but also because in a climate-constrained world like ours, the most profound economic issue, at least for rich countries, is not continual economic growth. As will be argued below, we already have enough total wealth for everyone to be able to live good, flourishing lives. What matters most is having steady employment so that everyone has secure access to a decent share of the wealth that already exists.

The Big Picture: Taxes and Growth

A skeptic might worry that the growth-harming effects of high taxes are going to outweigh the productivity-enhancing impacts of spending (since clearly many tax dollars are spent on things that have very little economic benefit). Is this right? The best way to answer this question is to look at the big picture: When taxes are high, does overall economic growth slow? After all, from a (narrowly) economic perspective, that is what matters most—it matters little if some work less, some dodge taxes, and some emigrate, as long as overall levels of growth, and therefore the material basis for general prosperity, remain robust. Luckily, there has been significant study of this issue, and so we possess ample econometric evidence to guide us.

That evidence, however, is mixed. On the one hand, there is evidence that higher taxes correlate with reduced growth. For instance, Padovano and Galli (2001) find that effective marginal income tax rates are negatively correlated with economic growth. Likewise, Afonso and Furceri (2010) find that a 1 percentage point increase in the government's share of total revenue decreases output by 0.12 and 0.13 percentage points for the OECD and EU countries, respectively (see also Vartia 2008). Bergh and Henrekson (2011) also find a negative correlation between growth of real GDP per capita and total government size over time.

However, there is also significant evidence pointing in the opposite direction.

First, consider US history. The data shows gigantic changes in tax levels over the years, with virtually no observable shifts in growth rate. From 1870 to 1912, the United States had no income tax, and total tax revenues were only 3% of GDP. By contrast, from 1947 to 2000, the highest marginal income tax rate averaged 66%, and total tax revenues averaged roughly 18% of GDP. And yet despite this remarkable increase in taxation, the growth rate of real GDP per capita was identical with the earlier periods (2.2% in each [Gale and Samwick 2016]). As Slemrod (2000, 3) says, "The fact that the golden years of modern American growth [3.1% from 1951 to 1963] occurred during the apex of marginal tax rates is, at a minimum, an embarrassing coincidence for those who believe that avoiding such a policy is the key to economic success."

More formally, Stokey and Rebelo (1995) show that the massive increases in income tax and overall tax revenues that started during World War II, and became more or less permanent afterwards, had no discernable impact on the long-term growth rate. Likewise, Hungerford (2012, 22) studied top US statutory tax rates over 65 years and found no statistically significant association between the top tax rate and real GDP growth: "The results of the analysis in this report suggest that changes over the past 65 years in the top marginal tax rate and the top capital gains tax rate do not appear correlated with economic growth. The reduction in the top statutory tax rates appears to be uncorrelated with saving, investment, and productivity growth. The top tax rates appear to have little or no relation to the size of the economic pie." More generally, Garrison and Lee (1992) as well as Mendoza, Milesi-Ferretti, and Asea (1997) find no effects of taxation on growth in developed countries. Piketty, Saez, and Stantcheva (2014, 232) studied the data from 18 OECD countries in terms of tax rates and economic growth from 1960 to 2010 and concluded that there is "no evidence of a correlation between growth in real GDP per capita and the drop in the top marginal tax rate."

Thus, the evidence is conflicting. A cautious conclusion would be that high rates of taxation *may* somewhat reduce economic growth, yet there seems to be little reason to think that this is inevitable or that the results of high taxes would be particularly calamitous.

Taxes and Inequality

Of particular interest for us is the fact that recent research has found that inequality itself can actually be detrimental to growth. Theoretically, as Stiglitz (2016) points out, there are several mechanisms through which we would logically expect inequality to undermine growth. First, inequality leads to weaker aggregate demand (since the wealthiest spend a smaller fraction of their income than the poorest, so the more a country's income is controlled by the wealthiest, the less of it is spent). Second, inequality of outcome reduces equality of opportunity for the next generation. And when those at the bottom lack good opportunities to learn and develop their capabilities, the economy suffers. Third, societies with greater inequality also tend to be low-tax societies, and that means they have fewer resources available for public investments into productivity-enhancing areas of public goods which can fuel long-term growth, such as infrastructure, public transportation, education, and developing new technologies.

Empirically, the evidence appears quite robust that inequality dampens growth. Cingano (2014) finds that income inequality has a negative and statistically significant impact on subsequent growth. What matters most is the gap between low-income households and the rest of the population; that said, he finds no evidence that the inequality between the top and the rest harms growth. Similarly, Biswas, Chakraborty, and Hai (2017) find that reducing inequality between low- and median-income households improves growth (whereas reducing inequality between median- and high-income households reduces growth). Papadimitriou, Nikiforos, and Zezza (2019) find that both a wealth tax (like that proposed by Elizabeth Warren) as well as a significant increase to income tax (like that proposed by Alexandria Ocasio-Cortez) would increase GDP growth.

Probably the most important and robust study on this subject in recent years, due to its comprehensive data set, comes from Berg et al. (2018). The authors attempt to separate the impact of *redistribution* on growth from the impact of *inequality* on growth. They conclude that "inequality is a robust and powerful determinant both of the pace of medium-term growth and of the duration of growth spells, even controlling for the size of redistributive transfers: more equal societies grow faster and more sustainably than less equal ones" (292). Redistribution appears generally benign in terms of its impact on growth. It is only when the levels of redistribution become very high that there is any evidence of a negative effect on growth.

Taking a step back, what shall we conclude from the evidence on taxes and economic growth? The most sensible conclusion is that a high-tax regime is unlikely to cause significant problems with growth. Reducing inequality, particularly at the bottom, may actually promote growth, though very high levels of taxation on the rich may somewhat undermine it. A cautious conclusion, therefore, is that a very-high-tax regime may lead to somewhat reduced growth, but would not likely suffer very much, if at all.

An Aside on the Costs of Transition: Capital Strike and Capital Controls

We have been considering the costs and benefits that would result from a new kind of high-tax, low-inequality market system. That is, we are considering the costs and benefits of an institutional arrangement that is already up and running. There is, however, a whole other set of questions which we have not engaged, questions of transition: How would a particular society actually *achieve* such changes? How could we realistically get there? Such questions are vitally important, but I must largely sidestep them here because questions of transition are inherently context-specific. The possibilities of transition to a high-tax regime in Canada or Sweden or Brazil or Indonesia would be extremely different in each case. And understanding the possibilities in each place would require deep and careful analysis of the specificities and idiosyncrasies of that context: What are the relevant social movements? What is the political culture? What are the existing economic institutions? What is the balance of class power at a particular moment? One of the most important issues for transition is the issue of economic sabotage. Will elites orchestrate widespread economic sabotage in order to derail a government's democratically mandated goals? Although we cannot address all the nuances of that question here, one general issue is so important that it requires at least some comment—this is the issue of capital strike.

Capital strike comes in two main forms: capital flight and investment strike.[11] Capital flight occurs when individuals send their money out of the country. This reduces the amount of capital available at home, so raises interest rates and thereby slows economic growth. If this occurs on a large scale, the country's currency will be devalued (as investors sell the domestic currency). This makes imports more expensive, and so to the extent that consumers and businesses rely on foreign products, they become poorer in real terms. Investment strike occurs when businesses decide to cut their investment and lay off workers, not for real economic reasons but for political reasons of wishing to destabilize the regime. These threats are uncommon, but they do happen.

In the early 1970s, Salvador Allende, the democratically elected socialist leader of Chile, faced investment strike, manifested in the intentional underproduction by domestic firms of necessary goods, as well as a credit squeeze from foreign investors (mainly American) who refused to lend money to the country, making it hard to import the basic goods the country relied upon (Boorstein 1977; Feinberg 1974).[12] Such factors contributed to the US-supported coup in 1973, which replaced Allende with a more business- and US-friendly dictator, Augusto Pinochet.

In 1981, François Mitterrand was elected in France promising "une rupture avec le capitalisme." Immediately financiers (institutional investors, short-term speculators, currency traders, bond traders, etc.) withdrew huge sums of money from the country to the extent that the capital flight measured $1 billion per day by inauguration. Massive speculation against the currency forced the country to devalue the franc again and again. At the same time, business owners led by the National Council of French Employers called for a hiring freeze and started to slow investment as their confidence in Mitterrand's ability (or desire) to protect their profits crumbled. Less than two years later, with inflation and unemployment skyrocketing, the government admitted defeat and reversed its socialist policies (Morray 1997; Singer 1988).

In 1999, Hugo Chavez was elected president of Venezuela and radically shifted the country's politics away from neoliberalism. He initiated various social programs and expansive antipoverty initiatives, providing education and healthcare, engaging with the Indigenous population, and redistributing the nation's massive oil wealth. In response, financiers engaged in large-scale capital flight—estimated at $26 billion from 1999 to 2001 (equivalent to roughly 12% of the country's entire GDP [Parker 2005]). Even more

devastating was the investment strike organized by the Venezuelan opposition and business elites. Businesses closed their doors and locked out
workers, and the oil industry was shut down. The investment strike brought
the economy crashing down—losing 24% of GDP in three months, close to
Great Depression numbers.[13]

These are massive economic costs. But it's difficult to determine what exactly we should think about the nature of these costs. After all, there is something ethically fishy about calling such sabotage a "cost" on the balance sheet
of inequality reduction. For example, if a conservative opposition, upset at
taxes, goes out and smashes public buildings, is that rightfully considered
a "cost" of the tax policy? Or if a new feminist law against sexual assault an-
gers men, leading them to take to the street in a rampage of assault, should
that be considered a "cost" and a drawback to the normative goal of reducing
sexual assault? Surely not. It seems much more appropriate to think of these
as obstacles in the way of *transition*, not costs of the *institutional proposal*
per se. In other words, we should always keep a clear distinction in mind
between the *achievability* of a proposal, in terms of whether it is within our
ability to transition to it, and the *viability* of a proposal, which refers to its
institutional soundness once it already exists (Wright 2010). Although undemocratic sabotage is a vital issue for questions of achievability, it should
not carry any weight in terms of this chapter's reflection on the viability of a
regime of economic equality that is already set up. Again, the point is that although achievability is undoubtedly a vital question, it's a very different question from the one of institutional viability.

The other point to make is that such dangers are not inherent in the specific question of high taxes and inequality reduction. After all, concerns of
economic sabotage from capital strike are concerns that must be confronted
by any and every proposal aiming to deeply challenge the economic status
quo. They are not problems specific to the issue of inequality reduction per se.

Nevertheless, any real-world movement for economic equality must invariably confront the real strategic questions of transition. Though we cannot
deal with such issues comprehensively here, it is useful to point out that, generally speaking, countries are not helpless against capital strike. In order to
mitigate the damage of investment strike, the main tool at a government's
disposal is increased reliance on public investment (supported by increased
borrowing, if necessary, but ideally by increased taxation). We have already
discussed the significant evidence of the positive economic potential of
such investment, so we will pass over that issue. In terms of capital flight,

the main tools that governments can use are capital controls (i.e., rules and regulations that restrict people's ability to bring money in or take money out of a country).

Capital controls have a long history. In helping to construct the Bretton Woods system after World War II, John Maynard Keynes strongly advocated them as a vital component of the new global economy. "Nothing is more certain," he said, "than that the movement of capital funds must be regulated" (quoted in Cohen 2002, 104). And indeed, in the postwar period almost every country followed his advice, using controls of some sort to guide their development and pursue independent policies. Capital controls were arguably a vital element of the development of many nations, including Japan, Korea, Sweden, and Germany (Crotty and Epstein 1996). The East Asian tigers used controls extensively, helping them to achieve the fastest economic growth in human history (Chang 2006; Stiglitz 1996). China has seen the fastest economic growth in the world for some time now, and has used extensive controls for many years.

In the mid-1990s, most mainstream economists were strongly opposed to the use of capital controls. The Asian financial crisis, however, dramatically changed their opinion. In 1996, five Asian countries (South Korea, Indonesia, Malaysia, Thailand, and the Philippines) received net private capital inflows amounting to a massive $93 billion. A year later they experienced an estimated outflow of $12 billion—a turnaround, in other words, of $105 billion in a single year, equivalent to more than 10% of the combined GDP of these economies (Rodrik 1998, 1–2). Not only were these unrestrained flows devastating to Asian economies, but it was hard to ignore the fact that the countries which recovered best from the crisis were precisely those that had used capital controls—such as China, India, and Malaysia (Epstein, Grabel, and Jomo 2003). Increasingly, influential economists started to support controls in certain instances, arguing that financial markets were very particular types of markets, characterized by asymmetric information, herd behavior, and self-fulfilling panics. They argued therefore that controls were often useful for maintaining a country's monetary autonomy, preventing instability, and warding off financial crisis (Bhagwati 1998; Kaminsky and Reinhart 1999; Krugman 1998; Magud and Reinhart 2006; Rodrik 1998; Stiglitz 2002).

The second major shock to the faith in free capital mobility came from the Great Recession of 2008–2010, when huge flows of capital wreaked havoc around the world. This led the World Bank to state, "In 1997–98, the words 'capital controls' were forbidden and stigmatized. Now the problem of capital is so systematic and huge globally, it has now become universally acceptable to have a certain type of temporary capital controls" (Porter 2010). Even the International Monetary Fund, in a remarkable about-face, declared in 2010 that "there may be circumstances in which capital controls are a legitimate component of the policy response to surges in capital inflows" (Ostry et al. 2010, 15). The era of implacable hostility toward capital controls has come to an end. Today many, if not most, economists believe capital controls are an important tool for governments to have at their disposal in order to re-duce instability (preventing massive inflows, followed by sudden outflows), reducing business-cycle booms and busts, and giving governments more independent policy space (e.g., allowing them to follow expansionary, pro-employment policy to reduce inequality).[14]

Are controls feasible? A major worry is that contemporary technology allows controls to be easily evaded, with evasion accelerating over time (Carvalho and Garcia 2008; Edwards 1999). Skeptics also worry that controls will inevitably lead to black markets as people try to profit by evading them.

Indeed it is definitely true that capital controls can and often do fail (Magud and Reinhart 2006; Saborowski et al. 2014). Nevertheless, the ev-idence shows that capital controls can work effectively provided they are designed and implemented well.

Capital controls tend to be more commonly used to prevent significant inflows (which are a danger to countries because they cause the currency to appreciate, thereby harming domestic businesses by making them less com-petitive internationally), and so we have more evidence about controls on inflows than outflows. The evidence is now extensive that controls on inflows can be effective (Chamon and Garcia 2016; Ma and McCauley 2008; Oatley 1999; Yeyati, Schmukler, and Van Horen 2008; and see Erten, Korinek, and Ocampo 2019 for a useful survey).

Moreover, it is not true that controls need be only short term, as the cases of China and Singapore demonstrate. Epstein, Grabel, and Jomo (2003, 39) conclude their survey of numerous countries' experiences with capital controls by advising "*cautious optimism* regarding the ability of developing countries to pursue various capital management techniques."

Our main concern, however, is less with inflows than with outflows. There is less evidence here, so we need to be more cautious, yet here too the bulk of the evidence appears to support much the same conclusion: that while controls can and often do fail, they can be successful if well implemented.

Two important examples are those of Malaysia in 1998 (Ariyoshi 2000; Edison and Reinhart 2001; Kaplan and Rodrik 2002) and Iceland in 2008 (Saborowski et al. 2014). In both cases, the countries succeeded in implemented outflow controls, successfully insulating themselves in order to keep interest rates low, thereby providing the room to enact expansionary policy to revitalize the economy (see Figure 3.2, though notice as well the two cases where controls failed).

The state-of-the-art evidence on the efficacy of outflow controls is from Saborowski et al. (2014). They studied 37 emerging market economies from 1995 to 2010 and found that capital controls can indeed be effective: "A tightening of outflow restrictions is effective if it is supported by strong macroeconomic fundamentals or good institutions, or if pre-existing restrictions are already fairly comprehensive" (7).

In terms of feasibility, the key insight is that, at the end of the day, there is nothing fundamentally different between implementing capital controls and collecting taxes (Crotty and Epstein 1996). Both can be evaded, both require a skilled bureaucracy to enforce, but both are fundamentally feasible. Critics are right to point out that controls can sometimes be evaded—indeed, all regulations and forms of taxation are evaded to some degree—but that is hardly a blanket argument against taxation per se. Controls appear to work best with strong macroeconomic fundamentals and require sufficient state capacity for comprehensive administration. Successful controls require nimble and dynamic application (i.e., closing loopholes, giving up on aspects of controls that are not working, etc. [Epstein, Grabel, and Jomo 2003; Valdés-Prieto and Soto 1998]).

In terms of the costs of capital controls, economists have found evidence of both economic costs and benefits.[15] Overall, the data shows no clear relationship between financial openness and growth (Rodrik 1998). Probably the most detailed and careful study of the literature from this vantage point is from Kose et al. (2009), who conclude that the cross-country evidence on the growth benefits of capital account openness is inconclusive and lacks robustness.

The penultimate point to make is that capital strike—in both its forms—is likely to be provoked by sudden shocks. This implies that the more that reforms can be instituted slowly, transparently, and gradually, the less likely they will lead to disruptive panic. Moreover, if governments can maintain the general economic conditions necessary for companies to make a profit—even if profitability is reduced—there is good reason to suspect that any

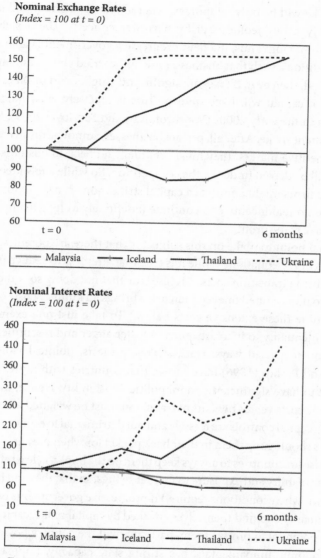

Nominal Exchange Rates
(Index = 100 at t = 0)

Malaysia — Iceland — Thailand ····· Ukraine

Nominal Interest Rates
(Index = 100 at t = 0)

Malaysia — Iceland — Thailand ····· Ukraine

Figure 3.2 Economic indicators following tightening of outflow restrictions (Saborowski et al. 2014, 5). The top graph shows that controls kept exchange rates low in Malaysia and Iceland (though not in the other two cases). The bottom graph shows that the imposition of controls allowed Malaysia and Iceland to maintain low interest rates. Note: t = 0 is the month in which outflow control restrictions were tightened.

capital strike will be only temporary. After all, most international investors are not driven by ideology but by narrower concerns about stability for their profit making. Thus, if a new, progressive government is able to create stable conditions, such that businesses are not worried about suddenly being expropriated, then even if taxes are significantly higher and profits are somewhat lower, capital will likely return. This is precisely what happened in Venezuela in the early 2000s (Weisbrot, Ray, and Sandoval 2009). Similarly for investment strike. After all, private businesses cannot be on strike forever. In a competitive market, they must eventually go back to business as usual or they will be driven under by the competition. So while a few ideologically motivated firms might continue a capital strike, none can do so forever, and most have no real incentive to continue indefinitely as long as they are still able to make some profit.

The final point to make on this subject is that there are potential costs on both sides of the equation. While it is true that attempts to reduce inequality may well bring transition costs, it is *also* true that not doing so—allowing inequality to be sustained or even increase—brings all kinds of costs of its own. (We examine these extensive costs below.) To take just one example here, allowing inequality to increase tends to foster anger and resentment, which may erupt in myriad ways: riots, strikes, protests, political violence, etc. Alesina and Perotti (1996) have shown that countries with more inequality also tend to have significantly more political instability. Hence, the balance sheet of the costs versus benefits of transition must be weighed accordingly.

In sum, capital controls are feasible and not detrimental to economic growth. Countries should keep them in their back pocket for when they are needed. (It may be wise for countries to always keep them on the books, at least at low levels to reduce volatility and exposure to market swings, so that they can be ramped up or down when conditions require.) If progressive governments begin to reduce inequality and find themselves attacked by capital strike, capital controls have the potential to protect them, particularly if the country possesses good macroeconomic fundamentals, has strong state capacity, imposes controls comprehensively, and reacts nimbly and quickly to holes.

Weighing Social Harms and Benefits

Up to this point we have been examining the *economic* costs and benefits of high taxes. But, of course, economic issues are far from the only ones that matter. So in this section we broaden the focus to consider the *social*, or noneconomic, harms and benefits accruing from increased taxation.

In terms of the noneconomic harms of high taxes, the only issues that really stand out are the ethical ones: the belief that high taxes represent a theft of one's property or a taking of what one rightly deserves. We will analyze those arguments in depth in Chapters 4–6.

There is much more to say on the other side of the ledger. In what follows I briefly, and without any claim of comprehensiveness, lay out some of the major social benefits of high taxes and low inequality.

Environmental Benefits

The environmental crisis is in many respects the defining issue of our age. The Intergovernmental Panel on Climate Change's (IPCC 2018a) latest report is that we have until 2030 to prevent catastrophic climate change. One estimate is that climate change could kill 184 million people in Africa alone before the century is over (McKibben 2007, 21). While many changes to our economies are required to ward off such disasters, high taxes and reduced inequality have significant potential to help.

Climate sustainability will require truly massive public investments; we need to create green transit systems (transforming the car and highway system into a train, bus, and bike system), green energy networks (transforming the fossil fuel sector into a clean energy sector), retrofit our homes and businesses, and more (Aronoff et al. 2019; Hahnel 2011; Klein 2014). None of this will be possible without substantial increases in public revenues. Where should such revenues come from? Not only do the rich have the necessary funds, but they are by far the worst polluters. According to Piketty and Chancel (2015), the world's richest 10% contribute 45% of total global emissions, whereas the poorest 50% contribute only 13%. Oxfam's (2020) estimates are even worse (see Figure 3.3): the richest 1% emit 175 times more carbon than the poorest 10%. In terms of their carbon footprint, the rich stomp across the world like King Kong.[16] Hence redistributing a portion of the wealth of the rich to be spent on public, low-carbon investments would represent a doubly impactful move toward sustainability because it would reduce high emissions at the top, and replace them with desperately needed low-carbon infrastructure.

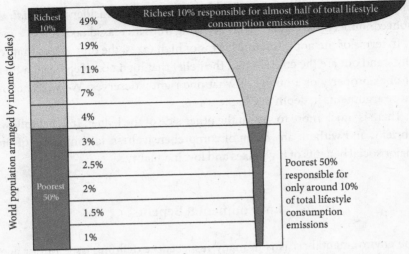

Figure 3.3 Percentage of global carbon emissions by income decile (Oxfam 2015, 4).

There are several additional mechanisms by which high taxes and reduced inequality may promote sustainability. First, wealthier households often "conspicuously consume" more goods and services (Veblen [1918] 2007). This drives less wealthy people to want to emulate the rich (working harder in order to trade in their subway pass and modest apartment for a fancy car and suburban mansion). Second, it is the wealthy who are, by and large, the owners of polluting firms, so the more they can gain control of the political system, the more they will be able to undermine the implementation of green regulations. Third, income inequality is "a predictor of work hours. . . . [I]ts effects are large, and estimates are robust across a variety of specifications" (Bowles and Park 2005, 399). And we know that longer working hours drive increased carbon emissions (Fitzgerald, Schor, and Jorgenson 2018; Fremstad, Paul, and Underwood 2019; Knight, Rosa, and Schor 2013). For instance, Fitzgerald, Schor, and Jorgenson (2018) find that a 1% increase in average working hours per worker is associated with a 0.552–0.668% increase in emissions (holding all else constant). For each of these reasons, it seems likely that reducing inequality will reduce emissions. In fact, recent research confirms that as economic inequality worsens, so too do carbon emissions (Jorgenson, Schor, and Huang 2017; Knight, Schor, and Jorgenson 2017). Knight, Schor, and Jorgenson (2017) studied 26 high-income countries from

2000 to 2010 and found that wealth inequality (measured as the wealth share of the top 10%) has a relatively stable positive effect on per person emissions.

Another important point is that the ecological crisis should dramatically change our attitude to "growth." Recall that essentially every concern with high taxes boils down to the worry that they will reduce economic growth. But is this really a bad thing? In fact, reduced growth is decidedly ambiguous (at least in the rich countries). Reduced growth means less of certain things that we do want (such as green energy and increases in general productivity) but also less of what we desperately need to avoid (such as carbon emissions, pollution, deforestation, species going extinct, etc.)[17]

In theory, it makes sense to aim to promote "good growth" while curtailing "bad growth." The problem is that in practice this distinction has been impossible to maintain. The reason is that economic output remains highly correlated with total emissions (Jorgenson and Birkholz 2010; Jorgenson and Clark 2012; Knight and Schor 2014).[18] It is revealing that in the past 60 years, we have witnessed significant decreases in total global carbon emissions in only four brief periods—1981, 1992, 2009, 2020—precisely the years in which the world was experiencing deep economic recession.[19] Capitalist prosperity has been fueled by fuel (Wrigley 2010). Even though a shift to sustainable and green production is occurring, it is happening far too slowly (Jorgenson and Birkholz 2010; Jorgenson and Clark 2012; Knight and Schor 2014). For example, from 1980 to 2006 global carbon intensity declined from just over 1,000 grams of carbon dioxide per US dollar to 770 grams. Nevertheless, total global carbon dioxide emissions from fossil fuels have actually increased by 80% since 1970. And obviously the environment does not care about our efficiency; it only cares about our total emissions (Jackson 2009, 71). In other words, total growth in economic output is continuing to significantly outweigh the improvements in efficiency, so that overall carbon emissions continue to rise. In Juliet Schor's (2010, 96) words, "[D]ematerialization, or delinking income and impact, is possible but it is proceeding far more slowly than the pace of ecological decline." The consequence is hard to avoid: reducing carbon emissions in the short term (which is the only time frame that really matters given the urgency of the ecological crisis) does seem to require a reduction in general economic activity. If not degrowth, we require at least stability.

Furthermore, in the rich countries of the Global North, the main requirement is not more economic growth. Our countries are already very rich. What we urgently need is redistribution. Recall the egalitarian thought experiment from the introduction: if the United States were to redistribute income and working hours evenly across the working population, every adult could have the same median income that exists today, while benefiting from even better public services than exist in Sweden, plus a generous unconditional basic income, with each worker needing to work only three and a half hours per day.[20] In material terms, our societies are already rich enough to provide the conditions for good and flourishing lives for all.

The real threat of reduced growth is that it will lead to recession and unemployment and their resultant miseries. In other words, the major goal should not be growth per se, but economic security. The task, therefore, is to find policies which can enhance economic security without relying on never-ending growth (Jackson 2009). Green economists have pointed to a number of important reforms here: full-employment policies from governments and Central Banks; universal public services and/or an unconditional basic income; policies for work sharing, whereby a firm's work hours are shared among larger numbers of workers, reducing hours worked per person and increasing employment (Baker and Bernstein 2013; Schor 2010); and perhaps most important, collective work-time reduction schemes, whereby workers and employers agree that increased productivity will be taken not as increased wages (as is standard) but as reduced work hours. This would mean that over time, as the economy's productivity slowly increases, workers will continue to see their lives improve, but in ways that are ecologically sustainable (Hayden 1999).

The bottom line is that in our climate-constrained world, growth of GDP can no longer be the alpha and omega of social policy. In the rich countries of the Global North, the immediate aim should be to reduce total emissions and redistribute wealth—those aims are far more important than GDP growth. If increasing taxes and reducing inequality can help to reduce total emissions and increase economic security, those benefits seem vastly more important than the mixed costs of reduced GDP growth (with the caveat, of course, that reduced growth can be successfully insulated from unemployment and economic insecurity).

Democratic Benefits

One of the most profound worries about inequality is that it threatens to undermine democracy. Political scientists have outlined a number of mechanisms through which this could plausibly occur (e.g., Christiano 2012). The first is *money for votes*, whereby rich people fund or lobby politicians in exchange for advantageous policies. The second is *money as gatekeeper*, whereby those with money are better able to fund political campaigns and run for office than those without. The third is *money as means for influencing public and legislative opinion*, whereby the rich are better positioned to pay for advertising, buy newspapers and TV stations, and direct think tanks. The fourth is *money as independent political power*, whereby owning large amounts of economic assets—such as corporations or financial assets—means that the rich can always threaten to leave the country or cut investment (costing jobs and risking economic downturn) if the government does not kowtow to their wishes.[21]

What does the evidence say? Like all complex issues in social science, there is never unanimity. A small minority of scholars are skeptical of the claim that inequality is damaging to democracy (e.g., Guntermann 2021; Kenworthy 2022; Ura and Ellis 2008).[22]

But the bulk of the evidence is strongly (if not overwhelmingly) on the other side. As I see it, there are two powerful lines of evidence demonstrating that inequality does indeed undermine democracy.

The first is what we might call the *money buys influence* principle. It seems undeniable that with increased wealth comes increased ability to purchase many things that can increase one's political influence. For example, the rich have far more ability than the poor to hire teams of activists to work for them, to host gatherings of like-minded people, to lobby, to donate, and to disseminate their political views through radio, TV, newspapers, social media, and think tanks. Since political campaigning requires funding, it invariably benefits the rich. For example, in the 2016 election, the richest 1% accounted for 40% of all campaign contributions (Robert Reich 2019).[23] We also know that business (which typically represents the interests of the rich) donates roughly 16 times more money to their preferred political candidates than does organized labor (OpenSecrets 2022). Recall the tremendous influence that the Koch brothers have had over American politics—spending hundreds of millions of dollars through a vast network of shadowy private foundations and conservative think tanks and acting as key players in mobilizing the anti-tax Tea Party movement (Goldmacher 2019). In the US context, such power has been significantly strengthened by the Supreme Court decision in *Citizens United v. Federal Election Commission* in 2010, which held that corporations were entitled to spend unlimited amounts of money on campaign financing on the grounds of free speech.

The *money buys influence* principle is also apparent in media ownership. In contemporary societies, the means of the production and dissemination of political information—newspapers, TV and radio stations, websites, blogs, think tanks, etc.—are typically privately owned by a small minority of the population (Cagé 2016; Herman and Chomsky 1988). In the United States, six companies own about 90% of the entire media landscape (Lutz 2012). In the United Kingdom four men (three billionaires and one multimillionaire) control roughly 75% of the press: Viscount Rothermere, Rupert Murdoch, Evgeny Lebedev, and Frederick Barclay (Ponsford 2021). This means that mainstream media information will typically have a conservative (pro-business, antiworker) political bias. In Canada, 95% of the daily newspapers supported the Conservative Party during the 2011 election (as did 71% in 2015 [Winseck 2015]). Likewise, a study of the major UK newspapers found overwhelming bias against the progressive Labour leader Jeremy Corbyn. The authors found "most newspapers systematically vilifying the leader of the biggest opposition party, assassinating his character, ridiculing his personality and delegitimising his ideas and politics" (Cammaerts et al. 2016, 12). More subtly, but no less insidiously, a number of studies have shown how the rich exert disproportionate intellectual and cultural influence through their ownership and control of think tanks (e.g., Mirowski and Plehwe 2009).

In addition, the superrich have significant power over society in terms of their control over investment, which is incompatible with democracy.[24] For instance, if a government wishes to pass progressive policy, the superrich can threaten to leave or go on investment strike. To see the problem here, recall that Elon Musk possesses $270 billion in wealth. If Musk were to live in a country the size of Norway (with a GDP of $357 billion), his total stock of wealth would be equivalent to fully 76% of the country's GDP. Annually, his income would be sufficient to employ 8.4% of the entire workforce (at the average income).[25] Any threats he issued to go on capital strike, or simply any indication whatsoever that he was unhappy with government policy, would be very serious indeed, as he could, at any moment, unilaterally crash the country into a depression should he so choose. Such power is not only incompatible with democracy at home; it is detrimental to other democracies abroad. If Musk were suddenly to decide to invest his tremendous wealth into the stock market of a small African or Latin American economy, or to suddenly pull it out, this would cause absolute havoc. Recall that the Asian

Financial Crisis of 1998, which devastated a whole region, was caused by the capital flight of roughly $170 billion in 2020 dollars (Rodrik 1998); Musk has about $100 billion more than that.

The bottom line is that increased wealth clearly buys increased political influence. Kenworthy (2022, 107) argues that "there is a tipping point" beyond which inequality has diminishing impact on political influence. That may be true, but even if the impact of each additional dollar is somewhat less than the previous one, the more important point is that with every extra dollar the rich still acquire *somewhat* more influence than the poor over the political process. More money can always buy more influence.[26]

The second important line of evidence comes from recent empirical studies. In their study of the responsiveness of political parties to low-income citizens, Rigby and Wright (2013, 563) determined that "the least fortunate in society have no independent voice in the formulation of party platforms." According to Flavin (2012, 29), "citizens with low incomes receive little substantive political representation (compared with more affluent citizens) in the policy decisions made by their state governments." Similarly, Bartels's (2016, 248) analysis "provides considerable evidence that elected officials are more responsive to the opinions of affluent constituents than those of middle-class or poor constituents." Perhaps most striking, Gilens and Page (2014) examined 1,779 policy debates between 1981 and 2002 in which a national survey asked the general public whether they were supportive or opposed to a particular issue. They found that "when the preferences of economic elites and the strands of organized interest groups are controlled for, the preferences of the average American appear to have only a minuscule, near-zero, statistically non-significant impact upon public policy" (575). Their conclusion is that "the majority does *not* rule—at least not in the causal sense of actually determining policy outcomes. When a majority of citizens disagrees with economic elites or with organized interests, they generally lose" (576). Such evidence demonstrates that significant inequality can actually break a democracy, gradually transforming it into a plutocracy, as has arguably already transpired in the United States.[27]

Much the same result has been found elsewhere. Rosset's (2013) study of the Swiss Parliament learned that relatively poor citizens are less well represented compared to citizens with high incomes. Elsässer, Hense, and Schäfer (2021, 1902) show that "the political decisions of the German *Bundestag* are biased in favor of the better off." Lupu and Warner (2022, 286), using a variety of methods and a data set consisting of 92,000 elite observations and 3.9 million citizen observations spread across 52 countries and 33 years, concluded that "representation may be more unequal in the United States, but it is still unequal elsewhere. Around the world, less affluent citizens can expect their preferences to be less well reflected among their elected representatives than are the views of their more affluent neighbors."

It is also striking that across the world elected representatives are nowhere close to being *descriptively representative* of the population—their demographic makeup is typically highly skewed toward the rich (as well as White people and men [Carnes 2012; Carnes and Lupu 2015]). The US Senate, for example, is a club for millionaires—the median wealth of senators in 2015 was a whopping $3,200,000, compared to the median wealth of citizens, which was only $45,000 (Luhby 2014; OpenSecrets 2018). Even Sweden's democratic system is seen by scholars as "representation from above." For instance, the Swedish Riksdag in the 1990s, when the country was significantly more social democratic than today, was still significantly overrepresented by the rich and underrepresented by the working-class: blue-collar workers made up 41% of the electorate and only 9% of MPs (Esaiasson and Holmberg 1996). It is quite stunning to reflect on the fact that although the majority of every country is composed of workers and caregivers, the system of electoral democracy has practically never produced a government wherein the majority of legislators themselves come from such groups. This overrepresentation of the rich matters because one's social location is likely to impact one's beliefs and political decisions. Carnes (2012) finds that American representatives with a working-class background tend to have more progressive economic preferences than legislators from higher class positions. Consequently, the underrepresentation of the working class in the legislature suggests that the preferences of the working class are underrepresented. When Carnes and Lupu (2015) examined 18 Latin American countries, they found that legislators from working-class backgrounds consistently made different policy decisions than richer ones, again implying that the numerical underrepresentation of the working class in parliaments reflects a substantive underrepresentation of working-class perspectives.

In sum, the evidence that inequality can undermine democracy is overwhelming. Nevertheless, one may still wonder whether it is possible to insulate money from political power so that inequalities in money are prevented from transforming into inequalities of political influence. Can we break the link so that even if the rich have great consumption ability they do not have great power? There are two reasons to think that the answer is no. The first is the wide-ranging empirical evidence canvassed above: everywhere we look, inequality does seem to undermine democracy. Second, and more fundamental, the democratic process itself—disseminating one's ideas, communicating one's opinions, mobilizing political movements—is inherently fostered and facilitated by money, and will therefore always be biased toward the rich. It's true that it is entirely possible to dampen the most egregious ways in which the rich control politics, such as by limiting private donations to political parties and enforcing campaign finance rules; these are good and worthwhile practices. Nevertheless, the key point to recognize is that there are stark limits to what can be done to prevent wealth becoming power so long as we wish to maintain freedom of expression and basic market freedom. As long as citizens have the right to spend their money as they wish, it will generally be impossible to eradicate the significant advantage that the rich have in mobilizing support for their preferred platforms, because they will always have significantly more power to hire activists to knock on doors, pay strategists and political experts, print materials to distribute, host lavish events to promote their message, rent office space for campaigns, give donations to allies in supporting causes, and so on. Likewise, it will be impossible to eradicate the advantage that rich people have in controlling and disseminating information, since private individuals will presumably always be permitted to produce pamphlets, books, newspapers, podcasts, websites, advertisements, and billboards sympathetic to their views, as well as purchasing their own TV stations and think tanks—all to a much greater extent than regular citizens.

As long as society retains a belief in freedom of expression, the rich will be able to use this right to influence politics more than the poor (Alì and Caranti 2021).[28] We might call this basic fact the "liberal democracy paradox": *economic inequality + freedom of expression (including normal market freedoms) = unequal political influence.* If the liberal democracy paradox is true, as I think it is, there are only two possibilities for sustaining a truly democratic system of (roughly) equal political influence. One is by banning freedom of expression, so that all individuals are equally barred from hosting gatherings, hiring employees, printing newspapers, producing websites, etc.—in other words, by giving up on liberalism (which is obviously a terrifying prospect). The other is to create substantial economic equality (or at least significantly reduce inequality), in other words, giving up on neoliberal capitalism. We can have capitalist inequality or democracy, but we can't have both (at least not so long as we also wish to retain basic liberal rights).

The starkness of contemporary inequality means that we must choose a side. Either we allow such inequality to continue, thereby giving up on democracy and the ideal of political equality, or we insist on the necessity of democracy and put an end to rampant inequality. We cannot have both.

Benefits of Equal Opportunity and Security

Another profound benefit of high taxes is that they enable society to provide more opportunities, as previously poor and marginalized people acquire the means to develop their capabilities and pull themselves up by their community's bootstraps. In this sense, higher taxes lead to more real freedom for society at large, because the reduced freedoms of the superrich to buy an additional car or yacht are, generally speaking, much less important than the freedoms of the poor to securely access university, child care, pensions, and so on. Higher tax countries, like the Nordic countries, provide more opportunity for their populations as a whole to access quality healthcare, child care, university education, paid parental leave, and decent pensions than low-tax neoliberal countries (Pontusson 2005).[29] Higher taxes enable society to fund a more generous welfare state, which guarantees not only greater opportunities but enhanced economic security—so that everyone knows that their basic needs will always be met.

Countries with less inequality also tend to have greater social mobility. (In other words, it's easier to "climb the ladder.") This is often referred to as the Great Gatsby Curve (see Figure 3.4).

The horizontal axis shows income inequality as measured by the Gini coefficient from about a generation ago. The vertical axis measures intergenerational economic mobility (specifically, the elasticity between paternal earnings and a son's adult earnings using data on a cohort of children born during the early to mid-1960s and measuring adult outcomes in the mid- to late 1990s). The slope of the graph is clear: more inequality means less social mobility. "In countries like Finland, Norway, and Denmark, the connection between parental economic status and the adult earnings of children is weakest: less than one-fifth of any economic advantage or disadvantage that a father may have had in his time is passed on to a son in adulthood. In Italy, the United Kingdom, and the United States, roughly 50 percent of any advantage or disadvantage is passed on" (Corak 2013, 81).[30]

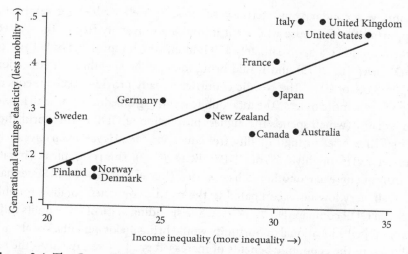

Figure 3.4 The Great Gatsby Curve: more inequality is associated with less mobility across the generations (Corak 2013, 82).

This is the basis of Wilkinson's (2011) famous quip that if Americans want to live the American dream, and not just dream it, they should move to Denmark. Inequality (and tax rates) play an important role in the level of social mobility because of their effects on the quality and accessibility of education, as well as the extent of family connections. We discuss inequality of education below. In terms of the importance of family connection, Corak (2013, 93) points out that a remarkable 70% of sons who are born to fathers in the top 1% at some point acquire a job with an employer for whom their father also worked. Likewise, Pérez-González (2006) examined over 300 CEO transitions and found that in 36% of the cases, the new CEO had a family connection to the company. Inequality breeds nepotism.

One of most important facets of equal opportunity is equal access to high-quality education.[31] The fact that access to education, particularly at the university level, remains a class privilege in many countries is deeply odious. Historically, one of worst crimes of inequality was the fact that the mass of people were kept not just in material deprivation but in mental squalor, stunted and ignorant, denied the opportunity to develop their faculties and unfold some of the myriad potentials of their personalities. An egalitarian, high-tax society could easily guarantee free education for all, including primary, secondary, and tertiary schools, as well as lifelong retraining opportunities for those who want it. Making university free in the United States would cost approximately $79 billion, which represents only 0.4% of GDP (Deming 2019) and would bring total public spending on education up to 3.6% of GDP. The Nordic countries already provide excellent education for all, more or less. The total public spending on education, at all levels, in Norway (which spends the highest proportion of GDP in the world after Costa Rica, offering high-quality, free education for all levels from daycare to university) is roughly 4.6% of GDP (OECD 2020c). This is significant, but it's hardly out of reach for other rich countries. (Recall that the United States has, overall, very low taxes compared to the Nordic countries, totaling roughly 25% of GDP compared to 42–47%, while spending 3.7% of GDP on its military.) Equal educational opportunity would bring major benefits. We already alluded to the economic benefits of increased productive capacity—the so-called human capital—that education brings. Beyond this there are the much broader benefits of allowing individuals to develop their personalities and intellectually flourish. Not to mention the benefits of social development, transforming individuals into competent citizens with a solid understanding of the social world and their place in it, and thereby more capable of self-governing (Brown 2011). After all, democracy surely means more than a mechanical structure of governance by elected officials; in its truest sense it expresses a form of social life whereby people cooperate as equals and make decisions as equals in the co-management of their shared institutions. This is clearly much more likely to be achieved with a population that is better educated and so less easily lied to, manipulated, or sidelined in the governance of public affairs.

Finally, equal opportunity is also a positive thing from the perspective of justice—at least insofar as a core element of justice is the luck egalitarian principle (elaborated on in Chapters 5 and 7), that it is wrong for some to have significantly better lives than others due to mere brute luck. Consider the astounding fact that American men in the bottom 1% of the income distribution have a life expectancy of 72.7 years whereas men in the top 1% have a life expectancy of 87.3 years. Rich people have almost 15 more years of life than the poor (Chetty et al. 2016). Indeed, as pointed out in the introduction, the poorest residents of Chicago have a life expectancy which is fully *30 years* shorter than the richest (Lartey 2019). Here the poor enjoy not only fewer of the good things in life but far less of that ultimate good: life itself. Such statistics are shrieks of unfairness, calling out for restitution. A just society, from an egalitarian perspective, is, among other things, one that takes seriously the equal moral worth and dignity of all its members and so refuses to allow some to live significantly better—or longer—lives than others due to the mere luck of being born a certain race or gender or into a rich family. To the extent that higher taxes provide everyone, regardless of their background circumstance, the essential requirements for living a good and flourishing life, they contribute to a more just society.

Benefits of Reducing Xenophobia, Racism, and Fascism

Another potentially profound benefit from high taxes is that if such taxes are spent increasing economic security, they could significantly douse the flames of right-wing populism. Fear is, after all, the lifeblood of the crueler impulses of our nature. Though right-wing populism has many complex causes, the evidence is clear that economic insecurity is a central and potent one (likely because insecurity increases fear that one's already precarious position will be worsened by competition from "immigrants" and "others" [Algan et al. 2017; Arzheimer 2009; Dal Bó et al. 2018; Guiso et al. 2017, 2019; Swank and Betz 2003]). There is strong evidence to indicate that societies with more economic security also have less right-wing extremism (Arzheimer 2009; Halikiopoulou and Vlandas 2016; Swank and Betz 2003; Vlandas and Halikiopoulou 2019). For instance, Swank and Betz (2003, 232) found that "an increase of +1.00 on our standard score index of universalism [meaning that more of the population is guaranteed social benefits and protections] (e.g. the difference between Italy (−.54) and Finland (0.45) in the early 1990s) is associated with a reduction of roughly five percentage points in the vote share for RRWP [radical right-wing populist] parties." Similarly, Halikiopoulou and Vlandas (2016) have shown that countries with more generous unemployment benefits have, other things being equal, lower support for far-right parties in European Parliament elections. Of course, even if more egalitarian countries produce less right-wing populism, that is not to say that they have no such problems. Even the Nordic countries have seen a precipitous rise in far-right activity over the past 20 years (though it has been relatively less severe than in other places) [Barry and Sorensen 2018; Widfeldt 2018]).

In addition to economic insecurity, a deep source of the xenophobic and populist backlash convulsing the world at present is the resentment that many (mainly White) working-class people feel at being humiliated by a so-called "meritocratic" society that constantly devalues them (Hochschild 2016; Sandel 2020). Central to the meritocratic ethos is the notion that you get what you deserve. Hence, those without a university degree (two-thirds of American adults) are frequently portrayed as ignorant and backward. And those with low-paying jobs are dismissed as having little inherent value: their financial wealth is equated with their human worth. Meritocracy says to regular working people—such as retail clerks, truck drivers, restaurant servers, and office administrators—that since one's pay reflects one's value to society, your low pay means that your work is unimportant, your labor has little value, and you yourself have little worth. People get what they deserve. This is what Sandel (2020) refers to as the "tyranny of merit." Such a narrative is of course deeply shaming and risks creating in the hearts of millions hurricanes of resentment, even rage.

By contrast, a more equal society would have much smaller gaps between the top and bottom; it would also provide a much higher and more generous floor of things guaranteed to all, no matter what. There would be far less of a chasm between the so-called winners and losers of the economic competition. Such a society would undoubtedly be one with less anger and resentment simmering under the surface, just waiting for a charismatic leader to funnel such rage into the explosive force of xenophobia or even fascism.

At this moment in history, the importance of this issue is hard to overstate. Several years ago the Italian prime minister Silvio Berlusconi referred to immigrants as an "army of evil" (Standing 2011, 4); the most widely read newspaper in the United Kingdom has called immigrants "vermin" (language which was common in Rwanda before the genocide [Williams 2015]). Trump declared that immigrants are "not people" but "animals" (BBC 2018) and enacted policies to lock immigrant children in migrant detention centers which have been likened to "concentration camps" (Datil 2019). Such omens are chilling to the core.

Low taxes and high inequality, therefore, provide a real material boost to racism, xenophobia, even fascism, and the terrors they bring in train.

Benefits of Reduced Social Friction

There has been an explosion of studies over the past couple of decades linking inequality to a variety of social problems related to social friction.

Unfortunately, the bulk of these studies are cross-sectional, meaning that they compare different places or countries at one fixed point in time; so although they can establish interesting correlations, they can't prove that inequality is truly *causing* the problems—there is always the possibility of reverse causation or that some other factor altogether is driving the association. For these reasons, Kenworthy (2016) argues that longitudinal studies (which look at how changes in inequality *over time* lead to changes in various outcomes) are more persuasive in terms of establishing causality. In what follows I rely on the longitudinal evidence where it exists. Where it does not, the reader should keep in mind the truism that correlation does not prove causation.

To date, the available evidence does suggest that inequality tends to erode social bonds and increase social friction. Paskov and Dewilde (2012) find that living in more unequal countries is associated with people being less "solidaristic" in the sense that they are less willing to contribute to the welfare of others (and this is true for respondents living in both low- and high-income households).[32] De Vries, Gosling, and Potter (2011) find an association between more unequal societies and less "agreeableness" (meaning that people are less helpful, considerate, and trusting, and more aloof, rude, and quarrelsome). Likewise, income inequality is associated with higher levels of intolerance toward homosexuality (Andersen and Fetner 2008).

Beyond these negative attitudes, inequality also appears to lead to all kinds of societal problems. For one thing, inequality appears to be inversely related to happiness at work: Clark and Oswald (1996) found that the satisfaction levels of British workers varied inversely with the wages of their peers. Inequality is also associated with reduced civic engagement (Lancee and Van de Werfhorst 2012; Solt 2008; though contrast with Uslaner and Brown 2005) and appears to cause more corruption (Apergis, Dincer, and Payne 2010; Policardo, Carrera, and Risso 2019; Uslaner 2008). Inequality also seems to worsen mental health: the most recent meta-analysis of the evidence reviewed 26 studies and found that "nearly two-thirds of all studies and five out of six longitudinal studies reported a statistically significant positive relationship between income inequality and risk of depression" (Patel et al. 2018).[33]

Worse inequality also leads to more crime. The bulk of the now voluminous cross-sectional evidence finds that income inequality is highly associated with many kinds of crime (Hsieh and Pugh 1993; Nivette 2011; Spencer, Mendez, and Stith 2019). Likewise, a review of the studies which use

time-series evidence finds that increased inequality leads to increased property crime, though the effect on violent crime is more varied (there is a relationship between inequality and homicide and robbery, but not for assault or
rape [Rufrancos et al. 2013; though note that Kenworthy 2016 is skeptical]).
Beyond normal crime, Krieger and Meierrieks (2019) find that higher levels
of income inequality are associated with more domestic terrorism, whereas
countries which redistribute more suffer less terrorism. The authors suggest
that this may be because more unequal countries produce more deprivation, more corruption, worse human rights records, and thereby more social
frustration.

A number of theorists have suggested that inequality is detrimental to
average levels of happiness, trust, and health (Uslaner and Brown 2005;
Wilkinson and Pickett 2010). However, I am somewhat skeptical about the
robustness of such evidence. Though this may turn out to be true (particularly for trust and health), the evidence at present is decidedly mixed, and
so it would be premature to take a confident stand one way or the other and
better to err on the side of caution.[34]

Benefits of Work Time Reduction

We saw that high taxes may lead to some reductions in working time for the
rich, though these would likely be quite minimal. Nevertheless, assume for
the sake of argument that the worst-case conservative predictions turn out
to be true and there are indeed significant reductions in working time among
high earners. Even in this case, the losses to economic growth would have to
be measured against the benefits that reduced work time can bring.

One such benefit is related to gender justice. A reduction in work hours
of people at the top—typically male managers and CEOs—could potentially help to soften the "ideal worker" norm that successful careers must involve very long hours. This long-hours norm is an important part of what
constitutes the glass ceiling for women; since women do the bulk of caregiving work in society, they are much less able to perform the uninterrupted
long hours that the expectation of the successful (but implicitly male) career entails (Nedelsky and Malleson, forthcoming; Schulte 2014; Slaughter
2012). And since the people at the top tend to have significant influence
over the cultural norms as well as the rules and regulations of the workplace,
they have significant latitude to shift the norms and the rules toward shorter

hours, if they so choose. A reduction of working hours by those at the top may well help to change the norms and rules about working time expectations, making it easier for people (particularly men) to work less and so share caregiving responsibilities more, resulting in improved gender equality as well as improved work-life balance.

Weighing Total Harms and Benefits

We are at last in a position to evaluate the overarching question of this chapter: Is it a bad idea to raise taxes to high levels in order to reduce inequality?

In terms of the costs, the major worry is that taxes will lead to reduced economic growth. On the one hand, we have seen that increased taxes would likely lead to only minor reductions in work effort, and perhaps moderate costs of reduced private investment. On the other hand, such costs are likely to be substantially offset by the economic gains accruing from increased public investment. The bottom line from the empirical growth literature is that a high-tax regime is not likely to cause significant reductions in growth. Reducing inequality, particularly at the bottom, may actually promote growth, though very high levels of taxation on the rich may somewhat undermine it. Moreover, given the gravity of the ecological crisis, reduced growth is not an entirely bad thing (at least for the rich countries, and at least to the extent that it can be disconnected from economic insecurity, which is of course no easy task).

In terms of the benefits of high taxes and low inequality, we have seen that there would likely be minor to moderate benefits of reduced debt and enhanced stability. There would also be mild to moderate benefits in terms of reduced social friction (more solidarity, more civic engagement, less corruption, better mental health, and less crime) and perhaps somewhat improved gender equality. Moreover, we can expect there to be major, fundamental benefits in four areas: environmental sustainability (from enhanced public, green investment), democratic equality, equal opportunity (and enhanced security from a more generous welfare state), and reduced racism and xenophobia.

In sum, the costs of high taxes and low inequality are likely to be only moderate, whereas the benefits are potentially enormous, a different order of magnitude entirely.

4

Do Rich People Deserve Their Income?

Remember that you are an Englishman, and have consequently won
first prize in the lottery of life.

—Cecil Rhodes

You can make it if you try.

—President Barack Obama (a phrase he used
140 times during his presidency)

Do Bill Gates and Elon Musk morally deserve to make billions of dollars?[1]
Do professional athletes deserve to make millions? Does the disabled population deserve to earn so little? More broadly, do the richest 1% of Americans
deserve their current 20% appropriation of national income (and 40% of national wealth [Piketty 2020])? Or is such income undeserved and therefore
rightly taxed and redistributed?

The meritocratic belief that people morally deserve the income they acquire in the market is the belief that such money rightfully belongs to them because of their actions and efforts, and so it would be wrong for the state to tax
it away. Such a belief is both powerful and deep-rooted in Anglo-American
societies. According to the World Values Survey, 60% of Americans think
that the poor are so because they are "lazy or lack willpower" (Bénabou and
Tirole 2006). More recently, a Pew Research Center survey from 2017 finds
that 56% of Republicans believe that poor people are poor because of a "lack
of effort," and 66% believe the rich are rich because they "worked harder," not
because of having other advantages in life (Smith 2017). The Tea Party, one of
the most prominent social movements in the 2010s, originated from a CNBC
editor's philippic against government subsidies for those he deemed *undeserving* "losers." Kathy Miller (a campaign manager for the Republican Party
in Ohio) publicly insisted, "If you're Black and you haven't been successful in
the last fifty years, it's your own fault" (quoted in Lewis and Silverstone 2016).

Against Inequality. Tom Malleson, Oxford University Press. © Oxford University Press 2023.
DOI: 10.1093/oso/9780197670392.003.0005

Likewise, US presidential candidate Herman Cain said, "Don't blame Wall Street. Don't blame the big banks. If you don't have a job and you're not rich, blame yourself" (quoted in Martinez 2016, 18). Similarly, but more politely, Greg Mankiw (2013), chairman of the Council of Economic Advisors under President George W. Bush and a leading intellectual figure in the Republican Party, wrote an influential article entitled "Defending the One Percent," centered on the idea that market incomes, even for the very rich, are morally deserved. Distributive "desert" (the philosophers' word for "deservingness") and meritocracy are widely held beliefs—they are the mortar between the bricks of society's foundation.

Is it true that markets provide individuals with an income that at least somewhat accurately reflects their economic contribution to society? Many have thought so. Since at least the time of John Bates Clark ([1899] 1956), a central pillar of conventional economic thought has been that of marginal productivity theory, which says that a competitive market will distribute income to each factor of production—each worker or each owner of a factor of production—in accordance with its marginal contribution. From this perspective, capitalism can be seen not simply as an efficient system but as a *moral* one, because it gives to each the value of what they create. This idea has long been central to conservative economic thought; the most recent articulation of which is Mankiw's (2013, 30) notion of just deserts: "In the standard competitive labor market, a person's earnings equal the value of his or her marginal productivity." The large incomes of Steve Jobs, J. K. Rowling, and the One Percent are morally deserved, he argues, because they simply reflect these individuals' enormous contributions to our welfare (21–22).

The prominent philosopher David Miller (1999, 184, 186) captures the common intuition well when he says, "People deserve the rewards of economic activity for their achievement, for the contribution they make to the welfare of others by providing goods and services that others want. . . . Over fairly large aggregates of people at least, the money they are willing to put up to acquire goods and services provides a reasonable estimate of the value of these goods and services, and so a reasonable estimate of the contribution of the providers" (see also Kershnar 2005). This line of thought is widely accepted, intuitively compelling, and logically coherent. Yet I will argue that it is deeply flawed.

This chapter examines the idea of distributive desert, specifically the notion that people deserve to be rewarded in rough proportion to their economic contribution as valued by the market. I put forward five critical arguments. Three of these are well-known. Since these have been adequately discussed elsewhere, I mention them here briefly and only for completeness. The bulk of the chapter focuses on two original arguments. Overall, my aim is to show that taking these arguments together, the case against distributive desert is overwhelming.

In brief, my argument is that in contemporary capitalism, income is not morally deserved because it typically stems from the luck of inheriting very unequal circumstances. In particular, some inherit far more power and class privilege than others in terms of money, geographic location (being born in a rich versus a poor country), access to advantageous schools and social networks, and so on. Another way of saying this is that wealth is not deserved—Anglo-American societies are not meritocracies, far from it—because there is nothing close to a level playing field. Moreover, the income that people receive in the market is in many ways morally arbitrary; far from being a simple reflection of talent and effort, income often derives from market failures, random spikes and crashes of various prices, and the myriad decisions of politicians and lawyers whose decisions necessarily shape the nature of the market system and alter the resulting pattern of distribution. Let us examine these arguments in more detail now.

The Luck of Unequal Opportunities

The most common argument against distributive desert is that it does not make sense to say that people deserve their income if they enter the labor market from very different starting points—that is, if they come from markedly different social classes and family backgrounds. Market desert is undermined, in other words, by unequal opportunity, because if opportunity is unequal, then the resultant competition between people is manifestly unfair. If the race is rigged to be easier for some and harder for others, the resultant victories and defeats are meaningless, null and void.

And indeed the evidence is overwhelming that opportunity is severely unequal (at least in the Anglo-American countries, which are our focus). In Canada, Indigenous people face myriad obstacles and barriers that don't exist for the majority White population, such as racial stereotypes of inferiority, intergenerational trauma from residential schools, frequently unsafe drinking water,[2] high rates of youth suicide, frequent disappearance and murder,[3] and ongoing theft of land and resources (Manuel and Derrickson

2015; TRC 2015). Indigenous people face twice the unemployment rate as the national average, earn 60% of the median income, have 10 times the incarceration rate, 2.3 times the infant mortality rate, and 2.7 times the high school dropout rate. (These rates are, by and large, even worse than those impacting African Americans in the United States [Gilmore 2015]).[4]

In terms of gender, women continue to face immense cultural pressure to perform the bulk of unpaid care and household work. Women are also seriously disadvantaged by the so-called ideal worker norm, whereby most workplaces base their expectations, as well as their criteria for salary and promotion, on the best employees being able to work long hours, whenever demanded, without significant interruption, for years at a time. Such expectations obviously severely disadvantage those with caregiving responsibilities (Hochschild 2003; Nedelsky and Malleson, forthcoming; Schulte 2014). The result of such factors is that women typically earn far less than men; it is commonly reported that women in the United States earn 80 cents to the dollar. Yet this statistic understates the problem because it is measured only over a one-year period. If we instead measure total earnings over a 15-year period (when more women are likely to take breaks from employment for caregiving), women actually earn only 49% of what men earn (Rose and Hartmann 2018).[5]

In the United States, access to quality education is strikingly unequal. Poor inner-city schools (often with large populations of racialized students) receive only $3,000 per student, while wealthy private schools (often with large White populations) cost up to $40,000 per year (Asen 2012; Tronto 2013, 134). In terms of university admission, despite all the rhetoric of "merit," the fact is that SAT scores are highly correlated with family wealth: a student from a family earning over $200,000 annually has a 20% chance of scoring 1400 on the SATs, whereas a student from a family earning less than $20,000 has only a 2% chance of getting the same score (Sandel 2020, 164). Moreover, the cost of doing an undergraduate degree at an Ivy League school in the United States is approximately $200,000,[6] which is clearly far out of reach for many families (since the median family income in 2019 was only $69,000 [US Census 2020].)[7] The result is that university is much more accessible for richer than poorer families. The data show that children born to the highest-income families in 1984 were 74.5% more likely to attend college than those from the lowest-income families (Chetty et al. 2014, 1).[8]

Perhaps the most obvious way in which the playing field is not level is inheritance. Some people start life with far more resources than others. Of the richest 400 people on the Forbes rich list, 42% inherited their way onto the list, and a further 13% started life with over $1 million (Hahnel 2002, 28). Piketty (2014) estimates that a massive 66% of all private wealth is derived from inheritance. In the race of life, inheritance represents being able to compete in a motorcycle while everyone else must compete on foot.

Relatedly, those who start life with a significant amount of wealth will typically find it much easier to accumulate more by simply reinvesting their existing wealth, which often pays more than actually working for a living. Recall the remarkable fact from Chapter 1 that owning a house in London will bring the average homeowner the same income (from increasing property value) in two days as the average worker will earn from labor in five (Chakrabortty 2016). More dramatically, Elon Musk could choose to sit back, put his feet up, and simply invest his $270 billion wealth. If he invested in generic mutual funds, he would likely earn a standard 5% return (if not substantially more), meaning he would earn roughly $13.5 billion per year for doing nothing more than sending an email to his money manager. (Musk's income in such a case would be equivalent to the wages of 432,000 minimum-wage workers laboring for 40 hours per week every week of the year.)

Factors such as these dramatically impact social mobility, so that today an American child born into the bottom fifth of the income distribution has only a 7.8% chance of reaching the top fifth (Chetty et al. 2014, 47; see also the discussion on the Great Gatsby Curve in Chapter 3).

There is no equal opportunity in the contemporary United States. Meritocracy is a lie.

The Luck of Global Unequal Opportunity and the Understructure

Much discussion of income desert has tended to focus on issues of unequal opportunity within a given country. I want to now make an analogous argument, but in terms of factors that have received far less attention in the literature, yet which play an even more significant role in terms of one's economic contribution. These are the accumulated factors of production and set of social infrastructures which foster and facilitate economic activity, which I will collectively call "the understructure." While the understructure plays an enormous role in fostering every individual's economic contribution, no one can claim individual responsibility for such contribution; it results from what

Ronald Dworkin (1981b) would call the "brute luck" of being born in a rich country.[9] To see this, let us take a small detour to discuss the understructure.

The Understructure of Market Production

Standard libertarian and neoclassical economic discourse tends to describe economic activity as if it were the result of individual Robinson Crusoes producing their own private property out of nothing, then trading it with others (Friedman [1962] 2002, 13; Grapard 1995; Narveson 2001, ch. 7; Rothbard 1982, 29). That is a deeply misleading picture. In this section I briefly lay out a more empirically accurate picture by focusing on the sociological reality of the production process in contemporary market economies. In particular, I want to draw attention to the inherently social and deeply interdependent nature of economic production. Whereas libertarians and neoliberals tend to visualize production by focusing on the foreground owners of production, I want to draw attention to the background enabling conditions which allow production to occur. The understructure refers to the complex of infrastructures—physical assets, institutions, laws, norms, intellectual concepts, emotional supports, natural resources, etc.—which underlie and enable market production. In short, all the historical and background human (and environmental) activity that make present production possible.

Consider the following seven elements of the understructure.

Physical infrastructure. This includes the range of public utilities (roads, bridges, railways, tunnels, water systems, sewers, electricity grids, telecommunication networks, and so on) as well as the stock of private buildings: houses, farms, factories, offices, skyscrapers, etc.) that can serve as fixed capital (i.e., capital that is not used up in the production of other goods). All such things were built by large numbers of people in complex chains of cooperation. They massively magnify the productive capacity of individuals participating in the economic system.

Political-legal infrastructure. It has long been known that the state provides a background infrastructure of social stability, predictability, and peace that is necessary for any market to function well.[10] Moreover, a fundamentally important insight from Karl Polanyi ([1944] 2001) is that market systems cannot exist on their own. There is no such thing as a literally "free market" (Murphy and Nagel 2002). All market systems are embedded in a political-legal infrastructure; they are shaped and defined by legal and political rules, regulations, and institutions (Ciepley 2013). These include, chiefly, a system of property rights which defines who owns what, what rights ownership conveys, what is allowed to be sold and what is not, as well as a police force to enforce such rights and a judicial system to adjudicate them; a system of business law to define the kind of firms that are permitted to operate in the market—such as corporations, partnerships, worker cooperatives, nonprofits, charities—and to specify their rights, responsibilities, and liabilities;[11] a treasury to maintain a safe and legitimate monopoly on the creation of money; and a central bank to reduce the risk of financial crises, as well as to manage the amount of money in the economy, which is vital for ensuring stable economic growth (i.e., without overly high inflation or unemployment).

The essential point here is that contemporary economic production could not happen without the political-legal infrastructure. This means that the state, and all the various workers who administer and maintain it—the politicians, lawyers, police officers, bureaucrats, administrative staff, janitors, office cleaners, and so on—are, as it were, "silent partners" in every business and in the production of every new piece of private property.[12] They are its co-creators.

Cultural infrastructure. All economic production takes place within a given cultural infrastructure. This includes the background of cultural norms, or what Durkheim ([1893] 1984) called the "noncontractual basis of contract." Such norms include trust (which reduces transaction costs by facilitating exchange), as well as broader cultural canopies such as the belief that the pursuit of profit is morally legitimate (Mokyr 2017; Putnam, Leonardi, and Nanetti 1993; Weber [1904] 2003).

More broadly, all production requires thinking, and all thought happens within a cultural and linguistic framework. We would not be able to produce anything at all were it not for the extensive cultural frameworks that shape the architecture of our minds and make the world sensible (allowing us to understand what objects are; how to understand norms, rules, and regulations; how to understand and operate in social situations). We rely on others to provide a cultural framework which forms the basis of our very ability to think and to act with intention. The limits of our language are the limits of our world, as Wittgenstein ([1921] 2014) would say. Yet individuals do not, for the most part, create their own language or concepts; they may adapt them, but they do not create the building blocks of their ideas out of nothing: they inherit them from the community. Even the most autonomous person is able to be so only because they have access to a range of diverse ideas and viewpoints provided by *other* people which provides the fodder for self-critique.[13] No one could be autonomous in a cultural vacuum, because no one grows their own worldview from scratch. No one is a self-sufficient farmer of their own mind. Even the exercise of autonomously choosing to distance oneself from one's original cultural community is only ever done on the basis of other concepts borrowed or adapted from other cultural communities.

Every time we think, we are inevitably doing so by using the concepts, definitions, norms, givens, and taken-for-granted assumptions that our community has given us. To think is thus to see the world through a cultural kaleidoscope, where many of the myriad reflecting mirrors are inherited from our community. Our cultural inheritance, in other words, provides us with the conceptual categories that we use to understand the world and to act in it. The upshot is that economic production is always and inherently a collective process because it happens on the basis of shared cultural infrastructures developed, maintained, and transmitted to individuals by the community of other people.

Knowledge infrastructure. For a long time, it was conventional wisdom that economic growth was due to increases in the inputs of labor, and especially fixed capital. But it is now widely recognized that a major source of modern prosperity (if not the most important source) is the accumulated collective knowledge that we inherit from the past (Kuznets 1971; Solow 1957). Many economists now agree with Abramovitz (1993) that roughly 80% of economic growth over the past century was created not by labor or capital inputs per se but by technological progress broadly understood.[14] As Alperovitz and Daly (2008) point out, this means that the bulk of our modern wealth cannot be attributed to the effort or investment decisions of isolated individuals but is rather the result of individuals building on the immense knowledge infrastructure that was passed down to us through vast networks of engineers, scientists, theorists, technicians, teachers, scholars, practitioners, and others.[15] And of course, the knowledge of the past was made possible not simply by the scientists but by the large numbers of nonscientists whose labor (growing food, providing public safety, printing books, cleaning offices, caregiving) made the specialized work of the knowledge producers possible in the first place. This means that the stock of knowledge which we inherit from the past is not due to a small class of inventors or academics but from society in general, understood as a complex system of social cooperation. Furthermore, the *proportion* of the output that could ever be attributed to oneself, compared to what comes from the labor of other people, is continually and constantly shrinking as society's knowledge base grows. For these reasons, the educational system of a country is a vital component of that country's knowledge infrastructure. The extent to which high-quality and accessible education is provided to the population at large will obviously have a direct and profound impact on collective productivity.[16]

Care infrastructure. Perhaps the most important of all economic infrastructures is the one that is most commonly neglected: the infrastructure of care (Fineman 2004; Kittay 1999; Tronto 2013). The care that is provided to young people is what enables them to be able to do anything at all. Care is, among other things, the production of human capacity. None of us could walk, talk, or think for ourselves were it not for our caregivers. Care is also fundamentally important for our psychological well-being. We become self-confident, healthy, stable, happy individuals only if we have received years of care and attachment (Cassidy and Shaver 2008). This is most obvious in early childhood, but it continues more subtly throughout our lives as we rely on friends, families, and lovers to provide emotional support and recognition through nurturance, empathy, love, and sexual care. Care is thus the invisible infrastructure—the ladder of congealed, mostly feminine, and often racialized labor—that we all climb on to reach our goals.[17] It is instructive to recall that even those who earn millions in the market, such as the basketball star Wilt Chamberlain (a favorite libertarian example whom we discuss further in Chapter 6) would not have been able to walk, talk, or sit upright (much less play amazing basketball) were it not for Olivia Ruth Johnson, his mother, and the broader web of care.

Related to the care infrastructure is the *healthcare infrastructure.* Having accessible healthcare as well as well-enforced health standards (such as safe drinking water, clean air, free testing for infectious disease) is of vital significance in keeping people healthy and thus productive. Moreover, health is, in many respects, a public, not a private, matter. As the COVID-19 pandemic made abundantly clear, one's individual health can be highly dependent on the level of community health. If your neighbors and coworkers get infected, your own risks become substantially elevated. In cases like this, my productivity will be very much influenced by your health (and vice versa). Individual productivity can thus be greatly impacted by public health issues and the robustness of the public health infrastructure. For example, one reason Canada suffered much less economic damage from COVID-19 than the United States can be traced, at least in part, to Canada's provision of universal healthcare (Coletta 2020).[18]

Natural environment. Although nature or "land" is often seen as a simple input in production processes, it is much more than this. Ecological systems are also a vital part of the understructure in that they provide the basic prerequisites for the continuance of life itself (Milman 2015). As ecological economists have long pointed out, the environment is a vital support, a container, and a fixed boundary for any and every economic system (Daly and Farley 2011).

Natural resources—in particular, energy resources (oil, gas, coal, wood, sun, wind)—provide the basic fuel for the economy to function. Recall that during the earlier agricultural era of human civilization, all production from human or animal muscle depended ultimately on vegetal raw materials. In Wrigley's (2010, 9) words, "the production horizon for all organic economies was set by the annual cycle of plant growth." This decisively changed with the discovery of mineral energy sources. Industrial society as we know it would not have occurred without being powered by the tremendous amount of energy locked up in coal (and now other fossil fuels, particularly oil). For example, to produce one ton of bar iron—a basic prerequisite of industrialization—required roughly 30 tons of dry wood in 17th-century England. If half of the entire surface of the country were used as woodland, it would still only produce 1.25 million tons of bar iron per year, not nearly enough for railways or steel ships or other necessities of industrial life. Yet by burning coal, England was able to produce 10 million tons of bar iron per year by the early 20th century (the equivalent of burning four times the size of the whole of England in wood every year), allowing for society-changing and eventually world-transforming industrialization (Wrigley 2010, 16–17). Where do these fossil fuels come from? During the Carboniferous era (roughly 300 million years ago), a portion of the annual plant growth (particularly in swampy areas) would decay and transform into stored energy in the form of coal. (Similarly, algae and plants in shallow seas would sink to the seafloor, become buried, and slowly form natural gas and oil.) This means that many of our cars, as well as heat, electricity, indeed much of industrial life itself, are able to exist only because they are powered by a massive natural inheritance of fossil fuels formed over a period of 60 million years.[19] And if we are able to transform our economies to use renewable energy, those economies will still be fed and sustained by the immense power contained within various natural resources.

In sum, the understructure is the complex of infrastructures which underlie and enable market production. The reason this all matters is that it demonstrates why productivity and property itself never emerge from the individual tout court. On the contrary, production is always a deeply social, interdependent process involving the background labor of much of the community. Instead of the commonplace understanding that production is due to individual action—for instance, that Adam Smith wrote the *Wealth of Nations* himself—what I am urging is instead a broader and more sociologically and empirically accurate understanding of how production really occurs. In fact, the *Wealth of Nations* was not produced by Smith alone, but also by Margaret Douglas, his mother, who cooked his meals and provided significant emotional sustenance (Marçal 2015), as well as the myriad other elements of the understructure whose labor enabled Smith to work in the first place by providing him a home, warmth, ink and paper, peace, quiet, knowledge, understanding, and more. Margaret Douglas, and all those others, were *partners*—in sociological if not legal terms—in the cooperative production of such famous writings. That is not to say that they had identical skills or did identical work, but that the final product was able to exist only because of their joint labor. This is what the understructure helps us to see: that all production is, in reality, social production.

It is easy to underestimate the truly vast contribution of the understructure to our quotidian economic activities. Consider one mundane example: every day in every city in the Global North, thousands of semi trucks shuttle back and forth carrying our goods. Each one of these trucks can carry roughly 78,000 pounds and can travel approximately 2,000 miles before needing to refill its tank. This stupendous feat is possible because of the immense underlying understructure: the endless ribbons of concrete highways, the years of labor that built them, and the generations of learning that developed concrete; similarly the trucks, with their thousand component parts, the incredible cultural and scientific developments necessary to develop the combustion engine, discover and mine the fuel, and so on. To get a sense of the potency of the understructure, we can ask what it would take for human beings to accomplish this one simple task *without the modern understructure*, i.e., by simply carrying the goods on our backs. The answer is that what one truck driver can accomplish in a single day would take an individual without the modern understructure about 2,700 years (or 990,500 people all carrying goods for a day)![20]

The Understructure Undermines Income Desert

Returning to the issue at hand, how is the understructure relevant for our discussion about the income that individuals morally deserve?

Consider the example of two brother farmers, Sam and Sami. Sam is brought up in an average working-class family in the United States. He received a small inheritance from his family and sufficient loans from the bank to allow him to buy some land, fertilizer, a tractor, and other factors of production. Sam works hard, grows his crops, sells them, and makes an annual income of, say, $30,000 a year (Martin and Costa 2017). Imagine also that 30 years earlier, around the time of Sam's birth, his father had a relationship with a woman in India, who bore a son named Sami. Sami does not know of Sam's existence but lives a parallel life. He is brought up in a typical family in rural India and likewise becomes a farmer, though atop a very different understructure. Sami can afford only a small plot of land because it is difficult to get loans. He works the land with traditional plows and sells his produce in nearby markets (since transportation costs are high over the unpaved roads). Sami earns the equivalent of $4,200 per year (in USD purchasing power parity [PPP]).[21] We assume that the two men have equal natural talent, similar levels of cultivated ability, and equal capacity to put in diligent effort. We also assume that they do in fact work equally hard.

The first thing to say about this example is that it is true to reality. Instead of discussing farmers, we could just as easily have taken another occupation.[22] For instance, the facts are similar for bus drivers: a bus driver in Sweden makes, on average, nearly 50 times more than one in New Delhi (Chang 2010, 24). Both brothers put in similar levels of effort and had similar skills, but Sam was lucky to be able to use a whole range of inputs that Sami did not have access to: bank loans, tractors, fertilizers, paved roads, and more. Sam rides a tractor while Sami pulls a plow. Sam is riding, literally and figuratively, on the historical wealth and knowledge of his society. His contribution does not come from *him* in any simple way. It comes mainly from the social structures—the understructure—for which he is in no way responsible.

The reason Sam makes so much more is because the US understructure is much wealthier and more developed. Consider only one aspect of the understructure: the store of accumulated business capital. The remarkable fact is that in the United States the amount of capital that exists in the private sector is roughly $438,000 per worker.[23] This is a major reason why American workers are so fantastically productive compared to workers in poor countries: each one (at least each one lucky enough to find employment) is privileged to work using materials worth roughly $438,000, which massively magnifies their productivity, whereas in India the comparable figure is only $30,340 (PPP).[24] Why are these aspects of the understructures so different? The answer has to do with their respective histories—the colonial control of India by Britain, the settler-colonial independence of the United States, their different trajectories of development in terms of center and periphery in global divisions of labor and production, and many other such factors. The central point is that no American today can claim responsibility for the development of the understructure that they enjoy (which hugely magnifies their personal income) because it is due to a historical accumulation that required the labor of millions of other people over hundreds of years.

Reflecting on this example brings to light the more general Polanyian point that people in the Global North make the income they do largely because they are lucky to be able to participate in extremely productive social systems; they are able to benefit from valuable societal inputs that immensely enhance their personal productivity.[25] Herbert Simon (2000, 755–756) makes the point forcefully:

> Consider the income that you or your family now earn . . . and compare it with the income that you would expect to earn if you were equally hardworking members of Chinese or Indian society, or the society of any other Third World nation. I expect that for most of you, the difference between the two incomes is one or more orders of magnitude, at least 10 to 1 and perhaps even more than 100 to 1. Now, I would like you to consider the causes for the gap between the 10 and the 1 or the 100 and the 1. How much of it do you wish to attribute to your superior energy, motivation, and application of effort as compared with your Third World counterparts? And how much do you wish to attribute to your good luck or good judgment in being born in, or joining, the highly productive and democratic American society? If we are very generous with ourselves, I suppose we might claim that we "earned" as much as one fifth of it. The rest is the patrimony associated with being a member of an enormously productive social system, which has accumulated a vast store of physical capital, and an even larger store of

intellectual capital—including knowledge, skills, and organizational know-how held by all of us—so that interaction with our equally talented fellow citizens rubs off on us both much of this knowledge and this generous allotment of unearned income.

Consider another aspect of the understructure—that of educational spending. A typical child born in Canada can expect to have the state invest $115,000 (USD PPP) into their primary and secondary education. If the same child were born in Ghana they would receive only $3,000 (USD PPP) for the same number of years of schooling.[26] Since the more educated are more productive and, therefore, other things being equal, able to command higher incomes, Canadian children will earn higher incomes at least partially because of their luck in inheriting a rich educational system.

Branko Milanovic's (2008, 2011, 2012) work is instructive in empirically demonstrating the degree to which the luck of geographical circumstance affects one's income. In studying global income distribution, he shows that the single most important factor in determining average income is not effort, or even the class one is born into, but the country one is born into. This fact alone accounts for between 66% and 87% of global inequality (Milanovic 2008, 12–13). He finds that personal effort is responsible for no more than 13–34% of income (and this is with the unrealistic assumption of perfect social mobility—that with sufficient effort anyone can rise to any class within one's country). In other words, he finds that the major determinant of income is the brute fact that most people are not free to migrate to places of greater wealth.[27] Consider the dramatic fact that only 3% of Indians are richer than the poorest 1% of Americans (Milanovic 2011, 118). This means that even if a poor American spent their life in total indolence, developing no skills, exerting no effort, and making no contribution to the economy (which almost never actually happens), they would still be richer than 97% of Indians. Milanovic concludes that if we assume reasonable levels of social mobility within countries (and attribute this mobility to "personal effort"), then "circumstance"—meaning, first, one's unchosen country of birth and, second, one's unchosen class of birth—explains 80% of income variability in the world today.

The essential point is this: one's total productivity comes in small part from *personal inputs* (such as talent and effort) but in large part from the *societal inputs* that one is able to access. Not only are the societal inputs much more important in terms of one's total productivity, but they are also a matter of luck, which dramatically advantages some over others, and so undermines any claim to desert. The understructure is, among other things, a vast social inheritance. This is one reason why the common distinction between inherited wealth and self-made wealth is highly exaggerated. What is called "self-made wealth" is possible only on top of the gigantic inheritance of the understructure, meaning it too represents a massive undeserved inheritance. This is not to say that inheriting a family fortune and inheriting a productive understructure are exactly the same things (since one who inherits a family fortune may never need to work again), but it is to insist that the "self-made" person is in reality much more similar to the trust fund baby than is typically acknowledged.

Similarly, for anyone who recognizes that, for instance, unequal access to education at a domestic level undermines desert (the first argument above), how can it be denied that the far greater inequalities of international education undermine desert even further? More generally, it is contradictory to believe that a personal inheritance of family background undermines desert, but social inheritance from national background does not. How can one's *domestic class position* undermine desert, but the much more severe and significant *international class position* be irrelevant? There are no good answers to such questions.

Many progressive thinkers like David Miller (1999) believe that market income would be deserved if it were earned from a level playing field. But even if we accept for the moment the dubious assumption that we deserve the rewards derived from our natural talents and efforts (Chapter 5 scrutinizes this assumption in depth), think what it would require to make the argument actually work. If we can gauge the level of deserved income only by imagining what would be earned from a more or less level playing field, then we have to imagine a *globally* level playing field (with roughly similar levels of accumulated factors of production and societal infrastructure). In such a context, the income that a typical worker would "deserve" would be close to the global median income—roughly \$2,600 per year.[28] Starting from such meager levels of background wealth, even highly talented individuals able to earn, say, 10 times more than the median person would still be making only \$26,000 per year. The difference between *this* income and the income that rich people in the Global North actually make is thus vast, and undeserved.

In fact, I think we can go even further than this. For the moment, let us continue to assume with desert proponents that individuals truly do deserve the income they derive from their efforts and talents. How much income is then deserved?

To get to the heart of the matter we need to imagine fully removing the individual from the understructure. Of course, this is impossible to do entirely because being a functional adult human being means that one has invariably already benefited extensively from years of cultural knowledge and care provided by others (not to mention benefiting from the natural environment). Nevertheless, for the sake of argument, let us be generous to the desert advocates and assume that in very simple societies, such as nomadic hunter-gatherer societies, there is basically no accumulated capital, technology, legal structures, or other infrastructures of any kind.[29] Let us take such societies to constitute a baseline of negligible understructure, thereby assuming that all the "income" generated in such societies stems entirely and completely from the talents and efforts of living individuals. We can then say that the income generated by individuals in such a society is completely morally deserved. Now, the key point that I want to make is that even if we grant this implausible assumption, the bulk of the income earned today is still not deserved.

What is an approximate average "income" for adults in such a society? In his influential work on the long sweep of human history, Angus Maddison (2007, 260) estimated subsistence income at $400 per person per year in 1990 international dollars. Adjusting those dollars to their 2011 equivalents gives $688 per person per year. Similarly, the World Bank defines "extreme poverty" or "absolute poverty" by the international poverty line of $1.90 (in 2011 USD PPP), which is $694 per year. So we can take $700 as a very rough approximation. We can compare this to the median income in the United States, which in 2011 was $27,000, and the average income of the top 1%, which was roughly $814,000.[30] If we assume similar work effort and talent across time, this means that 97% of the income of the contemporary median worker, and 99.9% of the income of the top centile, cannot be attributed to individual effort or talent but is in fact due to the social inheritance provided by the understructure, and therefore underserved.

Objection: Responsibility and Circumstantial Luck

David Miller (1989, 1999) has been one of the most philosophically astute defenders of distributive desert. He might seek to salvage the position by objecting that a certain amount of luck is always in the background of human actions and is not sufficient for undermining desert claims. In *Principles of Social Justice*, Miller (1999) responds to the concern that luck undermines desert by drawing a distinction between "integral" and "circumstantial" luck. Integral luck (i.e., luck that affects the performance itself) does, he concedes, undermine desert. However, circumstantial luck (i.e., the luck of having the opportunity to perform in the first place) does not. "Judgments about... deserts are not affected by the fact that other people in different physical and social circumstances may have very different sets of opportunities. Circumstantial luck always lies in the background of human performances"; it is what is *done* with one's circumstances that counts for grounding desert (146). In other words, his position would be that Sam's higher income may well come from circumstantial luck, but this does not undermine his desert, because he is still responsible for (and hence deserving of) what he does with these circumstantial opportunities.

To motivate this reasoning, Miller gives the example of a scientist who is lucky in acquiring a laboratory with which he does path-breaking work that results in winning the Nobel Prize. Miller claims that although the scientist is circumstantially lucky, he still deserves the prize. Circumstantial luck does not undermine desert. But notice that things look very different once the competitive aspect of the competition is more clearly emphasized. Miller (1999, 145) admits that if there were *other* scientists who might just as easily have made the discovery if they had been able to use the lab, then we will indeed "see the actual winner as less deserving." So Miller does not seem to be totally clear himself about whether circumstantial luck is truly irrelevant or not.

But let us go further. Imagine that in addition to the Nobel Prize there is another general Science Prize being offered to any scientist who can do a particularly difficult calculation. However, it turns out that this calculation requires use of the European Organization for Nuclear Research's (CERN) Large Hadron Collider, a particle accelerator located near Geneva. All that is required to perform the calculation is to press a big red button labeled "Go," and then write down the number that the screen displays. Since every undergraduate science student in the world is capable of doing this task, there are thousands of applications to work in the lab. So CERN picks a name out of a hat, and the chosen scientist does the calculation and consequently wins the Science Prize. In this instance surely no one would want to say that the circumstantially lucky scientist really *deserves* the eminent prize, because having access to the CERN calculator was due to mere luck, and so desert is undermined. Yet notice that this example is now closely analogous to the real-world example of Sam and Sami. The scientist's desert is undermined because there is no level playing field; they were simply circumstantially lucky—just as is Sam.

The conclusion is that, in competitions between people, circumstantial luck *does* matter because different circumstances confer different advantages and disadvantages on people's ability to perform. When these circumstantial advantages are due to luck, desert is indeed undermined.[31] The case of Sam and Sami, and the case of market income in general, clearly falls into this category of competition, and so Miller cannot avoid the conclusion that luck matters for weighing desert claims. Ultimately Miller (1999, 146) concedes that circumstantial luck can undermine desert "when it intrudes in a fairly clear and direct way on what different people achieve relative to one another." Yet the intrusion of luck into the determination of Sam's and Sami's incomes is about as "clear and direct" as could be.

Objection: Desert and the Relevance of International Comparisons

Another objection to consider is whether international considerations are relevant for thinking about income desert. Miller is perhaps even better known for his arguments about the necessity of a national context for discussions of justice (contra theorists of global justice) than for his arguments about market desert.[32] So it is easy to imagine him contesting the above argument by arguing that market desert is inherently state-dependent. The strongest version of this critique that I can imagine goes something like this: People in different countries (such as the United States and India) operate within different market systems. It only makes sense to talk about the economic contributions of Americans *in* the United States and Indians *in* India. It does not make sense to compare deserts across countries.

My response is that it is, empirically, simply not the case that income is a purely national thing. In the OECD, international trade of imports and exports accounts for an average of 41% of domestic GDP.[33] The income of wealthy individuals is especially integrated into the global economy since the richest 5% own 80% of all financial assets, and such assets tend to be highly diversified through investments in global markets (Blasi, Freeman, and Kruse 2013, 12). So if one wants to say that income is morally deserved, and given that domestic income is significantly affected by global competition, then it must follow that desert has an international bearing. If my income is determined in part by the economic actions of Indians (and other foreigners), then my desert must be relative to those Indians—in which case the Sam-Sami comparison holds. One cannot say, "The income that I have earned through exchange with Indians is deserved, *but* my desert is incomparable and incommensurable with their desert." That is incoherent.

A Note on Basic Income and "Something for Nothing"

Before moving on, note that recognizing the understructure as a vast and undeserved inheritance is illuminating for another reason: it helps us think more clearly about public services and Unconditional Basic Income. The standard critique of public services, and even more so of Basic Income, is that it involves giving people something for nothing. But once we recognize the existence of the understructure, we see that practically all contemporary wealth is actually due to the contributions of those long dead. The effort and talent of those living today contribute only a small amount. So this raises the question of *who should benefit from this immense social inheritance?* Who deserves to benefit from all the accumulated wealth, knowledge, and care of our forebears? Should rich people be the only ones to benefit?

Since no one alive today can take responsibility for more than a microscopic portion of the understructure, it seems obvious that the only acceptable answer is "all of us, more or less equally." Everyone should have, as a birthright, a share in the inheritance of the immense value of the understructure. From this perspective, public services and Basic Income look entirely different. They no longer represent "something for nothing"; instead they represent a fair way of distributing our social inheritance to everyone, not just a lucky few. At root, that is what such universal programs really are: *a fair and equal distribution to all of our social inheritance that is the understructure.* From this perspective, a cut to public services should not be seen as saving money by cutting off "undeserving" people, as conservatives often frame it, but should rather be seen as the theft of people's birthright for the benefit of the superrich, who have privately appropriated the value of other people's labor and refuse to pay back the rental payment on their use of the understructure.

Market Income Is Distorted by Market Failures

Recall Miller's (1999, 184, 186) defense of distributive desert: "People deserve the rewards of economic activity for their achievement, for the contribution they make to the welfare of others by providing goods and services that others want. . . . Over fairly large aggregates of people at least, the money they are willing to put up to acquire goods and services provides a reasonable estimate of the value of these goods and services, and so a reasonable estimate of the contribution of the providers."

We started this chapter by examining the idea that individuals deserve their income by looking at arguments of unequal opportunities and unlevel playing fields. We now turn to a second set of arguments, namely that the ways in which markets function in the real world means that the income that individuals receive often has no clear or sensible relationship to what they could plausibly claim to be their economic contribution.

One such argument, and the most common, is that market income will not reflect economic contribution if there are pervasive market failures—such as rent-seeking, externalities, monopolies, or public goods—because such failures mean that prices no longer reflect popular demand. As in the first argument, the debate here is mainly empirical: Are market failures widespread or are they marginal? While this is not the place to engage in this debate in depth, suffice it to say that there does seem to be significant evidence that, at least in the United States, the market contains extensive market failures (Foster, McChesney, and Jonna 2011; Stiglitz 2012).

Consider as well the most severe market failure of all: recession. Recall that according to the desert view, a low income means that there is little desire for your labor: your labor has little value to others. But in all recessions, a significant number of people abruptly lose their jobs. Are we to believe, therefore, that during, say, the Great Depression (not to mention the Great Recession or the COVID-19 pandemic), the US population all of a sudden saw no value in the labor of a quarter of the working population? Surely a more reasonable explanation for people's lack of income during this instance is not that they had nothing to contribute *as individuals*, but that major macroeconomic forces made it unprofitable for businesses to hire workers. In other words, individual contribution in the market can be totally submerged under the tidal waves of market cycles. It would be a mistake to shrug off this kind of market failure as an "abnormality" because as long as market systems have existed there have been continuous business cycles. There is no good reason to think that the top of the business cycle is any more "natural" than the bottom, or that income is more justly deserved at the peak of the business cycle than at the nadir. Yet if desert makes sense only in relation to markets that are operating in conditions of perfect equilibrium, it does not make much sense for the real world.

Market Income Is Distorted by Unpredictability

The next problem is this: the intuitive basis for market desert is the desire to reward people for making good economic choices that benefit others, but because the market is inherently unpredictable, the income that one ends up with is often due more to random chance than good planning.[34]

Consider two sisters who both work in juice factories. Alice works at an apple juice factory and Olga works at an orange juice factory. Initially, they earn the same income, yet after six months, random changes in the world market occur, perhaps due to drought in one part of the world and bumper crops in another, leading to Alice receiving a raise and Olga getting a pay cut, even though they both continue to do exactly the same work for the same hours and at the same intensity as before. It is hard to believe that their different income is morally deserved. Miller (1989, 167) would probably argue that people deserve their income because they have or should have predicted changes in the market: if one "chooses to become skilled at a task which he rightly foresees will become essential to the production of a valuable commodity, then he is surely properly rewarded for making that choice." But as Jeff Spinner-Halev (2017) notes, this misunderstands the nature of the market. To the extent that markets are unpredictable (and Spinner-Halev makes a persuasive case that they typically are), it is doubtful that people will be consistently or fairly rewarded for making diligent choices, precisely because it is very difficult to know beforehand what a diligent choice would be.

Consider also the oscillation of CEO pay in the United States. In the 1960s, a CEO earned roughly 20 times as much as a typical worker. That ratio rose slightly to 23:1 by the early 1970s, 58:1 by the end of the 1980s, 120:1 by 1995, 376:1 by the peak of the stock market bubble in 2000, and 351:1 by 2020 (Baker 2016, 132; Mishel and Kandra 2021). Overall, between the years 1978 and 2013, CEO pay increased by 937%, whereas pay of the typical worker grew only 10.2% (Reich 2015, 97). This means that if we are to believe that pay simply reflects productivity (as neoliberals argue), then we must believe that CEOs went from being 20 times more productive than typical workers to nearly 400 times more productive in the late 1990s to 351 times more productive today. The idea that such pay oscillation reflects an oscillation of real productivity is very hard to believe, to say the least.

Note that the third and fourth arguments cast doubt on desert by pointing out the ways in which real-world markets often do not conform to the textbook ideal of perfect equilibrium. While I find such arguments persuasive, a committed defender of market desert will be tempted to dismiss them as examples of market aberrations that are "atypical" or "unusual." When markets are working well, this defender might insist, then distributive desert still makes sense. With this in mind, I want to present my second original argument, which is that the *inherent nature* of the market is such that desert does not make sense. If I am right about this, then distributive desert will be very hard to maintain.

Market Income and the Political Nature of the Market System

A number of thinkers, such as Sadurski (1985) and Attas (2003), have critiqued distributive desert on the grounds that for workers in the public sector, wages are determined not by supply and demand but ultimately by political factors. Here I want to build on their insights to construct another argument against distributive desert. My claim is that market income is not deserved because prices in a market system are always affected by the political construction of the market, and are therefore always at least somewhat arbitrary from a moral point of view.

If there is a fundamental Polanyian insight, it is that there is no such thing as a truly "free market," and therefore no such thing as a neutral or objective price of things. Prices are determined in large part by the rules of the game, which are both contingent and variable. The market is not a neutral arena of supply and demand, but rather a complex set of political and legal institutions, parameters, and regulations that inevitably, deeply, and inextricably shape how the game is played and influence its outcome (Pistor 2019). Most people think of the market as a game, like Monopoly, where the rules are set in advance and individuals simply compete within the given framework of the rules. However, in reality, the market is actually a game where the rules themselves are constantly changing. Indeed, think how different a game it would be if Monopoly players were not allowed to accumulate more than a couple of properties each, or had to share the rents with others, or were allowed to periodically redistribute some of the wealth from the bank. In the real world, how does market shaping occur? In every market the *supply* of labor and goods is deeply shaped by labor laws (Are children allowed to work? Are the elderly forced to retire?), licensing regulations, intellectual property laws (such as copyright and patents), active labor market policies, tariffs and other trade barriers, and perhaps most profoundly in the contemporary context, immigration laws. Likewise, *demand* is deeply shaped by legislation determining what goods and services are permitted to be sold (usually not body parts, drugs, weapons, votes), also by tax rates (set by fiscal policy) and interest rates (influenced by monetary policy). So instead of price simply reflecting supply and demand, in fact what happens is that regulated-and-politically-influenced-demand interacts with regulated-and-politically-influenced-supply, resulting in inherently politicized prices.

What are the implications of this for moral desert? The constructed, regulated, *politicized* nature of the market means that price does not, contra desert theorists, simply reflect what the people want or what clever entrepreneurs are willing and able to supply. There is no clear connection between income and moral desert.

Consider some examples. Dean Baker (2006) has shown that an important part of the divergence of income between the middle and upper classes in recent years is due to the relative openness of immigration for low-skilled jobs (so that Mexican workers, for instance, are more able to compete for manufacturing and service jobs), while strong protectionism has been maintained for highly skilled jobs (so middle- or upper-class Mexicans are prevented from becoming American doctors, lawyers, academics, and so on, through tough licensing regulations). Politically increased supply has driven down wages at the bottom, while politically restricted supply has driven up wages at the top. There is nothing natural or neutral about this. The income divergence simply reflects a host of political decisions that in turn reflect the balance of political power at a specific time in American history.

Likewise, consider the example of Bill Gates, who, like Steve Jobs, is a favorite example of those wishing to advocate a theory of desert based on economic contribution. Gates is one of the richest individuals in the world. Is his income deserved? Desert theorists like to point to his immense economic contribution—the fact that millions of people voluntarily, and eagerly, choose to purchase his products. Yet his wealth is in no way a simple reflection of demand but is massively affected by the regulation of supply due to copyright protection. Copyright is a government-granted monopoly that can create huge amounts of money for its owner. But different market systems can and have used very different legal regimes for intellectual property. The particular regime of copyright law in use in the United States is not at all a natural thing. If it were replaced by (an arguably more efficient system of) open-source access with public funding and prizes to reward innovation, as suggested by Stiglitz (2007) and Baker (2005), then Gates's income would be dramatically reduced. In this alternative regime, we can imagine that his innovations might win prizes of, say, $10 million per year. But this would still represent a 99% reduction of his current income of over several billion dollars per year. The point is not that a prize system is necessarily better or worse than the present copyright system, but rather that Gates's income depends almost entirely on contingent market regulations, which are at least somewhat morally arbitrary because they are determined by a whole host of political and technical considerations, not pure economic contribution.

Many more examples could be given: income in the immensely profitable pharmaceutical industry is deeply affected by political decisions about patent laws; the income of doctors is deeply affected by political decisions about licensing laws; the income of manufacturing workers is deeply affected by political decisions about how easy it is to form a union and how open the sector is to international competition; the income of CEOs is deeply affected by the political rules of shareholder governance law, and so on.

More generally, the way the market is politically and legally shaped is hugely influential in determining the relative bargaining positions of employees and employers over wages. About 90% of workers work in multiperson firms or organizations, so their income is not set by the market in any direct way, but is always mediated through the employment relationship (Le 1999). Wages reflect bargaining power, and bargaining power is determined by the various ways in which the market is shaped (by rules about wages, hiring, firing, unions, codetermination, exit options in the form of welfare, basic income, etc.).

The essential point is that income can only ever be an indirect and opaque reflection of economic contribution because it is always refracted by the political nature of the market system and market prices. Since income always reflects the arbitrary rules of the game, there is never a clear amount of income that is obviously deserved. Consider the example that Miller (1989, 166) gives of the elderly neighbor: "If every month I clean the windows of my elderly neighbor's house, I deserve considerable gratitude; but if one month her grandson has forestalled me, I can't expect to be thanked as warmly if I go through my usual routine. Desert isn't merely a matter of good intentions; it also has to do with how much benefit you create for the recipients of your services, and in nearly every case that depends on the configuration of the world outside."

Miller's point is that a price change really does reflect a change in one's desert, because a change in price means that one's contribution to others has changed. But notice that what others do is in large part determined by broader political forces, and if their options for signaling their preferences are significantly shaped by these forces (as they always are), then the market cannot be seen as a simple reflection of what people want, and therefore cannot be treated as a conveyer belt of desert. Perhaps the elderly neighbor usually pays Miller $50 for cleaning her windows. But imagine in a different scenario that the state obliges her to pay a higher minimum wage, so he now earns $75. Or imagine in yet another scenario that the state suddenly relaxes its immigration controls so an additional million migrant workers enter the country, leading to many more people applying to clean the windows, and he gets offered only $20. In every case there is a clear and constant economic contribution—the windows have been cleaned—but which income accurately measures Miller's desert, the original scenario or one of the others? The point is that there is no correct answer to this question because price never reflects supply and demand in a straightforward way. The unavoidable conclusion is that price is not the neutral measure of contribution that desert theorists need it to be in order to ground their claims. If one were to enter a race only to find that as the race progressed the finish line was continually being moved closer to some participants and further away from others, one could be forgiven for having serious misgivings about its fairness.

One might wonder if the issue of political construction of the market that I'm pointing to is simply the familiar phenomenon of rent-seeking (i.e., the practice of manipulating a business or a public policy to increase profits). For example, Mankiw (2013, 23) argues that "the story of rising inequality . . . is not primarily about politics and rent-seeking [which he agrees is undeserved], but rather about supply and demand [which he thinks is deserved]." In other words, he wants to distinguish between the political manipulation of the market, on the one hand, and the interplay of what he sees as neutral economic forces of supply and demand, on the other. But quite apart from whether he is right about the empirical extent of rent-seeking in the contemporary United States (which he thinks is minimal), this way of framing the issue is conceptually misleading because the idea that there are neutral forces of supply and demand is wrong. Rents are the result of regulations, laws, policies, and institutions that cannot be separated out from the market. There is no such thing as a "true market" that simply has political policies glued on from the outside. This is the Polanyian insight: policies and politics are inherent to the market, through and through. Indeed, they *are* the market. Conceptually, we should not even talk of "the market" full stop; we should talk more accurately of the "market-state complex" (Malleson 2014a). It is conceptually confused to think that the goal could be to abolish rents per se: we can only strive to make sure that the market is shaped such that the rents which do occur are ones we consider just. To believe that there could ever be a market system without rent-seeking is to believe that it is possible to have a market unsullied by political regulation; it is to retreat from looking at markets in the real world to a fantasy land of general equilibrium and apolitical market forces that exist only in the utopian novels called microeconomics textbooks.[35]

Another way to see the issue here is to think about desert as it relates to the public versus the private sector. The contribution of public-sector workers (such as teachers) can never be determined simply by supply and demand but always depends on prior political evaluations: What is the social need for education? What are society's educational goals? What are the requirements of pay equity? Miller (1999) recognizes this but recommends that we try to salvage the notion of desert by finding ways to estimate contribution (e.g., he recommends doing surveys to figure out how much people would be willing to pay for such services). Nevertheless, he recognizes that the supply of public goods will always contain an ineliminable political element and so is always somewhat arbitrary: "I want to conclude by conceding, however, that whenever someone's work involves the production of a public good, there is likely to be some indeterminacy in estimating the size of his or her contribution" (197).

This concession, however, is not minor at all. It actually undermines his entire argument for distributive desert. Note first of all that the public sector is in no way a marginal part of modern economies. Across the OECD (2020a), total government spending in 2020 was around 50% of total economic activity (up to 61.6% in France). Contemporary economies are very much mixed economies. Given the size of the public sector, and the fact that prices in the public sector directly or indirectly affect large swaths of the private sector, because the outputs of the public sector are often the inputs of the private sector, the partial arbitrariness of public-sector income will invariably seep into the arbitrariness of private-sector income.

The more profound issue is that the same features that undermine desert in the public sector—the arbitrariness of income due to the political shaping of supply and demand—are precisely the same features that exist in the private sector too. As we saw, there is no such thing as an apolitical market economy. Every economy is inextricably politically shaped. Supply and demand do not exist naturally but are always created and constituted by the political and legal institutions of the state. So the arbitrariness which Miller concedes exists in the public sector cannot be analytically cordoned off from the private sector. To think that it can is to commit the naturalistic fallacy of assuming that a market system can exist independently of the state. In sum, the private sector is deeply affected by inherently political decisions in the same way as the public sector, even if it is affected less directly. Therefore, the income generated in the private sector has, at root, the same elements of inherent arbitrariness as public-sector income. Consequently, *all* income, whether public or private, is at least partially arbitrary and contingent, which means that it cannot be an appropriate measure of moral desert.

The conclusion is that income always reflects a range of political and morally arbitrary factors that can never be weeded out, analytically or in practice, to arrive at a notion of pure contribution. This means that income is never a clear measure of economic contribution, and therefore is never a reliable measure of desert.

Summary

The most common ethical justification of economic inequality is the notion that individuals rightfully deserve the very different incomes they receive in the market. This chapter has placed this idea under a microscope. We have seen five arguments as to why differences in income are not in fact deserved. On the one hand, income differentials are not deserved because they are largely the result of luck, in particular the luck of inheriting an advantageous position in the class hierarchy. Income differentials stem from the dramatically unequal circumstances that people find themselves in with regard to inheritance, education, job opportunities, race, gender, national understructure, etc.—all of which are profound on a domestic scale and enormous on a global one. On the other hand, the income that people receive in the market is in many ways morally vacuous—due to market failures, unpredictable and random vacillations of various prices, and the political nature of the market, that is, the continual shaping and reshaping of the rules and parameters of the market system by politicians and lawyers in ways which fundamentally influence the income that different groups will receive.

Of course, some readers may well disagree with one or two of the arguments presented here. But since each argument is by itself a sufficient critique of desert, the desert advocate must resist and be able to demonstrate why all five arguments are wrong. That seems extremely implausible, to say the least.

5

Do the Skilled and Hardworking Deserve More Than Others?

Obliged to submit to the law of the majority, the classes that call themselves superior can preserve their political hegemony only by invoking the law of the most capable. Because the walls of their prerogatives and tradition are crumbling, the democratic tide must be held back by a second rampart made up of brilliant and useful merits, of superiority whose prestige command obedience, of capacities of which it would be folly for society to deprive itself.

—Émile Boutmy, founder of Sciences Po, in 1872

Democratic modernity is founded on the belief that inequalities based on individual talent and effort are more justified than other inequalities.

—Thomas Piketty, *Capital in the Twenty-First Century*

It seems to be one of the fixed points of our considered judgments that no one deserves his place in the distribution of native endowments any more than one deserves one's initial starting place in society. The assertion that a man deserves the superior character that enables him to make the effort to cultivate his abilities is equally problematic; for his character depends in large part upon fortunate family and social circumstances for which he can claim no credit. The notion of desert seems not to apply to these cases.

—John Rawls, *A Theory of Justice*

In the previous chapter we saw that individuals do not deserve their income—and society is not a meritocracy—because there is nothing like a level playing field in contemporary capitalism.[1] But this raises a difficult

Against Inequality. Tom Malleson, Oxford University Press. © Oxford University Press 2023.
DOI: 10.1093/oso/9780197670392.003.0006

question: *What if society were to become more equal?* What if there really were equal opportunity between people, so that everyone had access to similar educational opportunities, there was far less class hierarchy, much reduced racism and sexism, and so on? Should we, in this case, embrace meritocracy and affirm that those who are more successful in the market competition rightly deserve their income on the grounds that it is the result not of privilege but of merit? And similarly, that the poor deserve their poverty because it is the result not of unfortunate circumstance but their own failures? If there truly were a level playing field, then would we want to say that those who have more skill or work harder or make better choices deserve more than the untalented, lazy, or weak-willed?

Some on the left seem to think so. For instance, the most famous book from the left in recent years—Thomas Piketty's (2014) *Capital in the Twenty-First Century*—assumes that the income earned in a fair market is morally deserved; Piketty's powerful critique of contemporary society is not that there is anything wrong with desert or meritocracy per se, but that inheritance and inequality have become so great as to "radically undermine the meritocratic values on which democratic societies are based" (1). Piketty reflects the conventional social democratic wisdom when he says that "democratic modernity is founded on the belief that inequalities based on individual talent and effort are more justified than other inequalities" (241). Indeed, he seems to believe that insofar as deservingness is concerned, there is a fundamental distinction to be made between "*self-made wealth* (for which individuals can be held responsible, at least in part)" and "*inherited wealth* (for which individuals can hardly be held responsible)" (Piketty, Saez, and Zucman 2013, 6–7, emphasis added). In other words, inequality stemming from "self-made wealth" is morally acceptable.[2] This kind of belief in what we might call "genuine meritocracy" is widespread among prominent social democrats. For instance, Nobel Prize winner Joseph Stiglitz (2012, 266, emphasis added) believes that "the bottom 99% by and large are not jealous of the social contributions that some of those among the 1 percent have made, of their *well-deserved incomes.*" Likewise, Robert Reich (2015, xi–xii) reminisces about what he sees as the golden age of US capitalism in the 1950s and 1960s, when CEOs made only 20 times more than their workers and "hard work paid off . . . [and] those who contributed most reaped the largest rewards." Indeed, the typical opinion of meritocracy from social democrats is not "We oppose" but "It doesn't yet exist," which appears to reinforce the notion that the ideal itself is a good and valuable one.

Socialists too often support a version of desert, though their position is more complicated. While there is clearly a long history of socialist thought that is adamantly needs-based (rejecting desert),[3] there's an equally long tradition that is firmly desertist. This is the tradition which emphasizes the exploitation of workers and the parasitism of capitalists. The problem with capitalism from this perspective is that workers do not receive what they rightly deserve from their toil (whereas bosses, and particularly rentiers, receive far more than they rightly deserve for their relative lack of work). Indeed, the basic socialist concepts of "exploitation" and "parasitism" are, arguably, deeply interwoven with, and animated by, the notion of deservingness (Cohen 2000).[4]

In other words, while many are rightly skeptical of the claim that meritocracy *currently exists today,* most people, including many on the left, continue to believe that the ideal of meritocracy is valid. In particular, many people (including on the left) share the core meritocratic intuitions: first, that people should be rewarded for the fruits of their skills; second, that people have control over their efforts and choices, and therefore hard work and good choices deserve greater rewards than laziness and poor choices. Indeed, these core meritocratic intuitions are interwoven with some of the foundational notions of Western (and other) culture that stretch back hundreds, if not thousands of years, such as the belief that individuals make their own choices, criminals deserve punishment, hard work deserves reward, and underlying them all, the conviction that individuals inherently possess "free will," which is what differentiates them from the beasts and allows them to be rightly held responsible—that is, praised or blamed, rewarded or punished—for the free choices they make.

In this chapter my aim is to challenge these common intuitions, with the hope that the reader will be persuaded to take a second look at their allegiance to ideas of deservingness and meritocracy. I will argue that even if circumstances were more equal, we should still reject meritocracy. The problem is not simply that meritocracy is not yet realized (as many on the left seem to think) but rather that the idea itself is inherently unjust and should be abandoned. I defend the admittedly radical position that we should be extremely skeptical of the idea that certain individuals ethically deserve more or less income from their work than others. True, some are more talented, some are more able to exert effort, and some are better able to shape their personality in productive ways—but all of this is ultimately due to luck. Rewarding people with significantly greater means to live a good life due to luckily possessing more talent or effort or self-cultivating skill than others is akin to rewarding people for having white skin or blue eyes: it is arbitrary and unfair.[5] *At its heart, meritocracy is a doctrine of ableism* (by which I mean that it discriminates and disadvantages people on the basis of their bodily abilities [Kristiansen, Vehmas, and Shakespeare 2009]). Like racism, meritocracy ranks people in a social hierarchy on the basis of characteristics that are arbitrary from a moral point of view. It should therefore be firmly rejected.[6]

I admit from the outset that this is a radical position, and one which clashes with many people's deep intuitions about deservingness, free will, and moral responsibility. But even if you, dear reader, are not willing to go all the way with me in abandoning desert altogether, I hope that by the end of this chapter you are at least more suspicious of it.

To reiterate, the central argument in the previous chapter was that desert is undermined because there is nothing like a level playing field in terms of opportunities. This chapter argues that *even if* there were a level playing field in terms of class and economic opportunity, individuals would still not deserve their income because of the luck of possessing uneven mental resources and capacities. The playing field of *internal capacities*, in other words, is inevitably unlevel all the way down, and so the competition that exists between people is inherently unfair. I agree that people do have the ability to make choices, exert effort, and improve their capacities; what they do not have is anything like equal ability to do such things. (There is no magical capacity of "autonomy" or "will power" that all humans equally possess.) People differ in their abilities to exert effort or self-improve just as dramatically and just as arbitrarily as they do in their ability to run fast or sing in perfect pitch. Since there is no level playing field, we should be deeply skeptical of the notions of desert and meritocracy. Ultimately, the aim should be to distribute essential economic goods as equally as possible (or perhaps according to need). Practically, of course, it will often be necessary for there to remain a certain level of income inequality in order for a market system to function well (because we want to create appropriate incentives for people to work hard, innovate, shift to working in jobs that are in high demand, etc.). Nevertheless, the justification of such inequalities is that of social usefulness; they are not ethically deserved.

To develop these arguments, the first section examines the question of whether we deserve rewards on the basis of skills; the second section examines whether effort is an appropriate basis for desert; the third section addresses whether individual choice legitimately grounds desert. In every case my answer will be no. The fourth section considers some objections, and the final section steps back to look at the big picture.

Before beginning, let us clear some conceptual ground. Even though this chapter is critical of desert, there are many areas of social life where it is perfectly reasonable, and even important, to talk about what people "deserve," as long as we're very clear about what precisely we mean. The crucial distinction to keep in mind is that of *institutional entitlement* versus *moral desert* (Olsaretti 2003). Entitlement means that one "deserves" a reward simply because that is what the rules of the game or institution in question dictates. So it makes sense to talk about someone "deserving" the gold medal because they won the race, or the worker "deserving" a promotion because they put in the required two years of service, or the politician "deserving" the powers of prime minister because they won the election. Entitlements play all kinds of roles in society, often highly useful ones, because setting up institutions to grant entitlements for abiding by specific rules can have highly beneficially consequences (e.g., entitling people to promotions for achieving certain results can be a good way to motivate them to strive to obtain such results).

Entitlement aside, most people believe that there is a different and more fundamental kind of desert, which is not institutional but moral (sometimes called "pre-institutional desert"). Here desert refers to the idea that it is morally right (or intrinsically good) for someone to receive a reward based on their performance of an activity, regardless of whether or not the performance exists within any set of institutional rules. Whereas entitlement is a purely sociological or empirical matter (about what the institution in question dictates), desert is a normative notion; it is about an appropriate *fittingness* between the individual and the action. Sometimes entitlements and desert can come apart. For instance, if a society institutionalizes a rule whereby men are legally paid more than women, then even if a man is "entitled" to such payment, one may well say that it is not truly deserved because men do not actually work harder or perform better than women. Desert advocates, like David Miller (1999), typically argue that the way we judge the validity of entitlements is by viewing them through the lens of moral desert.

Now my argument will be that there is no problem, in general, with desert in the sense of entitlement (since entitlements are often very useful). It is fine to say, loosely and colloquially, that those who pass the bar exam "deserve" to be lawyers and that the winners of the race "deserve" the prizes.

Likewise, there are good practical reasons for allowing a certain amount of inequality. There are good reasons for allowing jobs and offices to be allocated on the basis of skills and effort (i.e., "merit") because we want jobs to be done by people who are well-qualified for them. Similarly, it is fine for there to be a small amount of inequality in wages, since these are useful for providing motivation. However, where I differ from the mainstream is in denying that such differences are morally deserved (even if they are practically necessary)—*that* kind of desert does not exist. The upshot is that while small inequalities in income may be necessary, large ones are not. What is unacceptable is for different jobs to have great differences in pay. As much as possible, incomes should be highly compressed, and the essential elements necessary for people to live good and flourishing lives (such as having economic security), should be guaranteed to all.

Do We Deserve Income on the Basis of Skills?

Consider two individuals, Mark and Jada. Mark grew up in a loving, stable family, where he was exposed to chess at a very early age and developed an obsession with it. His family supported his devotion—buying him countless chess books, hiring coaches, taking him to tournaments. He became a chess prodigy by the age of five. Mark was loved and nurtured through secure attachments; he attended schools where teachers fostered his confidence, taught him how to diligently complete tasks, and praised him for doing so. He frequently won chess tournaments as a teen, which fueled his ambition and single-mindedness. He entered adulthood as an enthusiastic and optimistic young man, with significant self-confidence, obsessive interest in chess, and extreme ability to concentrate on chess problems for many hours at a time without fatigue, distraction, or disinterest. Mark went on to become a Grand Master in his early 20s, earning many millions of dollars per year from winnings and sponsorships.

On the other side of town, Jada grows up in a household that is just as well-off materially as Mark's but is significantly worse off in terms of emotional and psychological well-being. Her single mother is frequently absent, short-tempered, and emotionally detached. As a child Jada experienced the profound trauma of sexual abuse from an uncle. She also has cerebral palsy; she has typical cognitive functioning but uses a wheelchair and can speak only slowly and with difficulty. She also suffers from chronic pain, which leads to bouts of depression and low self-confidence.[7]

Due to the brute luck of her bodily impairments it is difficult for Jada to compete in the marketplace for many jobs. As a result, she ends up earning a typical income for disabled people, say, $25,000.[8] The key point, which should go without saying, is that Jada is fully and completely a human being. She experiences the full range of human joys and fears, of existential terrors and delights. She dreams about loving relationships and fulfilling work, worries about insecurity, illness, and climate change. Her life is precious and has just as much moral worth as that of Mark or any other human being. However, in any market system (even a more egalitarian social democratic one), Mark will earn much more than Jada (in this case, 100 times more), and so society is essentially rewarding Mark for the luck of being immensely skilled while simultaneously punishing Jada for the misfortune of being impaired.[9] Mark is rewarded with the material conditions to live a full and rich life—he owns a mansion and multiple cars, eats delicious exotic foods, has top-notch healthcare and complete economic security, and is able to fulfill practically any and every desire. Jada, on the other hand, is deprived by society. In the social democratic society we are imagining, she would not starve or go homeless, but she would still face considerably more hardship than Mark: living in a small, dilapidated apartment, surviving off cheap food, stressed from long hours of work and little leisure time, and suffering the stigma of being poor.

My claim is that it is wrong—unfair and unjust—for such differences in life to be due to luck. Mark doesn't deserve his skills. Jada doesn't deserve her impairments. Such differences are the result of mere brute and brutal luck. To allow Jada to live a significantly worse life than Mark due to differences in luck is to manifestly fail to treat her with equal respect and equal concern. In effect, society is saying to her, "We regard you as less worthy. We see no problem with you suffering due to arbitrary reasons which are no fault of your own." This lack of equal respect is the essence of ableism, which is just as noxious as racism or any other system of institutionalized arbitrary prejudice. Indeed, remunerating people on the basis of skills is morally equivalent to rewarding people for having white skin. Of course, rewarding people for the lucky possession of skills is not exactly the same as rewarding people for skin color, since there may well be instrumental and pragmatic reasons as to why society would want to set up entitlements to reward skill or productivity in ways that do not apply in the case of skin color. Nevertheless, the point remains that from a noninstrumental, purely moral point of view, distributing income on the basis of luck—whether of skin tone or natural talents—is morally egregious.

Deserts Due to Effort and Hard Work

While many can agree that natural talents are innate and arbitrary, most people strongly believe that skills are not because they have to be developed through hard work. For many, the major reason that some are more deserving than others is that they have exerted more effort.[10] Hasn't Mark worked hard to develop his genetic potential? Didn't he make the hard choice day after day to painstakingly cultivate his skills? Hasn't he put in enormous effort to get where he is? Although people frequently recognize the arbitrariness of ability when it comes to their own failings, when it comes to their successes, suddenly everyone becomes a meritocrat, proudly proclaiming personal responsibility for their achievements.

Yet such arguments are often quite disingenuous. The astronomical paychecks of the rich and famous—LeBron James, J. K. Rowling, Lionel Messi, Bill Gates, etc.—are often defended on the ground that these people work hard. But no one can seriously claim that such people work harder than many, many others who earn far less. I have no doubt that LeBron James works hard at his basketball training. But surely he works less hard than very many working-class people who are driving trucks or flipping burgers, who work not only longer hours than James but in worse conditions and at less pleasant jobs. (James's effort, after all, consists in playing a game that he loves, for immense financial reward, as well as iconic status and celebrity.) If James had a brother who trained twice as hard as he but had no basketball talent whatsoever, would desert advocates say that the brother should get paid more? Most would not. Insofar as that is the case, they're not genuinely advocating desert on the basis of effort, just using the rhetoric of "effort" as a veil to justify rewards on the basis of (morally arbitrary) genetic predispositions.

Nevertheless, let us take the idea of effort seriously. It is undeniably true that some individuals work harder than others. Should they therefore deserve greater rewards? Many will want to say yes. It is a widely held intuition in Western culture that everyone can choose how much effort to exert, and so those who choose to work harder are more deserving.

Yet although this intuition is common, it is wrong. The fundamental problem is that effort is not something that lies within one's control. There is no level playing field in terms of effortability—in fact, different people have very different abilities to exert effort, and such differences are infused with luck and arbitrariness.

This is so for two reasons. First, the total amount of energy at any individual's disposal is significantly outside their control. Some people have bodies capable of exerting tremendous amounts of physical energy, while others do not. Mark is healthy, fit, and energetic, finding it easy to work long days and requiring only a few hours of sleep. Jada, in contrast, is easily fatigued and frequently depleted by chronic pain. More generally, consider people undergoing chemotherapy or those with chronic fatigue or severe depression; they have very limited amounts of effort at their disposal—even getting out of bed in the morning might be exhausting. It would be preposterous to assume that such people have the same amount of effort at their disposal as others.

Second, one's psychological temperament, one's ability to choose to exert conscientious effort is also significantly outside one's control. Some people, like Mark, are blessed with temperaments that make it easy to exert effort for long periods of time, such as enthusiasm, excitement, self-confidence, self-efficacy,[11] pride in their work, self-discipline, tenacity, and the ability to focus without getting distracted or bored. Indeed, many prolific academics and other successful professionals are lucky in just this regard: they are filled with energy, enthusiasm, and self-confidence, so that their work is enjoyable and their effort often effortless.[12] Those who benefit from such things are frequently uncomfortable to admit it, but if they are honest with themselves it is hard to deny that possessing such personality traits is not generally planned or cultivated but is largely a matter of luck.[13] On the other hand, many people, like Jada, have very different attributes. Through no fault of their own they have personalities that suffer from low self-confidence, from being easily discouraged and demoralized, or from chronic pain, making every activity difficult and making it hard to concentrate for long stretches at a time. At the extreme some individuals develop "learned helplessness," believing that they are entirely powerless to change things (Miller and Seligman 1975). All bodies and temperaments are different; there is no level playing field of effortability.

The key point is that one's ability to put in effort—one's "effortability" or "perseverance," "concentration," "discipline," or other such characteristic—is just a different kind of skill; we might call such higher order self-improvement skills "metaskills." Just like any other skill, metaskills originate from people's specific developmental trajectory and unique combination of genes and social environment. Therefore, they are just as arbitrarily possessed as other skills, be they LeBron James's ability to shoot baskets or Mozart's ability to play the piano. Mark happens to have significant ability in terms of perseverance, whereas Jada's skill is limited in that area. But neither of them are morally responsible for possessing those attributes—they are just differentially lucky. To say that Jada, whose perseverance skill is arbitrarily lower, deserves lower income (and therefore less ability to live a flourishing life) than Mark, who arbitrarily has great skill in this regard, is no different from saying that people who arbitrarily possess black skin deserve worse lives than those with white. There is no level playing field: we human beings differ in our abilities all the way down, including in our ability to exert effort. The seemingly progressive approach of saying "Let's reward people according to the amount of effort they exert" actually invisibilizes, and thereby naturalizes, the arbitrary advantages of some and the disadvantages of others. In saying this I'm disagreeing with mainstream proponents of meritocracy, and also with that meritocratic strain of socialism which sees effort as a legitimate basis for differentiating people's rewards (e.g., Albert 2003; Roemer 1998).[14]

Deserts Due to the Autonomous Choice of Self-Cultivation

At this point the only path left open to the advocate of desert is to insist that Mark truly does deserve more than Jada because his effortability is not, in fact, arbitrary, but is due to his own "good choices." Mark *chose* to become the kind of person who has great perseverance and concentration; he exercised his autonomy; he self-cultivated and shaped, at least partially, his own personality. Jada, on the other hand, did not. She failed to shape herself into a hardworking person and therefore must take responsibility for her character flaws and resultant life failures. It is thoughts like this which lead to the common (though I think incorrect) clichés that "Winners make their own luck" and "It's not the cards you're dealt that matter, but how you play your hand."

This line of thought is both empirically false and conceptually flawed. Empirically, the notion that we create our own personality and character is false or at least highly exaggerated. Does anyone really believe that Mark, as a five-year old, chose to have a personality that was obsessed with chess? The reality is that we human beings do not, generally speaking, choose our temperament, the things that give us pleasure or pain, our visceral reactions of shame and disgust, our degree of introversion or extroversion, our emotional responses to stimuli, nor a multitude of other characteristics that make each of us who we are.

Even our abilities to make "good choices" (to work hard, study diligently, reason well, avoid conflict, engage in healthy activities, etc.) are hugely variable, and arbitrarily so. The scientific evidence for this is abundant and growing stronger every day. Indeed, part of my claim here is that as scientific and psychological understanding progresses, the grounds for believing that we are in control of our personality correspondingly shrinks. To see this, let's consider some of the psychological factors which impact all of our abilities to make so-called good choices and engage in good actions.

- *Implicit bias* refers to the various ways in which all of us subconsciously stereotype others, and ourselves, particularly based on culturally significant hierarchies of race and gender (Nosek et al. 2007). In one famous and heartbreaking study, both White and Black children preferred playing with White dolls to Black dolls. Even Black children thought Black dolls were uglier than White ones (Kenneth and Clark 1947). Similar results continue to be found today (Banks, Eberhardt, and Ross 2006). None of us chooses to have the implicit biases that we do. And that is the point: such biases impact our choices and actions even though we are unaware of them.
- *Intellectual abilities.* Some people have highly elevated analytical and cognitive abilities, while others do not. Some have high levels of deliberative ease—they find the weighing of arguments, the analysis of evidence, the examination of costs and benefits, and so forth, to be enjoyable and easy activities, whereas some experience these as stressful and uncomfortable (Cacioppo et al. 1996). Some people have significant capacity for higher-order reflectiveness (Frankfurt 1971) and long-term planning, while others don't. Some have significant ability to concentrate on a task with diligent "stick-with-it-ness," while others find themselves easily distracted or bored. Likewise, many people have varying degrees of cognitive impairment (such as learning difficulties or attention deficits) or behavioral disorders (such as being on the autism

spectrum). Such differences significantly shape people's ability to reflect, deliberate, and come to good decisions.

- *Emotional abilities.* Individuals have marked differences in their degree of self-control (Moffitt et al. 2011). This too substantially impacts one's choice-making ability. For instance, it is well-known that the ability to self-regulate emotions, particularly anger, is highly correlated with crime (Roberton, Daffern, and Bucks 2014). In addition, people's choice-making capacities are powerfully influenced by their level of internal stress and anxiety, as well as the ability to empathize and feel compassion. Some are so empathetic that they feel driven to devote their lives to the reduction of others' suffering (MacFarquhar 2015), whereas at the other extreme, sociopaths are completely unaffected by others' emotional well-being.

- *Situational factors* similarly play a deep role in people's choices. For instance, it is well-known that even minor situational changes can significantly impact people's thinking and acting (Doris 2002). Isen and Levin (1972) found that the mere act of finding a dime led people to be more generous in helping to pick up dropped papers at a later time. Relatedly, there is significant evidence that merely coming to occupy a new social role will deeply impact one's choices and behaviors. The classic example here is Milgram's (1963) electric shock experiments, where individuals were willing to induce extreme pain on others simply because they found themselves in a role where they were told to do so by an authority figure.

- Our choices are also deeply impacted by brain processes happening *subconsciously.* Psychologists tell us that much of what is going on in our brains actually happens below the surface of consciousness, in what is referred to as the domain of "System 1"—the subconscious part of brain activity that is quickly sorting and filtering information, making snap decisions, seeing patterns, drawing instant connections between phenomena, etc. As Daniel Kahneman (2011) points out, the main source of our conscious beliefs and choices, as well as the bulk of our decisions and actions, do not come from the conscious thinking part of ourselves (System 2) but are actually driven by the subconscious System 1. One famous example is the study of an office with an "honesty box" for putting in change when you help yourself to a cup of tea or coffee. Every week above the box there were pictures of either flowers or human eyes. Researchers found that during the weeks with the pictures of eyes, staff paid almost three times more for their drinks than they did during the weeks with flowers (Bateson, Nettle, and Roberts 2006). In other words, the mere subconscious recognition that your actions might be noticed by others—even pretend others—is enough to induce significant changes in action. Kahneman's (2011, 25) conclusion is that, "in summary, most of what you (your System 2) think and do originates in your System 1." But if this is true it creates profound trouble for normal ideas of deservingness. After all, why should the person who acts more considerately in paying for their coffee deserve more praise simply because there happened to be a different picture hanging on the wall that week? In the words of neuroscientist David Eagleman, "Your consciousness is like a tiny stowaway on a transatlantic steamship, taking credit for the journey without acknowledging the massive engineering underfoot" (quoted in Martinez 2016, 9–10). Mainstream culture, as well as much philosophical discourse on deservingness, tends to vastly overestimate the extent to which we—the thinking, deliberating, conscious part of ourselves—are fully in control of our brain and personality. Western culture suffers from a widespread megalomania of the conscious self.

- One's choices and actions are also profoundly impacted by changes in one's *brain biochemistry*. A fascinating example is the case of a happily married man who started developing pedophilic desires, which turned his life upside down, ending in arrest. It turns out that the man had developed a brain tumor. When the tumor was removed, the pedophilic desires disappeared; when the tumor returned, so did the pedophilic desires (Martinez 2016).[15]

The empirical evidence is clear and becoming clearer every day: human beings differ markedly in their cognitive capacities. (And the source for much of the difference is arbitrary in the sense that it is due to factors beyond anyone's control.)

Taking a step back, it should come as no surprise that autonomous capacity is not a level playing field between people. What really is autonomy or self-cultivation? It is, just like effortability or perseverance or any other metaskill, simply another kind of skill (one might call it a meta-metaskill) that some arbitrarily possess more of than others. There is no fundamental difference between the skill of making good choices to cultivate parts of oneself and the skill of playing piano. They are both just skills that some individuals are better and some are worse at. Due to all kinds of arbitrary reasons relating to his genetics and social history, Mark has more ability to "self-cultivate" than Jada. But so what? He didn't choose to have such abilities; they were just there. Why should he be rewarded for such luck? Likewise, it's not Jada's fault that she has fewer skills of self-cultivation, so why should she be punished for it? To believe that everyone, deep in the recesses of their soul, has the same innate capacity—whether it's called "autonomous choice" or "self-cultivation" or "effort exertion"—as everybody else, regardless of the specificity of their genes and particular historical trajectory, is to abandon naturalistic accounts of how human bodies and minds actually develop and is to fall into a kind of transcendental mysticism. It is apotheosis aspiration: the desire to see a flickering of the divine in the mundane (socially and historically constituted) human shell (Waller 2020).

The only way out for the desert advocate is to insist that the bedrock of one's deservingness is one's "autonomous choice"—that below every personality trait, there is, somehow, a pure choosing entity that willed it into being. But this is absurd. It cannot be choice all the way down. We do not choose to become choosers. As naturalistic creatures, we do not will ourselves into being. We do not (to use Nietzsche's evocative phrase) pull ourselves "up into existence by the hair, out of the swamps of nothingness" (quoted in Martinez 2016, 13). At some point—most conspicuously in the years leading up to adulthood—our vastly different abilities to engage in reflective choice, higher-order self-improvement, and even higher order self-cultivation, like every other ability, simply emerge. They develop from the normal human processes of learning and development; such abilities to think and choose are *not* themselves the result of choice. At bottom, the bedrock of "autonomous choice" which desert advocates require, turns out to be distributed no more evenly than any other human capability—indeed, how could it be otherwise, given that autonomy is no magic thing but simply another kind of human capacity like any other?

In sum, there is no level playing field between human beings. Human performance, in every regard and along every axis, is ultimately due to the arbitrary luck of genetics and social history that together shape one's personality, providing different people with more or less ability to self-improve or self-cultivate.[16]

Now, none of this is to imply that individuals are unable to make choices. Most people do have (varying) capacities to reflect, deliberate, and make choices. Indeed, many people have wonderful abilities to learn new things, change their opinions, act differently, develop new sides of themselves, and become strikingly different people. I do not dispute that. What I do dispute is the notion that being "autonomous" in this everyday sense of the word makes one morally deserving.

While it's true that most people do indeed have the capacity to reflect, make choices, and exert effort in specific directions, the key point is that *they manifestly do not have anything like the <u>same</u> capacities in these regards.* There is no level playing field. Some people have vastly more of these skills and mental resources than others. Moreover, people have different amounts of these skills for entirely arbitrary reasons—ultimately due to the brute luck of their genes and social history. Desert is undermined not by the absence of choice-making ability but by the absence of a level playing field. The reason why it is wrong to reward Mark so much more than Jada is not that Jada lacks autonomy, but that Mark's possession of advanced skills of reflection (and other mental resources) and Jada's relative lack of such skills are ultimately due to luck. Doling out rewards or punishments on the basis of luck—as the system of desert does—is inherently unfair. At the end of the day, one can value desert or value fairness, but not both.

This is a crucial point, so let me say it differently. The heart of most people's belief in desert, I suspect, is the strong feeling that "I am autonomous! I can make choices!" and therefore "I deserve something in the light of my choices." The problem is that this conflates autonomy and desert, which are not the same thing. Autonomy is a feature of the individual—one's contingent abilities to reflect, deliberate, and so on. But deservingness is not about whether the individual can make choices; deservingness is about how one person performs *in relation to others*. Autonomy is grounded in features of the individual, whereas desert is grounded in features of the competition. So the reason that we should reject desert is because when we closely examine the competitions between people, we see that they are never truly fair: some individuals inevitably have arbitrary advantages over others. What undermines desert, therefore, is the fact that there is never a genuinely level playing field, never a truly fair competition between human beings who arbitrarily differ in their capacities all the way down. That is why it is perfectly reasonable to agree that people by and large are autonomous (though variably so), yet also insist that that fact has no bearing on their deservingness. When we reject desert we are not rejecting autonomy; we're rejecting unfair competitions.

The bottom line is that we human beings do not choose our personalities, proclivities, or mental capacities in large part. We are largely the outcome of unchosen genetic, social, and historical forces. We are not responsible for who we are. Even our varying ability to self-cultivate and partially shape our own personality does not rescue desert, because such higher-order skills, like every other skill, are themselves determined by forces outside our control. Individuals can take no more credit for their higher-order skills than for their ability to run fast or sing well or for having white skin. Autonomous abilities are not things that everyone possesses in equal measure—they are not some innate imprint of human essence—but simply naturalistic skills like any other, which some arbitrarily possess to a greater extent than others. The system of desert is thus a system of rewarding and punishing on the basis of arbitrary luck, and is therefore inherently unfair. From a moral point of view there is no fundamental difference between inheriting a fortune from a parent, inheriting talent from one's genes, or inheriting advantageous personality traits (like perseverance) from the complex interaction of genes and environment. To reward someone who is lucky in their possession of mental resources, and deprive another for being unlucky, is to reward the already fortunate and punish the already unfortunate. It is to reify the inevitable differences among human beings into institutional inequality.

The last point to emphasize here is that ideas of desert and meritocracy are, at root, fundamentally ableist (in the sense that they involve harming, discriminating against, or disadvantaging people due to arbitrary differences in their bodily abilities). To see this, imagine an egalitarian society with genuine equal opportunity for all: everyone has their material needs met, including adequate food, housing, and healthcare; everyone has access to high-quality schooling from daycare to university; everyone has caring teachers and safe neighborhoods, and so on. Even in such a society there would still inevitably be deep differences in people's abilities. Humans will continue to exist in wonderfully diverse shapes, sizes, capabilities, and attributes. Some will be anxious, some energetic, some will have strong perseverance, some will have ADHD, some will be self-confident, some will be depressed, and on and on. For each and every skill imaginable, we will find that some people possess more of this skill and some less. The distribution may be that of a bell-shaped normal distribution, but in any case it will be a spectrum. And this is just as true whether we're considering regular skills (like playing chess or singing in perfect pitch) or metaskills (like perseverance) or meta-metaskills of self-cultivation. The key point is that where a specific individual falls on this spectrum is due to luck (of genes, social environment, natural environment, etc.). Through no fault of their own, certain people will come to possess fewer physical or mental resources than others. (Perhaps one had a life partner pass away and becomes deeply depressed; perhaps someone else has a random serotonin deficiency in their brain.) Individuals with comparatively fewer physical or mental resources will tend to perform worse than others in all kinds of contests, and so desert-based theories like meritocracy will naturally conclude that they deserve less. For instance, desert advocates must hold that the way Jada's life has turned out is her own fault, that despite her chronic pain and cerebral palsy she should have simply tried harder or made better choices. But this is precisely what makes meritocracy so noxious: it looks at those who have been disadvantaged by fortune, and instead of responding with compassion, declares it to be their own fault. By blaming the victim, the doctrine of meritocracy acts to heap disrespect onto already existing misfortune. For these reasons, desert and meritocracy are, at their core, inherently ableist. It is deeply unfair to provide some people with the economic means for a significantly better life than others due to the arbitrary luck of possessing more or less bodily ability. As disability activists have long insisted, biology (including the impacts of society and historical circumstance on biology) should not be destiny.

Of course, differences in bodily ability should, in some cases, lead to different outcomes. We wouldn't want everyone to be licensed to perform brain surgery; obviously society benefits tremendously by allowing only certain people to do these jobs—those who have the specific skills, dexterity, etc. The key point, however, is that while only a small minority can be brain surgeons, these people, already blessed by fortune, should not be doubly blessed by society in being paid vastly more than anyone else, because their skills and talents are ultimately due to luck.[17] Many people, through no fault of their own, are not able to become brain surgeons, but they should not suffer deprivation because of that. Differences in ability should lead to different occupations, but not to differences in status or income. A meritocratic society is one in which arbitrary differences in bodily abilities lead some to be severely deprived and others to be extraordinarily rich. In contrast, a just society, I am suggesting, would be one that ensures that everyone, regardless of their bodily abilities, has secure access to the essential conditions for living a good life, and where all jobs pay roughly similar wages.

Objections

One way to frame the argument of this chapter is to use a straightforward syllogism:

> Premise 1: Moral desert requires a level playing field.
> Premise 2: There is no such thing as a truly level playing field between human beings.
> Conclusion: Therefore, there is no validity to moral desert.

The first premise is that comparative desert claims are valid only if there is a level playing field. To see this, call to mind any obvious example of when a reward or prize in a competition is clearly undeserved. For instance, a boxing match where A, a 300-pound heavyweight, defeats B, a 110-pound flyweight; or when C ends up much more successful than D because C inherited millions of dollars and lives off the accumulated interest, while D was born into deep family poverty from which they were never able to escape; or E, who ends up a rich lawyer due to inheriting family contacts which got them into Harvard, compared to F, who was unable to afford university and so ended up working a retail job for low wages. In such cases, rewards are not deserved because the playing field is not level. A, C, and E all possessed unfair advantages over B, D, and F, and it is precisely this fact—that the competition is unfair—that undermines desert; this is the crucial fulcrum around which the validity of desert turns.

Indeed, the first premise is essentially the definition of a fair competition. If there is no level playing field, then an individual's performance will inevitably be skewed by morally arbitrary facts about the competition (in the above examples, arbitrary facts about weight, inherited capital, and educational opportunities), and so desert is rendered meaningless. The lack of a level playing field undermines desert because it is wrong for people to be rewarded for arbitrary advantages (or punished for arbitrary disadvantages).

The second premise is justified on straightforward empirical grounds: human beings are naturalistic creatures shaped by the confluence of genes and environment and so vary in every which way. There are no shared abilities—mental or physical—that all members of the species inherently possess to the exact same degree.

From these two premises the conclusion follows logically. So it is no accident that those who wish to defend moral desert tend to do so by denying one of these premises. In what follows we will look first at arguments denying P1 and then at arguments denying P2.

Desert without a Level Playing Field

Probably the most common way that defenders of desert respond to the kind of argument that I have been advancing is to deny P1 and insist that people can be morally deserving even if there is no level playing field between them.

For instance, David Miller (2004) provides three arguments for why people can luckily possess very different internal abilities without that undermining their just deserts. The first is that the luck of possessing natural talents is irrelevant because talents are always interwoven with choice and effort, and so as long as choice and effort are involved, desert is valid.[18]

There are two problems with this. First, as we have already argued at length, choice and effort are themselves interwoven with luck. So Miller is wrong to simply assume that choice and effort unproblematically ground desert. Second, even assuming for the sake of argument that choice/effort really do ground desert, it is mysterious why mixing a deserving basis (choice/effort) with an arbitrary basis (natural talent) renders the final product wholly deserved. Consider a contest between X, who has immense talent but puts in little effort, and Y, who has very little talent but has put in lots of effort. Imagine that X wins the contest. Miller's position is that X deserves the reward because at least *some* effort was involved. But that seems strange. Surely the fact that the outcome was determined more by arbitrary factors than nonarbitrary factors should matter. If I start life with millions of dollars of inheritance and live a life of luxurious indolence, but once a year work for 20 minutes updating my paperwork to purchase new mutual funds, then by Miller's rationale I morally deserve all of the capital income that I accrue for the rest of my life, even if this is vastly more than my unlucky neighbors. That is hard to believe.

His second argument is that there is a significant difference between external luck and luck that is internal to the body. He gives the example of a mountain climber. If the climber fails to scale Everest because of bad external luck, such as poor weather or a broken rope, they deserve to have their achievement commemorated. However, if they fail to reach the top because of bad internal luck, such as being "physically weaker," then they do not (Miller 2004, 194). However, this too is a weak argument. Why should the source of the luck matter? Whether it is inside or outside the body, it is still arbitrarily impacting one's performance compared with that of other people. It seems bizarre and arbitrary to say that if a rope breaks randomly that really is bad luck, but if your genes are such that on the day you were climbing your body suddenly develops asthma, making the climb impossible, that is not bad luck; it's just your fault. Miller seems to be assuming that whatever happens within a body is irrelevant for desert. But that is simply wrong. As we have seen, much of what goes on under our skin and inside our skull is beyond our control or responsibility yet deeply impacts our performance. True, internal bodily luck is often more subtle and harder to see than large external things like ropes breaking or lightning flashing, but it is just as real, and just as consequential all the same.[19] What really matters is not whether luck is internal or external but whether or not it arbitrarily advantages some over others.

Miller's (2004, 193) final argument is that we shouldn't try to disentangle arbitrary luck from performance, because this would "sabotage the whole notion of desert." He points out that if we start allowing into our consideration all of the deeper kinds of luck that we have been discussing in this chapter (e.g., the ways that luck leads to differing levels of effortability, perseverance, self-improvement skills, etc.), then "desert shrinks to within a tiny fraction of its normal range" (195). If we nullify desert every time that luck is involved, this would mean that we can no longer talk as we conventionally do about athletes deserving medals, workers deserving wages, etc.—and that, he thinks, would be a disaster. "If we decide that we want to keep the concept in a form that captures most of the desert judgments people actually make, then we cannot hope to find a basis for desert that is untouched by contingency" (195).

Now it is true that my antidesert argument is radical, but it is not outlandish. Even if society were to cease making any claims of moral desert, it would still be possible to have all kinds of institutional entitlements (Olsaretti 2003). Athletes could still be entitled to gold medals; workers could be entitled to periodic raises. Likewise, society could still create all kinds of systems and institutions to incentivize (or disincentivize) various types of behavior, justified on consequentialist grounds. Hence there could still be income differentials to encourage work effort, and even prisons to discourage crime (though hopefully this would be minimized, as we discuss below). That said, a world without moral desert would indeed be significantly different from (and, I believe, significantly improved over) our current world. In particular, wealth and income differences would be very much more compressed. Income differences of 5:1 or even 10:1 may be practically necessary for the smooth functioning of a market system, but the current 351:1 differences existing between the average CEO and worker would be abolished (Mishel and Kandra 2021). Hence a society that abandons distributive desert would be much more equal, providing material resources to people on the grounds of what they *need* to live good, flourishing lives, as opposed to what they *deserve*.

The final response to Miller is to point out that radicalness in itself is hardly evidence of being wrong. Miller's belief that we should hold on to conventional notions of desert simply because it complies with popular opinion is deeply conservative. The job of philosophy is to critically examine cultural beliefs, not defend them on the grounds that they're popular. Miller is right to recognize that taking luck (and the idea of a level playing field) seriously does indeed sabotage desert. But the right response is not to dig in our heels and pretend that unfairness doesn't matter for social life; the right response is to admit that if indeed conventional notions of desert are intrinsically unfair, then so much the worse for desert.

Another common objection to P1 is to point to the example of sports. Daniel Dennett (2015) points out that in sports certain players are going to be slightly better than others, due ultimately to luck. Nevertheless, that doesn't negate our belief (he says) that the winning player rightfully deserves their victory (104–105).

I agree that there is no problem with saying that Usain Bolt "deserves" the gold medal for winning the 100-meter dash, as long as that is just an informal, colloquial way of saying that he is *entitled* to the medal. The competition in question has a set of rules, and the rules dictate that whoever wins is entitled to a gold medal. There's no problem with that because sports are about fun and entertainment, and there's no harm in having prizes of this sort.

However, matters are entirely different as soon as we shift from thinking about games to thinking about matters of real moral urgency. Imagine if a society, call it the society of True Merit, is constructed so that from the ages of 18 to 21 every individual is forced to compete in a number of tests in order to determine their place in society's hierarchy for the rest of their lives. We can even imagine very high levels of equal opportunity up to the point of competition. One of the tests is the 100-meter dash. Unsurprisingly, some people do very well (those who have strong bodies and a love of training), while others do poorly (especially those who have bodily impairments that make it hard to run, and depression making it hard to train). In the society of True Merit winners are celebrated and guaranteed high levels of income, excellent healthcare, educational opportunities, and so on, while the losers are publicly humiliated and systematically denied housing, healthcare, good jobs, and opportunities of all kind; they are forcibly segregated into poor, dirty shantytowns at the margins of the cities and compelled to carry a passport proclaiming their inferior status. Now surely Dennett would not say that the barbaric results of *this kind* of sporting competition are morally deserved.

In such a circumstance we have clearly moved far away from the terrain of inconsequential entertainment to the terrain of deadly serious matters of social justice. And as soon as we are talking about real issues of social concern, then we absolutely should reject any talk of desert. We should insist that just because the competition is formally fair (in that all competitors start at the same point), there is no substantive fairness in this apartheid society because there neither is, nor ever could be, a genuine level playing field between people's running abilities.

Some naturally suffer from muscular dystrophy, while others, such as virtuoso sprinters, luckily possess ACTN3 "sprinting genes," amazing fast-twitch leg muscles, and obsessive personalities which allow them to train all day long, every day, as well as myriad other unchosen factors that contribute to their ability. Such luck nullifies their claim to distributive superiority. Allowing luck to play a significant role in determining who gets prizes in sports competitions is no big deal because unfairness doesn't really matter in such cases. (The purpose, after all, is not fairness or justice, but fun and games.) But sports is not life. The appropriate metric of social and economic life is not entertainment, but fairness, which is why Dennett's analogy is unpersuasive.

The bottom line is that positions which reject P1 boil down to saying that luck-based differences are legitimate grounds for differential rewards. But it is just wrong, and inherently unfair, to reward or punish people for arbitrary reasons. Allowing major life chances to be determined by arbitrary luck is, at the end of the day, the morality of feudalism.

John Roemer's Defense of Desert

Perhaps the most sophisticated objection to my critique of deservingness comes from John Roemer (1993, 1998, 2003). His position is complex, but the essential points are as follows. Although individuals do differ in the total amount of effort that they possess, as autonomous adults they nevertheless all share the capacity to exert more or less effort. In other words, he thinks that everyone has complete control over the *degree of effort* they exert. Hence Roemer is implicitly denying P2; he believes that there *is* a true level playing field between all human beings: the ability to control the degree of effort that they exert. One useful metaphor for this idea comes from David Alm (2011), who invites us to think of our effort as a fuel tank; although individuals possess different sizes of tank, we nevertheless all have the same autonomous ability (supposedly) to choose to use, say, a quarter, half, or all of our tank. Along these lines, Roemer tells us to conceive of effort not in absolute terms (which are out of our control and therefore unsuitable for desert), but in proportional terms (which he believes are within our control, and are therefore a suitable basis for desert).

This is an ingenious attempt to ground desert claims. However, it is not successful. The problem is that individuals are *not* in fact in control of the degree of effort that they exert. This is a sleight of hand; since it is true that all individuals can exert more or less effort, it is tempting to jump to the conclusion that we all do so with equal autonomy. But that is false. The decision to exert some, most, or all of one's energy is itself a decision that will be largely influenced by one's individual personality—one's proclivities, desires, pain thresholds, temperament, etc. Does Roemer really believe that someone who is clinically depressed can "autonomously choose" to exert the exact same degree of effort as a healthy and happy person? That would be absurd. The truth is that different people have, contra Roemer, very different abilities to exert not just a total amount of effort but a degree of effort too. (It's a sleight of hand because Roemer plasters over the different abilities to exert degrees of effort that different individuals possess by simply labeling *all* such abilities, great or small, as the same mystical thing: "autonomy.")

If it were true that everyone, universally, shared the same ability to autonomously choose their degree of effort, then it would follow that everyone would be able to exert, say, 10% of their total effort one hour, and then 20% of their remaining effort for the second hour, then 30% of their remaining effort for the third hour, and so on, in this careful, disciplined, meticulous way. But that is clearly not equally possible for everyone. Being able to choose the precise degree of effort that one exerts on a particular activity, or for a particular amount of time, is itself a kind of skill that different people will possess to different degrees. This shows that even the "propensity to exert degrees of effort" is not a transcendental faculty that all humans magically possess but is simply a human character trait, which, like every other, some possess more than others due to luck, and therefore cannot serve as a basis for moral desert.

We can see the problem by reexamining Alm's metaphor of the fuel tank. Alm (and Roemer) conceive of autonomy as the supposedly universal ability of each of us to use more or less of our "fuel tank." But this raises the question, Who is driving the car?! Actual (empirically variable) human beings, or transcendent god-like beings? The purpose of the gas tank metaphor is to give a naturalistic account of our empirically differing capacities. But if everyone, universally, regardless of their individual personality, genes, or upbringing, is somehow equally capable of pushing the accelerator/brake of the car to the exact same degree as everyone else (as the metaphor implies), this brings a ghost into the machine through the back door.[20]

The bottom line is that Roemer cannot escape the fundamental fact that effort-exerting abilities, like every other ability, differ arbitrarily between people. Therefore, rewarding or punishing someone due to their "propensity to exert effort" is still to reward or punish them for arbitrary features like inheriting a family fortune or white skin.

In sum, we have seen that there are two main avenues open to those who wish to uphold moral desert. The first is to deny that a level playing field between people is necessary; people can be deserving even if they are luckily advantaged over others. But that is to simply shrug and admit that unfairness is okay. It allows luck and arbitrariness to play a determining role in how people's lives are allowed to go. Such a cavalier attitude may be appropriate in certain domains (such as sport), but it is unacceptable for matters of grave importance like income or access to pensions or quality child care. Such a position retains the feudal belief that an arbitrary fluke—such as the characteristics of birth, class, gender (and, I would add, bodily talent and effortability)—is a legitimate basis for determining one's life prospects. The second approach is to deny P2 and insist that there really is a level playing field, such as a supposedly universal capacity to exert effort. But this is just empirically false and risks falling into a kind of religious mysticism. In other words, the defender of desert faces a fork in the road: one path leads to feudalist morality, the other to mysticism. Both avenues for defending desert are dead ends.

Other Objections

One concern with desert skepticism is whether it will demotivate people and lead to generalized apathy. One may ask, If I am just the product of my genes and environment, why should I bother trying to improve at anything?

The answer is that just because each of us is the product of our environment does not at all mean that we cannot learn, develop, and grow. Of course, some of us will be able to learn and change more than others (through no fault of our own), but none of us can ever know *in advance* what we're capable of. Practically all human beings have at least some capacity to learn and develop; indeed, most brains and personalities have impressive amounts of plasticity and openness to change (Barker 2015; Doidge 2010), and furthermore, everyone is slowly being changed (whether they want to be or not) by their changing environment and social milieu. The crucial point is this: because the extent to which we can change is never known in advance, all one can ever do is try. As long as they are alive no person is entirely fixed or frozen. There are always new circumstances and new environments which may provide new possibilities for change and growth. Again, since no one can know in advance what they are capable of in each new circumstance, there is no reason not to try.

Another important objection is that of criminal responsibility. Are we no longer able to blame and punish a criminal for, say, stealing or committing physical assault? Are they no longer responsible for their choices?

The problem with the notion of criminal responsibility is the same as with economic desert: it's inherently and inextricably unfair (Waller 2018). Although the legal system is based on a naïve binary threshold, whereby everyone who is neither a child nor insane is perceived as having the same amount of full legal responsibility, in fact real human beings come in all shapes and sizes, and the ability to make ethical decisions and follow the law, like any other human capability, exists on a spectrum, coming in vastly differing amounts, which different people possess arbitrarily. Some are mentally ill. Some find it very difficult to contain their anger. Some are less able to reason through the consequences of their actions. Some have been socialized into violence and rely on it habitually. Some have faced years of sexual or racial trauma that builds up to the point where it is liable to explode at the latest microaggression, and on and on. (Not to mention the most important source of crime, which is the vast deprivation of respect and resources and opportunities that some people routinely face.) If we simply shrug our shoulders and continue to punish heterogeneous people according to a homogeneous standard, we will be punishing them for things that are out of their control. (We might as well punish people for the color of their eyes or their sexual preferences.)

This is not to say that we should do nothing when crime occurs—far from it. In fact I think that we should do much more than we currently do. The point is that we should dramatically change our focus and respond to crime very differently. Instead of punishing people because it's what criminals "deserve," the overriding aim of the judicial system should be to restore and repair the community from harm (as well as to transform the conditions that cause crime in the first place, including, importantly, material deprivation and social inequality). If jails have to be used at all, they should be aimed at deterrence, quarantining dangerous people, and rehabilitation, and hence should be as infrequently used and as nonpunitive as possible. (Norway's humane Halden prison, with its focus on reintegrating people into society through education, job training, and therapy—including access to nature, good food, and ceramics workshops—is an instructive example [Benko 2015].)[21]

The final objection to consider is the worry that my line of argument, which denies that all people have the same inherent capacity for autonomy, leads to problematic consequences in implying that not everyone has equal moral worth or dignity. If people have different levels of autonomy, doesn't this mean that people must have different degrees of dignity—and doesn't that then undermine much of the basis of democratic citizenship and human rights?

This conclusion follows only if moral equality depends on everyone possessing equal autonomy—but that is a problematic move. Of course, determining the ethical basis of human equality is an old and difficult question. The liberal tradition has tended to answer "autonomy" (or related ideas of "reason" or "will power"). But if autonomy is to ground human equality, it must be presupposed that all humans possess autonomy in equal measure. So in an honorable attempt to establish a foundation for human equality, the liberal tradition has been forced to defend a factual absurdity: that all actually existing human beings have the exact same capacity for choice and reflection—which is obviously false.

It is far more reasonable to presume that people have differing levels of autonomy, just as they differ in terms of every other human capacity. (How could it be otherwise for real, nonmythological, empirical beings?) But given differing levels of autonomy, how can we hold on to the notion that all human beings are of equal moral worth? There is no insurmountable problem here because there are other ways to buttress a belief in equal moral worth. One approach is to simply insist that equal moral worth is a nonnegotiable starting premise. It is a basic axiom of morality and so doesn't require any further justification.

My preferred approach is to recognize that equal moral worth flows from the fact that all human beings share the same fundamental ontological and cosmological conditions: those of *finitude* and *uniqueness*. Each of us lives a short and finite existence. Given the extremely improbable conditions that must occur in the universe in order to sustain life in the first place, we are all incalculably lucky to have been born at all. We live on this ball of spinning rock in a remote corner of the Milky Way; we briefly experience consciousness—with the possibility of loving, creating, exploring, under-standing, struggling, and enjoying—before our awareness is extinguished forever. Death is, as far as we know, a 100% certainty and is absolute, irrevo-cable, permanent, and forever; our bodies will all too soon die and rot. Each of us, therefore, has only this one momentary, fleeting chance at life. Yet not only do we all share this same fundamental finitude, but each of us is also wonderfully unique. Though we are all deeply shaped by circumstance, all forged in the caldron of social life, each and every individual emerges per-fectly unique. No two individuals will ever share the same precise complex combination of genes and social environment; each of us is a unique swirl of fortune enfleshed. Each individual possesses a unique life that has never been lived by anyone before and never will be again. It is these facts of equal finitude and equal uniqueness which together constitute the moral fact that each and every human being is equally precious, or, if you prefer, of equal moral worth. It is this notion of equal moral worth that is the moral basis for insisting that each of us should be entitled to equally good lives (as much as possible); likewise, this is the basis for condemning as wrong the fact that some live significantly worse lives than others.

Few have described as powerfully as Bertrand Russell (1923, 22–26, em-phasis added) this fundamental equality of the human condition:

> We see, surrounding the narrow raft illumined by the flickering light of human comradeship, the dark ocean on whose rolling waves we toss for a brief hour . . . [u]nited with his fellow-men [*sic*] by the strongest of all ties, the tie of a common doom. . . . One by one, as they march, our comrades vanish from our sight, seized by the silent orders of omnipotent Death.

Very brief is the time in which we can help them, in which their happiness or misery is decided. Be it ours to shed sunshine on their path, to lighten their sorrows by the balm of sympathy, to give them the pure joy of a never-tiring affection, to strengthen failing courage, to instil faith in hours of despair. *Let us not weigh in grudging scales their merits and demerits, but let us think only of their need.*

We have now reached the pinnacle of the ethical argument of this book. The ultimate and fundamental reason why economic inequality is wrong is that human beings are of equal moral worth and therefore should be equally entitled to access the material conditions necessary for living a good or flourishing life. An equivalent way of saying this is that we should abandon entirely the idea that some individuals *deserve* to possess significantly better or worse material conditions for their lives than others due to their contributions, even those stemming from skill or effort, because the ability to contribute is dependent on the arbitrary luck of genes and circumstance. The resources and opportunities that people receive in life should not be based on (morally arbitrary) empirical facts about what each of us is able to do, but on the moral fact of who each of us *is*: an equal member of the human family, precious and unique.

The conclusion is that equality should be the default position of social and economic affairs. That said, for a number of important practical reasons, complete equality is neither feasible nor desirable. Let us see why.

What Should Be Done?

The central example of Mark and Jada is designed to highlight one crucial point: income differences are not morally deserved. Yet even if you accept this example, you may well wonder what such ethical arguments imply in the real world. In this final section I attempt to illuminate this by asking the question—really the central question that all egalitarians must answer—of what kinds of inequality are legitimate and what kinds are not.

The central thrust of this chapter has been that since people's talents, skills, and efforts are arbitrary from a moral point of view, their economic rewards should be largely equalized. All people, regardless of their skill or effort, should be guaranteed the essential goods necessary to live a good and flourishing life. I call this position Good Life Egalitarianism (Malleson 2022).

What are these essential goods? That is a very difficult question, based as it is on one's perspective of what constitutes good and valuable human lives. Here I will only suggest (but not defend) the proposal that we should recognize two main categories of essential goods. First, everyone should be assured good opportunity rights, that is, the means to self-determine, so that they can live the life that they autonomously value. The essential prerequisites for this include physical security, civil rights, education, economic security, and free time. The level at which these things can be provided will depend on the context, but in the rich countries of the Global North, they should include, above and beyond the standard package of liberal rights, universal healthcare, access to free (or heavily subsidized) postsecondary education, income security (such as through a Basic Income and extensive public services such as affordable housing, public transit, universal child care, and pensions), and rights to quality part-time work, all of which must be accessible to neurodivergent and differently abled bodies. Second, everyone should be assured good relationship rights, that is, the goods necessary for ensuring egalitarian social relationships (so that workplaces, families, and the state treat their members with equal respect, equal status, and, where appropriate, equal democratic rights).[22]

The heart of Good Life Egalitarianism, in other words, is that because people's capabilities are fundamentally arbitrary, what people receive should be based primarily not on what they as individuals *do* or *deserve* but on what they *need*. Providing the essential goods on the basis of need is thus a central pillar of distributive justice.

However, even though the moral aim is equality, practically speaking, complete equality is neither feasible nor appropriate. There are two reasons for this.

First, on straightforward consequentialist grounds, having some inequality is likely necessary to provide basic incentives. If everyone were guaranteed the same exact income regardless of whether they worked 40 hours per week or none, clearly most people would cease working. (Most jobs, after all, contain a substantial amount of drudgery.) Indeed, it seems likely that no realistic society could have completely equal income; there must also be monetary incentives to encourage people to expend effort on their work.[23] Moreover, allowing some wage inequality can be useful to motivate people to seek work in areas of high demand, to work longer hours, and to upgrade their skills; allowing higher wages for such jobs can produce numerous positive benefits for society as a whole.

That said, although the scale of inequalities between people should not be totally extinguished, they can and should be significantly compressed. In the case of income, the market clearly requires some inequality to function. But it absolutely does not require the huge 351:1 pay differentials currently existing between American CEOs and their workers (Mishel and Kandra 2021). The goal should be to compress these differences as far as is possible without suffering too great losses in efficiency or productivity.

Similarly, there are good practical reasons for allowing some inequalities in terms of positions and offices. Basing job applications, promotions, grades, and so forth, on the possession of relevant skills and aptitudes is obviously socially sensible (as long as there is a baseline of robust equal opportunity). The important point to remember, however, is that the rewards that people acquire for holding such positions should be thought of as entitlements, not moral deserts. Their justification is that of social usefulness, not inherent rightness—indeed, they are not deserved. Therefore, differences in employment positions should not lead to marked differences in social status or life prospects. It is legitimate to prevent a person working as a janitor from performing brain surgery, but it is wrong for the janitor to be treated as inferior to the surgeon or denied the same essential goods to live a good and flourishing life or paid significantly less.[24]

Second, it makes good sense to allow inequalities in nonessential goods so as to provide ample scope for individual preference and choice. For example, if X prefers to work more hours so as to go on expensive vacations, whereas Y prefers to work less and have more leisure at home, Y cannot complain that they deserve compensation for ending up less rich.[25] As long as both are equally guaranteed robust economic security, no serious "inequality" results from individuals choosing to work different amounts or from spending their disposable income in different ways. Likewise, if Z chooses to live an ascetic life in a monastery, their relative poverty is not something that society need mitigate (as long as Z always has secure access to a Basic Income, jobs, housing, and educational opportunities should they desire them in the future). As long as these preferences are playing out in the realm of nonessential goods, we need not be overly worried about the differences that accrue.

Likewise, it is fine for there to be a range of noneconomic inequalities between people (as long as they too are inessential for a good life). For example, in any society people will differ in terms of their level of attractiveness, the amount of love they possess, the amount of charm, their height, etc. Such differences are ultimately derived from luck, and so, strictly speaking, are ethically undeserved. But should we care? The answer depends on two things. On the one hand, are such goods "essential" to individuals living a good and flourishing life? And on the other, would equalization impose such severe harms on people that the harms would dramatically outweigh the benefits of equalization? (It should go without saying that even though equality is a fundamental good, it is not the only thing we should care about.) For instance, any polity that tried to level the amount of attractiveness of its citizens through forced body modification would clearly be terrifying and tyrannical. While there is very little harm done to millionaires by forcing them to pay higher taxes (since they would still possess all the essential freedoms necessary to live good and flourishing lives), the harms of forced bodily modification would be horrific indeed (see Chapter 6).[26]

With these two caveats in mind, we can now formulate the practical ideal of an egalitarian society. This would be one which guarantees to all the entitlements necessary to live a good and flourishing life; there would be a general expectation for all able-bodied adults to reciprocate by working at least part time;[27] and annual market income should be highly compressed.

The society we are describing might be envisioned as a kind of democratic socialist society, where everyone is guaranteed the essential goods necessary to lead a flourishing life: hence there are extensive public services, a Basic Income, widespread workplace democracy, with typical employment being that of flexible, quality part-time work of, say, 15–30 hours per week. Annual wages are significantly compressed between people, and everyone is free to choose (within standard parameters) the number of hours they prefer to work. This could occur by implementing steeply progressive income taxes or by introducing maximal allowable pay ratios between the lowest and highest paid, so that, for instance, the highest paid are allowed to earn only 10 or 20 times the minimum wage, as well as introducing a general right of workers to adjust their hours. Substantial differences in the accumulation of wealth over the life course should be mitigated by a wealth tax, and inheritance taxes should be used to prevent parents from passing on significant advantages to their children. (Recall the upshot of the notion of the understructure from Chapter 4: the social inheritance provided by the understructure should be shared equally by all.) The details of such a vision are well beyond the scope of this book, but the important point here is that Good Life Egalitarianism envisions a robust social minimum, accessible to everyone—not merely a meager safety net, but a much more significant guarantee of the conditions for a comfortable, relatively affluent, flourishing life for all.

Though ambitious, I do not claim that this would be a perfectly just distributive system. As a market system it would still arbitrarily reward those with above-average talents and skills.[28] It would also arbitrarily benefit those with above-average effortability (those who are lucky to possess large "fuel tanks," energetic bodies, and enthusiastic dispositions). Nevertheless, such a system would be highly attractive. Most important, it would be far less arbitrary and unfair, with far smaller inequalities. We saw that in conventional market systems, Mark earns over 100 times more than Jada, due (among other things) to his immense natural talents and effortability. But in the system discussed here, their incomes would be much more equal. Such a society would be basically an egalitarian one, where the floor of guaranteed goods is high, and the ceiling of top incomes is significantly lowered. The default distributive position would be that of equality, and the dominant ethos would be provision according to need (not desert). If such a system were to be created, it would successfully expunge the greater part of arbitrariness, ableism, and inherent unfairness that plagues contemporary market systems. Yet such a system would retain the most desirable features of market systems. In particular, it would retain a sensible incentive structure to foster efficient production (encouraging people to work hard and develop their skills), as well as allowing wide scope for the expression of personal preferences. (People would be free to work as much or as little as they want in whatever line of work they desire and are able to find employment.)

Let us wrap up by taking note of a few illustrative contrasts between Good Life Egalitarianism and the now dominant theories of egalitarianism. Consider all of those who, for whatever reason, suffer a difficult period in their lives. Maya "chooses" to drop out of university due to depression. Luke, suffering from the trauma of residential schools and racial stigma, "chooses" to seek solace in drugs and alcohol, eventually ending up on the street unable to pay their rent. The logic of luck egalitarianism[29] (though I suspect not the heart of many of the humane, really existing luck egalitarians) is to simply say "Too bad; you made your bed; you must lie in it." Relational egalitarianism[30] does somewhat better, but perhaps not much. The logic of this position is that such circumstances are only a problem—and support should only be offered—to the extent that such people risk disrespect and domination. Do they? Perhaps, but perhaps not. For instance, what Anderson (2007) says about education makes it seem that her version of relational egalitarianism would offer little support to Maya. And what Anderson (1999, 325) says elsewhere about poverty implies that as long as Luke can acquire "basic capabilities" and is not a "peon," then no additional support is required. There are also cases, such as Jamila's suffering a bodily impairment and being forced to quit her job, where relational egalitarianism appears even more cold-hearted than luck egalitarianism, as it is unattuned to misfortune, and so would seem to allow Jamila to live a life that is significantly worse off than her luckier colleagues as long as she is not disrespected or dominated.

By contrast, Good Life Egalitarianism performs significantly better. In guaranteeing such people perpetual access to the essential goods, regardless of their past "bad choices," it insists that such choices should not define their future lives. It is thereby a theory of considerable warmth and compassion, even, if it is not too much to say, of structural love. All desert-based theories, be they luck egalitarian or neoliberal, tend to be moralistic and harsh, admonishing people for making mistakes and implying that their situation is their own fault. That is no accident; such moralism flows directly from the very DNA of a desert-based philosophy; indeed, it is the very point. The antidote to such moralism is compassion and loving kindness, since the primary impulse of compassion is its nonconditionality, its unconditional warmth, its desire to focus not on a person's faults but on their humanity, emphasizing the flickering, all too brief existence of a human life and the overwhelming need for it to be as good as possible.

Good Life Egalitarianism is thus motivated at the deepest level by two primary impulses: an emotive sense of love and compassion (driven by the recognition that so many people today live lives of pain, suffering, and deprivation even though their finitude and uniqueness make them precious) with an analytical skepticism of desert (that such suffering could be attributed to their own fault or responsibility). These two impulses merge in the desire for a robust safety net, which says to all, "We have your back. If and when you fall in life, it's okay, we will support you." Like loving parents to their children, Good Life Egalitarianism says to its residents, "No matter what choices you make in your life, no matter what accidents or misfortunes befall you, you will be (nonpaternalistically) cared for and supported because your life is precious. Even if we dislike your choices, indeed, even if, in extremis, we must occasionally restrain your choices to prevent harm to others, you will still never be abandoned to the winds of fortune."

To update the old Leveler slogan, Good Life Egalitarianism might say, "We believe that even the most wayward they have as much a life to live, as the greatest they."[31]

Summary

If there were a more level playing field in society, would individuals then deserve the income that accrues as a result of their skills and efforts? I have argued no. Individuals cannot be said to morally deserve their income, because their talents and efforts and self-improvement abilities are all ultimately skills which some arbitrarily possess more than others due to luck. Since real, empirically variable human beings differ all the way down, the playing field can never be level, and the competition never truly fair. Disadvantaging people on the basis of arbitrary facts about their body and mind, as meritocracy does, is inherently ableist. We should, therefore, be highly skeptical of the twin notions of desert and meritocracy. Those who explicitly defend desert, merit, or personal responsibility are implicitly defending unfair advantage and sanctifying biocultural privilege.

Society should aim to distribute income and wealth not on the basis of what people "deserve" but equally (or on the basis of need). We should aim not for absolute equality of income but for a highly compressed income scale with robust guarantees for everyone to access the social and material conditions necessary for good and flourishing lives.

I grant that these are radical claims which conflict with many people's deep-seated intuitions, and so I clearly cannot hope to convince everyone. Nevertheless, even if the reader rejects my wholesale attack on deservingness, I hope that they will at least be persuaded that the everyday claims about what people "deserve" must be much more modest than is generally the case. The more that society downplays the role of fortune in individual abilities, or overestimates the degree to which the playing field is truly level, the more that unfairness will reign.

6

Does Voluntary Exchange of Private Property Justify Inequality?

Taxation is theft!

—Libertarian slogan

[C]apital comes [into the world] dripping from head to foot, from every pore, with blood and dirt.

—Karl Marx, *Capital*, (1867) 1933

A common justification for inequality is the libertarian belief that it is legitimate because it is simply the inevitable result of individuals freely exchanging their private property with others, either as gifts or as part of market exchange. On this view, individuals inherently possess very strong rights, or what I will call "absolute" rights, over their property; such property is fully and completely *theirs*. They can exchange it however they like, and as long as the exchanges are voluntary—involving neither force nor fraud—then the resulting distribution of ownership is perfectly just, and the state has no right to interfere or redistribute, regardless of the extent of inequality that transpires.

In this chapter I argue that the libertarian perspective is wrong because property rights should not be seen as absolute but as contingent on what justice requires. There are three reasons why. First, the property and wealth that actually exist today are interwoven with a long history of violence, coercion, fraud, theft, domination, and injustice. This means that redistribution is in many cases completely justified, even required. Second, other people's needs matter, and these needs should sometimes outweigh the individual's right to have complete control over their property. Third, the rights that individuals have over their property should be seen as very different from, and typically much weaker than, the rights that individuals have over their bodies; it's

Against Inequality. Tom Malleson, Oxford University Press. © Oxford University Press 2023.
DOI: 10.1093/oso/9780197670392.003.0007

perfectly legitimate to insist that income and wealth can (and often should) be frequently redistributed, whereas one's body parts should not be. Let us examine each of these arguments in turn.

The Violent Origins of Property

Although the number of self-avowed libertarians is quite small, many of the core assumptions—what might be called "everyday libertarianism" (Murphy and Nagel 2002)—remain very common. For instance, most people take it for granted that owners should have near total rights over their goods in relation to others: they should possess the unique right to control, use, manage, alienate, destroy, transfer, or gain income from their property (Narveson 2001; Nozick 1974).[1] In Blackstone's evocative words, private property means that individuals should possess "sole and despotic dominion which one man claims and exercises over the external things of the world in total exclusion of the right of any other individual in the universe" (quoted in Christman 1994, 18). I will refer to such a view as one of "absolute" property rights, and contrast it with a view that I take to be preferable, which says that property rights are contingent, i.e., not absolute, and sometimes trumped by other moral considerations. Whereas libertarians see property rights as *natural rights—* rights that human beings just naturally have, which preexist any actual state, and which set important moral limits on what the state may reasonably do (e.g., Rothbard 1982)—I will instead argue that we should see property rights as merely conventional, and secondary to more primary considerations of justice. The kind of property rights that we should institute are whatever we need to make a just (and, I would argue, egalitarian) society possible.

For libertarians, inequality in a market society is the normal state of affairs and may well be perfectly legitimate, so long as the transfers themselves are legitimate (meaning they involve neither force nor fraud). In Nozick's (1974, 149) words, "What each person gets, he gets from others who give to him in exchange for something, or as a gift." The distribution that results "is just if it arises from another just distribution by legitimate means" (151). Perhaps the most powerful illustration of this principle is Nozick's famous example of Wilt Chamberlain. Nozick instructs us to start by imagining any just distribution of property that we would like. From this baseline, such as a socialist or an egalitarian one, we imagine that a large number of basketball fans freely wish to pay Chamberlain for the pleasure of watching him play. The fans voluntarily transfer some of their private property (over which, it is assumed, they have absolute rights) to Chamberlain, who becomes the new owner of such property, making him very rich. Nozick's claim is that given the voluntary nature of these exchanges, the wealth (and inequality) that results is completely legitimate. If the state were to forcibly redistribute Chamberlain's wealth, that would be unjust, a form of theft. (Indeed, Nozick [1974, 169] describes taxation in the language of "forced labor," while Narveson [2001, 250] talks of "armed robbery.")[2]

Now, it is important to notice that the legitimacy of this private property rests on the fact that it was voluntarily transferred from someone else who had absolute property rights. But this immediately raises the question, Why did *that person* have absolute ownership rights over it? Because, we are told, it in turn came from sellers who themselves possessed absolute ownership rights, and on and on. In other words, the libertarian view is "dizzyingly circular" (Christman 1994, 72). Private property is justified because it comes from other private property that is assumed to be justified. So, to justify the existence of exclusive private property the libertarian must be able to demonstrate how such property rights emerged in the first place.

For this reason, libertarians spend much time and energy trying to persuade people that absolute property rights could have originated in a perfectly just manner in some distant past "state of nature," and then be passed on, via innumerable pristine transfers over the centuries, to eventually become the property that exists today. Hence much of the philosophical debate over libertarianism revolves around this issue of "just acquisition." How did an absolute property right emerge in the first place? What constitutes it? Is it really legitimate for individuals to permanently appropriate bits of the earth for themselves if they are the "first occupiers" or if they leave "enough and as good" left over (e.g., Arneson 1991; Cohen 1995; Kymlicka 1990; Narveson 2010)?[3] Libertarian writings are full of discussions of how property could have emerged justly in a state of nature. Rothbard (1982) takes Robinson Crusoe as a useful model; Otsuka (2003, 22) asks us to think about initial acquisition by imagining "hypothetical cases in which childless adults with no worldly resources on their persons have washed ashore on an uninhabited and undiscovered . . . island"; and practically every libertarian author spends much time considering the appropriation of land by imagined homesteaders at the American "frontier."[4]

My view is that far too much attention in the philosophical literature has been devoted to these (historically fanciful) thought experiments about initial acquisition, whereas far too little attention has been paid to the real history of property acquisition. On this question, the philosophers are typically of less relevance than the historians. What we see when we study actual history is that the genesis of contemporary property (at least in North America, if not more broadly) is interwoven through and through with all kinds of brutal violence and injustice, and so libertarians are wrong to see it as belonging absolutely to the individuals who happen to currently possess it. Before delving into the history, let me set the stage by considering a stylized contrast to the typical libertarian story of the homesteader who diligently farms their land and thereby becomes the legitimate absolute owner of their property.

Imagine a gang of pirates roams the coast, raping and pillaging, and over time comes to acquire immense wealth and property, becoming some of the richest 1% of the country. The pirates eventually settle down, change their names, establish legal businesses on the basis of their immorally acquired wealth, and pass on their wealth to their heirs. Now at some point the state decides to levy a 75% income tax on the top tranche of their income, meaning that the pirates still remain very wealthy. Nevertheless, the pirates are furious, claiming that the tax is "turning them into slaves," "is on a par with forced labor," and "is an abhorrent theft, no different from cutting out their eyeballs to redistribute them." Should we take such claims seriously? Clearly not. The pirates' claims have no resonance because their money was not rightly theirs to begin with (and the harm done to them through taxation in terms of their real freedoms is, we assume, quite minimal).

For another example, consider the case not of pirates but of lottery winners. Smith wins a lottery, but then is forced by the state to pay a tax. Smith responds in the same vein as the pirates, claiming that the tax amounts to armed robbery. Again, such claims ring hollow because Smith's property was not morally his in the first place (it was due to luck), and the harm done to him through taxation is (we assume) extremely minimal.

These examples are important to keep in mind because they show that the libertarian claim that tax is theft only makes sense given the implicit (and often hidden) assumption that the property was morally the rightful possession of the individual in the first place. Once that assumption ceases to hold, as the pirate and lottery-winner examples make clear, our intuitions about the wrongness of taxation substantially shift.

Granted these stories of pirates and lottery winners are thought experiments, just like the state of nature, Robinson Crusoe, and homesteaders.

The real question is which of these metaphors is closer to the historical truth. And the answer is easy. No serious historian would deny that the emergence of the wealth of rich countries is drenched in blood, domination, and even genocide (Galeano 1973; Harman 1999; Hobsbawm 1987; Tilly 1985; TRC 2015; Zinn 1996). The accumulation of wealth in North America came in no small part from stolen land and stolen labor, which was then passed down over generations, leaving some families significantly advantaged and others significantly deprived, in ways that are extremely obvious and apparent today. As Thomas Mautner pointed out years ago, libertarian arguments about the inviolability of property apply *even by libertarian lights* only to that property which could be traced by a series of just steps to an original just acquisition, whereas the actual facts show that "force and fraud have reigned supreme in the history of mankind" (quoted in Widerquist 2010, 18).

In North America the evidence is clear that the accumulation of great wealth was undergirded by a number of deeply coercive historical processes, including colonialism, slavery, rapacious industrialism, and patriarchy.

In terms of colonialism, the countries that are now called Canada and the United States were created by the arrival of European settlers beginning in 1492 and subsequent methodical theft of the land from the myriad Indigenous nations existing since time immemorial across Turtle Island. Occasionally the settlers signed treaties with the Indigenous nations—though often in circumstances of duress (Saunt 2021). Even then, the treaties were almost always broken by the colonizers. The US government signed over 400 treaties with Indigenous nations, and broke every single one (Pruitt 2020; Zinn 1996). In many cases, no treaties were ever signed, and the land was simply stolen outright—as is the case for large areas of western Canada which remain to this day unceded, occupied territory (McIntosh 2020; Pasternak and King 2019). In both countries, Indigenous populations were decimated through war and disease, the peoples removed from their traditional territories and relocated to small, usually unproductive "reservations"; federal laws were implemented to oversee their lives and suppress their sovereignty; and all kinds of government policies—from residential schools to racist social service adoption policy—were used in an attempt to assimilate the people (in the case of the residential schools, to "kill the Indian in the child").[5] The fundamental facts are these: in 1492 there were roughly 60 million people living in what is now called the Americas; by 1600 over 90% had perished (Koch et al. 2019). In Canada, before contact, 100% of the habitable land was controlled by Indigenous peoples; today Indigenous peoples, via the reserves, control only 0.2%, whereas settlers (and their government) control 99.8% (Manuel and Derrickson 2015, 7–8).

Narveson (2010, 131) offers the typical defense of colonialism: "[W]e can argue, as capitalists have for so many centuries, that growth in farming and manufacturing, and entrance into the exchange economy, will ultimately benefit the hunters and gatherers far more than enough to 'compensate' them." As if the genocide of your people, the loss of your land, the continual multicentury attack on your culture, the systematic abuse of your children in residential schools with the mass graves of babies,[6] and the ongoing denial of any fundamental rights of sovereignty are compensated by the ability to buy a modern car or dishwasher.[7]

For several hundred years, slavery and then Jim Crow were institutionalized in order to provide cheap Black labor for the US economy.[8] It is estimated that 10 million people were stolen from Africa and forced to work as slaves in the United States. By 1860, slaves as an economic asset were worth more than all of America's manufacturing and all of the railroads put together (Coates 2014). Simultaneously, state policy for hundreds of years was explicitly designed to benefit White people (over Black and Indigenous people) in settling the land and accumulating White wealth. For instance, the 1618 Headright system and 1862 Homestead Act were designed to encourage Europeans to settle the land; the 1944 GI Bill sent White veterans to college; and in the 1930s to 1960s Federal Housing Administration provided extensive support for White families to get home mortgages and build their family wealth.[9] The consequence of all this theft and injustice remains clearly visible today: *the average Black household has a net worth which is 13 times, or $800,000, lower than the average White household* (Darity and Mullen 2020). White Americans own 90% of the national wealth, whereas Black families (which constitute 13% of the population) own only 2.6% (Moore 2017). In other words, unless one wishes to argue that Black people are systematically less productive, intelligent, and hardworking than White people (an undeniably racist position), the only alternative explanation for this stunning wealth gap is that it is the result of a history of racial oppression.

One of Nozick's (1974, 198, 160) central arguments against redistribution is that property and wealth are not "manna" from heaven but rather "come into the world already attached to people having entitlements over them." Now he's right that property is not manna, but wrong about the entitlements, since much of property has come into the world wet with tears and stained in blood. In terms of historical veracity, then, Marx's ([1867] 1933, ch. 31) account is much more accurate than the state-of-nature stories that libertarians tell:

> The discovery of gold and silver in America, the extirpation, enslavement and entombment in mines of the aboriginal population, the beginning of the conquest and looting of the East Indies, the turning of Africa into a warren for the commercial hunting of black-skins, signalised the rosy dawn of the era of capitalist production. These idyllic proceedings are the chief momenta of primitive accumulation. . . . If money, according to Augier, "comes into the world with a congenital blood-stain on one cheek," capital comes dripping from head to foot, from every pore, with blood and dirt.

One might object that the property that is being created today is free from violence and oppression. Yet that would be incorrect. The opportunities that different people have to acquire property in contemporary markets are structured in ways that are often deeply unjust. We discussed many of these in detail in Chapter 4 and need not repeat them here. It will suffice to simply recall the many ways in which economic opportunities remain (unjustly) deeply unequal. One aspect is that of vastly unequal inheritance. Recall that in the United Kingdom, Hugh Grosvenor, the Duke of Westminster, inherited £9 billion at the age of 25 and now owns half of London (SkyNews 2016). Indeed, it is estimated that fully two-thirds of all the land in England is owned by a mere 0.36% of the population (Shrubsole 2019).[10] In the United States, roughly 66% of all private wealth is derived from inheritance (Piketty 2014). Another crucial dimension of unequal opportunity is educational: whereas only about 20% of poor people (i.e., in the bottom decile) have access to higher education, this increases linearly to more than 90% for those whose parents have the highest income (Piketty 2020, 34). Opportunity also continues to be distorted along unfair racial and gender lines. Black people face twice the unemployment rate as Whites (Paul, Darity, and Hamilton 2018), and Black job applicants without criminal records enjoy roughly the same chance of getting hired as White applicants with criminal records (Coates 2014). In Canada, Indigenous children are far more likely to grow up in poverty, far less likely to attend university, far more likely to get incarcerated, and far more likely to go missing or be murdered than the settler population (Gilmore 2015; Manuel and Derrickson 2015). Women are still expected to perform the bulk of unpaid and devalued care labor, with the result that only 3% of Canadian CEOs are women (Joseph 2018; Nedelsky and Malleson, forthcoming). All this to say that much of the new property that emerges today continues to be interwoven with injustice and so cannot have the absolute halos around it that libertarians desire. Whereas Nozick (1974, 151) believed that "[w]hatever arises from a just situation by just steps is itself just," in the real world exchanges happen on the mountaintop of rampant injustice and overwhelming historical violence.

Of course, libertarians will want to argue that even if *some* property is tainted by historical violence, surely much of it is not. But this is wrong both conceptually and empirically. Conceptually it's wrong because the violent systems that we've been pointing to are *systemic*, meaning that they underlie and impact all property. For instance, as I am writing this book on my computer in my room it may seem that this new property is emerging without any obvious injustice. But the fact is that my computer was made in unjust sweatshop labor conditions; the chair that I sit on may well have been built by a company whose wealth was accumulated during Jim Crow; the electricity that warms me and the food that sustains me were produced on the basis of a patriarchal division of labor; and my house itself sits on stolen land. New property created today is built on the basis of an understructure which is interwoven with injustice—that is what it means to call such injustice "systemic." Hence the accumulation of property based on historical violence *plus* the ongoing creation of new property within structures of unjust and unequal opportunity means that no one (at least in the rich countries) can claim that their property rights are pristine. The point is not that every single piece of property is the direct result of violence and injustice tout court but that the threads of violence and injustice are integral and everywhere interwoven into it. Empirically, the objection that tainted property is marginal is wrong because the ongoing patterns of profound wealth disparity (by class, race, gender, ability) continue to be reproduced across society in every new generation, demonstrating the indisputable ongoing legacy of colonialism, slavery, and other forms of injustice.

Property Is Not Inviolable Even after Rectificatory Redistribution

To their credit, libertarians typically recognize a need for rectification if there is past injustice (though they tend to be vague and minimizing about the extent of injustice they believe really has transpired in capitalism, or how much rectification is needed).[11] Nozick (1974), for instance, is clear that if there has been past force and fraud, then rectification is necessary. Hence he suggests that it may be acceptable for society to engage in significant redistribution, at least "in the short run" (231). So we can imagine a powerful version of the libertarian argument going like this:

> Since there has been significant historical injustice, we accept the need for a one-time large redistribution of property. After that, however, property rights should be regarded as absolute and inviolable. Now, from this point on, invariably what will happen is that individuals will freely choose to ex-change their property in varying ways. X will get paid for performing his job; Y will buy a farm and plant crops to sell on the market; basketball stars will agree to play basketball for payment from fans; some individuals will prefer to work little and relax a lot, while others will prefer to work hard and save frugally for decades, coming to accumulate substantial wealth (we might call this "clean accumulation"). All of which will generate inequality that is perfectly just, and therefore the state must not interfere. So even if contemporary inequality cannot be said to be completely just, future ine-quality would be. Liberty upsets patterns.[12]

At first glance this seems to be a powerful argument, but let us look deeper. The first point to make is that there is something deeply unsatisfying, if not insincere, about the way that libertarians typically discuss rectification. For Nozick (1974), in his famous 82-page chapter on distributive justice, the first 81 pages are devoted to *defending* private property rights; it is only on the last page that rectification is mentioned. It is incredible that even though rectifi-cation is presented as one of the three major principles of distributive justice, presumably just as important as just acquisition and just transfer, nowhere in the chapter (or in the book as a whole) does he consider any historical evidence of how existing property in the United States actually emerged. He says absolutely nothing about colonialism or slavery or union smashing or patriarchy; he simply avoids any discussion of real-world historical property accumulation. His gesture toward rectification on the final page, therefore, seems insincere. Similarly for Narveson (2001); even though he formally claims allegiance to the principle of rectification, his entire book consists of an elaborate defense of *existing* private property. There is not a single men-tion of "Indigenous land," "aboriginal land," or "colonialism" in the entire manuscript. If libertarianism were truly the philosophy of freedom it claims to be, then surely it would trumpet the manifest unfreedom of the multi-tude of Black and Brown bodies destroyed in the historical accumulation of contemporary property; instead it usually passes over such unfreedoms in silence. Indeed, it is noteworthy that despite their proclaimed allegiance to rectification, in practice libertarians are typically at the vanguard of *opposi-tion* to calls for reparations (e.g., Calton 2018; Epstein 2014).

The other point to notice is that the way libertarians frame the issue is rigged. Recall the Wilt Chamberlain example. Nozick instructs us to start by imagining any just distribution of property that we would like. From this baseline (such as an egalitarian one), we are then told to imagine that a large number of basketball fans freely wish to pay Chamberlain for the pleasure of watching him play, the conclusion being that the resulting inequality is supposed to strike us as obviously legitimate. This indeed is a provocative argument. However, where the argument fails is simply assuming (with no argument or explanation) that the fans must possess full property rights to begin with. In other words, what is misleading in the Chamberlain example is Nozick's presumption that no matter what a just distribution is, it must be based on libertarian property rights. In so doing, Nozick simply assumes as true what the whole debate is in fact about. In fact, we should completely reject this assumption. A just society, I will argue below, would *not* have ab-solute property rights; it would have only contingent ones. Kymlicka ([1990] 2000, 103) hits the nail on the head: "If we realize that Nozick is saying, 'Here are some absolute rights to property—distribute them as you like,' then we should politely refuse his offer. For the legitimacy of such rights is precisely what is in question."

These two caveats aside, let us address the heart of the matter: in a just so-ciety (after sufficient rectification to deal with past injustices), should prop-erty rights be treated as absolute? In other words, would a just society refuse to interfere with individuals exchanging their property in any way they see fit—should it allow, and refrain from interfering with, "capitalist acts be-tween consenting adults"?[13] My answer is no, for two reasons.

The first important point to make is that even after a significant one-time redistribution, individuals would not, generally speaking, have deep moral rights to the property they acquire. As we saw in Chapter 4, even if there were a fair starting point from which certain individuals could cleanly accumu-late substantial wealth, this would still not make it morally deserved because such wealth would primarily stem not from any individual's own skill and effort but from the understructure—the accumulation of capital, technology, and institutions deriving from the labor and care of *other* people, most of them long dead—as well as from the amoral workings of the market system (with its wild fluctuations and political machinations).

Furthermore, as discussed in Chapter 5, even in a situation of clean accumulation, rich individuals would not morally deserve the results of their skills or efforts, as those too are ultimately due to the luck and unlevel playing field of genetics and fortunate circumstance.

Hence even in a post-redistributive society, a Chamberlain-type figure would not deserve his income because he would be arbitrarily lucky to possess extreme basketball skill (and the perseverance to train hard), lucky to have had all the people around him who nurtured, cared for, and trained him, as well as lucky to live in a particular time and place that has great demand for his particular skillset, and lucky again for there to be such scarcity of supply of equivalent skills. If he had been born a Kenyan or Chinese person instead of a Black man in Philadelphia, he would likely never be able to become a famous basketball star in the first place.

If the arguments of Chapters 4 and 5 are correct, then there is actually no deep moral right to one's income or property whatsoever, and therefore one's ownership rights are only ever contingent and secondary—they depend on what justice requires (see also Fried 1995). Of course, people should normally possess relatively strong property rights over their money (so that it's wrong for someone to deduct money from your paycheck without your consent), but these rights are contingent and secondary in the sense that they should be respected only *after* the primary task of establishing the conditions of social justice has been accomplished.

The second and perhaps most fundamental reason why libertarians are wrong to think that property rights should be inviolable after a large-scale redistribution is because other people can have a legitimate claim over one's property if their need is sufficiently acute. For this reason as well, property rights should be seen not as absolute but as contingent (i.e., contingent on what is required to provide the conditions for everyone in society to live good and flourishing lives).

A strange aspect of libertarianism is its extreme one-sidedness. Individuals are taken to have extremely strong negative rights (not to be harmed or aggressed upon in any way), but on the flip side, they have zero positive obligations to aid others, no matter what. So if I see a child drowning in a pond who is moments away from certain death, and I am the only person who could possibly save them, and could easily do so without any harm occurring to myself except for ruining my shoes in the mud, libertarians insist that I still have absolutely no obligation to save the child's life. (I should feel charity, perhaps, but cannot be ethically compelled in any way, shape, or form.) Yet this is surely wrong. Of course compulsion is bad, but so too is easily avoidable suffering and death. The problem, as Arneson (2010, 2011) rightly points out, is that the libertarian sees property rights as absolute trumps, completely outweighing any other concern. Yet surely other moral considerations should at least sometimes, and at least in some instances, outweigh such rights. A more sensible position is that property rights are not absolute but contingent: our right to not be harmed or coerced by others must be balanced by obligations to support and care for others.

What are some cases when another's needs should outweigh the "inviolability" of private property? There are, I believe, many instances when this is true, but probably the most obvious case is that of basic needs. Consider the context of a rich country (leaving aside for now the more complex questions of global justice), where a relatively small number of residents do not have their basic needs met—they are hungry, sick, injured, homeless, or disabled without the accommodation necessary for basic functioning. Narveson (2001, 100) argues that there is no obligation to support any such people, not even with a basic right to life: "We come into the world equipped with the right not to be harmed, not to have our liberty violated. But we don't come equipped with a positive right to any resource. And in a desperate circumstance, this could be taken to mean that we do not come equipped even with a 'right to life.'" In Naverson's view, a situation is more just in which a handful of billionaires are permitted to keep all of their money—even though children are starving, disabled individuals are being left to rot without any aid, people suffering from mental health crises are sleeping on the street, and elderly persons cannot afford the heat to warm their homes—than an alternative situation in which the superrich are compelled to pay a tax of a small percentage of their wealth to ensure that these people have their basic needs met. It is hard to see much morality in such a position, at least for those of us for whom morality is interwoven with compassion and care and concern for the well-being of others, particularly the worst off.

The case of individuals living with a disability is a particularly striking challenge to libertarianism. The basic libertarian premise of course is that those who are injured or disabled have no claim on the resources of their fellow citizens. Nozick's (1974, 160) principle is "[T]o each according to what he makes for himself (perhaps with the contracted aid of others) and what others choose to do for him and choose to give him of what they've been given previously." In Narveson's (2001, 266) words, "[T]hose who do not [work] don't obviously merit payment for their leisure." In neither book is there a single mention of the "disabled" or "handicapped." A libertarian society, therefore, would allow the disabled to suffer poverty, deprivation, stigma, humiliation, and all in all a much worse life than others for no reason other than that they have been differently lucky in terms of bodily abilities. Of course, libertarians claim that the disabled can be adequately cared for by private charity. But not only is that empirically doubtful (I am not aware of any case in any country in all of Western history where disabled individuals have been supported entirely by private charity up to the level of the median income); it also leaves them entirely at the mercy of the charitable inclinations of the rich and any capricious fluctuations in their benevolence. Living one's life at the mercy and whim of donors is no good way to live. The egalitarian position is surely preferable: disabled individuals have as much right to live a good and flourishing life as anyone else because they are *human beings*, because they have just as much human dignity and their lives are just as precious as any others; they should therefore be guaranteed a wide range of entitlements. To deny them the material conditions to live good and flourishing lives, as libertarianism does, is really to deny that their lives are as valuable as the able-bodied.

Another telling case is that of young children. For the libertarian, children have no inherent rights of support.[14] Hence in a libertarian society, whether children flourish or perish will depend on the arbitrary happenstance of whether their parents were, in the first place, lucky enough historically to accumulate their own private resources and, in the second, whether they happen to be positively inclined to use such resources to support the child's flourishing. For the egalitarian, by contrast, allowing luck to play such a preponderant role in a child's well-being is appalling. Notice again the strange asymmetry at the heart of libertarianism: there is an intensive focus on the rights of adults with their present holdings, but no interest in the rights of future adults—those count for nothing. From an egalitarian perspective, by contrast, it is the fluke of parental history that should count for nothing for the life prospects of a baby. The life prospects of children should be sheltered from the storms of misfortune and the arbitrariness of family context by being guaranteed the conditions for a stable, secure, and flourishing life. Yet in many cases, guaranteeing access to good life opportunities for children will be possible only by taxing the wealth of existing adults.

The libertarian view of taxation is another example of how extreme and one-sided their view of property rights is. As we have seen, Nozick (1974, 169) describes taxation in the language of "forced labor"; Narveson (2001, 250) talks of "armed robbery"; and as we will see below, most libertarians compare taxation to forcible removal of body parts. For libertarians, infringement on property rights is about as absolutely wrong as anything could be. The deprivation of the poor, starving children, abandoned disabled people, homelessness, elderly people shivering in their homes—such things are seen, by contrast, as mere misfortune, a pity, but no great moral problem. The libertarian in effect shrugs and looks away.[15] A much more sensible view, it seems to me, is one which says that both property rights and basic needs matter. So we as a society must compromise. On the one hand, we want people to be secure in their ownership of their property (so that they can enjoy the security and autonomy that such control brings). But on the other hand, we also care about meeting people's basic needs, which will at least sometimes clearly outweigh the importance of individual property rights (particularly when significant harm is at stake, and especially when no comparable harm occurs by virtue of taxation).[16] Given this, having a system with regular, transparent taxation on income and wealth, combined with a legal system that protects one's rights to one's private property after such redistributions, seems a sensible compromise.

Basic needs are the most obvious area where other people's needs can and should trump property rights, but there are other areas too where the benefits of redistribution likely outweigh the harms suffered by the property owner, such as providing access to the essential opportunities required to live a good or flourishing life (e.g., affordable housing, higher education, child care, transportation, a minimum income guarantee, free time, access to nature and art); ensuring that important egalitarian relationships, such as political democracy, are not undermined by extreme inequalities in private wealth; and providing public goods, such as the basic infrastructure that everyone depends on and which markets will typically fail to adequately provide (a well-functioning legal system, public safety and security, public health, environmental sustainability, etc.).

Now of course there is much room here for legitimate disagreement about the extent to which these goods outweigh private property rights and exactly how much tax is the right amount. Should rich countries provide free university education in addition to high school? Should we provide everyone with a pension but not a basic income? Should we provide only temporary shelters so that poor people probably won't die on the street (at least not in large numbers), or should we actually guarantee a home for all (Cohen et al. 2019)? Whatever one's position on such issues, the crucial point is that as soon as one accepts the basic proposition that *some things* legitimately do outweigh individual rights to property, then the game is up. As soon as one admits that property rights are not inviolable, the foundation of the libertarian edifice crumbles. At that point the debate is no longer one of deep moral principle— everyone agrees that property rights are not absolute and redistribution is, at least sometimes, justified—so the debate becomes one of the degree and extent of appropriate taxation. The reasonable debate, in other words, is between socialists and liberals; libertarianism is beyond the pale.

Given this, what should we make of the libertarian claim that "liberty upsets patterns," i.e., that "no end-state principle or distributional patterned principle of justice [such as equality] can be continuously realized without continuous interference with people's lives" (Nozick 1974, 163)?

It is simply not true that instituting "patterns" of distributive justice (such as regular taxation) necessarily reduces freedom. On the contrary, small reductions in the freedom of the rich due to taxation (such as the reduced ability to, say, afford a private yacht) may actually generate much more freedom, and more important kinds of freedom, for the poor (such as the freedom to eat, to have clean drinking water, to go to school, to have healthcare and stable housing [Cohen 1995]). State policies and "patterns" can reduce freedom, of course, but they can also increase it by providing the material basis for people to live good and flourishing lives. Indeed, there is good reason to believe that an egalitarian society would in fact provide substantially more freedom for many people (see Chapter 3). An egalitarian society would have more taxes, more redistribution and public services (or a basic income), and hence more real freedom for people to live the lives that they value (Van Parijs 1995). Just as a typical citizen of high-tax Sweden has significantly more real freedom (such as the opportunities to go to university, acquire healthcare, balance work and care through generous parental leave, and access affordable day care) than a typical citizen of the low-tax United States, so would most citizens in an egalitarian society have more freedom, other things being equal, than in libertarian society.

By insisting on the inviolability of property, libertarianism actually undermines the real freedom of many, such as by preventing the poor from meeting their basic needs. Ironically, countries that have sought to protect "liberty," in the sense of absolute property rights, have tended to thereby create very real historical patterns—patterns of domination—whereby White people have been systematically richer, Black people and women systematically poorer, generation after generation. This is why G. A. Cohen (1995) concluded that libertarianism is not, at root, primarily concerned with "liberty" at all but with justifying property rights (hence the doctrine should not really be called "libertarian" but "propertarian"). Despite its name, the doctrine turns out to be mainly apology and apologia for wealthy property owners.[17]

In a just society, individuals would not have carte blanche over their property—property rights would not be recognized as absolute. Instead of protecting private property rights, the primary goal of the state should be to foster just relationships between people so that everyone has guaranteed access to the material (and cultural) requirements to live a good and flourishing life. This will require regular redistributions of the property that is currently allocated in such arbitrary ways by the market. What is fundamental is not property rights, but justice. We should derive the former from the latter, not the other way around.[18]

Redistribution of Property Is Deeply Different from Redistribution of Body Parts

One of the most famous, or perhaps infamous, libertarian arguments is that the redistribution of private property is morally akin to the forced redistribution of body parts. Libertarian writings are scattered with nightmarish analogies of the state forcibly removing people's kidneys or eyeballs in order to redistribute them. For example, Samuel Wheeler (1980, 189) argues that "no significant moral difference in kind obtains between eliminating my ability to play softball by taking my knees away and eliminating my ability to play the market by taking my money away. . . . Theft, taxation, and disembowelment are different forms of the same kind of violation of rights." [19] When most people hear this argument for this first time they tend to think it extreme or even outlandish. And while I agree that it is, ultimately, wrong, it can't be dismissed out of hand. The power of the argument stems from the fact that most people do share with libertarians the strong intuition that my body is indeed *mine*. This intuition resonates with many people's sense of why autonomy is valuable: I should be completely in charge of what happens to my own body; it is I and I alone who should rightly be able to decide whether

I eat unhealthy food, take drugs, abort a fetus, or commit suicide; it is wrong for others to decide what happens to my body; my body, my choice.[20]

What do these rights over one's body have to do with ownership of economic resources? The standard version of the libertarian argument is that property in the world emerges out of a more basic kind of property: property in the person (which libertarians refer to as "self-ownership"). In other words, people supposedly are natural self-owners, and then come to own property by using their body on the world, or "mixing their labor" with parts of the world (Locke [1689] 1980; Widerquist 2010). We have already discussed and dismissed the idea that actually existing property arose ethically. Nevertheless, there is still a strong version of the libertarian objection that we can imagine, which goes like this: "You egalitarians have said that property is not morally deserved, and so can be redistributed. Yet surely no one can claim to morally deserve their body. (It's just good fortune that one has working eyeballs, kidneys, etc.) But if it's acceptable to redistribute property, this implies that you must also support redistribution of body parts, which shows the absurdity of the egalitarian position."

The problem with this line of thought is that there are real and profound differences between body parts and pieces of external property. First, the relationship between an individual and their body is much more basic and primary than the relationship between an individual and their money because one's body is much more tightly connected to oneself than is one's money. From the day I'm born until the day I die, my body is there, attached to me, significantly (though not entirely) coextensive with me. In most cases, individuals possess their eyes and kidneys throughout their whole life. Property, income, wealth, and possessions are very different. The income that individuals possess isn't attached to them in anything like the same way. After all, one is born with neither income nor possessions, and the amount of property that one has may well fluctuate tremendously throughout one's life. The income that one acquires comes not from the self in any simple way but derives from participation in systems of large-scale social cooperation—i.e., from *other* people. If you are a bus driver in San Francisco earning $50,000 per year who is suddenly transported to rural India, your income would dramatically change due to the radically different understructure, but your body would not; you would still be you.

The second and most important difference between body parts and property is that the harm involved in redistribution is, generally speaking, very different in the two cases. One's body is much more vital and integral to one's selfhood than is one's income. My body is a vessel of my agency and the carrier of my personality and so is coextensive with my *self* in a way that my income is not. This means that the harm involved in interfering with my body is typically much more extreme. The state tying me down in order to forcibly cut out a kidney to share it with another is a nightmarishly deep and violent infringement of *me*. In contrast, the act of taxation, whereby my employer reduces the number on my paycheck (to automatically deduct income tax from the source) is at least one step, if not several big steps, removed in terms of the severity of harm involved. Of course, taxation may be passionately disliked, but as long as it is of the kind that we have been discussing (i.e., modern progressive taxation, where poor people pay little or nothing at all, and therefore no one is significantly deprived of their basic needs due to such taxation), it is hard to believe that the harm it causes is in any way analogous to that of permanent body modification through invasive surgery.

Here again, the key is not sweeping assertion but careful nuance. What matters in distinguishing the kind of rights people should have over their bodies versus their money is the character of the harm done. Does it deprive people of the ability to live good or flourishing lives? Does it involve severe pain or humiliation or degradation? Are there viable alternatives? Does the harm enable society to rectify more pervasive and serious harms elsewhere? Those are the kind of important questions that we must consider in order to arrive at a justified position on when redistribution is legitimate. For example, it's easy to imagine various kinds of taxation of property—for example, a state taxing every single penny that an individual has so that they are left to starve, which truly *would be* terrible and unjust. It's also easy to imagine kinds of bodily taxation (such as the state requiring a microscopic hair or flake of dead skin from every living person), which, if it is completely painless to remove, and is not a body part that anyone has any deep ethical or religious attachment to, and which could for some reason medically save the lives of many others—would appear quite unobjectionable. In hypothetical (and extremely far-fetched) cases like that, the usual state of affairs would be reversed, and bodily taxation might actually be more justified than property taxation. That said, in the real world, public policy needs to deal with general regularities. In normal circumstances, it seems generally true that monetary taxation (of the progressive sort that we've been discussing, where richer people pay higher rates and such funds are used to guarantee everyone's basic needs) is vastly less harmful than taxation of eyeballs or kidneys or other bodily infringements. Forcible redistribution of body parts would typically be so ghoulish, degrading, and harmful that even if it's possible to imagine theoretical examples that aren't so terrifying (e.g., redistributing flecks of useless skin), it makes good sense for public policy to simply enact a broad rule that the body is (at least in all normal circumstances) simply out of bounds for redistributive justice. Generally speaking, the rights that individuals have over their property should be seen as very different from, and typically much weaker than, the rights that individuals have over their bodies; it's perfectly reasonable to insist that property can (and often should) be frequently redistributed, whereas one's body parts should not be.

Summary

Libertarians justify inequality on the ground that individuals possess absolute rights over their property, which, through voluntary exchange with others, will naturally create inequality. In this chapter we have seen that this perspective is deeply flawed. The property and wealth that actually exist today did not come into the world through peaceful "first ownership" or clean accumulation in a mythical state of nature, but rather from a long history of violence, coercion, fraud, robbery, domination, and injustice. This means that redistribution is in many cases completely justified, even required.

Moreover, even if we were to redistribute property so that everyone started from a fair position, it would still be wrong to treat property rights as inviolable because other people's needs matter, and these needs should, at least sometimes, outweigh the individual's right to have complete control over their property.

Finally, the rights that individuals have over their property should be seen as very different from, and typically much weaker than, the rights that individuals have over their bodies; redistribution of the former is typically legitimate, while redistribution of the latter should almost always be forbidden.

In sum, property rights should be seen as contingent, not absolute. Whereas libertarians typically see property rights as natural things that constrain what a society can and cannot do, we should actually take the opposite perspective. Property rights are *derivative*. The fundamental thing is justice—establishing good relationships between people whereby everyone has the means and ability to lead good and flourishing lives—*that* is what matters. The kind of property rights that we should institutionalize, and the distribution of property itself, should flow from the requirements of justice, not the other way around. In most cases, economic inequality is not at all legitimate because it undermines social justice. Hence property can and typically should be redistributed in order to guarantee everyone access to good and flourishing lives.

7

How Much Inequality Is Acceptable?

The Case for Maximum Limits on Income and Wealth

Inequality is the difference between those who have little and those who have much. For those who believe that there is too much inequality in society, the goal is to narrow this gap. This can be done by raising the floor or by lowering the ceiling. Most people are very familiar with the idea of raising the floor, but we are much less familiar with the opposite direction. Should there be a top ceiling on income and wealth that people are actually barred from surpassing? We have a minimum wage, but should there be a maximum wage as well?

It is not intrinsically bad to be a rich person (depending on how the wealth was acquired), but a society which allows individuals to accumulate tremendous wealth does lead to unjust consequences. I argue, therefore, that we should impose maximum limits on income and wealth because individuals having too much wealth is a major problem for society for two principal reasons: the rich undermine democracy, and the rich privately appropriate the resources that we desperately need for other things, such as providing basic needs, essential opportunities, green investment, and economic security to reduce xenophobia and populism. The maximum limits could take the form of a maximum ratio, whereby the richest are banned from earning more than, say, 10 or 20 times the minimum wage (after which, individuals would face a 100% marginal tax rate).

The first part of this chapter outlines such arguments, drawing on the wonderful work of Ingrid Robeyns (2017) on "limitarianism," which is the doctrine that it is immoral for the rich to possess too much wealth. Yet even if these normative arguments are persuasive, many people will undoubtedly remain skeptical on practical grounds. Are such limits really economically feasible? Again, the answer is yes (though here much caution is required). Although we have not yet witnessed an example of a market economy imposing egalitarian limits on what its members are allowed to accumulate, the

Against Inequality. Tom Malleson, Oxford University Press. © Oxford University Press 2023.
DOI: 10.1093/oso/9780197670392.003.0008

empirical evidence nevertheless suggests that there is nothing impossible about doing so. Instituting such limits against the wishes of the powerful will of course be extremely difficult, but if successfully instituted, limits could indeed work well and without severe costs to our economic well-being.

The goal of this chapter is thus to synthesize the two sides of the coin: the normative arguments for maximum limits with the political-economic evidence of their feasibility.

Before beginning, there is one important point to make, which is that thinking about limits to wealth is not nearly as outlandish as it might first appear. Note that anyone who believes that there must be *some* upper limit to acceptable inequality is also thereby implicitly committed to the notion that there must be some limit on maximum allowable wealth. Presumably most people do believe that there is some threshold at which inequality becomes too high. For some this might be when the top 1% controls 10% of national wealth; for others it might be 20% or 40% or even 99%. Whatever this threshold may be, keeping inequality below that threshold logically necessitates imposing a limit on the total amount of wealth that one can acquire (because if one's wealth can expand indefinitely, there will be no limit on the amount of inequality). This means that as a matter of logic, having a belief in unacceptable levels of inequality (which most people do have) necessarily implies a policy of imposing maximum levels of wealth.[1] Or, to put the argument the other way around, anyone who refuses to countenance the idea of a maximum limit to wealth is thereby committing themselves to the principle that there should be no limit whatsoever to the extent of inequality. Such a person is thereby committed to taking as acceptable a society in which the rich own everything and the poor own nothing. Yet such a position is patently untenable. The bottom line is that egalitarians need to become more comfortable and forthright in arguing for maximum limits. Limits are actually intrinsic elements of what egalitarianism means. Coherent egalitarianism actually embodies limitarianism.

The Necessity of Limits for Protecting Democracy

In her groundbreaking work on limitarianism, Robeyns (2017) advances two main arguments in favor of imposing limits on maximum income or wealth, one based on democracy and one based on urgent unmet needs.

The first argument is that the rich undermine democracy. As we saw in detail in Chapter 3, any society which allows billionaires to exist will inevitably be one in which they have significantly disproportionate influence over public policy. This is because electoral democracy is an inherently competitive system based on people's abilities to lobby, to mobilize a political campaign (to spread one's ideas widely and mobilize large numbers of activists to work for the campaign), and to generate and disseminate political ideas and opinions. And since the rich will always be strongly advantaged in these areas, the electoral system will always be tilted in their favor. Campaign finance reform and other such policies are useful, but they will never eradicate the fundamental advantage that rich people have in any liberal society where free expression and market freedoms exist.

This means that there is and will always be an insoluble tension between wealth and democracy. The rich are a Trojan horse within the walls of our democracy. This is the first reason to support limitarianism. Hence the first limitarian argument is that imposing limits on the rich would mean that society benefits hugely from a more robust (representative and egalitarian) democracy, whereas rich individuals would suffer only slightly from their reduced affluence, and so the benefits far outweigh the harms.

Let us try to formulate this argument a bit more precisely. To keep things simple, we will focus simply on material means, bracketing all the other important aspects necessary for a good life. In general, the more money one has, the more one is able to lead a good or flourishing life. However, it is not the case that more money always provides the same degree of life improvement at any level. At low levels, more money can make a huge difference in the quality of life, as it can mean the difference between starving and surviving, whereas for the billionaire, an extra thousand dollars means essentially nothing. This is the familiar phenomenon of the so-called declining marginal utility of money.[2] If we were to create a very simple classification system, we could say that if someone has *no money*, facing imminent bodily harm, we can define them as "destitute." The threshold above this is being able to meet one's *basic needs*—food, shelter, clothing, etc.—but little more; such people may be called "poor." Somewhat above that there is the important threshold of being able to access some but not all of the *essential opportunities* to live a flourishing life. What exactly these are will vary across societies depending on different people's evaluation of what constitutes a flourishing life, but presumably in the rich countries of the Global North they include healthcare; child care; primary, secondary, and tertiary education; housing; pensions;

transportation; employment opportunities; free time; and a modest disposable income for pleasure (not to mention the vital nonfinancial goods of social respect and recognition). We can call such individuals the middle class. Next, individuals who have sufficient money to acquire all of the essential opportunities and more we will call "rich." The final threshold is that of *great wealth*, whereby individuals are able to enjoy all of the essential opportunities many times over; we will call such people "superrich" (see Figure 7.1).

The superrich live lives of opulence: private jets, multiple vacation homes, yachts, luxury cars, domestic servants of all sorts—gardeners, chefs, cleaners, caregivers, assistants—jewelry, art, wine cellars, designer clothing, and storage rooms stuffed with toys.[3] If superrich individuals lose some money—a billionaire becomes merely a multimillionaire—they lose a (relatively unimportant) ability to buy toys, yet their (very important) essential opportunities to lead flourishing lives remain largely the same. Moreover, recall that the superrich actually spend only a small proportion of their money on such toys. Most of the wealth of the 1% is not actually consumed but is reinvested for future income. In other words, the bulk of the wealth of the superrich is not actually contributing to their day-to-day well-being (aside, perhaps, from the joy that the businessman in Saint-Exupéry's *Le Petit Prince* experiences from continually counting and recounting his money). It is

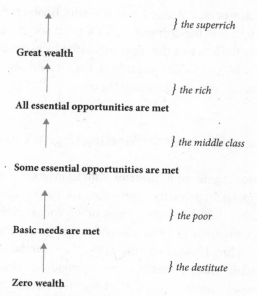

Figure 7.1 Thresholds of wealth.

simply reinvested again and again, with no purpose except that of endless accumulation. But since the superrich are so rich that the growing income will, for the most part, never be used for actual consumption, it is hard to make the case that much of this wealth is concretely important to their well-being, beyond the subjective (and ethically dubious) sense of superiority that it brings. For regular people, we rightly refer to the act of keeping money in the bank as "saving," but for the superrich this is no longer an accurate description, since such money will likely *never be consumed*. It's more accurate to see the bulk of their actions therefore not as saving in the sense of deferring consumption, but as either "gambling" or "power expansion" (e.g., through buying companies and exerting greater influence over other people's lives). In either case, we should feel very little sorrow about its redistribution.

If rich or middle-class individuals lose sufficient wealth so that they can no longer afford the essential opportunities needed to flourish, they have become "poor." This is a serious loss indeed because they are now significantly unfree and deprived.

And if poor individuals lose even more money so that they can no longer afford to meet even their basic needs, this is catastrophic; such people are "destitute," and their position cries out with the loudest moral urgency.

With this simplified—but sociologically realistic—background sketch in mind, we can see clearly the force of the limitarian argument. The superrich undermine our democracy. Reducing their wealth is vital for protecting political equality, which is the cornerstone of a good society and immensely valuable, whereas the loss that the superrich suffer by becoming merely rich in terms of their abilities to lead flourishing lives is minimal. Therefore, the benefits of imposing limits far outweigh the costs.

The Necessity of Limits for Meeting Urgent Unmet Needs

The second major argument in favor of limitarianism is that the rich, and a fortiori the superrich, privately appropriate the resources that we desperately need for other things. What are these other things? Here I will point to four main issues, though I make no claim that these are the only such things that matter: providing basic needs, providing the essential opportunities to flourish, advancing green investment, and providing economic security.[4] In each case the argument is straightforward: redistributing from the rich would substantially improve these problems, and such redistribution is justified because the importance of such needs far outweighs the need that the superrich have for their excess wealth (i.e., the wealth that they possess far above and beyond that which is needed to flourish).

The first and most obvious case is that of basic needs, which we defined as the ability to meet the bare requirements of survival: food, clean water, shelter, clothing, basic healthcare. Currently, 900 million people live on less than the World Bank's (2015) poverty level of $1.90 per day. Seventeen thousand children die every day from poverty-related illness (WHO 2018).[5] At the same time, the world contains roughly 2,200 billionaires. The unnecessary deprivation suffered by the poor in the Global South compared to the relative opulence of the population in the Global North is arguably the single greatest injustice in the world today.

Two elements make the case for limits here particularly powerful. On the one hand, the moral urgency of meeting people's basic needs is overwhelming. No one can deny that providing people with the basic ability to survive is of the very highest ethical concern, particularly when nothing of comparable importance is sacrificed. And indeed, the loss that would be suffered by the superrich to meet everyone's basic needs is so vanishingly small that the issues are about as morally black and white as can be imagined. The empirical facts are quite stunning: recall from the introduction that if we were to redistribute merely 2% of the wealth of only the world's billionaires, thereby leaving 99.99997% of the world's population completely untouched by such taxation, it would be possible to entirely eliminate extreme poverty around the world. Moreover, the billionaires would barely notice, as 2% is substantially less than they likely earn in a year, meaning that this tax could be levied annually and still their total wealth would actually continue to increase. In the United States, if we taxed only two individuals—Jeff Bezos and Bill Gates—at 2% of their wealth it would be possible to completely eradicate homelessness in the country (and once again their total wealth would not even diminish).[6]

The second important issue is that of essential opportunities. In the rich countries of the Global North, many people are deprived of the opportunities needed to lead a flourishing life because they lack access to one or more of the essential opportunities necessary. In Canada, 20% of people lack access to affordable housing (defined as less than 30% of pretax income [CMHC 2018]). In the United States, 9% of people lack health insurance (US Census 2018a), and 63% of full-time working parents cannot afford child care (Baldiga et al. 2018, 7).

The urgency of these essential needs is less than for basic needs, but meeting such needs is still of utmost importance. Without them, one cannot flourish because one is not economically secure. When people's essential needs are not met they are left in a desperate scramble to get by, filled with worry and anxiety, their life plans, goals, and aspirations displaced to the margins of their existence. Robust economic security is necessary because, as Franklin Roosevelt (1936) once remarked, "necessitous men [sic] are not free." A certain level of material security and stability is a prerequisite for life planning. Without it, one is constantly worried, distracted, and unstable. Without it, one is not really living; one is merely surviving. Indeed, there is much psychological evidence showing that most human beings are unable to pursue their projects (and so are not meaningfully free) unless their basic needs are secured (Deci and Ryan 2000; Maslow 1943; Tay and Diener 2011).

The third area of urgent unmet needs is that of environmental investment. As discussed in Chapter 3, preventing catastrophic climate change will require immense public spending: building a green energy infrastructure, redesigning urban spaces to revolve around public transit and dense housing, retrofitting old businesses and houses, etc. (Aronoff et al. 2019; Davis 2010; Klein 2014; Schor 2010). Poor countries will require significant financial support from rich countries to help them develop in ways that are not reliant on fossil fuels. Here too the issues are particularly stark. The benefits from imposing limits on the wealthy to be spent on the environment are enormous. It is not clear how to measure the value of preventing cataclysmic climate disaster—how does one measure the worth of a livable planet, not only for ourselves but for our children and grandchildren? What is clear is that the cost of failing to act will be immense. The current scientific consensus is that continuing business as usual will likely result in a 3.7–4.8°C increase by 2100 (IPCC 2018b, 8). Such changes are predicted to sink many places (e.g., a sea rise of one meter is projected to permanently flood 21% of Bangladesh, de-housing millions of people [Monbiot 2006, 21]), turn large swaths of farmland in Africa into desert (Cline 2007), dry up a number of vital rivers (such as the Ganges, which 500 million depend on [Davis 2009]), and increase the prevalence of extreme weather events, such as floods, fires, storms, and hurricanes. All told, researchers are warning that climate change could kill 184 million people in Africa alone before the century is over (McKibben 2007, 21). That represents double the numbers who died in World War I and World War II combined.

The fourth area of urgent unmet needs is economic security. We already discussed the importance of economic security for flourishing. But here I want to point to a different issue, which is the importance of economic security for reducing the appeal of the far right. As we saw in Chapter 3, although the worldwide growth of populism, xenophobia, the alt-right, and outright fascism cannot be simply reduced to economic insecurity (other issues, such as fear of status loss and cultural backlash against multiculturalism, feminism, and queerness also play important roles), the evidence is clear that insecurity does much to fuel such movements (Algan et al. 2017; Arzheimer 2009; Dal Bó et al. 2018; Guiso et al. 2017, 2019; Swank and Betz 2003). Once again, the issues are quite stark. The benefits to society that would accrue from imposing limits on maximum wealth in order to improve economic security may well be gigantic. It is not possible to put a numeric GDP value on such things, but clearly the dangers of the rise of the far right are hard to overstate. In the United States, the populist rise of Trump led to immigrant children being separated from their families and kept in cages which some likened to "concentration camps" (Datil 2019), a palpable increase in fear for the 10 million undocumented people, and a 30% rise in hate crimes (SPLC 2019). Across Europe, support for far-right parties has tripled over the past 20 years, reaching roughly 16% of the population today (Tartar 2017). Ominously, these are levels of support which have not been seen since the 1930s.

In all four cases, the benefits of imposing maximum limits on wealth—acquiring many more resources so as to ensure basic survival for the world's poorest, providing the essential opportunities needed to flourish, reducing the risk of climate catastrophe, and dampening the rise of the far right—are truly immense. The cost of doing so is the cost of making the superrich only rich. It is hard to argue that such costs are a major concern. The superrich may lose some marginal ability to consume extravagantly, but they would remain very comfortable, still possessing the material conditions necessary to flourish, and would still be far richer than most. They will also lose some power by way of their reduced economic clout—but from the perspective of a democratic society, that is a benefit, not a cost. Thus the conclusion here too is that limitarianism is an attractive policy.

Before moving on, let me briefly mention two more attractive features of limitarianism.

One additional virtue is that it focuses our attention directly on the rich, which is useful because in much philosophical discussion of distributive justice, as well as much mainstream conversation, most of the focus tends to rest either on the "poor" or on "everyone," while the rich, as a distinct and important social class, are strangely absent. For Nozick (1974), and libertarianism more generally, the rich are not a separate category or class at all; they are conceptually indistinct from everyone else, simply regular people who are just more successful in market exchange. For Rawls (1971) the focus of his first principle and the first part of the second principle is on everyone, whereas the difference principle focuses on the "least advantaged." Here too the rich are not highlighted as a particularly important or salient social category; they are barely mentioned at all and appear to be conceptualized as not meaningfully different from anybody else, except in having somewhat more resources. It's noteworthy that the only real attention given to the rich in Rawls's theory comes in terms of the importance he attaches to not being overly disruptive to them due to the worry of worsening their incentives. Likewise for much of egalitarian theory such as in debates about expensive tastes, luck egalitarianism, and the appropriate currency of justice, there is very little explicit focus on the rich (e.g., Brighouse and Robeyns 2010; Cohen 1989; Dworkin 2000; Lippert-Rasmussen 2015).[7]

A major reason for this is that much of contemporary political philosophy occurs in the realm of ideal theory. And here the rich are assumed to either not exist or are portrayed as simply regular-people-with-more-talent or regular-people-with-more-resources; they are *not* seen as a separate class in antagonistic relations to others, nor are they viewed as a group that is actively trying to take advantage, dominate, appropriate resources, and exercise power over others. Such actions are typically ruled out by definition of the conditions of ideal theorizing.[8] For instance, Rawls frequently says things like "Ideally, society will be organized to allow the fair value of political liberties for all"; he does not say "The rich today are actively undermining democracy, and so democracy requires reducing their wealth," since he would see such framing as mere distraction by the noise of nonideal theory. Yet note how different these two framings are. The first is abstract to the point of being depoliticized, whereas the latter is deeply political in highlighting real-world existing political struggles, pointing out the source of the problem, and highlighting ways to make the situation better.[9] So a strength of limitarianism is that it foregrounds the old socialist insistence that the rich matter; they are necessarily central subjects of social justice and injustice; they are purposive agents, who in many ways actively strive to accumulate power over others and to take resources and opportunities from others. If limitarianism is correct, then the success of the rich, indeed their very existence represents a failure of social justice. Their existence cannot be ignored.

A final strength of limitarianism that is worth highlighting is that its policies have the possibility of enhancing social solidarity and at least somewhat mitigating class conflict (Pizzigati, 2018). This is because the central policy of limitarianism—imposing maximum limits—would typically work by establishing a limit on the basis of some top-to-bottom ratio, for instance, by setting the maximum income at, say, 10 times or 20 times the minimum or median wage. Consider the impacts of such an income policy. If top managers, CEOs, and other elites knew that their own income was tied to the income level of those at the bottom (or middle), this would significantly change their own incentive structure. In place of the standard drive to minimize the income of their employees in order to maximize their own wealth, their incentives would become more aligned—managers would have more desire to actually see a raise in minimum (or median) income. This may well soften some of the conflict that is inherent in union negotiation and wage bargaining more broadly. Across society, economic elites might become somewhat less hostile to popular wage increases and more sympathetic to government policies aimed at working-class income growth (such as full-employment fiscal and monetary policy).

For all of the aforementioned reasons (protecting democracy, meeting urgent needs, drawing attention to the societal impacts of the rich, and enhancing social solidarity), we should be forthright in emphasizing the importance of establishing maximum limits on income and wealth. These limits are an effective way of institutionalizing the normative aspiration that life is a common endeavor, that we live in a community of equals, and that we share each other's fate.

The Sufficientarian Objection

A major objection to my focus on the superrich is the sufficentarian one, which says that the important ethical impulse is to help those who are badly off; once everyone has the means to live a sufficiently decent life, it becomes irrelevant that some are richer. In other words, our attention should be on lifting up those at the bottom; we need not be concerned with the superrich.[10] For instance, Frankfurt (2016, xi) encourages his readers to "appreciat[e] the inherent moral innocence of economic inequality"; "if everyone had enough, it would be of no moral consequence whether some had more than others" (Frankfurt 1987, 21). Likewise, Axelsen and Nielsen (2015, 111, emphasis added) tell us that "one of the main attractions of ideals of sufficiency . . . [is] that they reject this focus [on the billionaires] entirely. Not only do they think the Buffett/Gates example is beyond the scope of justice; they also carry with them an inherently political dimension in stating, '*Do not look to claims made above the threshold; such claims do not deserve the attention of political philosophers*.'"

To concretize things, let us picture a society (not, perhaps, too different from contemporary Nordic social democratic societies) where everyone is guaranteed a comfortable material level of existence. There are also some rich people and a handful of billionaires. The question, then, is whether the existence of the rich matters.

I believe that, yes, the existence of the rich, particularly the superrich, is still a significant problem. There are three reasons why.

Most important, this sufficientarian society would be problematic in terms of those goods that are inherently relational in nature. In particular, the superrich undermine democracy. As we saw in Chapter 3, any society which allows billionaires to exist will inevitably be one in which political democracy is undermined. Sufficientarianism, therefore, cannot prevent the distortion of democracy by the rich; only limits can.

Axelsen and Nielsen (2016) attempt to avoid this conclusion. They call for equality of certain relational goods such as political influence, yet they insist that the grounds for doing so are strictly sufficientarian, not egalitarian, because for goods of this sort "one's relative place in the distribution has a large impact on one's absolute capabilities to succeed" (114). "In some areas, then, securing that everyone is free from significant pressure against succeeding will require an equal or almost-equal distribution—but, this is for reasons of sufficiency, and not, as egalitarians would have us believe, due to egalitarian considerations" (Axelsen and Nielsen 2015, 407).

In other words, their argument is that for relational goods like political influence, we should interpret "having enough" as meaning "having equal amounts." Their position is that equality is only instrumentally valuable; what really matters, they claim, is not equality per se, but that each has enough. (It's just that for goods of these types, having enough typically means having equal amounts.)

The problem is that it does not make sense to conceptualize the amount of political influence that one person in the relationship has (ignoring all others), since the amount that one person has will be directly proportional to and directly determined by the amount of influence that the others have. For relational goods, it is incoherent to aim for "enough" for those at the bottom because such goods are inherently dyadic—achieving them means, by their very nature, that a certain relationship is realized between the two sides; what matters is not the bottom per se, but the bottom vis-à-vis the top and the top vis-à-vis the bottom. It makes little sense to focus on only one side of an inherently two-sided relationship.

What does it mean for deprived individuals to acquire "enough" or "a sufficient level" of political influence? According to Axelsen and Nielsen, it means that they acquire equal amounts of influence so as not to be dominated. I agree. But notice that this shifts the goalposts: the goal has now become, for all intents and purposes, equality. Their official goal is to give everyone sufficient influence. But because political influence is a relational good, giving more to some inevitably means taking away from others (and vice versa). Hence, just as much as powerless people need more political influence, powerful people need their influence curtailed. In both cases the aim is bringing everyone closer to an equal level. In other words, as soon as we recognize that there's an unbreakable chain between "the political influence of the bottom" and "the political influence of the top," it makes no sense to say that what matters is only the bottom. In fact, what matters is *everyone* having roughly the same amount so that the relationship is of the right nondominating character. But as soon as we say this, we've switched from talking about sufficiency to talking about the egalitarian character of the relationship.

Relational goods are best conceived as seesaws, or perhaps the scales held by Lady Justice (see Figure 7.2).

The defining feature of seesaws and scales is that their two sides are interdependent; they are inherently in relationship. Lifting one means, by its very nature, reducing the other. Reducing one is the functional, operational, and therefore moral equivalent of increasing the other. The sufficientarian is free to declare that they care only about one side of the scale. But conceptually

Figure 7.2 Seesaw and scales of justice.

there is no meaningful distinction. Semantics aside, their position (at least insofar as it applies to relational goods) is not meaningfully distinguishable from egalitarianism.

We've been talking about the importance of reducing inequality for protecting democracy, but it's important to point out that the same argument holds for other relational goods. For instance, as we saw in Chapter 3, a number of other important goods, such as social solidarity, civic engagement, reduced corruption, mental health, and reduction of certain types of crime, all appear to be relational goods. That is, they are driven not fundamentally by poverty but by the inequality—the gap in status and income—that occurs between people living in proximity to one another.[11] This means that for such goods, sufficiency is inadequate. A social democratic sufficientarian society that allows the superrich to exist thereby worsens social solidarity, civic engagement, corruption, mental health, and certain crimes. Such a society will fare worse on these issues than would an egalitarian society without the superrich.

The second problem with a social democratic sufficientarian society is that it is deeply unfair and unjust because it would allow people to be significantly disadvantaged for things beyond their control. Recall the case of Mark and Jada from Chapter 5. Mark is enthusiastic, optimistic, and self-confident, with an obsessive interest in chess and extreme ability to concentrate on chess problems for many hours at a time without fatigue, distraction, or disinterest, leading him to become a rich and successful chess player. Jada has cerebral palsy and chronic pain, with bouts of depression and low self-confidence. Now the sufficientarian intuition is that as long as Jada is materially comfortable, it doesn't matter how much better off Mark is. But can that really be right? Jada is not at all horribly off. In the social democratic context that we are imagining, she has a secure but modest existence, in a one-room apartment, in a town that she rarely leaves. Mark, on the other hand, has much, much more: he has a beautiful house full of toys and aesthetic pleasures; he eats at all the fancy restaurants; he has numerous personal doctors, masseurs, nutritionists, and exercise consultants to help him feel fit and happy; he frequently goes on holidays and travels to a diverse range of places, experiencing a wider range of the human condition. In sum, Mark has significantly higher well-being and more opportunity for joy and flourishing—all due to arbitrary luck. I grant that if Jada is not severely deprived, much of the sting of the situation is removed. Nevertheless, if her position is fixed while Mark becomes ever richer—100 times better off, 1,000 times, 10,000 times—and we compare his opulence and extensive opportunities of every kind imaginable to Jada's much more limited set of possibilities, surely our sense of fairness is perturbed. Arbitrary inequality matters because it offends our sense of fairness. It offends the egalitarian conviction that every human being has only one life to live, and so their life is just as precious and matters just as much as any other. Yet could anyone truly believe that Jada's life is being treated with as much care or concern as Mark's? The bottom line is that a sufficientarian society with billionaires allows for extremely large differences between people on arbitrary and ableist grounds.

The third and final issue with social democratic sufficientarianism is that it would fail to provide everyone with sufficiently good lives. Good Life Egalitarianism, I suggested in Chapter 5, would insist on a substantially higher threshold of guarantees than a social democratic society (including higher security from a generous basic income, much more extensive public services—such as free transit and, importantly, high-quality affordable public housing—as well as substantially more free time, and so on). In my view, social democratic sufficientarianism also fails to adequately deal with workplace injustice. The superrich are often business owners, which means that they possess significant unaccountable and arbitrary power over their workers—dictating what they do, how they do it, and if they will continue to have a job at all. Of course, social democratic societies would have unions and legislation protecting workers' rights, but this does not address the fundamental issue that most working-class people spend most of their lives in undemocratic workplaces where they are, essentially and structurally, servants.[12] Good Life Egalitarianism would differ from social democracy by making it far easier for workers to escape such servitude by having the option to choose to work in a worker cooperative (as opposed to a conventional hierarchical firm [Dahl 1985; Malleson 2014a]).

Moreover, these expensive goods should be funded first and foremost by redistributing income and wealth *from the billionaires* (which would effectively abolish them). As Robeyns (2022) points out, whereas sufficientarianism is essentially recipient-oriented (focusing on what we want poor people to have), limitarianism is contribution-oriented: it is concerned with who should contribute and how much. In other words, we should not be neutral with respect to who pays for Good Life Egalitarianism—we should start by redistributing wealth and income from the billionaires and, if more funds are needed, move down the income scale from the top.

Now, one might argue that Good Life Egalitarianism is really just a form of sufficientarianism with a particularly high threshold. There is an element of truth in that, but it is a threshold which is far higher than that which social democracy provides. Moreover, raising the bottom to such a high level would require lowering the top so much that the end result would be so much more *egalitarian* than what presently exists that it becomes largely semantics whether we call this ideal society "sufficientarian" or "egalitarian."

In sum, a social democratic sufficientarian society is inadequate. I have no problem with the notion that we should give priority to those with the most pressing needs (e.g., Parfit 2000). I also accept that a sufficientarian society would be one in which much of the outrage that egalitarians feel is diminished. But it would not diminish all of it. By itself, sufficiency is insufficient.[13]

Laffer's Objection

Probably the most frequent objection to the idea of imposing maximum limits is that it would actually be counterproductive for meeting urgent needs. If high taxes end up leading to more avoidance, evasion, and reduced incentives to work, then higher taxes might actually lead to lower total government revenues—this is the infamous Laffer curve. This objection is powerful since the goal of limitarianism (and egalitarianism more generally) is presumably to redistribute *more* resources, not fewer.

Indeed, there is something to this objection. There has now been much study of so-called optimal levels of taxation, with most experts estimating that the level of income tax that would result in the highest revenues is in the range of 70–80% (Diamond and Saez 2011; Piketty and Saez, 2013; Piketty, Saez, and Stantcheva 2014). If this is accurate, unmet needs would actually be better met by *not* imposing tax rates above this.

That said, although this objection clearly does have some force, we should not concede the point too quickly because the issues here are actually much more nuanced than is commonly recognized.

The first point to make is that the Laffer curve conflates two very different reasons for why tax revenues may fall: individuals may choose to work less *or* they may evade taxes more. The problem with this conflation is that we should make very different moral evaluations of these two very different types of behavior, and so should react to them very differently. Consider first the issue of avoidance by itself. On these grounds, the objection to limitarianism is, ethically speaking, very murky, as it is not based on the worry that limits would reduce genuinely valuable activities (such as hard work); the objection is that such limits will increase *unethical activity* (such as avoidance and evasion). In other words, the objection takes the following form:

Premise 1: Limitarians aim to meet urgent unmet needs.

Premise 2: Imposing limits will inevitably lead to unethical activity (as the rich will avoid and evade).

Premise 3: This unethical activity will undermine the goal of meeting unmet needs.

Conclusion: Therefore, limitarians should abandon limits as the mechanism for achieving their goal.

But that is a troubling argument. To see why, consider an analogy:

Premise 1: Antiracists aim to end racism against Black people (among others).

Premise 2: Passing antiracist policy (such as desegregating schools) will inevitably lead to a backlash and upsurge in racism.[14]

Premise 3: This unethical activity will undermine the goal of reducing racism.

Conclusion: Therefore, antiracists should abandon desegregation of schools as a mechanism for achieving their goal.

What is problematic in both arguments is, of course, P2. We should not simply accept that unethical activity is a fait accompli, inevitable and unchangeable. Antiracists should not abandon the tool of desegregation merely because there is a risk that it will inflame racist backlash; rather the goal should be to reduce such backlash (by doing the things that antiracists conventionally do, such as education, protest, political mobilization). Likewise, limitarians should not abandon their tool of imposing limits. They should instead work to end, or at least minimize, the unethical behavior of avoidance and evasion. The problem, in other words, is not the limitarian *mechanism* of imposing maximum limits; the problem is the *unethical behavior* of the rich. The point is that to the extent that raising taxes increases avoidance, our response should not be, contra Laffer, to reduce taxes but to increase enforcement. In the case of avoidance, there is actually no one Laffer curve; there are actually infinitely many different

Laffer curves depending on how seriously a society chooses to deal with enforcement.

The second reason that higher taxes may lead to lower revenues is if they lead people to work or invest less. Even though this is the objection that most people have in mind when they worry about high taxes, it's important to recall that empirically this phenomenon—at least of working less—is actually far rarer than the morally problematic phenomenon of avoidance (see Chapter 3). Conservatives often use the image of hardworking people choosing to work less in emphasizing the Laffer curve, when what actually occurs much more commonly in the real world is rich people responding to taxes by simply hiding their money and shifting it from one bank account to another. Nevertheless, we should accept that there is some point at which marginal tax rates will be so high that significant numbers of rich people will indeed choose to work or invest less. What is crucial to notice about this is that two important consequences follow. One consequence is that total tax revenues fall. And that is indeed a bad thing from a limitarian perspective, as it means there is *less revenue* available to meet urgent needs. However, the second and less noted consequence is that in choosing to work or invest less, rich people themselves end up somewhat poorer. But notice that this consequence is actually positive for egalitarians because it results in a society with *less inequality* overall. This means that being on the "wrong side" of the Laffer curve actually has some real benefits. First, there are relational benefits: it is good for democracy, as there would be less inequality in political influence between rich and poor, and it is likewise good for reducing social friction (improving social solidarity, civic engagement, corruption, mental health, and crime) as well as distrust in society which stems (among other things) from the gap between the rich and the poor. Second, it is good from a fairness and anti-ableist perspective, since people will have less luck-based differentials in terms of their income and economic security (and so less luck-based differences in their ability to live good, flourishing lives).

Two conclusions follow from this. The first is that we should be forthright that there are actually real virtues in being on the "wrong side" of the Laffer curve. Or, to put the issue a different way: we need to be more explicit about the one-sidedness of the Laffer curve. It is a model of tax revenue only. It is not a model of inequality tout court. The Laffer curve should always be supplemented with an "Inequality curve" which measures tax-and-enforcement rates against levels of inequality (such as the income share of the top 1%; see Figure 7.3). This curve looks very different: as taxes-and-enforcement

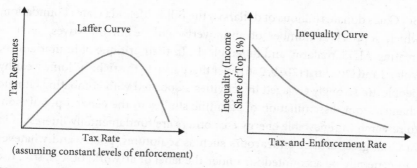

Figure 7.3 The Laffer curve and the Inequality curve.

increase, inequality continuously drops. Whereas the point of the Laffer curve is to show that increased taxes are counterproductive, the Inequality curve shows the opposite: increasing taxes consistently leads to increasingly positive outcomes of reduced inequality.

A second conclusion is that, as Robeyns (2017) has pointed out, there is an interesting tension between the two major arguments for limitarianism. The argument for meeting urgent needs logically requires slightly lighter taxation at the top (i.e., being on the "right side" of the Laffer curve) since the goal is to maximize revenues; the argument for protecting democracy implies the need for stronger taxation at the top (i.e., being on the "wrong side" of the Laffer curve, or being further along the x-axis of the Inequality curve). This means that limitarians will have to set tax rates according to their evaluation of how best to balance these conflicting desires. One attractive solution (though by no means the only one) is to follow the path of Franklin Roosevelt in the early 1940s: impose high progressive tax rates across most of the income spectrum (with the goal of maximizing revenues) and, at the very top, impose even higher "confiscatory" rates (or, I would suggest, impose wealth and inheritance taxes, with the aim not of revenue maximization but of inequality reduction, in particular reducing the power of the superrich). Such a strategy would allow limitarians to come close to having their cake and eating it too.

The Philanthropy Objection

A final normative objection to limitarianism is that rich people often do valuable things with their money in the form of private philanthropy. For example,

Bill Gates donates billions of dollars to the Bill & Melinda Gates Foundation, which supports a number of antipoverty and health initiatives, such as treating AIDS, malaria, and tuberculosis. In their critique of limitarianism, Volacu and Dumitru (2019, 256) offer this paean to the rich: "[S]ome wealthy people are strongly engaged in activities associated with combating climate change, from dissemination of scientific studies to the general population, to research in renewable energy etc.; others are fundamentally interested in funding great artistic endeavours such as sculptures, poetry and whatever can generally be accounted for under the label of artwork; others, still, use their wealth in order to contribute to the establishment and development of democracy-building non-governmental organizations in countries that are in a process of transition from autocratic or totalitarian regimes to democratic ones."

There is nothing wrong with the act of private charity, and by many accounts Bill Gates himself is a kind and generous man. However, it is a mistake to consider such good deeds in an overly abstract way. Of course, it is better to treat disease than to not treat disease. But that is not the point. Consider the case of the kindly king in the feudal era. The king is a king—he claims divine right to rule over others, and his wealth derives from perpetual, systemic domination of the masses of peasants. Yet in his personal interactions with his peasants he is benevolent. He provides some financial relief to starving peasants after a bad harvest and directs some of "his" resources to setting up a handful of hospitals for sick peasants to visit, as well as building beautiful churches for them to pray in. Now of course it's true in the abstract that it is better if the king is kindly than cruel. But it's also true that this is missing the bigger point. The real ethical issue here is not the virtue of an individual action in the abstract, but whether the social system is a good one. Should kingdoms exist, or should they be abolished and replaced by an alternative system, such as a democratic system? Likewise, the real question in our case is not whether it is right or wrong for an individual to donate to the fight against malaria, but whether the current form of big private philanthropy—directed and controlled by the superrich—is better or worse than an alternative arrangement of public philanthropy (where instead of receiving tax breaks, the rich are forced to pay taxes that the government then democratically directs to philanthropic causes).

The answer, I believe, is that a public system is significantly better. The first reason is that private philanthropy is undemocratic and paternalistic. The Bill & Melinda Gates Foundation, for instance, has an endowment of over $50 billion—larger than the entire GDP of some African nations. The sheer size of such foundations means that we are not talking about a simple "good deed"; we are talking about power. How this money is spent, who receives it, and who is cut off after previously having received it will have serious impacts on many people's lives. Yet the money is not allocated with any public accountability. Neither the American public (which would have received the money if not for the tax breaks) nor the African public (which may receive such money if the donor benevolently deigns it so) nor the various NGOs whose projects and employment stability will rise and vanish with a flick of the Foundation's pen, will have any say over how this money is allocated. These huge resources are simply directed, unilaterally, from the top, according to the wealthy individual's view of what is best. Indeed, big philanthropists do not even need to be transparent about how they spend their funds. For example, the $8 billion Simons Foundation International does not even have a public website (Madrigal 2018). For such reasons Rob Reich (2018) is right to argue that "big philanthropy is an exercise of power, and in a democracy, any form of concentrated power deserves scrutiny, not gratitude" (Reich quoted in Madrigal, 2018).

The second reason to prefer a system of public, democratically accountable philanthropy is that, on the whole, it is likely to make better-quality decisions. Government decisions are clearly not flawless or unbiased—far from it—but at the very least a public, accountable system has to justify and give publicly scrutinizable reasons for their actions. Private philanthropists do not.

Moreover, we have very good reason to suspect that the rich will often be particularly poor decision-makers and narrow in their worldview. The psychological evidence shows that compared to average people, the rich are statistically more solipsistic (Kraus et al. 2012), more hypocritical (Lammers, Stapel, and Galinsky 2010), more entitled and narcissistic (Piff 2014), more favorable toward greed (Piff et al. 2012), less generous, trusting, or helpful (Piff et al. 2010), and, importantly, less compassionate (Varnum et al. 2015). For instance, richer individuals display fewer physiological signs of concern (such as heart rate deceleration) and report less compassion when observing a video depicting others' suffering, relative to lower-class individuals (Stellar et al. 2012). Rich individuals tend to be more antisocial, unethical, and dishonest in a number of ways. The powerful tend to cheat more in games (Lammers, Stapel, and Galinsky 2010) and also cheat more on their spouses (Lammers et al. 2011). The rich tend to shoplift more frequently (Blanco et al., 2008). They are also more likely to cheat on exams, take office supplies from work, lie to customers, cut off others in traffic, accept bribes, cheat on taxes, and avoid paying fares on public transit (Piff et al. 2012; Wang and Murnighan 2014). The rich are even more likely to take candy that would otherwise go to children (Piff et al. 2012).[15] Clearly these are not the kinds of psychological traits that we want in someone making important social justice decisions.

Ken Stern (2013) points out, "Of the 50 largest individual gifts to public charities in 2012, 34 went to educational institutions . . . like Harvard, Columbia, and Berkeley, that cater to the nation's and the world's elite. Museums and arts organizations such as the Metropolitan Museum of Art received nine of these major gifts, with the remaining donations spread among medical facilities and fashionable charities like the Central Park Conservancy. Not a single one of them went to a social-service organization or to a charity that principally serves the poor and the dispossessed." A democratic system of public philanthropy has to be accountable to a much wider group of people than just the rich, and so its aims are likely to benefit from the epistemic superiority that comes from including broader perspectives—such as including poor and racialized people, or at least their representatives—in decision-making.

A further advantage of public philanthropy is that it is more adaptable than private philanthropy. Government-managed philanthropy can change direction when new needs or new evidence arises. Private philanthropy, on the other hand, is typically more rigid because the donor's intent must be respected in perpetuity, even long after the initial foundation was set up or the donor has died.

None of this is to imply that private individuals should be banned from making private donations; such acts are kindly ones and should be encouraged. The point is simply that the act should not be tax-exempt. We shouldn't rely on the rich to solve the world's problems. Far better to tax the rich and solve them ourselves. Private philanthropy abounds today because we live in an era of remarkable wealth idolatry. Consider the never-ending stream of television shows, blogs, podcasts, and social media memes admiring Bill Gates, Jeff Bezos, Elon Musk, Warren Buffett, and Steve Jobs. Such people are widely revered. Yet the problem with Netflix shows discussing, for instance, how smart Bill Gates is,[16] or memes celebrating his generosity, is not that they are wrong per se. It's that they obfuscate a more important truth, which is that a society which allows any individual to accumulate billions of dollars from the collective labor of the many is deeply unethical. Such media are distasteful because they celebrate what should be criticized. Their celebration acts as an implicit defense of that which should be rejected. They are analogous to the priests of earlier eras, singing hymns to the magnanimity of the king. The point is not that the superrich are individually evil; it's that their existence is structurally immoral. As individuals they should not be harmed, but their social position—like that of feudal kings—is incompatible with a just society and should be abolished.

The Practical Case for Imposing Limits

Let us now turn to the practical side of the issue. Would such limits work in the real world? To give the conversation more definitiveness, let us propose a specific limit of maximum income and wealth. Clearly, deciding on an appropriate limit is a very difficult question and should be subject to intense democratic deliberation. A limit that is too high will undermine the benefits that limitarianism is supposed to bring, whereas a limit that is too low risks severe economic costs (not to mention the political difficulties of appearing overly harsh). There is no perfect answer to this question. But for the sake of clarity, and to get to the heart of the matter, let's envision a maximum personal income that is ambitious but not outlandish, say, in the range of $200,000 to $400,000 per year (i.e., roughly 10 to 20 times the minimum wage),[17] and a limit of maximum personal wealth in the range of $20 million to $40 million (i.e., roughly 200 to 400 times the median wealth).[18] Let us bracket the difficulties of transition and assume that such policies are enacted with a strong popular mandate and with relatively little turbulence (perhaps by being initially imposed at significantly weaker levels, and then gradually strengthened over time, through repeated democratic mandates, in a fashion similar to the rise in taxes in Nordic countries in the mid-20th century following several decades of social democratic rule).

There is an interesting policy question as to whether it would be preferable to anchor such limits to the *median* income or the *minimum* income (i.e., the minimum wage). The advantage of using the minimum as the baseline is that it fits better with the normative vision of a community of equals. If the goal is to ensure that poor and rich live in the same community, with similar essential opportunities to flourish, then the reference point needs to be the distance between bottom and top. The advantage of using the median income, on the other hand, is that it creates pressure for elites to care about the well-being of the population in general—pushing them to be more amenable to universal policies such as public services and union rights—rather than creating pressure to raise the minimum wage alone, which impacts only 2–3% of workers. Another solution would be to anchor the maximum income to a larger pool of people at the bottom of the economic ladder than the very poorest, for instance, the average income of the bottom 33%.[19] In any case, this is an issue that must be left to future research.

Potential Market Distortions from Maximum Limits

Would a 100% marginal tax on income or wealth create troubling market distortions? Historically, we have seen successful examples of very high marginal income taxes—even in the 90% range—but one might wonder if there is a significant qualitative difference between marginal tax rates of 90% and 100%.

Materially, there is very little difference. At first glance one might suppose that a 100% marginal tax rate means that an individual is left with *nothing*, but that of course is incorrect. In the example above (footnote 17), the top rate of 100% goes into effect only at $600,000. So a person earning, say, $650,000, will still walk away with the maximum income of $400,000. Even though they are paying a 100% marginal rate on the top portion of their salary, their overall effective tax rate is significantly less than 100%. (In this case, they would be paying only a 38% effective tax rate.)

Below we will consider the two most prominent areas of economic concern: incentives and disinvestment. But beyond this, there are clearly a few industries that would face significant distortions from maximum limits.

A first area of concern is with those very particular industries, like professional sports and Hollywood, which are characterized by having extremely highly paid employees. In these cases, the maximum limits would clearly be very disruptive. Consider the case of the National Basketball Association. The average salary is currently $4.9 million, often with multiyear contracts worth dozens of millions of dollars. All of this would be rendered illegal by the adoption of maximum limits. The danger here is not really one of incentives—it is hard to believe that many athletes would quit playing basketball if they were going to get paid "only" $400,000 in order to get a regular job of, say, truck driving (the most common job for men in the United States) for $50,000. The actual danger is that the very top players would emigrate en masse to foreign leagues. Indeed, there is some empirical evidence showing that this already happens to a certain degree, as Kleven, Landais, and Saez (2013) demonstrate with regard to European soccer players.

Is this a significant problem? On the one hand, many fans would be sad to see the top players leave the league. On the other hand, it's doubtful that the actual quality of play would drop very much. After all, the difference in skill level between the very best 0.0001% athlete and merely exceptionally good 0.001% athlete is rare enough to generate huge income differentials in the bizarre marketplace of professional sports, but is actually very small in absolute terms. For the fans, the quality will remain almost as high.[20] Moreover, the reduced salaries could mean that tickets become significantly cheaper, rendering the sport as a whole more accessible to fans. In sum, we would expect the domestic sporting league to survive despite significant emigration of the top athletes. After all, the Canadian Football League has existed for many years, with a devoted fan base, despite the fact that the best players often emigrate to the more lucrative NFL. Likewise, poorer countries like Brazil and Argentina still have thriving domestic soccer leagues which provide immense pleasure to local fans, despite the fact that the all-stars invariably leave for more lucrative contracts in Europe. The bottom line is that given there is no actual shortage of talented potential employees in these areas, the emigration of the very top stars would be a sad thing for some, but not particularly damaging to the industry as a whole. So we can expect there to be some real costs here—both financially and emotionally—but ones that must be weighed against the gains in terms of democracy and meeting urgent needs. Clearly such costs are worth it.

A second potentially problematic distortion is the housing market. To see the problem here, imagine that an individual purchased a house in Vancouver or San Francisco 20 years ago. It is now worth millions of dollars. If that person now sells the house, they will receive a sudden, one-time influx of income of several million dollars. Will that be taxed at 100%? If it is, that would of course immediately freeze the housing market. What, then, should be done in cases like this?

There are good reasons for imposing high taxes on property income. As Henry George ([1879] 1910) famously pointed out long ago, the value of one's property is not primarily due to anything that the owner has done, but is largely, in most cases overwhelmingly, due to the value that the land acquires by virtue of the community that it is a part of. A completely vacant lot on the west side of Vancouver, consisting of nothing but dirt, is still worth millions of dollars. It is obviously not the dirt that has such value, but its proximity to the stability, safety, job opportunities, infrastructure, fixed capital, rights, liberties, and other goods that the community provides. And since it is the community writ large which has produced the value in the first place, it has every right to claim repayment of that value through high rates of property tax. Indeed, the normative argument from Chapter 4, based on the idea of the understructure, is really just an extension and generalization of the Georgian insight that the production of value is inherently collective.

Nevertheless, even if high property taxes are normatively attractive, we still presumably want to avoid freezing the housing market. One possibility is to use income averaging (Pizzigati 2004). In this case, if you sell a house and receive a large inflow of income, you would be permitted to average this income out over a several-year period, paying tax only on this reduced amount. Another approach would be to exempt house sales from income tax altogether, instead collecting the wealth tax, which would include housing assets. This too is an important area for future research.

The Feasibility and Cost of Maximum Limits

The major questions with respect to maximum limits are feasibility and cost. Would limits be disastrously damaging to the functioning of the economy? In considering this question, the first point to realize is that while such limits would undoubtedly impact the economy in various ways, the proportion of people directly impacted would be small. Limits at the level we are discussing would impact only the top 1% or 2% of the entire working population. Continuing with our previous example (footnote 17), a maximum wage of $400,000 (after tax) has a top maximum threshold which kicks in at $600,000. But given that the top 1% currently earns an average of $539,000 (Stebbins and Comen 2020), we can see that this top threshold would directly impact less than 1% of the total working population (though of course the thresholds at lower levels would touch many more, so much depends on how high those intermediate tax rates are). Assuming, conservatively, that the new very high taxes impact roughly 5% of the population, 95% of the workforce will not be impacted at all. Thus 95% of the population have no incentive to work less, invest less, or do anything differently than before. (In fact, the only difference for such people are positive, such as having somewhat improved infrastructure and educational opportunities from the enhanced public spending.)

Moreover, the maximum limit applies only to the portion of one's income *above* the highest threshold, so one's total effective tax is often significantly less than the maximum. We saw that an income of $650,000 implies an effective tax rate of only 38%—far, far less than the 100% maximum.[21] Furthermore, these maximums apply to *individuals* (they are limits on personal income, not corporate income), so firms could continue to grow forever, and earn billions of dollars, so long as their ownership is not overly concentrated. In other words, the limits envisioned here would not prevent giant firms from operating—the Amazons or Apples of the world—but they would prevent ownership of them from being highly concentrated in the hands of a few billionaire CEOs.

The question of feasibility has several dimensions: Is it possible to prevent wide-scale avoidance? Is it possible to prevent wide-scale emigration? Is it possible to prevent wide-scale evasion via tax havens? In Chapters 1 and 2 we reviewed the evidence pertaining to such questions. We saw that high taxes are possible, though only if they are complemented by a number of well-designed policies, such as making extensive use of third-party reporting, broadening the tax base by closing loopholes, ensuring that rates of capital income are taxed at similar rates as labor income, increasing enforcement efforts, taxing citizens' global income, imposing an exit tax, and cracking down on tax havens. Even with well-designed policies it is unlikely that limits would work perfectly; there would undoubtedly remain some leakage through avoidance and evasion, but there is no reason to think that such leaks will be so severe as to invalidate the possibility of limits working reasonably well. After all, the existing income tax in most countries is quite leaky too, but no one concludes that it is therefore infeasible or unimportant.

In terms of costs, we saw in Chapter 3 that high taxes may have a modest but not likely a major impact on work effort or business start-ups. The biggest concern is the impact that maximum limits would have on private investment and business growth.[22] To see the danger, consider a young firm with significant growth potential. In the first few years of business, the firm is very successful, so that the owner is quickly earning a total income of, say, $350,000. (Assume that the maximum income is $400,000.) Now, the owner is considering a major new investment to take production to the next level. This is risky and could end in failure, but if successful it could create millions of dollars of value, lead to many new jobs being created, and result in a new innovation rippling through the economy. The problem is that the maximum limit significantly changes the risk-to-reward ratio. If the investment requires borrowing $10 million from the bank, the owner faces significant downside (if the investment fails, they will have lost everything) but only modest upside (if the investment succeeds, they will stand to make only $50,000 more). In such a scenario it would be rational to not bother risking the investment, much to the detriment of society at large. And the problem is similarly severe in the case of the wealth limit. If the firm is capital-intensive, so that even a small firm is worth, say, $9 million, and the wealth limit is $10 million, then a successful investment would mean that even if the firm quadruples in value (to $36 million), the owner must pay back the bank $10 million (plus interest) and then the wealth tax, ending up with only $1 million more. Why would anyone take a $10 million gamble for a maximum reward of $1 million? There is thus a sharp tension between limits and the growth of new firms (particularly ones that are capital-intensive and solo-owned).

So there is a real trade-off here. We want promising firms to grow in order to benefit consumers, provide employment opportunities, enhance government revenues, and increase the overall productivity of the economy. But we also want limits in order to protect democracy and meet urgent needs. There is no simple solution. Comparing, for instance, the benefits of democracy with the costs of reduced GDP is comparing apples to oranges. One rule of thumb might be to allow firms with single owners to become "medium" size. That is important in order to demonstrate that an idea and a product are commercially viable. But it does not seem necessary, from the perspective of the economy as a whole, that any single-owner firm itself become massive (leading to a very rich CEO). Once firms are successful at a medium size, they will be copied by others, and so larger businesses with broader ownership can scale up the idea; in that way the economy can still benefit without any particular individual becoming very rich. Another possible approach would be to exempt wealth from being taxed insofar as it is tied up in business ventures. This will incentivize rich people to stash more money in the tax-exempt business, which may benefit employment and productivity (Bjørneby, Markussen, and Røed 2020); however, the evidence from the European wealth taxes suggests that this is a dangerous road to go down, as it leads to all kinds of gaming incentives. So probably a better approach would be to set a higher maximum limit but then disallow any exemptions whatsoever. In any case, we must leave as an open question how to best solve this difficult trade-off. I can only speculate that based on current economic conditions, a wealth limit of $5 million seems too constraining and too dangerous to business growth and job creation, whereas a $100 million limit seems too timid and allows too much inequality. The most sensible approach would be for a government to introduce limits cautiously, starting at a high level, and then gauge the impacts before gradually lowering the maximum limit. Once citizens have seen in real time the results of imposing limits, they will be in a better position to judge whether or not the benefits outweigh the costs.

Since we do not yet have any empirical evidence of countries imposing limits, we must be extremely cautious about making sweeping predictions of their impacts. The most relevant evidence that we do have, relating to moderate levels of tax and economic growth (canvassed in Chapter 3), suggests that redistributive taxes generally do not lead to significant reductions in economic well-being. This is because reductions in private investment can be largely offset by increased public investments. A society with maximum limits would have fewer billionaire CEOs able to gamble on risky but potentially important innovations, but it would provide more opportunity for far greater numbers of smart, ambitious people to acquire the skills and education and start-up capital to become innovators themselves.[23]

What is the best prediction of economic costs in terms of the maximum income and wealth limits envisioned here? The state-of-the-art evidence from Berg et al. (2018) suggests that redistributive taxes probably promote growth, at least until such taxes get to very high levels, at which point they probably lower it. However, the higher the taxes, the more scope for public investment, which should continue to stimulate economic growth (presumably better infrastructure and education will always be economically beneficial) even though such things may become marginally less useful at high levels. A cautious and conservative conclusion, therefore, is to expect that the limits we are discussing may well lead to moderate reductions in economic growth. Yet even this cautious conclusion requires three significant caveats.

The first is to repeat that we are discussing unchartered territory, and so we must be upfront in admitting that we do not know with a high degree of confidence whether real-world experience will be significantly better or worse than predicted. The second caveat is that a major unknown is the degree of economic sabotage unleashed by economic elites—particularly from capital flight and investment strike—which has the potential to derail any progressive project by causing severe economic costs (not to mention undermining the democratic will of the majority). Such threats do not undermine the normative attractiveness of maximum limits, but they do necessitate careful strategic reflection from any government and social movement that wishes to pursue them despite the intimidation. The final caveat is that some reduction in GDP growth need not be an entirely bad thing—it might actually be a positive thing in a climate-constrained world. In the rich countries, at least, we must confront growth fetishism head-on; we can no longer simply assume that growth is good. The real danger of reduced growth is not that GDP stays constant or even slightly falls—after all, rich countries are already sufficiently rich enough for everyone to lead good and flourishing lives. The real danger is that reduced growth leads to instability and widespread unemployment, so that poor and working-class people suffer profoundly even though they live in a rich country. Note, however, that this danger could be significantly attenuated by a society with maximum limits because there would be more government revenue to spend on economic security (e.g., ensuring public services, affordable housing, or even a basic income for all). Additionally, the downturns would likely be less severe because there would be more countercyclical public spending, as well as more redistribution, which increases aggregate demand (due to poorer people's higher marginal propensity to consume). For all these reasons, a society with maximum limits might manage just fine with lower GDP growth, while simultaneously doing its part to prevent catastrophic climate change.

Summary

Should we impose maximum limits on income and wealth? This chapter has argued in the affirmative. Distributive justice should not be concerned only with the condition of the poor, but should also be concerned with the condition of the rich. It is a real problem and serious injustice when the rich have too much. Limits to maximum income and wealth are necessary for two major reasons: to protect democracy and to enable us to meet urgent needs, such as providing basic needs to the world's poorest, providing the essential opportunities of those in the rich countries, enhancing green investment to prevent catastrophic climate change, and providing economic security to reduce xenophobia and the threat of far-right populism.

For many people, however, the major objection is not ethical but practical. And indeed, limits in the range that we have been discussing would undoubtedly impact the economy in numerous ways (though how much is uncertain given that only a small percentage of the population would directly face the higher taxes). Any substantial progressive reform such as this also risks provoking backlash and sabotage. Aside from this, the limits will be feasible only if they are introduced in conjunction with a number of complementary reforms to tighten the tax system (in order to make avoidance and evasion more difficult). The international comparative evidence surveyed in earlier chapters suggests that such reforms are entirely workable. If such maximum limits are effectively enforced, they will likely impose some costs on the economy in terms of the impacts on a few industries with very high-paid employees, and there may be more significant costs in terms of reduced incentives and particularly reduced private investment, which is the most serious concern.

How significant these costs are overall remains unclear. The evidence on taxes and growth implies that there should not be extreme costs. That said, the taxes that we have been considering are at substantially higher levels than those which the data covers, so we cannot know for sure. A sensible and cautious conclusion would be that there may well be moderate costs in terms of economic growth. Whether these costs outweigh the benefits—particularly given the overarching need for reduced growth in a climate-constrained world—remains an open question. The best approach would be for a society to enact such limits at weaker levels and then gradually enhance them in a way that is bold but not reckless, allowing the citizenry to judge for itself whether the benefits outweigh the harms. Such caution is not only safer; it is inherently more democratic, and thereby intrinsically aligned with the normative impetus of this book. To know whether, at the end of the day, the benefits of imposing maximum limits on income and wealth will exceed the costs of doing so, we must wait and see. At the levels that we have been discussing, I suspect they will.

Conclusion

Contemporary inequality is vast. I began this book by noting that eight individuals currently control the same amount of wealth as half the entire global population (Oxfam 2017). We live today in a world where, at one pole, over 700 million of our fellows—brothers, sisters, and nonbinary siblings of our human family—are struggling to survive, living on less than $1.90 per day, the World Bank's (2020) measure of extreme poverty;[1] they stand precariously upon the precipice of starvation, death by disease, homelessness, destitution, and all the evils that come in their train, such as despair, insecurity, vulnerability, and susceptibility to domination. At the other pole, there are over 2,000 billionaires. Each with far more wealth than could be spent in a hundred lifetimes—lavish vacation homes, yachts, personal jets, multiple cars, art, jewelry, every fancy toy imaginable, and the ability to guarantee immense privilege for their children, grandchildren, and beyond. Extreme wealth also constitutes extreme power as the richest individuals possess greater wealth than the GDP of medium-size countries. The superrich stride the world like giants, and the rest of us quiver in their wake. This polarization is the reality of our world and a defining issue of our age. Inequality constitutes the major fault line of the socioeconomic order in every country and across the globe. It is already one of the major battle lines of political conflict, and I predict it will become even more so throughout the century to come.

Is such inequality justifiable? No one objects to very small differences in income between people. But what happens when the differences widen? A ratio of rich to poor of 2-to-1 is one thing. But what about a society that permits income inequalities of the order of 10-to-1 or 100-to-1 or 1,000-to-1 or, as currently exists in the United States, comparing Elon Musk to his neighbor on welfare, 900,000-to-1?

There are two basic answers to such questions. On one side of the divide are those who share the dominant neoliberal perspective that, from an ethical point of view, there is no important difference between a world where the richest are twice as rich as the poorest or a million times richer. The latter is

Against Inequality. Tom Malleson, Oxford University Press. © Oxford University Press 2023.
DOI: 10.1093/oso/9780197670392.003.0009

not necessarily any less just than the former and, indeed, may even be more so (if it is more respectful of private property or just deserts). On the other side are progressives who, from socialist and feminist perspectives, see such a position as absurd. As inequality grows, so too do many social problems. As inequality becomes enormous, severe societal tensions emerge. And when the fabric of community is stretched too far between the bottom and the top, it inevitably begins to rip and tear.

There are four major justifications for inequality, two of which are practical and two of which are ethical. These are the four cornerstones, the foundation blocks on which is built the edifice of neoliberal and conservative economic thought, at least as it pertains to issues of economic distribution. The overarching aim of this book has been to scrutinize these justifications in detail.

The first and most prominent justification of inequality is that it is simply not feasible to reduce inequality through the tax system—the rich will always be able to avoid taxation through loopholes, sending their money to tax havens, or emigrating. Raising taxes, according to this argument, is like squeezing one part of a giant balloon: the money will simply move somewhere else. Nothing can be done. However, we have seen that this is simply not true. The historical and comparative evidence shows that raising taxes is indeed feasible. Moreover, we have a clear understanding of what is required to institute a more or less effective high-tax system, such as implementing extensive third-party reporting, a broad tax base with limited exemptions and loopholes—particularly to ensure that capital income is taxed at rates similar to labor income—increased enforcement efforts, including policies to tax global income, crack down on tax havens, and impose an exit tax on those wishing to expatriate.

The second argument is that even if it were possible to reduce inequality by raising taxes, doing so would create more costs than benefits, since it would prompt the rich to work less, invest less, and innovate less, resulting in slowed economic growth, unemployment, and ultimately reduced prosperity for all—including the poor. In fact, we have seen that while high taxes on the rich may lead to a minor reduction in incentives to work and moderate costs of reduced private investment, that is only half the story. Such costs are likely to be at least somewhat offset by the economic gains accruing from increased public investment. And even if there does turn out to be significant economic costs from high taxes, it is hard to believe that such costs compare to the truly enormous benefits that such taxes could bring—particularly in terms of environmental sustainability, democratic equality, equal opportunity with enhanced economic security, and reduced racism and xenophobia.

The third argument is that people (and particularly, rich people) morally deserve their income because it reflects their contribution to the economy. The truth, however, is that one's income is profoundly shaped by the arbitrary workings of the market—such as the contingent ebbs and flows of supply and demand and the political-legal shaping of the market system—which has no clear or consistent correlation with personal deservingness. Even more profoundly, one's income is largely determined by the inequalities in bargaining position and power, in particular the size and shape of the social inheritance that each of us is lucky enough to acquire by virtue of our relationship with the understructure. Indeed, we saw in Chapter 4 that 99.9% of the income that rich individuals make today cannot be attributed to their effort or skill but in fact derives from the understructure, and so is undeserved. Furthermore, the income that individuals are able to earn is inextricably interwoven with luck. Luck significantly and arbitrarily impacts everyone's abilities to do anything, including making money, advantaging some and disadvantaging others for reasons that are arbitrary from a moral point of view. Human beings have bodyminds that differ all the way down, so treating us as if we are all the same, or all compete on a level playing field, is inherently unfair. One can value deservingness or one can value fairness, but not both.

At the most foundational level, the chapters on deservingness suggest that we need to shift our most basic understandings of what human beings really are. In place of the conventional view of individuals as fully responsible and deserving, we should see the human self as a node of unchosen characteristics within a constellation of unchosen social relations, a unique and unreplicable knot tying together the myriad genetic and social threads that compose the singular history of each of our lives. As historically and socially constructed creatures, we do not create ourselves ex nihilo. We are shaped through and through by our environments, history, and social context. That does not mean that we cannot change or grow or learn new things, but it does mean that our very ability to reflect, consider, exert effort, and make choices is neither transcendental nor a level playing field with the abilities of others. Even our meta-abilities to learn, self-improve, and self-create are, like any other talent, arbitrarily distributed among us. Some of us possess more than others, and none of us can take credit for their possession. Hence those who explicitly defend personal responsibility and merit implicitly defend unfair advantage and sanctify biocultural privilege. For these reasons, we should abandon the notion of moral desert altogether. A better question is not what arbitrarily different individuals morally *deserve*, but what each of us *need* in order to lead good, flourishing lives (as well as what we can each contribute to the communities we are part of).

These chapters sought to undercut the dominant view of economic production as consisting of atomistic individuals engaged in self-interested exchange with the property they are solely responsible for. This is the insight from the metaphor of the understructure, which is meant to illustrate that we are, fundamentally, interdependent, social beings. Our very identity is constituted in relationship to others; all our abilities, actions, and opportunities are deeply dependent on the previous actions of others. Everything we do, we do on the shoulders of other people. Indeed, to live in a society is to be a beneficiary of an immense social inheritance, painstakingly built and maintained by the labor (often dominated and invisibilized) of our past and current community. We are not responsible for the understructure that we are born into, and so we cannot take credit for the immense productive powers that it bestows upon us. Hence the very idea of purely individual action is at best a myopic simplification and at worst an ideological obfuscation. The economic actor is not the independent producer, but the social individual cooperating on a vast understructure of congealed labor. We should not picture the production process via the metaphor of the self-sufficient farmer; a better image is of an individual sitting in the operating cabin at the top of a giant tower crane (which represents the understructure). This is important because once we shift our view of what an economy truly is and how production really occurs, our evaluations of the justice or injustice of existing economic distributions invariably shift as well.

The fourth and final argument, the subject of Chapter 6, is that individuals possess full and absolute rights over their private property, including the right to voluntarily exchange it (e.g., in the market for other goods or services). Such exchanges typically generate inequality, though, it is argued, of a fully justified kind. This conclusion is mistaken because property rights should actually be seen as contingent, not absolute. Property often emerges through various forms of injustice, and other people's needs can trump ownership rights. The kind of property rights that we should embrace, and the distribution of property itself, should flow from the requirements of justice, not the other way around.

* * *

A major aim of this book has been to help illuminate and clarify the distributional harms and injustices which flow from contemporary capitalism. We have seen that market systems as they currently exist in the Global North are characterized by at least four deep distributional injustices.

The first is that of class hierarchy. There are huge differences between people in terms of their initial starting place and opportunities in life due to family background, inheritance, social capital, and educational opportunities (not to mention nationality), all of which are interwoven with race and gender hierarchies. These factors mean that the wealth people end up with is, to a significant degree, a function of the class privilege passed down to them by their parents. Class hierarchy in a democratic society is a historical anachronism; it is feudalism in a business suit, with as little justification as the divine right of kings. It follows from this that a first pillar of distributive justice is to flatten the class hierarchy by dramatically limiting inheritance and establishing, as much as possible, genuine equal opportunity, so that regardless of initial family circumstance, everyone has similar access to education and opportunities to obtain desirable jobs.

So far, so familiar. What is less commonly appreciated is that *even if* capitalism were reformed to provide equal opportunity, significant injustices would still remain. The second major injustice that we have seen is that of ableism. The harm here is to that class of people who, through no fault of their own, have less bodily ability, skill, or effortability than the norm, such as the disabled, the unwell, and the elderly (though sooner or later this category encompasses all of us). Such people will typically suffer significant disadvantages in market systems because markets generally work by paying people on the basis of their productivity (though of course this will be more or less egregious depending on the extent to which the market system is regulated and essential goods are decommodified). This is inherent in the very logic of conventional market systems, which is why they are inherently ableist. A market society is one in which the lives of the people, their opulence or desperation, will be governed to a large degree by the vagaries and caprice of brute luck. It follows from this that a second pillar of distributive justice (though in many ways the primary one in terms of overall importance) is the provision of essential goods to all people on the basis of need, regardless of their personal abilities.

The third injustice is limitless wealth. Contemporary capitalism has allowed for the accumulation of stunning levels of wealth for a few lucky individuals; Piketty (2014) and others have shown that if radical changes are not instituted, such levels of wealth will likely continue to spiral out of control. Left to their own devices, market systems seem incapable of regulating the amount of inequality they produce. The problem is that a society which allows limitless wealth thereby condones limitless inequality. The harm of limitless wealth is widespread: to the poor who are unnecessarily deprived, all those who suffer from the worsening of inequality (such as the undermining of democracy, social solidarity, civic engagement, mental health, and public safety), and everyone else who would deeply benefit if the private resources held by the rich were spent on the public good—such as protecting the environment and enhancing economic security to reduce right-wing populism. This is why a third principle of distributive justice is to institute maximum limits on income and wealth.

In short, Equal Opportunity, Provision for Need, and Limits are three crucial principles of distributive justice (which is to say that they matter, but not that they are the only things that matter).

Another way to frame the issue is to ask the big-picture question: Why should one be an egalitarian? This book has provided four powerful answers. The primary ethical reason is that the differences in income and wealth that accrue between people are arbitrary from a moral point of view. Much of the differential is due to differences in power and privilege stemming from class hierarchy, and the remainder is due to personality factors which are likewise morally arbitrary, deriving as they do from a host of genetic and environmental factors that no one is responsible for. This arbitrariness means that it is deeply unfair for some to live significantly better lives than others. Combining this moral principle with the fact that all human beings are of equal moral worth, propels us toward equality. The second reason to be an egalitarian is that it is ethically wrong for the poor to suffer deprivation, particularly when society as a whole is so rich, and given that in most cases the reductions of well-being to the rich that would be caused by redistribution are so minor and inconsequential compared to the vast improvements for the poor. The third reason to be an egalitarian is that it is wrong for the rich to have so much since their wealth undermines democracy, as well as a number of other relational goods that are undermined by inequality (such as social solidarity, mental health, and reductions in crime). The final, and perhaps strongest reason to be an egalitarian is the practical one: a society with more equality would, all things considered, be an immensely better place to live. It would have only minor drawbacks (in terms of economic growth) but overwhelming benefits, especially in terms of environmental sustainability, democratic equality, equal opportunity and security, and reduced racism and xenophobia.

Of course, the three principles—Opportunity, Need, and Limits—might not always push in exactly the same direction; that is the difficulty for any realistic theory of justice which recognizes a plurality of goals: there will invariably be some messiness. Things would be much cleaner if we accepted only one supreme principle, but then we would lose much nuance and sensitivity to a wide range of issues of social concern. It seems to me that such a loss is too great a price to pay for the prize of intellectual parsimony. Nevertheless, in most instances, most of the time, these three principles all point toward the same conclusion: we should have vastly less inequality.

How might it be possible to institutionalize these three principles into a viable functioning society? This book has not attempted to sketch any kind of comprehensive vision of what a just future economy could or should look like. Nevertheless, the broad contours of such a society are, perhaps, slowly becoming visible. We can envision a viable democratic socialist society with the following elements: highly progressive income taxes, including an inheritance and wealth tax (as well as the necessary complement of regulations for enforcement and closing tax havens); maximum limits on income (perhaps in the range of $200,000 to $400,000 per year, roughly 10 to 20 times the minimum wage), as well as limits on wealth (in the range of $20 million to $40 million, roughly 200 to 400 times the median wealth); extensive public spending on entitlements for all (healthcare, day care, education, pensions, public housing, public transit, free time, etc.), as well as an income guarantee such as a basic income; guaranteed rights for all workers (at least in medium-size workplaces) to choose how many hours they work;[2] substantial numbers of well-paid public-sector jobs for the production of public goods; and significant predistributive regulations of the market to reduce inequality, such as strengthening unions. And though it has not been a major focus here, we also require new systems of ownership and control over firms in order to expand democratic accountability over the economy, perhaps through combinations of Employee Share Ownership Plans, codetermination, economic bicameralism, worker cooperatives, and consumer cooperatives (Alperovitz 2005; Ferreras 2017; Malleson 2014a; Schweickart 2011; Wright 2010).

In such a system, the principles of Need and Opportunity would be guaranteed through public spending on entitlements. And the Limit principle would be institutionalized through the 100% marginal tax rate and the wealth tax. Clearly such a system would not be perfect. There are many other aspects of social justice (such as environmental justice, racial justice, Indigenous sovereignty, and many others) that we have not attended to and that would need to be included in various ways. Nevertheless, we have good reason to believe that such a society would be economically viable, stable and a dramatic improvement in terms of equality and distributional justice.

Let us wrap up by briefly noting how the system advocated here differs from the most prominent alternatives of Rawlsianism and social democracy.

Elsewhere I have argued that there is much more common ground between Rawls's ultimate position, which he calls "property-owning democracy," and democratic socialism than either liberals or socialists typically recognize (Malleson 2014b). Rawls's (2001, 43) two major principles are, first, that "each person has the same indefeasible claim to a fully adequate scheme of equal basic liberties," and, second, that "social and economic inequalities are to satisfy two conditions. . . . [T]hey are to be attached to offices and positions open to all under conditions of fair equality of opportunity . . . [and] they are to be to the greatest benefit of the least-advantaged members of society."

At the abstract level of general principle, there is clearly much overlap. In particular, Rawls's (1971, 72–75, 100–104, 310–315) arguments about arbitrariness and against desert are, I think, very powerful (see Chapter 5). However, I go much further than Rawls in insisting that the arbitrariness of human capabilities—the moral irrelevance of the differences in our skills and aptitudes—should be taken as a central premise of egalitarianism. Rawls himself doesn't do this. Though he develops a powerful antidesert argument, he sees such arguments as offering only intuitive confirmation for his principles, which he sees as primarily deriving from the abstract thought experiments which drive his theory (which he calls the "Original Position" and the "Veil of Ignorance" [Rawls 1971]). This difference reflects a deeper methodological difference between Rawls's preference for ideal theory and my preference for thinking about justice as starting from and improving the actually existing world (so-called nonideal theory, or what Robeyns 2022 calls "problem-driven philosophy").

Probably the biggest difference between our approaches is that Rawls's work is almost entirely theoretical, with very little engagement in concrete institutional questions of what a just society would actually look like, whereas this book is based on the presumption that any convincing account of social justice must interweave normative ideals with practical possibilities—hence the deep focus in this book of institutional design, from wealth taxes to income limits.[3] In addition, I am much more concerned than Rawls was in carefully considering the ways in which other forms of injustice—such as ableism, patriarchy, colonialism, racism—constantly interact with and are co-constitutive of economic injustice. Another important divergence is that Rawls is insufficiently attentive to the existence of the superrich.[4] As mentioned in Chapter 7, operating in abstract ideal theory blinds him to the existence of the superrich in our "nonideal" world and the deep problems that their existence poses for society (in terms of monopolizing resources that are desperately needed elsewhere, undermining democracy, etc.). For such reasons he fails to adequately appreciate the importance of limitarianism for distributive justice.

The egalitarian vision outlined in this book also differs from Nordic social democracy (cf. Kenworthy 2020, 2022). Although Nordic social democracy represents a vital historical achievement and a marked improvement over the neoliberal countries, it hasn't gone nearly far enough in reducing inequality. These countries were at their most successful in reducing inequality in the 1970s and 1980s; they are less impressive today, though they still perform significantly better on this score than the Anglo-American countries.

The first limitation is that contemporary Nordic countries still possess significant class hierarchy, which allows for substantial differences in opportunities for children of the rich versus the poor. In Sweden, the top 1% own about 20% of the entire country's wealth (Piketty 2014, 345). Since 2004, billionaires do not have to pay any inheritance tax when they pass on their gigantic fortunes to their children. In contrast, 6% of households across the Nordic countries continue to live in poverty (defined as living on less than 50% of the median income [Pontusson 2011]). We also see that morally arbitrary factors (inheritance, educational achievement, talents, etc.) continue to play the predominant role in determining how people fare in society. Those who are disabled, unwell, and low-skilled earn far less money and have much less access to the essential goods required for a flourishing life than do the wealthy elites. In Sweden a welfare recipient will receive roughly $12,000 per year; at the same time, the country permits billionaires to exist (there are currently over 30). This shows that taxes are far too low and entitlements too stingy (not to mention the deep problems that the Nordic countries are facing in terms of racism, particularly toward Muslims and migrants [Widfeldt 2018]). Last, social democratic countries have no maximum limits on wealth accumulation. (They typically aim to be more sufficientarian than limitarian.) As we have seen, this is problematic not only for preventing resources from being spent on raising the floor for everyone, but also for democracy—for instance, even in Sweden, democracy has long been significantly biased in favor of the rich (Esaiasson and Holmberg 1996)—as well as other goods that are relational in nature.[5]

In terms of practical tools for reducing inequality and expanding distributive justice, Nordic countries should strongly raise their income tax rates and make them steeper; they should make more use of inheritance and wealth taxes (plus rigorous anti-evasion and anti–tax haven policies); they should institute maximum limits on income and wealth; they should expand entitlements and implement stronger time sovereignty legislation to enable workers to have more control over the number of hours they work;[6] and, importantly, they should expand democratic ownership and control over workplaces and the economy more broadly.

In sum, though Nordic social democracy continues to represent a vital beacon of what is possible, a source of optimism and hope, even inspiration, it should not be seen as the ultimate goal. Nordic social democracy is the halfway point which we are happy to reach but compelled to move beyond.

* * *

My ultimate hope with this book is to persuade the reader of two big ideas. First, for all the reasons mentioned above, substantial inequality is morally wrong: it is unjust and unfair.

The second big idea is that the benefits of reducing inequality outweigh the costs, likely by far. Practically all of the economic concerns with high taxation boil down to one thing: a worry about growth rates measured in terms of aggregate GDP. The need for never-ending economic growth is the siren song of our age, hypnotizing us into driving faster and faster though the road is narrowing and the edge of the cliff is fast approaching. My hope has been to persuade the reader that the costs of reduced growth are overblown. On the one hand, the economic costs of imposing high levels of taxation are very unlikely to be catastrophic (due to the growth-promoting potential of public spending); on the other hand, the seriousness of the ecological crisis—its existential game-changing nature—means that slowing GDP growth is not obviously a bad thing, and may in fact be a good thing (at least for the rich countries, and at least to the extent that it can be disconnected from unemployment and economic insecurity by smart redistributive policy).

Beyond this, I hope to convince the reader that the benefits of high taxes and inequality reduction are truly massive, much more significant than is commonly appreciated. We have seen a number of important, though perhaps secondary benefits, such as reducing government debt, enhancing economic stability and employment (which, after all, is the real danger of reduced growth, not reduced GDP per se), reduced social friction (more solidarity, more civic engagement, less corruption, better mental health, and less crime), and perhaps somewhat improved gender equality. On top of this, there are at least five areas of enormous benefit: meeting the urgent needs of the world's poorest, mitigating climate catastrophe, protecting democratic equality, reducing the threat of far-right populism and fascism, and expanding equal opportunity and security. Such benefits are difficult to overstate.

If I am right about the relative costs and benefits, then it follows that we should seriously consider imposing concrete limits on maximum income and wealth. Without these, society is implicitly declaring that there is no ethical limit to inequality. Imposing such limits is serious business; it may well be costly and should be done with much care and caution. But boldness is required too. After all, the scale of any proposed solutions must match the scale of the problems they are meant to rectify—and the problems of contemporary inequality are truly vast. Indeed, it is those reform proposals that are mild and moderate which are truly unrealistic and utopian—not in the sense that they could not be implemented but in the astounding belief that their mildness is any match for the scale of the problems currently facing us. One of the chief follies of our age is the stubborn conviction that minor reforms can solve major problems, as if a sinking Titanic could be bailed out by using a bucket. Radical problems require radical solutions.

The wealth of the economy is ours. No individual truly deserves more than any other, and so it should be collectively owned and shared. Though much economic wealth is currently being privately appropriated by the superrich, we should strive to take it back. Some level of inequality is inevitable because market economies require financial incentives, and different individuals should be free to make different choices in terms of how much they prefer to work, spend, and save. But while we do require a basic incentive structure and a small wage inequality ratio, we do not require the superrich. The superrich are pirates, pillaging the common wealth. We can and should abolish them. Imposing maximum limits is one way to accomplish that; it is one way to embed in our institutions and social structures the ethical truth that each of us is equally precious and has a life of equal moral worth. Such maximum limits are thus one mechanism for giving real structural form to the ethical aspiration that we human beings can live together in a true democratic community of equals.

Notes

Introduction

1. This is as of January 1, 2022 (Bloomberg 2022).
2. This is based on the median income in 2014 of $36,000 (Piketty, Saez, and Zucman 2018) and assuming a 5% return on Musk's wealth.
3. This statistic is from 2010 and is based on "surveys, adjustment for underreporting, and adjustment for hidden wealth."
4. Originally devised by the Dutch Economist Jan Pen (1971).
5. It is important to remember that this parade reflects annual income. If it reflected total wealth it would be significantly more unequal. In this case, during the first 12 minutes everyone would be less than 3.5 inches tall! By 20 minutes they are still only 1.6 feet. At 30 minutes we see the median person (representing the median household) with wealth of $121,000. By 40 minutes, people are about 12 feet tall, and by 50 minutes they are over 31 feet. The top 1% in the final 36 seconds are 503 feet tall—the height of a skyscraper. In the final four seconds we see the top 0.1%—they are about 2,000 feet tall, the equivalent of the Statue of Liberty perched on top of the Empire State Building. Elon Musk is a stunning 2,317 miles tall, meaning that from head to toe he would stretch from New York to L.A. This data comes from 2014, for individual adults over 20 years old (Piketty, Saez, and Zucman 2018); the estimate for 40 minutes is based on an approximation from the data. Data for the wealth parade is from 2020, for households (not individuals), from the Federal Reserve Survey of Consumer Finances (PK 2020).
6. Author's calculations based on data from US Census (2018b).
7. Author's calculations based on data from the Federal Reserve (PK 2020). Since this data does not record the total wealth owned by the very richest, it is likely that the Parliament of Wealth actually underestimates the share owned by the richest third.
8. This is based on the total wealth of the 2,200 billionaires of $9.1 trillion (Neate 2018), and Jefferey Sachs's (2005) estimate that eliminating global poverty would cost $175 billion per year for 20 years.
9. This is based on the combined income of Gates and Bezos at $257 billion (Collins 2019) and an assumed cost of eliminating homelessness of $10,000 each for 550,000 people (US Department of Housing and Urban Development 2018), which requires a total of 2.1% of their wealth.
10. The median adult income in the United States in 2020 was $41,535 (US Census 2021a). To get the disposable income, we reduce this figure by the effective tax rate, which for this income was roughly 25.5% (ITEP 2020). This gives us a rough estimate for median personal disposable income of $30,944. In 2020, average labor productivity

in the United States was $80.5 per worker per hour (in current US dollars) (OECD 2020b). The US public sector is funded through taxation representing roughly 26% of gross domestic product (GDP) in 2020, whereas one of the world's most generous public systems is Sweden's at 43% (OECD 2020d). This high level of taxation allows for universal day care, free primary and secondary education, free university, an excellent system of public healthcare, good pensions, extensive public transport, 16 months of parental leave, generous welfare and disability benefits, retraining programs for workers to find new work, and more. So let us imagine that a radically egalitarian society funds its public sector at the rate of 55% of GDP. This represents a 12% improvement over Sweden's level of service provision, more than double the current US spending on social services. This would be enough to fund public services at a level even better than current Swedish levels, in addition to a generous unconditional basic income (PBO 2018; Widerquist 2017). If, for the sake of simplicity, we assume that all taxation comes from a single income tax, then each worker would require an income of $69,000 pretax to end up with the basic amount of $31,000 posttax. At prevailing rates of productivity, this income requires an average of only 857 hours of work, i.e., 18 hours of work per week, or 3.6 hours per day (assuming four weeks' holiday and the same percentage of population in the labor force as currently). Furthermore, it should be noted that all this is possible with redistribution of income alone; far more would be possible with a redistribution of wealth as well.

11. Some of the most powerful answers to this question, which have been formative and inspirational for this book, include (among many others) Tawney (1952), Baker (1987), Cohen (1995), Waller (2011), Stiglitz (2012), Saez and Zucman (2019e), and Piketty (2014, 2020).

12. Philosophers use the strange word "desert" to mean "deservingness." It is pronounced *DE-sert*, in contrast to the usual pronunciation of the word *DES-ert*, meaning a sandy dry area.

13. That said, different sufficientarians envision the threshold of what counts at "sufficiency," at very different levels.

14. A similar dynamic can be seen in the international arena. In the World Trade Organization, for example, the agenda is often set by the rich states of the Global North, which are able to use their power to shape the rules of the global market in ways that further enrich themselves (Cabrera 2010).

15. The main thrust of this book is negative in the sense of critiquing the dominant justifications of inequality. If the reader leaves this work with the judgment that inequality is much less justified than they previously thought, I will be very satisfied. Readers looking for a full-blown description of an alternative political-economic system will be disappointed, as I do not develop that here so as not to distract from the main themes. Nevertheless, there is a vision of such an alternative lurking in the background, which is a democratic socialist society based on, among many other things, high levels of taxation, a highly regulated (and ecologically sustainable) market system, generous universal public services, a guarantee of economic security and free time for all, and economic democracy. Some leading lights in this regard are Wright (2010), Schweickart (2011), Schor (2010), and Gornick and Meyers (2009b). My own

efforts to develop this vision are explored in my previous book on economic democracy (Malleson 2014a).

16. Howard Zinn (1999, 47) once expressed a similar thought in these words: "Give people what they need: food, medicine, clean air, pure water, trees and grass, pleasant homes to live in, some hours of work, more hours of leisure. Don't ask who deserves it. Every human being deserves it."

17. In other words, I will argue that there are two conceptually distinct (but complementary) goals of equality. One is the "sufficientarian" goal of reducing poverty, i.e., bringing the bottom up. The rationale for this is the importance of providing everyone with sufficient material means to live a good and flourishing life. The other is the "limitarian" goal of reducing the wealth of the rich, i.e., bringing the top down. The rationale for this is maintaining a healthy democracy, as well as overall fairness. We require both.

Chapter 1

1. The minimum wage varies by US state, with the 2014 federal minimum established at $7.25 per hour. So here we take $10 per hour as a rough overall average.

2. The statutory tax rate is often referred to as the "marginal" rate—it is the rate that one must legally pay on the last dollar earned. For example, if the marginal income tax rate is 20% for the first $100,000 earned, then 40% above this, the marginal rates are what one must pay between each income bracket. In contrast, the "effective" tax rate is the total amount of tax that one pays. So if someone earned $150,000, their tax bill would be $20,000 (i.e., $100,000 taxed at the marginal rate of 20%) plus $20,000 ($50,000 taxed at the marginal rate of 40%), totaling $40,000. The effective rate would be 27% ($40,000 divided by $150,000).

3. Further evidence of this comes from Piketty (2020), who finds that combining all taxes, the United States had an effective tax rate on the very rich (top 0.01%) of between 60% and 75% from 1930 to 1960.

4. There is one partial exception to this, which is Iceland's total tax take of 50.81% of GDP in 2016, which was a one-off anomaly. (The following year its taxes were down to 37%, which was far more typical.)

5. Technically, "avoidance" refers to legal activities, whereas "evasion" refers to illegal ones. In practice, the distinction is often quite blurry, so I will for the most part use these words interchangeably. In what follows, both of these words will refer to any and all activity that has for its aim simply the reduction of tax liabilities (as opposed to real economic activity).

6. A fourth important factor is the ease with which the wealthy can make use of tax havens (such as sending their money to secret Swiss bank accounts). This is a very important issue, which we will thoroughly explore in the next chapter.

7. While differential tax rates for different kinds of income is the most pressing issue, there are other significant loopholes that also need to be closed to broaden the tax

base. In the United States, one notorious issue is known as "stepped-up basis," whereby an individual is able to avoid capital gains tax entirely if they hold on to their property until death, when it can get inherited tax-free. This loophole should be repealed immediately, so that unrealized capital gains are taxed at death (Hemel 2019). Other important loopholes in the United States that should be closed are deferrals, 1031 exchanges, and carried interest (Hemel 2019; Kamin 2015; Sarin and Summers 2019).

8. This has been done before. For instance, in Spain in the pre-1960 period, the government audited a very significant fraction (10–20%) of individual tax returns (Atkinson, Piketty, and Saez 2009, 35).

9. We should always hesitate to do anything which reinforces the use of the prison system, which in the United States, with its mass incarceration, is grotesque. The country jails a higher proportion of its citizenry than any other country in the world. Indeed, fully one-third of all Black men in their 20s are "in the system"—behind bars, on probation, or on parole (Barry 2005, 100). Moreover, treatment in the system is often inhumane, with punishments of solitary confinement rising to the level of torture (Hresko 2006). Progressives should aim to radically reduce, if not abolish, the prison system (Alexander 2010; Davis 2011). If there need to be prisons at all for deterrence or public safety reasons, then these should be of the Scandinavian variety, i.e., much more focused on rehabilitation and much less harsh and punitive (Benko 2015).

10. David Gamage (2019) sensibly suggests that government should adopt a "strict liability" penalty regime, so that relying on lawyerly tax advice or expert appraisal does not suffice to excuse the principal of the penalties.

11. The Big Four are Deloitte, Ernst & Young (EY), PricewaterhouseCoopers (PwC), and Klynveld Peat Marwick Goerdeler (KPMG).

12. For countries that impose a tax on residents' worldwide income, it is standard for them to offer reductions for taxes already paid in a different country so as to avoid double-taxation.

13. According to Piketty, Saez, and Zucman (2018), inequality in the 1980s and 1990s was driven by a boom of the labor income of the top 1%, whereas since the 2000s, it has been driven more by an upsurge in capital income. In other words, the main drivers are no longer the "supermanagers" but the capitalists and rentiers.

14. Moreover, unions play an important role in terms of economic inclusion for racialized people. Rosenfeld and Kleykamp (2012) show that the decline of unions has been an important factor in the worsening of racial pay gaps between White and Black workers.

15. In addition to union density, Koeniger, Leonardi, and Nunziata (2007) find that stricter employment protection legislation, more generous benefit replacement ratios, longer benefit duration, and a higher minimum wage are all associated with lower wage inequality. They report that changes in such institutions explain a substantial part of the changes in male wage inequality—at least as much as is explained by measures of technology or trade. They conclude that "if the regulatory flexibility of all institutions in the studied countries were changed to match that in the United States,

wage inequality would increase between . . . 50% and 80% in continental European countries" (352–353).

16. It is sometimes argued that unions make workers lazy because there is less threat of being fired. However, what appears to the employer as laziness (such as workers having rights to take breaks, sit down, go on vacation, go on parental leave) will appear to the employee as security against exploitation. True, it's a good thing for workers to feel motivated. But the negative incentives of fear (from the threat of unemployment and poverty) is not the only way to motivate people. The alternative is to motivate workers through positive incentives, for example, through higher wages, profit sharing, inclusion in decision-making and responsibility, and joint ownership. The point of unions isn't to demotivate but to force employers to rely less on negative incentives and more on positive ones (Malleson 2016).

17. As I am writing this, the news is reporting that Starbucks has summarily fired a group of workers in a Memphis location who were attempting to unionize (Lakhani 2022).

18. In Canada, private sector unionization levels have decreased over the past couple of decades, but public sector levels have actually increased.

19. Traditionally, Nordic unions have had a much greater say in the shaping of national labor policy through the use of regular, institutionalized dialogue between union representatives, employer representatives, and the government.

20. The notion of a "caring state" comes from the exemplary work of Joan Tronto (2013).

21. For arguments that CEOs really are paid what they "deserve," based on their performance, see Kaplan (2012), though compare with Bivens and Mishel (2013).

22. For such reasons, shareholders very rarely remove or discipline directors. An analysis of director elections in 2012 by Investor Shareholder Services found that 99.6 percent of the 17,081 directors nominated by management were approved (Baker, Bivens, and Schieder 2019, 10).

23. Correa and Lel (2016) conducted a large, cross-country study and found that say-on-pay laws are indeed associated with lower CEO compensation.

24. Other important tools that we do not discuss here include cutting financial markets down to size, reforming Central Banks to care more about employment, and facilitating easier immigration for high-wage jobs.

25. Even though pharmaceutical companies like Pfizer and AstraZeneca have made massive profits from the production of COVID-19 vaccines, the vast majority of the underlying research was actually paid for by public sources. For example, of all the research in the 20 years leading up to the Oxford-AstraZeneca vaccine, 97–99% of identifiable funding came from public and charitable sources (Cross et al. 2021).

26. For instance, if a renter possesses $50,000 in wealth, while a rich homeowner owns a house worth $1,000,000, and then house prices go up by 10%, the renter will still only have $50,000, while the homeowner will now have $1,100,000 in wealth. Not only this, but the increase in property values will put pressure on the renter's landlord to increase the rent, reducing the availability of affordable housing.

27. In the United Kingdom, between 1931 and 1980 real house prices increased by 66%, whereas in the shorter period of 1980–2017, they increased by 242% (Christophers

2019). Why are house prices rising in many cities? Scholars point to the combination of insufficient supply of new (particularly affordable) builds, alongside huge demand, stimulated by increased migration to cities as they become increasingly dominant engines of economic growth, state policies promoting and subsidizing homeownership (such as the US practice of allowing tax deductions on mortgage interest [Cho and Francis 2011]), as well as the widely held cultural and status-driven desire to own a home (Christophers 2019).

28. Desmond (2012) shows that rising property prices have led to a situation in which many poor families in the United States pay a shocking 80–90% of their income on rent. This then leads to widespread (racialized) evictions and the reproduction of urban poverty.

29. For example, in Toronto, real estate investors have bought 39% of recently completed homes (Punwasi 2022).

30. It has been estimated that fully one-third of the mansions on the prestigious Bishops Avenue in north London are sitting vacant (Booth 2014).

31. It is important to point out that during its heyday, from 1934 to 1962, 98% of the $120 billion from the Federal Housing Administration and the Veterans Administration went to White people (Lipsitz 1998, 6), one of the many examples of White-based affirmative action throughout US history (Katznelson 2005).

32. Keeanga-Yamahtta Taylor (2018) points out that the 2008 housing crisis wiped out decades of financial gains of Black people. By 2014 more than 240,000 Black Americans had lost their homes. This greatly exacerbated inequality: before the crash the median White family had eight times the wealth of the median Black family; by 2013 the figure had risen to eleven times.

33. In the mid-1960s, the Swedish Social Democratic Party launched a program to build one million affordable homes in 10 years. This was an extremely ambitious program, given that at the beginning of the launch the entire population of the country was only eight million. Though not without its problems, the program did successfully meet its target, building 1,006,000 homes in a decade.

34. In most OECD countries fathers devote fewer than one-quarter of the hours devoted by their female counterparts to routine housework, and less than half to caregiving (Gornick and Meyers 2009b, 10).

35. Another important mechanism is that of Universal Basic Services (Portes, Reed, and Percy 2017). Universal Basic Income and Universal Basic Services have different strengths and weaknesses; for a careful comparison, see Malleson and Calnitsky (2021). Our analysis shows that for a Basic Income to be attractive, it must *complement* extensive public services, not replace them.

36. Calnitsky and Gonalons-Pons (2021) find a significant negative relationship between Basic Income and property crime. They also provide fascinating evidence suggesting that Basic Income can reduce domestic violence (Gonalons-Pons and Calnitsky 2021).

37. Another major obstacle is conservative beliefs about "undeserving people," which we discuss in depth in Chapters 4 and 5.

38. On the right, conservatives appreciate what they see as the expansion of self-reliance and workers' capitalism; on the left, progressives appreciate the sharing of wealth and the expansion of economic democracy (Mackin, forthcoming).

39. Jeremy Corbyn proposed giving workers 33% of board seats. Elizabeth Warren's Accountable Capitalism Act proposed that workers elect 40% of the board, while Bernie Sanders's Corporate Accountability and Democracy Act proposed that workers elect 45%.

40. Vitols (2021) finds that companies with board-level employee representation do indeed have a higher effective tax rate than companies without workers on the board.

41. I am aware of only one study that investigates whether codetermination impacts inequality across society as a whole (controlling for other factors, such as union power). This is a working paper (not a peer-reviewed article) from Hörisch (2012), who finds a strong equalizing effect of codetermination on the distribution of income, independent of union power.

42. Even in German firms larger than 2,000 workers, there is only "quasi-parity": workers get half the seats, but in case of a tie, the deciding vote is cast by shareholders, which enables them to retain their dominance. The one exception to this is firms in the mining, coal, and steel industries with more than 1,000 employees. These have genuine parity and shareholders do not have a tiebreaking vote (Jäger, Noy, and Schoefer 2021, 861). Moreover, it's important to recall that wages are typically *not* subject to bargaining by employee representatives in codetermined firms; this bargaining occurs elsewhere in other institutions (in particular, the trade unions at the industry level), which partially explains the low impact of codetermination on inequality (Gorton and Schmid 2004).

43. Although an inspiring model in many ways, Mondragon has struggled in the past couple of decades to retain its democratic character due to challenges from globalization and the acquisition of large competitors, which has led to a majority of its total workforce becoming conventional employees, not cooperative members (Malleson 2013; Whyte and Whyte 1988).

44. Democratic theorists have long pointed out the tension, if not outright contradiction, when Western societies conceive of themselves as "democratic"—insisting that the exercise of public power requires public accountability—and yet, although there are obvious power relations in the workplace, and the economy more generally, such societies do not have workplace or economic democracy (Dahl 1985; Malleson 2014a).

45. The number of worker co-ops comes from Prushinskaya (2020), and the number of total employing businesses comes from the Small Business & Entrepreneurship Council (SBECouncil 2018).

Chapter 2

1. Assuming a modest 5% return on his wealth of $160 billion (Au-Yeung 2018).

2. This is the major reason why relying on reforming income taxes—such as new and improved capital gains tax, which some authors prefer to a wealth tax (e.g., Adam and Miller 2021)—is fundamentally misguided. True, other taxes can be important and effective (and indeed superior) to wealth taxes at raising revenues. But only a wealth tax can deal with extreme inequality by aiming squarely at the stock of the accumulated wealth of the superrich.

3. The total burden of income and wealth tax from a Spanish resident cannot exceed 60 percent of their total taxable income (Chamberlain 2021, 605).

4. In the United States, the debate over the wealth tax also involves the issue of its constitutionality (Gamage 2019; Johnsen and Dellinger 2018).

5. Indeed, we know this to be the case. See page 78.

6. Expensive art and jewelry are often insured, so one possibility here is for the government to seek records from insurance companies to gauge value.

7. Valuing direct contribution pensions is generally quite straightforward, whereas valuing direct benefit pensions is trickier. See Saez and Zucman (2019b), Chamberlain (2020), and Daly, Hughson, and Loutzenhiser (2021) for discussion of how this could best be done.

8. The first five studies, with larger estimates of avoidance, all use a methodological approach called "difference-in-differences," whereas the three latter studies, with smaller estimates of avoidance, use a methodology called "bunching." See Advani and Tarrant (2021) for a discussion of the pros and cons of each.

9. While there is no third-party reporting in Switzerland, there is a 35% federal withholding tax which is applied to income from financial assets (mainly interest and dividends). These withheld payments are returned once tax reports, accompanied by bank statements, are submitted, thus providing some incentive for honest tax reporting.

10. In their study, Troup, Barnett, and Bullock (2020, 4) argue that based on their experience with UK tax authorities, compliance with a wealth tax is likely to be "broadly consistent with other taxes on capital and a tax gap of the same order of magnitude (i.e. around 10%)."

11. One possible solution from Gamage (2019) is that young businesses which are not yet profitable could be forced to pay the wealth tax but offered the option of spreading their tax payments over a period of years so as not to discourage investment and growth.

12. By "strong evasion" the authors are assuming that the tax base of real estate is reduced by 20%, financial assets by 48%, directly held companies by 26%, and other assets by 100% (Kapeller, Leitch, and Wildauer 2021, 18). Note that this is significantly more evasion than is predicted by the state-of-the-art prediction of 7–17% from Advani and Tarrant (2021).

13. For debate on the feasibility of recent American wealth tax proposals, see Summers and Sarin (2019) and Saez and Zucman (2019d).

14. In 2012, four scholars attempted to create anonymous companies through 3,700 incorporation agents all over the world. In roughly one quarter of the cases, they were

able to do so without providing any identification document whatsoever (Zucman 2015, 28).

15. According to Angel Gurría, secretary-general of the OECD, "developing countries are estimated to lose to tax havens almost three times what they get from developed countries in aid" (quoted in Dietsch 2015, 51).

16. For example, in 2014 the Central Bank of Iran was able to dodge US sanctions via a financial institution in Luxembourg, enabling Iran to hold $2 billion in US securities. It was able to do this because there was no requirement to register beneficial ownership for owners of listed companies and investment funds (TJN 2022).

17. The biggest criticism of the FATCA is that it creates administrative burdens on many law-abiding US taxpayers and financial institutions. So there is a risk that foreign banks may prefer not to deal with Americans so as to avoid FATCA regulations (Zucman 2015). Another significant problem is that the FATCA doesn't require the United States to exchange beneficial ownership information with other countries. (Thanks to Andres Knobel for pointing this out to me.)

18. One issue is that the OECD currently insists that the exchanges be fully reciprocal, so in order for a poor country in Africa to receive any information, it must also supply it. But that seems unreasonable. Certain African countries may not have the administrative capacity to provide information, but they should still be given the information from richer countries. After all, elites in poor African countries are a major source of tax fraud, whereas very few rich Europeans or Americans are hiding their money in Africa. So although ideally every country should participate reciprocally, the OECD should allow poor countries to receive unilateral information even if they are not yet able to provide it.

19. For years, the Tax Justice Network has been making the important point that to the extent that there is international coordination on tax policies, such coordination happens through the OECD, which is essentially a club for rich countries. The UN would be a better, and more democratic, forum for global tax discussions (e.g., Cobham 2020).

20. Such proposals are far more convincing in the case of democratic governments. For nondemocratic, authoritarian governments, there are good reasons why citizens might be very wary of their governments having full access to their financial information—such as which NGO or political party they donate to.

21. One of the most egregious ways this happens is when governments allow select corporations (usually in secret) to pay less tax than the law mandates. For example, the LuxLeaks scandal showed that Luxembourg occasionally signed confidential agreements with private companies, allowing them to avoid taxation (Piketty 2020). This is essentially government for sale.

22. Another common method of avoiding taxes is "thin capitalization," whereby a firm acquires finance through debt instead of equity. In other words, instead of issuing shares, a high-profit subsidiary takes a loan from a different subsidiary in a low-tax jurisdiction. The high-profit subsidiary can then write off the interest payments on the loan from its tax bill; the other subsidiary must pay taxes on the interest earned, but since it's located in a low-tax jurisdiction it can avoid this as well (Dietsch 2015, 41).

23. Another possibility is Avi-Yonah's (2016) proposal for countries to impose their normal rate of corporate tax on the *entire profit* of all the multinationals that are headquartered within the country (including the profit of all the subsidiaries that are managed and controlled by such firms). This would then be balanced with tax credits for multinationals that have already paid taxes to foreign jurisdictions, up to the level of tax in the residence jurisdiction.

24. Indeed, if the G20 were to agree to such a system, that would represent 80–90% of the global economy, more than enough to profoundly diminish tax havens. The primary arguments against formulary apportionment are that different countries would inevitably adopt inconsistent formulas, leading to double taxation, and that it would involve undue administrative capacity (Durst 2016). Yet these problems seem possible to overcome. Having similar formulas is important, but given that countries will remain free to impose any level of tax they want—which, after all, is the crucial issue for tax sovereignty—it seems perfectly conceivable that they could agree to use similar formulas. Administrative capacity seems unlikely to be a huge problem either, particularly for the rich countries, as evidenced by the experience of the United States and Canada, especially if the formula is relatively straightforward and easy to calculate. Moreover, given that most states have a lot to gain from implementing such a system, it is hard to believe that if they really wanted to, they could not find the capacity to impose such a tax.

25. An increasing bulk of economic activity nowadays—from restaurants to healthcare—provide inherently localized services and so are not threatened by global mobility or a race to the bottom. Locally oriented economic activity is already estimated to represent 60% of the US economy—and this is continually growing. In the words of Paul Krugman, "although we talk a lot these days about globalization, about a world grown small, when you look at the economies of modern cities what you see is a process of localization: A steadily rising share of the work force produces services that are sold only within that same metropolitan area" (quoted in Alperovitz 2005, 126). Nontradable economic activity is estimated to represent 70% or more of the US economy (Lombardo and Ravenna 2012, 560). Though this is smaller for smaller countries. Lombardo and Ravenna calculate the size of the nontradability sector using a few different measurements and give estimates for the OECD ranging from 34% to 56% (560).

26. The OECD states, "There is a consensus in the literature about the main factors affecting (foreign) investment location decisions. The most important ones are market size and real income levels, skill levels in the host economy, the availability of infrastructure and other resource that facilitates efficient specialisation of production, trade policies, and political and macroeconomic stability of the host country. . . . [Tax incentives] play only a limited role" (quoted in Shaxson and Christensen 2016, 281).

27. Bjørneby, Markussen, and Røed (2020) find that the Norwegian wealth tax actually increases employment because it encourages the rich to shift their wealth out of unproductive assets (such as multiple houses) into businesses (because those are taxed less).

28. Although the agreement represents a watershed moment, tax justice advocates have argued that there is still much room for improvement: arguably the level of 15% is too low (as Figure 2.2 shows, 15% is significantly less than OECD countries typically levy now, even after decades of decline), the distribution of tax revenues is unfair (privileging the rich countries at the expense of the poor), and it's insufficient to apply formulary apportionment only to a small portion of total corporate profits (Cobham 2021).

29. Though it should be pointed out that even in the 1970s the Swedish inheritance tax was by no means an unmitigated success. Henrekson and Waldenström (2016) show that the inheritance tax typically collected only 0.1% of national income. They are thus quite skeptical about whether the tax was particularly effective at reducing inequality.

30. Consider a family business worth a couple million dollars. If the parents wish to pass on this wealth, their choice is to pass the whole business on to the children, in which case the children would have to pay a significant amount of tax. Alternatively, the parents could choose to spread the ownership of the business more broadly (perhaps including the long-term workers as well as the children). That would reduce the total taxes that need to be paid. Such an outcome would also be a positive thing from the perspective of inequality (and may well be beneficial in terms of productivity too, as we discuss in the next chapter).

Chapter 3

1. To take one example, consider the case of Kati Kariko, the scientist who developed much of the mRNA technology underlying the Pfizer and Moderna COVID-19 vaccines. She worked long hours at the University of Pennsylvania for 40 years, loving being in the laboratory, even though she never earned more than $60,000 a year (Kolata 2021).

2. Though of course this doesn't apply to those whose primary motivation is being the richest, not only among their neighbors, but in the whole world.

3. Slemrod's (2001) "hierarchy" is the idea that economic actors respond to taxation in different ways: they are most responsive in terms of the *timing* of their activities; somewhat less responsive in terms of *avoidance* issues; and are least responsive in terms of *real* changes to economic activity (such as actually working less).

4. It is worthwhile to reflect on the fact that one of the most innovative societies in all human history—ancient Athens—was strikingly egalitarian (Patriquin 2015). Many societies have had slaves and many societies have been imperial centers without coming close to Athens in its fantastic productivity: in drama (Aeschylus, Sophocles, Euripides), comedy (Aristophanes), politics (Pericles), sculpture (the Olympia Master and Phidias), poetry (Demosthenes and Simonides), history (Thucydides and Herodotus), philosophy (Protagoras, Socrates, Plato, Aristotle), science and math (Aristotle, Democritus), medicine (Hippocrates)—all of which occurred within a relatively short time span of just 100 years in a city of only a couple hundred

thousand people, a mere town by today's standards. What made Athens different was not slavery or imperialism per se; its distinctness lay in the fact that no other ancient society of its size had such radically democratic egalitarianism among male citizens. When society was based on egalitarianism, we saw one of the most brilliant blossomings of human genius the world has ever known. It is, of course, possible that this was entirely coincidental. But it is also a possibility—and an intriguing one—that egalitarianism itself was a driving force in the cultural flourishing (cf. Finley 1973; Patriquin 2015).

5. It's also worth pointing out that high taxes may induce people to shift careers, and this may well bring social benefits if the old high-paying careers involved negative externalities. For instance, many of the brightest young minds today are attracted to the financial world because of the extreme rewards; they spend much of their time refining fancy econometric models for the purpose of enriching a small number of speculators (often at the expense of other people). In 2007, almost 50% of Harvard seniors took jobs on Wall Street (compared to only 8.8% who engaged in some form of public service [Binder 2014]). High taxes may well induce bright students to do more useful things with their talents.

6. In their sample of advanced economies, the authors find that a 1 percentage point increase of GDP in investment spending raises the level of output by about 0.4% in the same year and by 1.5% four years after the increase (Abiad et al. 2014).

7. Mokyr (2017) argues that what launched capitalism—the fundamental reason why Europe's economic production exploded several centuries ago, instead of China's, even though the latter was more technologically advanced in many ways—was the expansion of knowledge through the growing scientific networks of what he calls the "republic of letters." The growth in scientific knowledge and technical know-how was key.

8. For more evidence, consider Mani et al.'s (2013) study of poor sugar cane farmers in India. (Since their income is largely tied to the harvest, these farmers annually go through cycles of more and less poverty and insecurity, providing a clear case study.) The authors tested the cognitive abilities of the farmers at different times of the year and found that poverty reduces cognitive ability: being poor means being constantly worried and anxious, which leaves one with fewer mental resources for other tasks. They concluded that "the poor are less capable not because of inherent traits, but because the very context of poverty imposes [a] load and impedes cognitive capacity" (980). The size of the effect is equivalent to three-quarters of the size of losing a full night of sleep, or roughly 13 IQ points.

9. Supportive evidence for this comes from Gareth Olds (2016), who finds that the expansion of food stamps in the United States significantly increased entrepreneurship. It appears that simply knowing that they could fall back on food stamps if their venture failed was enough to make many individuals take the risk of starting new businesses (see also Frick 2015).

10. The top 10% in the United States control over 80% of all financial assets (Blasi and Kruse 2012, 4).

11. This section draws heavily from Malleson (2014a).

12. In order to undermine Allende's regime, President Nixon instructed his policymakers to "make the [Chilean] economy scream" (Navia and Osorio 2017, 1).

13. For a good analysis of the Venezuelan economy during the Chavez years, see Weisbrot, Ray, and Sandoval (2009). Although these actions came close to toppling the government, Chavez was eventually able to renationalize oil, implement capital controls, and reassure private businesses that they would not be expropriated, resulting in a return to stability and substantial economic growth in the subsequent five years.

14. The idea is that controls allow a government to engage in expansionary policy—in particular, lowering interest rates to stimulate borrowing and investment—in order to increase employment. Without controls, lowering interest rates in a time of panic is likely to lead to even more money fleeing the country in search of better returns elsewhere.

15. For the former, see Edwards (1999), Forbes (2007), Prasad et al. (2003); for the latter, see Krugman (2009), Ostry et al. (2010), Prasad, Rajan, and Subramanian (2007), Reinhart and Rogoff (2009).

16. And this is even more true for the superrich: the richest 20 individuals emit 8,000 times more carbon than the billion poorest people (Oxfam 2022).

17. This is why GDP is such a problematic measure for our societies to rely on. Since it is completely unclear whether an increase in GDP is, at the end of the day, a good or bad thing overall, it is neither a useful measuring stick nor a rational target. In a certain sense a McDonald's hamburger is "good" for health (it provides calories and prevents starvation), yet in many other senses it is clearly deleterious (it is high in fat, sugar, and sodium and not particularly nutritious); surely it would be insanity to measure an individual's overall health by counting the "number of burgers eaten"—yet that is precisely what GDP does vis-à-vis the health of our economy. A better measure of economic prosperity would take into account environmental (and other) factors, such as some sort of Genuine Progress Indicator (Stiglitz, Sen, and Fitoussi 2009).

18. This is especially true when emissions are measured with reference to consumption as opposed to production (since rich countries have significantly offshored their production [Knight and Schor 2014]). In their study in 1990–2012, which accounts for business cycle effects and also takes into account consumption based on international trade, Cohen et al. (2017) find that almost no country (with the exception of Germany) has been able to decouple greenhouse gasses from GDP over time.

19. See "Year-on-Year Change in Global CO_2 Emissions" in Ritchie and Roser (2020). The data goes to 2019; I have added 2020 to account for the recent downturn associated with COVID-19.

20. See footnote 10 in the introduction.

21. An additional plausible mechanism is that inequality may impact who participates. Inequality could plausibly discourage the poor from participating (though of course, it might just as well have the opposite effect).

22. For instance, Kenworthy (2022) shows that the correlation between economic inequality and the influence of the rich is far from perfect, pointing to examples such as California between 1979 and 2015, when inequality worsened but the political influence of the rich did not obviously increase. However, no one claims that there must

be a perfect correlation between these things, such that every time the Gini coefficient increases 1 point there must be a perfectly corresponding increase in influence of the rich. The world is far too complex for that. The real claim is that, in general and over time, as inequality worsens, the power of the rich over the political system will tend to increase.

23. In 2020, 55 large US corporations paid nothing in federal corporate income taxes, yet those same companies spent $450 million on lobbying and political contributions in recent years (Fonger 2021). Is it likely that these two facts are unrelated? Kenworthy (2022, 101) doubts that "campaign contributions and lobbying influence policy outcomes." But if this were true, then we must believe that these companies are simply acting irrationally and spending huge amounts of money for no reason at all, which is hard to believe.

24. Classic works on the tension between private control of investment and democracy include Block (1977), Lindblom (1982), and Cohen and Rogers (1983).

25. This is based on a rough annual income for Musk of $13.5 billion (i.e., a 5% return on his wealth), an average Norwegian income of $56,705, and a workforce of approximately 2,834,618 (the last two figures are from 2019 from the OECD (2021) and the World Bank (2022), respectively).

26. For hundreds of years, from roughly the time of Aristotle to Montesquieu (in the 18th century), political philosophers in the West took it as an obvious empirical fact about political life that electoral democracy was inherently biased toward the rich (Manin 1997). Aristotle (1998, bk. 4, ch. 9) was simply reiterating the common wisdom when he said, "The appointment of magistrates by lot is thought to be democratic, and the election of them oligarchic."

27. Andersen's (2012) study of 35 contemporary democratic countries finds that places with lower levels of income inequality tend to have higher levels of support for democracy (and vice versa).

28. For these reasons a number of scholars have argued that sortition—i.e., a legislature by lot—has the potential to actually be more democratic than conventional elections (Gastil and Wright 2019; Malleson 2018; Manin 1997).

29. While this is well-known for income taxes, an interesting recent study from Norway finds that the wealth tax can also increase equality of opportunity: children of wealthy parents ended up with a labor income that is closer to that of their nonwealthy peers than would otherwise have happened (Berg and Hebous 2021).

30. In the United States, more than half of the sons raised by a father in the top decile fall no further than the eighth decile, whereas roughly half of those raised by bottom-decile fathers rise no further than the third decile (Corak 2013). In other words, in the contemporary inegalitarian United States, there is a relatively rigid class hierarchy: rich families typically stay rich, and poor families stay poor.

31. In their fascinating study, Siddiqi et al. (2012) examine the educational outcomes of 119,814 students, 5,126 schools, and 24 countries. They find that "not only is income inequality a significant determinant of ARL [adolescent reading literacy] scores, but direct spending on education and overall national economic prosperity are not" (11).

32. Of course, it may be that the direction of causality runs the other way (whereby more solidarity creates the social basis for increased taxation and reduced inequality) or, as the authors suggest, runs in both directions simultaneously.

33. Layte (2012) tested whether poorer mental health could be due to more public spending as opposed to worse inequality. He found no support for explanations involving public spending, but did find support for the "psychosocial hypothesis": more equal countries seem to have better mental health at least partly because their populations are less anxious about status and are more involved in social networks that involve reciprocity, trust, and cooperation. (Along similar lines, see Wilkinson and Picket 2018.)

34. In terms of happiness, the cross-sectional evidence is very mixed (Ngamaba, Panagioti, and Armitage 2018). For trust, the cross-sectional evidence does typically find a clear association with inequality (Gustavsson and Jordahl 2008; Stephany 2017); however, the longitudinal results are much more ambiguous (Fairbrother and Martin 2013; Hastings 2018; Kenworthy, 2016). Likewise for health measures such as life expectancy: whereas the cross-sectional evidence is strong (Wilkinson and Pickett 2006, 2010), the longitudinal evidence is weak (Hill and Jorgenson 2018; Kenworthy, 2016). As mentioned above, however, the evidence that inequality is detrimental to mental health seems to be more robust.

Chapter 4

1. The quote from Rhodes appears in Milanovic (2008, 1); the remark about Obama is in Sandel (2020, 23).

2. As of 2020, there are currently about 80 Indigenous communities with boil water advisories.

3. According to the RCMP (2014), there were 1,181 missing and murdered Indigenous women, girls, and two-spirit people between 1980 and 2012.

4. The evidence that Black people in the United States face significantly reduced opportunities compared to their White counterparts is extensive and well-known. To take just a couple of examples: Black people are incarcerated at higher rates for the same crime (Alexander 2010); Black teens are 21 times more likely than White teens to be killed by police (Vitale 2018); Black people are discriminated against in the labor market (Bertrand and Mullainathan 2004); Black students are suspended from school and disciplined at higher rates than White students for the same infraction (GAO 2018).

5. Another major inequality in opportunity is that many individuals living with a disability lack sufficient accommodations to enter the workforce at par with others. Subsequently they have much higher unemployment rates and much lower incomes (Kraus et al. 2018).

6. Tuition is roughly $35,000 to $40,000 and room and board is another $10,000 to $15,000 for a typical four-year degree.

7. At Yale and Princeton, only 2% of students come from poor families (i.e., the bottom 20%). Things are somewhat better at Harvard and Stanford, which offer free tuition, room, and board to any student whose family makes less than $65,000 (Sandel 2020, 167).

8. Compare this evidence with Mankiw's (2013, 26) astonishing claim that "the educational and career opportunities available to children of the top 1 percent are, I believe, not very different from those available to the middle class."

9. Dworkin (1981a, 1981b) famously distinguished between "brute" and "option" luck. In the next chapter I will reject this distinction on the grounds that all luck is, in actual fact, ultimately attributable to brute luck. See note 16.

10. As Hobbes ([1651] 2002, XIII, 9) famously said, without a state there is "no place for industry, because the fruit thereof is uncertain."

11. To take just one example, recall how important the legal invention of limited liability was for the successful growth of modern corporations (Bowman 1996).

12. The idea that the state is a "silent partner" of every business comes from Edmund James (Fried 1995).

13. Charles Taylor (1989, 39) once pointed out that our very ability to have an identity at all is dependent on being embedded in "webs of interlocution."

14. That said, this view is not unanimous. For instance, Jorgenson, Ho, and Samuels (2014) have argued that the bulk of economic growth is due not to knowledge innovation per se but to the replication of established technologies through the growth of capital and labor inputs. Nevertheless, these authors would not dissent from the view that knowledge accumulation is a major source of economic growth.

15. Isaac Newton once said, "If I have seen further it is by standing on the shoulders of giants." Likewise, Albert Einstein remarked, "[M]any times a day I realize how much my outer and inner life is built upon the labors of my fellow men [and women], both living and dead" (quoted in Calaprice 2011, 14).

16. For example, in 2018, 58% of Canadian adults (age 25–64) had completed a tertiary degree—the highest proportion in the world. In South Africa, by contrast, the rate was only 7% (OECD 2019a).

17. In a related vein, Nina Banks (2020) powerfully describes the care infrastructure of nonmarket (unpaid) collective work that has often been performed by Black women in their communities.

18. Thanks to Chi Kwok for highlighting this point for me.

19. It is not much of an exaggeration to say that capitalism exists today because it found a way to access the energy created over a period of 60,000,000 years, and burn it in a mere 200.

20. Based on an assumption that in a day a person carries 15 pounds for 3 hours at 3.5 miles per hour.

21. This figure is calculated from the OECD's 2017 calculation of the Indian-to-US PPP of 17.813 and a figure of average monthly farming income of Rs 6,223 (Raghavan 2017). Purchasing power parity is a way of comparing prices from different countries by using the prices of specific baskets of goods to compare the absolute purchasing power of different countries' currencies. In other words, PPP takes into account the

differing prices of basic commodities in order to provide a reasonable comparison of costs across countries.

22. Amartya Sen (1982) once made the same point about barbers.

23. This is based on a calculation of total financial wealth (stocks, bonds, pensions, life insurance, etc.) of $55.6 trillion, divided by the 127 million workers in private industry (Roemer 2020, 27).

24. This is a rough calculation based on total financial wealth of 262.11 trillion rupees, converted by the OECD's PPP ratio for India in 2019 of 18.381, then divided by the nonstate workforce of approximately 470 million (Statista 2020).

25. A related debate in the literature is whether in contemporary conditions of complex production it is possible to separate the strands of one individual's contribution from everyone else's. For the perspective that it is, see Moriarty (2003). For the perspective that it is not, see Sen (1982) and Stiglitz (2012).

26. These figures are rough estimates. In Canada, public spending per student on primary education is CAN$10,758 and $11,489 for secondary education. So the above figure comes from multiplying an approximate figure of $11,000 for 13 years of education (kindergarten through grade 12 [StatisticsCanada 2012, 16]). The Canadian figures are then adjusted to USD PPP using the OECD's 2012 ratio of 1.245. In Ghana the government spends US$215 per student for secondary education (Omojuwa 2012), so the total was estimated by multiplying this figure by 13 years.

27. Although many people in the Global South presumably desire to migrate to richer countries, few are able to actually do so. In 2015, 85 million people migrated from the Global South to the Global North, which represents only 1.5% of the population of the Global South (Kingsley 2016).

28. This is based on the daily 2019 median income of $7.15, measured in 2011 USD PPP (Hill et al. 2021).

29. Although hunter-gatherer societies were very poor in material terms, they had all kinds of accumulated knowledge, often including incredible expertise about their land and animal behaviors. Moreover, they were not necessarily unfree or unhappy (Scott 2017). Indeed, in terms of their leisure time, some anthropologists believe they were the first affluent societies (Sahlins 2005).

30. The median income is from the US Census (2021b). Average household income of the top 1% comes from Khimm (2011). To convert household income into individual income I apply the ratio of individual-to-household income ($26,588:$50,045 or 1:1.88) that existed in 2011 according to the US Census Bureau.

31. Miller recognizes that the income of a nobleman in the Ancien Régime, or that of a person today who inherits a fortune, is not deserved. But he can offer no good or principled reason for why *those* circumstances undermine desert but other situations of circumstantial luck—like that of Sam and Sami—do not.

32. For his work on the national scope of justice, see Miller (2000, 2007). For important commentary on this work, see Bell and de-Shalit (2003).

33. This ranges from 12.5% for Japan to 83% for Ireland (OECD 2011). So does Miller therefore believe that the Japanese deserve their income but the Irish do not (because

a sufficiently large percentage of their economy is open to global competition and so subject to my objection)?

34. An early version of this argument comes from Henry Sidgwick ([1907] 1999). For a contemporary version, see Olsaretti (2004).

35. Daniel Attas's (2003, 93) critique of Miller along these lines is apposite: "A restriction of the theory [of marginalist notions of desert] to 'perfect competitive markets' makes it entirely irrelevant to real issues of distributive justice."

Chapter 5

1. The epigraph from Boutmy is quoted in Piketty (2020, 711); the second epigraph is from Piketty (2014, 241); the third epigraph is from Rawls (1971, 104).

2. To be fair to Piketty, his most recent book, the brilliant and ambitious *Capital and Ideology* (2020), is far less meritocratic. Indeed, he is scathing of attempts to use the rhetoric of "merit" as an ideological defense of inequality given the reality of pervasive and deep inequalities in life opportunities. Nevertheless, he still appears to believe that if there really were a level playing field, then meritocracy would be justified.

3. For instance, recall Howard Zinn's lovely invocation to provide people with what they need on the basis of their humanity (see the introduction, footnote 16).

4. Notice how central ideas of deservingness are in that paradigmatic socialist song "Solidarity Forever": "It is we who plowed the prairies / Built the cities where they trade / Dug the mines and built the workshops / Endless miles of railroad laid / Now we stand outcast and starving / Mid the wonders we have made / But the union makes us strong. . . . They have taken untold millions / That they never toiled to earn / But without our brain and muscle / Not a single wheel can turn / We can break their haughty power / Gain our freedom when we learn / That the union makes us strong."

5. The line of thought developed in this chapter shares with luck egalitarianism the belief that inequalities stemming from brute luck are unacceptable, but it diverges from the luck egalitarian belief that inequalities stemming from "choice" are acceptable, since choice-making ability is itself always interwoven with luck (Malleson 2022).

6. For arguments along similar lines, though more focused on questions of free will and moral responsibility rather than economic desert, see Pereboom (2014), Levy (2011), and in particular Waller (2011, 2020), to whose wonderful work I am particularly indebted. I am among the growing ranks of free will skeptics who hold that the conventional beliefs of free will and moral responsibility are no longer appropriate for a scientific and secular age. Yet given the depth at which such ideas are sunk into the foundations of the culture, no changes are likely to be made easily or quickly; nevertheless, I hope that this chapter can serve in some small way to enhance the efforts of all those attempting to challenge some of the oldest dogmas of Western culture.

7. Note that the issue of material luck has been bracketed to enable us to see clearly the issue of luck-based differences in *mental resources*. I assume that differences of this kind are inevitable in any and every society, even a future egalitarian one. The point,

of course, is that although mental resources are distributed arbitrarily within a population, they can significantly impact one's life prospects.

8. In the United States, individuals living with a disability earn, on average, $22,047 (Kraus et al. 2018). We can assume earnings would be somewhat higher in the social democratic society that we are envisioning.

9. In a future society we can hope that many common impairments would not translate into severe disabilities, because society would become much more efficacious at providing myriad accommodations. Nevertheless, I assume that any plausible future society will still be one in which various impairments still act to disadvantage certain individuals compared to others.

10. For discussion of effort as a desert basis, see Sadurski (1985), Milne (1986), Sher (1987, 2003), Lamont (1995), Roemer (1998, 2003), Olsaretti (2004), Alm (2011), and Malleson (2019).

11. Self-efficacy refers to the confidence that one has the knowledge and ability to make decisions and complete tasks effectively (Bandura 1997).

12. As an illustrative anecdote, I once asked the amazingly prolific and successful scholar Erik Olin Wright (past president of the American Sociological Association) how he was able to produce so much—how he was able to sit at his desk for so many hours each day. His honest and humble response was that he didn't think it had much to do with anything that he was responsible for, but rather was attributable to the luck of possessing significant energy, enthusiasm, ability to concentrate, and a disposition that allowed him to derive continual enjoyment and pleasure from his work. These are wonderful attributes, clearly, but they are due to luck.

13. Consider chess geniuses like Bobby Fischer and Magnus Carlsen. They presumably started life with a certain amount of raw talent, but their genius was developed through spending tens of thousands of hours as young adults sitting alone in their bedrooms playing game after game after game of chess. The jaw-dropping amount of effort that they put into chess was possible only because they possessed idiosyncratic temperaments that made them devoted, excited, single-minded, and almost pathologically obsessive about the game. Their skill reflected their effort, which in turn reflected the arbitrary possession of certain strong (and strange) personality traits (which in turn are the result of the interaction of complex genetic and environmental factors).

14. The specific thread of socialism that I'm questioning here is one that relies heavily on a concept of "exploitation," meaning that a group of people (e.g., workers) has the value of their labor and effort appropriated by another group of people (e.g., capitalists). According to this strain of thought, exploitation is immoral because the value created by workers should properly belong to them—they *deserve* it by virtue of their effort and labor—and so the boss is essentially stealing from them; the boss is a social parasite.

Although there is much that is intuitively compelling in this narrative, ultimately I think we must reject it. There are two reasons why. First, as we saw in Chapter 4, workers don't actually deserve the fruits of their labor or efforts, because such fruits are primarily due to the vast understructure of *other* workers long dead. Second, the skills and efforts of workers are arbitrary from a moral point of view. To see this, imagine that instead of the two standard characters—the worker in the factory or mine or field, and the capitalist relaxing on the beach—there is a third character, a disabled person unable to work, living in a small home paid for by taxes redistributed from income tax on the worker. According to the canonical Marxist view, the disabled person living off the labor of the workers is, at least from a technical point of view, an "exploiter" too. (See Roemer 1988 for a deep discussion of these issues.) But I see that as deeply wrong. The worker and the disabled person possess different levels of skill and effort that are arbitrary from a moral point of view. Saying that the worker deserves significantly more than the disabled person is inherently ableist. The heart of what's wrong with the notion of exploitation, in other words, is that it's interwoven with laborism—the idea that *laboring* grounds rights/entitlement/ownership. But since people's ability to labor is arbitrarily unequal, laborism leads to ableism. (What actually gives one rights, in my judgment, is not the act of laboring, but the fact of being human.) Hence we see that there is a deep clash between Marxist ideas of exploitation and egalitarian ideas of anti-ableism.

This is a complex problem, and I don't claim to have any decisive answers. My sense is that insofar as ideas of exploitation are based on notions of desert, they are untenable. It would probably be better to drop the language of "exploitation" and instead talk in terms of workers being *dominated* at work and how the situation derives from unjust *inequality* (both in terms of unequal opportunities and especially in terms of unequal outcomes). Inequality and domination, in other words, are the core problems. We would do better to avoid the ableist, desert-infused language of exploitation since we can express our moral outrage at the unfairness and wrongness of the oppression of workers without it.

15. Another example is that one's ability to exert self-control (or what philosophers often refer to as "will power") is in fact highly contingent on one's level of blood glucose, which is the main fuel for the brain. Some people, for reasons that are entirely arbitrary from a moral point of view, are simply more effective than others at transporting glucose to the brain in times of cognitive demand, and are thus able to exert more self-control (Gailliot and Baumeister 2007). A final example is that people's cognitive abilities are not only impacted by brain biochemistry but, incredibly, by gut biochemistry as well. What happens in the gut's microbiome actually has "multiple effects on affect, motivation and higher cognitive functions, including intuitive decision making" (Mayer 2011, 453). The microbes of the gut "majorly impact on cognitive function and fundamental behavior patterns, such as social interaction and stress management" (Dinan et al. 2015, 1).

16. Ronald Dworkin famously distinguished between "option luck" (which is the result of consciously choosing to gamble) and "brute luck," arguing that people deserve compensation for bad brute luck but not bad option luck. However, this distinction must be abandoned because option luck is invariably infected with brute luck. We can never extricate the impact of brute luck from psychological decision-making; it is baked in from the very beginning. The gambler's ability to make a reasonable judgment about what actually constitutes a risky gamble (the definition of option luck)

is itself a matter of brute luck (cf. Voigt 2007). Similarly, we must discard Dworkin's distinction between "ambition" and "endowment" because ambition is always inextricably impacted by endowment.

17. There should also be wide opportunity available and extensive accommodations made so that practically everyone could, if they so desired, have a fair shot at entering medical school (i.e., ensuring medical school is affordable, the classes and buildings are accessible for differently abled people, and so on).

18. "According to the concept of desert being defended here, people can deserve benefits only on the basis of intentional performances, so though the performance may depend on natural talent. . . . [I]t also requires choice and effort" (Miller 2004, 193).

19. Moreover, supposing that there is a deep difference between the external natural world and the internal human world implies that the human body is somehow not part of nature and not subject to the same laws, which is a deeply antinaturalistic and antiscientific point of view.

20. The ghost in Roemer's (1993, 165–166, emphasis added) account comes across most clearly when he says things like this: "Behind the . . . [desert] principle . . . lies, I think, the view that *there is a core of human nature common to all.* . . . All people would have, in particular, the same *capacity* to exercise equal degrees of responsibility for their actions." Such a view commits Roemer to a belief in something nonempirical and transcendental, which magically exists for all people. Such a view is, against his own intentions I am sure, no longer a scientific, naturalistic account of human beings.

21. While it is far beyond the scope of this chapter to examine this in detail, much excellent work has been done in recent years in mapping out alternatives—both philosophical and practical—to punishment-based carceral systems (Caruso 2016; Pereboom 2014; Waller 2018; Zehr 2015).

22. Important examples here are policies like campaign finance rules (or more radically, citizens' assemblies, so that the rich are less dominant in the political sphere), nondiscrimination laws (so that White people, men, and heterosexuals do not stigmatize people of color, women, and queers), strong unions and/or enhanced supports to form worker cooperatives (so that employers cannot dominate workers), and child care supports, alimony, and no-fault divorce rights (so that husbands cannot dominate wives). One important caveat to the guarantee of essential goods for all is the case of serious crime. If, for example, a sociopath murders someone, it may well be pragmatically necessary for society to protect itself by confining that person (though hopefully in a hospital rather than a prison cage). And even here the losses should be as minimal as possible, the goal more rehabilitative than punitive, and the perpetrators' essential rights should be restored as soon as possible.

23. Without monetary incentives to bribe people to work, the only real alternative is coercion (Nove 1991). (Though Joseph Carens 1981 has famously argued that it is possible for an egalitarian society to have complete financial equality by relying on moral rather than financial incentives.)

24. Likewise, in terms of the allocation of power in institutions, it is acceptable (and often socially necessary) for there to be differences, but everyone should be seen as possessing fundamentally equal status and dignity. For instance, in the running of

large workplaces, it is acceptable (and sensible) for there to be managers with powers and prerogatives over other workers. However, every worker should be treated with respect and dignity, and the powers exercised by the managers should always be accountable to the workers. Hence the need not just for political democracy but economic democracy too (Anderson 2017; Malleson 2014a).

25. An important complication here is the issue of who in society is responsible for doing the unpaid care work. Currently, many men "choose" to work long hours in the market while many women "choose" to work less (ending up substantially poorer), due to all kinds of norms, cultural pressure, and expectations about the division of labor (Nedelsky and Malleson, forthcoming).

26. That said, it's perfectly plausible to imagine a community deciding that, for example, attractiveness is generally so important for people to find love or have sex or develop deep romantic relationships that it really does constitute an essential good, in which case certain public interventions (such as plastic surgery for burns or disfigurement, or on body parts contributing to severe dysphoria) may well be justifiably publicly subsidized for those who desire them.

27. As well doing at least some unpaid care work (Nedelsky and Malleson, forthcoming).

28. This fact is the crux of the debate between G. A. Cohen and David Miller concerning the desirability of market systems for future forms of socialism (Miller 2014).

29. "Luck egalitarianism" refers to the belief that while inequalities in brute luck should be rectified, those which result from personal choice are legitimate. This key distinction between luck and choice thus constitutes the heart of luck egalitarianism (Arneson 1989; Cohen 1989; Roemer 1993).

30. Relational egalitarians believe that the goal of equality is not extinguishing bad luck but establishing nondominating, non-disrespectful human relationships (Anderson 1999; Fourie, Schuppert, and Wallimann-Helmer 2015; Scheffler 2003, 2005).

31. Thomas Rainsborough's original Leveler formulation from 1647 stated, "I think that the poorest he that is in England hath a life to live, as the greatest he" (quoted in Foot 2005, 28).

Chapter 6

1. In Narveson's (2001, 64) words, a property right over x is "the right to determine the disposition of x" or to "control" it.

2. For insightful discussion of the Chamberlain example, see Cohen (1995), Fried (1995), and Kymlicka ([1990] 2000).

3. Libertarians typically argue that absolute property rights emerge when a "first occupier" seizes a parcel of unowned land (so long as doing so doesn't harm others). For egalitarians, the basic objection is that this seems an extremely weak basis for granting perpetual, absolute ownership rights. Why should the lucky act of being the "first" person to stumble on to some land grant perpetual and absolute rights, whereas everyone else who comes forever after has no right to it at all? If one group of people

puts up fences over all the land, leaving nothing for another group (as well as nothing for all future generations), how is that just? Libertarians can only reply that it's acceptable because the private property rights will (they assure us) result in such productivity benefits that everyone will come to benefit. To which the egalitarian will be extremely doubtful: surely some of the propertyless will actually be far worse off than they could have been in situations of other property regimes. (Compare the well-being of the British peasants during the feudal era, living on the margin of starvation, to that of the Haudenosaunee, for whom property rights were more communal, and so no one starved [Brown 1970]). Quite aside from the lengthy debates about what constitutes "harming others," for many people the very notion that land can be turned into private property for individuals to own forever, to the exclusion of all others, and over which the owners can do absolutely anything they like (including polluting or destroying, as long as it doesn't infringe on the property rights of others), will be seen as extremely controversial if not manifestly reprehensible. For instance, many Indigenous peoples across Turtle Island would reject such a worldview out of hand. For them, land is the heart of communal life, and not something that can be privately appropriated by any individual. Individuals may have rights to use the land, temporarily, but not to permanently own it; even this temporary usufruct involves strict limitations on what one may do with the land, as well as stringent responsibilities to care for it (Kimmerer 2013; Pierotti 2010). Increasingly, many greens are coming to adopt similar positions, arguing that the correct relationship between humans and the land is not private ownership and dominion but communal stewardship. Hence the growing movement to endow certain lands and waterways with their own political rights—a view which is entirely antithetical to basic libertarian presumptions.

4. One of the striking things about libertarian theory is how pervasive the focus is on the ahistorical construct of the "state of nature," where original property is presumed to have emerged, and then been transferred in a perfect unbroken chain of voluntary transfers to today. It is jarring that these philosophically sophisticated defenses of capitalist inequality say so little about the real history of actual capitalism and actual colonial settlement of the land, instead focusing intently on thought experiments of a counterfactual state of nature (though of course using the conclusions from such thought experiments to justify actually existing state of affairs).

5. This phrase is often seen as the unofficial goal of the residential schools (e.g., Hanson 2020). It is commonly (though incorrectly) attributed to the Canadian Duncan Scott, who expanded the residential school system in the 1920s and 1930s; in fact, the phrase seems to derive from a letter written by Lt. Richard Henry Pratt, an American (Sniderman 2013).

6. Residential schools often created graveyards for the children who died during their time there. Typically the graves were left unmarked (unless a White person, such as a teacher, was buried). In 2021 an unmarked mass grave of 215 children was discovered at a residential school in Kamloops, British Columbia, containing the bones of children as young as three (Lindeman 2021). By 2022 the remains of another 1,000 children from different schools had been found.

7. In addition to colonialism, a major source of national wealth, particularly for the United States, has been due to imperialism. To give just one of dozens of possible examples, recall the US overthrow of the democratically elected leader Jacobo Arbenz in Guatemala in 1954 on behalf of the United Fruit Company (now Chiquita, the largest banana-selling company in the world). That wealth extracted from Guatemala passed to American shareholders, and from there into the broader US economy, becoming interwoven with everyone's property (though not of course in any kind of equal way). Much the same could be said of the US coup removing Prime Minister Mohammad Mosaddegh of Iran in 1953 in order to steal the country's oil (US companies subsequently became owners of 40% of Iranian oil fields), or the overthrow of President Salvador Allende in Chile in 1973 for copper (Blum 2002; Galeano 1973; Mitchell and Schoeffel 2002).

8. Slavery, it's important to point out, existed in Canada for 150 years, as did forms of legal segregation, such as Black-only sections in theaters until the 1940s (Maynard 2018).

9. The Headright system, created in England, provided any European willing to settle the land with 50 free acres. The Homestead Act transferred a massive 10% of the entire landmass of the United States to private citizens, mostly White (Blacks were excluded because many were not formally recognized as citizens). From 1944 to 1971 the US GI Bill spent $95 billion helping veterans attend college. Although the law didn't mention race explicitly, the money overwhelmingly went to White students as there were few Black schools that veterans could attend. The Federal Housing Administration provided low-interest mortgage rates to families (mainly White families via the notorious practice of "redlining"). Between 1933 and 1962 approximately $120 billion was given in home and business loans, worth roughly $2 trillion today. Fully 98% of the loans were given to White people (Painter 2010; Strand and Mirkay 2020; Zinn 1996).

10. In the United Kingdom, remarkably, almost a third of the total land is still to this day owned by the handful of families descended from the nobles associated with William the Conqueror's original theft of the land in the 11th century (Shrubsole 2019).

11. Whatever one might think of Nozick's arguments, he at least acknowledges the need for rectificatory or compensatory justice. Can the same be said of John Rawls?

12. The idea that liberty upsets patterns comes from Nozick (1974, 160).

13. This phrase comes from Nozick (1974, 163).

14. For instance, Rothbard (1982, 100) argues that "the parent should not have a *legal obligation* to feed, clothe, or educate his children, since such obligations would entail positive acts coerced upon the parent and depriving the parent of his rights. . . . [T]he parent should have the legal right *not* to feed the child, i.e., to allow it to die."

15. Hence Brian Barry's (1975, 332) scathing review of Nozick's book as "proposing to starve or humiliate ten percent or so of his fellow citizens (if he recognizes the word) by eliminating transfer payments through the state, leaving the sick, the old, the disabled, the mothers with young children and no breadwinner, and so on, to the tender mercies of private charity, given at the whim and pleasure of the donors and on any terms that they choose to impose."

16. There is an underlying premise here that the marginal harm done by taxing the rich is typically significantly less important or serious than the marginal harm of having

basic needs go unmet. Here I leave this argument implicit, though in the next chapter I develop it more explicitly.

17. For more evidence that libertarianism is unconcerned with liberty in general, consider the recurring theme in Narveson's (2001) book of the scary "knock on the door" from the police, the agents of the state, who he tells us are at every moment threatening to take away our property or impose a form of life on us against our will. This is indeed a scary thought, but notice what Narveson does not talk about. In Canada, where Narveson lives and works, the most brutal and historically consequential "knock on the door" has been that of the police ripping Indigenous children from their homes in order to force them into systems of cultural genocide in residential schools. (Interestingly, the Truth and Reconciliation Commission's report on residential schools is also entitled *A Knock on the Door* [TRC 2015].) Yet this kind of knock—this most profound and extreme deprivation of freedom—gets not a single mention in his book on "liberty."

18. There is a long line of thinkers, from Hume to Rawls, who have argued in this vein, against the Lockean tradition, that property is not natural but conventional (Waldron 2020). In Hume's words, "Our property is nothing but those goods, whose constant possession is establish'd by the laws of society; that is, by the laws of justice. Those, therefore, who make use of the words property, or right, or obligation, before they have explain'd the origin of justice, or even make use of them in that explication, are guilty of a very gross fallacy, and can never reason upon any solid foundation. A man's property is some object related to him. This relation is not natural, but moral, and founded on justice. Tis very preposterous, therefore, to imagine, that we can have any idea of property, without fully comprehending the nature of justice, and shewing its origin in the artifice and contrivance of man. The origin of justice explains that of property. The same artifice gives rise to both" (quoted in Waldron 2020). The argument of these pages is very much in line with this train of thought (see also Murphy and Nagel 2002).

19. For an overview of the debate, see Mazor (2019).

20. While I agree that we should insist that individuals possess strong rights of autonomy, we should refrain from using the libertarian language of "self-ownership." The problem with the language of self-ownership is that it implies that one's control over one's body is inviolable—you have absolute rights of noninterference and zero obligations to others. But as argued above, such an extreme position cannot be maintained. Yes, individuals should have strong rights over their bodies, but not absolute rights in all contexts no matter what. For instance, if redistributing a fleck of skin or a single hair could save hundreds of lives (and the process of redistribution was perfectly harmless), it seems dogmatic in the extreme to insist that such redistributions must be forever banned no matter what the consequences. As Arneson (2010, 184) remarks, "nothing worth caring about in any sensible ideal of personal freedom is secured by the dogmatic and shrill insistence on the full property rights over each and every part of my body that the self-ownership thesis affirms." For this reason, it is preferable to insist on strong rights of "autonomy" or "bodily integrity" as opposed to "self-ownership" per se.

Chapter 7

1. Technically, it is possible to reduce inequality without imposing top limits if the wealth of those at the bottom is increasing faster than the wealth at the top. This is a logical possibility, but since in the real world it is not possible to increase the wealth of the bottom ad infinitum, we can ignore this possibility. In the real world, setting limits on total inequality will mean setting limits on maximum wealth.

2. Conservatives sometimes object to this notion by claiming that it is not possible to compare well-being between different people on the grounds that interpersonal comparisons of well-being are impossible to make. This amounts to the incredible claim that we cannot say that it is generally true that bread for the starving is more important that an extra car for the superrich. That is clearly absurd. Of course, it may be true that specific individuals have such different preferences for things that it is possible for a particular idiosyncratic rich person to feel more sadness from losing the ability to purchase an additional car than a poor person does from losing some bread (if, say, the poor person has been so crushed by a lifetime of poverty that they are simply accustomed to being hungry). Nevertheless, this shows only the problem of using subjective preferences as the right metric for interpersonal comparisons—as Amartya Sen (1992) has long argued, people adapt their preferences to their circumstances. A better metric would be capabilities (or, in my preferred language, real freedoms) to live good and flourishing lives. By that objective measure there is no problem with interpersonal comparison: the opportunity for the poor person to eat bread clearly outweighs the opportunity for the rich person to have an additional car in terms of the importance in fostering good and flourishing lives (Brighouse and Robeyns 2010).

3. For instance, the Russian businessman Roman Abramovich owns a yacht worth £724 million, which is reputed to contain "two swimming pools (one of which has an adjustable depth that allows it to be converted into a dancefloor), an exterior fireplace, a leisure submarine, armour plating, bulletproof windows, a missile defence system and an anti-paparazzi shield designed to dazzle digital cameras" (Batty 2016).

4. My framing of these issues overlaps with Robeyns's (2017) but is not identical. She focuses on three issues: global extreme poverty, local disadvantage, and urgent collective action problems.

5. Oxfam (2022) estimates that inequality contributes to the deaths of at least 21,300 people each day.

6. See the introduction, page 7, for sources and calculations.

7. There are, of course, a number of important exceptions to this, such as the socialistic contributions of Cohen (2000), as well as some parts of the relational egalitarian school of thought, though even here it's notable how absent the rich are from discussion in the most prominent works of Anderson (1999) and Scheffler (2003, 2005).

8. Others have made an analogous argument about race. For instance, Charles Mills (2013) points out that it's no surprise that very few Black scholars make use of Rawlsian theory, because the Rawlsian ideal theory framework invisibilizes actually existing racism and thereby tends to obscure the need for rectificatory justice.

9. For related critiques of ideal theory, see Goodhart (2018), Mills (2013), and Sen (2009). For a different perspective, see Simmons (2010).

10. Sufficientarianism is now a complex family of theories, with much internal diversity among its branches (Axelsen and Nielsen 2015, 2016; Benbaji 2005; Crisp 2003; Frankfurt 1987; Herlitz 2018; Huseby 2010; Kanschik 2015; Nielsen 2017; Shields 2012, 2020; Timmer 2021).

11. This may well also turn out to be true for trust and for other kinds of health outcomes (such as life expectancy). However, at the present time, the evidence remains unclear.

12. This is because most working-class people have very limited alternatives to signing a conventional employment contract due to the relative unattractiveness of relying on welfare and the lack of employment opportunities in worker cooperatives. For most jobs, the fundamental thing that a contract does is establish the worker's "duty of obedience" (which is the standard common law understanding of the employee's essential duty). Since no contract can enumerate all of the myriad possible tasks that an employee might be required to do, the fundamental purpose of the contract is to establish a general power structure of (inegalitarian) authority and obedience. Indeed, it was not too long ago when the standard language used in legal discourse reflected this fact more honestly than it does today, by referring not to "employers" and "employees" but to "masters" and "servants" (White 2019).

13. At the end of the day, should we be egalitarians, sufficientarians, or limitarians? This is a complex question. I doubt that there is a simple answer and suspect that Robeyns (2022) is right that the best answers will likely be hybrid and pluralistic. Although I do not claim to have worked out all the details, my sense is that in the short term we require sufficientarianism (at a low threshold) to respond to abject poverty, and limitarianism to resist the undermining of democracy by the superrich. In terms of long-term ideals, I suspect that egalitarianism is the ideal for social relationships, and sufficientarianism (at a very high level) is the ideal for nonrelational goods.

14. Recall, for instance, the wave of brutal racist violence and the surge in Ku Klux Klan membership that followed the *Brown v. Board of Education* verdict mandating desegregation in 1954 (Zinn 1996).

15. In this study, participants filled out a survey and were then told to wait in a hallway before the second part of the study would commence. In the meantime, the experimenter presented participants with a jar of individually wrapped candies, telling the participants that these were intended for children participating in studies in a nearby laboratory. The experimenter told participants that they could take some if they wanted. The jar contained about 40 pieces of candy and was labeled with a note stating that it was to be taken to a specific child-research laboratory. The experimenter then left the participants alone with the candy jar for roughly 30 seconds. The experiments found that "participants in the upper-class rank condition took more candy . . . than did those in the lower-rank condition" (Piff et al. 2012, 4087).

16. See, for instance, the Netflix show *Inside Bill's Brain*.

17. If a society wishes to set a maximum income at $400,000 it could do so in two ways. One way would be to have income taxes which get progressively steeper until they

reach 100%. For instance, one (artificially simplistic) way of doing this would be to create a tax schedule with rates of, say, 20% on income from 0 to $100,000, 50% on income from $100,000 to $200,000, 75% from $200,000 to $400,000, 90% from $400,000 to $600,000, and 100% on income over $600,000. In such a case, the maximum income would be $400,000, although the top marginal rate would only kick in at $600,000. An interesting alternative approach would be to set tax thresholds based not on dollar values but on *ratios* (such as multiples of the median or minimum income). For instance, a person with an income at or below the median income could be taxed at a rate of 10%; someone earning from the median to twice the median income would pay 20%; someone earning three times would pay 30%; someone earning five times would pay 50%; someone earning 10 times would pay 75%; someone earning 20 times would pay 90%; and someone earning 30 times or more the median income would pay 100%. These two approaches could be made to be functionally equivalent, in which case the only difference would be symbolic: in the latter case the clear and transparent aim of the tax is to reduce inequalities between people.

18. Elon Musk currently possesses more than *two million* times the median wealth (assuming, roughly, a median wealth in the United States of $120,000 and Musk's wealth of $270 billion).

19. In terms of maximum wealth limits, one option would be to set this as a multiple of median wealth. Note that in this case it wouldn't make sense to tie it to the minimum wealth, since this is zero. (The bottom 40% of Americans have zero wealth; many actually have negative net worth as they are in debt [Wolff 2010].) On the other hand, a maximum wealth limit could be conceived as a sum (not a multiple) of the minimum. For instance, the maximum limit could be set at something like $20 million more than the average wealth of the bottom third of the population.

20. Similarly in the case of acting. Hollywood may lose the occasional superstar, but does anyone doubt that there are not a thousand struggling actors who are almost as good, and who would be thrilled to take on any vacated acting roles for a salary of "only" $400,000 per year?

21. At an income of $1 million, the effective tax rate would be 60%; at $10 million it would be 96%; and at $100 million it would be 99.6%.

22. There are also important potential transition costs of economic sabotage from capital strike and flight. See Chapter 3 for a discussion of these.

23. Recall the scientific advancements that led to the Pfizer and Moderna COVID-19 vaccines. These were accomplished not by business entrepreneurs but by academics at universities. The mRNA technology underlying these vaccines was mainly developed by Kati Kariko at the University of Pennsylvania, who loved the science and worked hard for many years but never made more than $60,000 a year (Kolata 2021). To the extent that a society with maximum limits funds more public research of this sort, it will become more innovative and productive.

Conclusion

1. Half of the entire world lives on less than $5.50 per day (World Bank 2018).
2. On the feasibility of increasing time sovereignty, see Hayden (1999) and LaJeunesse (2009).
3. An important attempt to give Rawlsian ideas more institutional form is the excellent volume by O'Neill and Williamson (2012).
4. At least in his formal theory. In his informal writings he clearly recognized the dangers (Rawls and Parijs 2003).
5. Though I cannot defend it here, I would suggest that Nordic social democracy, though inspiring in many regards, is still inadequate in terms of our long-term ideals. Beyond what has already been said, it is arguably also inadequate in terms of the prevalence of compulsory workplace servitude and the inaccessibility of workplace democracy; the lack of economic democracy more broadly; insufficient leisure time and time sovereignty; the insufficiently democratic nature of the political system (which remains biased toward the rich, nondescriptively representative, insufficiently deliberative, and lacking in mechanisms for popular participation); the unequal gender relations (women still do far more caregiving work and earn less in the market); unjust relationships with and insufficient sovereignty for the Indigenous peoples (such as the Sámi); the still extensive use of prisons and punitive, carceral systems, and so on.
6. The current leader in this regard is the Netherlands (LaJeunesse 2009; Visser 2002).

Bibliography

Abbas, Mohammed. 2011. "London Rioters Resent Media Image of Hooded Teen Thug." Reuters, August 10. https://www.reuters.com/article/idINIndia-58723220110810.

ABC News. 2012. "Warren Buffett and His Secretary on Their Tax Rates." January 25. http://abcnews.go.com/blogs/business/2012/01/warren-buffett-and-his-secretary-talk-taxes/.

Abiad, A., A. Almansour, D. Furceri, C. Granados, and P. Topalova. 2014. "Is It Time for an Infrastructure Push? The Macroeconomic Effects of Public Investment." *International Monetary Fund*, 1–52.

Abramovitz, Moses. 1993. "The Search for the Sources of Growth: Areas of Ignorance, Old and New." *Journal of Economic History* 53(2): 217–243.

Ackerman, Bruce, Anne Alsott, and Philippe Van Parijs, eds. 2006. *Redesigning Distribution: Basic Income and Stakeholder Grants as Alternative Cornerstones for a More Egalitarian Capitalism*. London: Verso.

ACLU. 2013. *A Living Death: Life without Parole for Nonviolent Offenses*. New York: American Civil Liberties Union.

Adam, S., H. Miller. 2021. "The Economic Arguments for and against a Wealth Tax." *Fiscal Studies* 42(3–4): 457–483.

Addison, J. 2009. *The Economics of Codetermination: Lessons from the German Experience*. New York: Palgrave Macmillan.

Advani, A., and H. Tarrant. 2021. "Behavioural Responses to a Wealth Tax." *Fiscal Studies* 42(3–4): 509–537.

Afonso, A., and D. Furceri. 2010. "Government Size, Composition, Volatility and Economic Growth." *European Journal of Political Economy* 26(4): 517–532.

Agrawal, D., D. Foremny, and C. Martinez-Toledano. 2020. "Paraîsos Fiscales, Wealth Taxation, and Mobility." Barcelona: IEB Working Papers 15. http://diposit.ub.edu/dspace/bitstream/2445/175660/1/IEB20-15_Agrawal%2BForemny%2BMtnezToledano.pdf.

Ajdacic, L., E. M. Heemskerk, and J. Garcia-Bernardo. 2021. "The Wealth Defence Industry: A Large-Scale Study on Accountancy Firms as Profit Shifting Facilitators." *New Political Economy* 26(4): 690–706.

Akcigit, U., S. Baslandze, and S. Stantcheva. 2016. "Taxation and the International Mobility of Inventors." *American Economic Review* 106(10): 2930–2981.

Albert, M. 2003. *Parecon: Life after Capitalism*. London: Verso.

Albouy, D., and M. Zabek. 2016. "Housing Inequality." NBER Working Papers 21916, Cambridge, MA. https://econpapers.repec.org/scripts/redir.pf?u=http%3A%2F%2Fwww.nber.org%2Fpapers%2Fw21916.pdf;h=repec:nbr:nberwo:21916.

Alderman, Liz, and Steven Greenhouse. 2014. "Living Wages, Rarity for U.S. Fast-Food Workers, Served Up in Denmark." *New York Times*, October 27.

Alesina, A., and R. Perotti. 1996. "Income Distribution, Political Instability, and Investment." *European Economic Review* 40(6): 1203–1228.

Alexander, M. 2010. *The New Jim Crow*. New York: New Press.

Algan, Y., S. Guriev, E. Papaioannou, and E. Passari. 2017. "The European Trust Crisis and the Rise of Populism." *Brookings Papers on Economic Activity*, no. 2: 309–400.

Alì, N., and L. Caranti. 2021. "How Much Economic Inequality Is Fair in Liberal Democracies? The Approach of Proportional Justice." *Philosophy & Social Criticism* 47(7): 1–20.

Alm, D. 2011. "How Much Effort Can We Make?" *American Philosophical Quarterly* 48(4): 387–397.

Alperovitz, Gar. 2005. *America beyond Capitalism: Reclaiming Our Wealth, Our Liberty, and Our Democracy*. Hoboken, NJ: John Wiley & Sons.

Alperovitz, Gar, and L. Daly. 2008. *Unjust Deserts*. New York: New Press.

Alstadsæter, Annette, Niels Johannesen, and Gabriel Zucman. 2018. "Tax Evasion and Tax Avoidance." December 28. http://gabriel-zucman.eu/files/AJZ2018b.pdf.

Alstadsæter, Annette, Niels Johannesen, and Gabriel Zucman. 2019. "Tax Evasion and Inequality." *American Economic Review* 109(6): 2073–2103.

Alvaredo, F., and E. Saez. 2009. "Income and Wealth Concentration in Spain from a Historical and Fiscal Perspective." *Journal of the European Economic Association* 7(5): 1140–1167.

Andersen, R. 2012. "Support for Democracy in Cross-national Perspective: The Detrimental Effect of Economic Inequality." *Research in Social Stratification and Mobility* 30(4): 389–402.

Andersen, R., and T. Fetner. 2008. "Economic Inequality and Intolerance: Attitudes toward Homosexuality in 35 Democracies." *American Journal of Political Science* 52(4): 942–958.

Anderson, E. 1999. "What Is the Point of Equality?" *Ethics* 109(2): 287–337.

Anderson, E. 2007. "Fair Opportunity in Education: A Democratic Equality Perspective." *Ethics* 117(4): 595–622.

Anderson, E. 2017. *Private Government*. Princeton, NJ: Princeton University Press.

Andrews, D., and A. Leigh. 2009. "More Inequality, Less Social Mobility." *Applied Economics Letters* 16(15): 1489–1492.

Apergis, N., O. C. Dincer, and J. E. Payne. 2010. "The Relationship between Corruption and Income Inequality in US States: Evidence from a Panel Cointegration and Error Correction Model." *Public Choice* 145(1): 125–135.

Aristotle. 1998. *Politics*. Translated by C. D. C. Reeve. Indianapolis, IN: Hackett.

Ariyoshi, A. 2000. *Capital Controls: Country Experiences with Their Use and Liberalization*. Washington, DC: International Monetary Fund.

Arneson, R. 1989. "Equality and Equal Opportunity for Welfare." *Philosophical Studies* 56(1): 77–93.

Arneson, R. 1991. "Lockean Self-Ownership: Towards a Demolition." *Political Studies* 39(1): 36–54.

Arneson, R. 2010. "Self-Ownership and World Ownership: Against Left-Libertarianism." *Social Philosophy and Policy* 27(1): 168–194.

Arneson, R. 2011. "Side Constraints, Lockean Individual Rights, and the Moral Basis of Libertarianism." In *The Cambridge Companion to Nozick's* Anarchy, State, and Utopia, edited by R. M. Bader and J. Meadowcroft, 15–37. Cambridge: Cambridge University Press.

Aronoff, K., A. Battistoni, D. A. Cohen, and T. Riofrancos. 2019. *A Planet to Win: Why We Need a Green New Deal*. London: Verso.

Arundel, R. 2017. "Equity Inequity: Housing Wealth Inequality, Inter- and Intra-generational Divergences, and the Rise of Private Landlordism." *Housing, Theory and Society* 34(2): 176–200.

Arzheimer, K. 2009. "Contextual Factors and the Extreme Right Vote in Western Europe, 1980–2002." *American Journal of Political Science* 53(2): 259–275.

Asen, R. Scott. 2012. "Is Private School Not Expensive Enough." New York Times, August 23. http://www.nytimes.com/2012/08/24/opinion/is-private-school-not-expensive-enough.html?_r=1&.

Atkinson, A. B. 2015. *Inequality: What Can Be Done?* Cambridge, MA: Harvard University Press.

Atkinson, A. B., T. Piketty, and E. Saez. 2009. "Top Incomes in the Long Run of History." NBER Working Papers 15408, Cambridge, MA. https://www.nber.org/system/files/working_papers/w15408/w15408.pdf.

Atkinson, A. B., and J. E. Søgaard. 2013. "The Long-Run History of Income Inequality in Denmark: Top Incomes from 1870 to 2010." EPRU Working Paper Series, 2013-01, University of Copenhagen. https://www.econstor.eu/bitstream/10419/82127/1/wp-13-01.pdf.

Attas, D. 2003. "Markets and Desert." In *Forms of Justice: Critical Perspectives on David Miller's Political Philosophy,* edited by D. A. Bell and A. de-Shalit, 85–106. Lanham, MD: Rowman & Littlefield.

Au-Yeung, A. 2018. "How Jeff Bezos Became the Richest Person in America and the World." Forbes, October 3. https://www.forbes.com/sites/angelauyeung/2018/10/03/how-jeff-bezos-became-the-richest-person-in-the-world-2018-forbes-400/#4f9502d01bee.

Auten, G., D. Splinter, and S. Nelson. 2016. "Reactions of High-Income Taxpayers to Major Tax Legislation." *National Tax Journal* 69(4): 935–964.

Avi-Yonah, R. 2013. "And Yet It Moves: A Tax Paradigm for the 21st Century." Ann Arbor: Law & Economics Working Papers 59. https://repository.law.umich.edu/cgi/viewcontent.cgi?article=1169&context=law_econ_current.

Avi-Yonah, R. 2016. "Hanging Together: A Multilateral Approach to Taxing Multinationals." In *Global Tax Fairness,* edited by T. Pogge and K. Mehta, 113–128. Oxford: Oxford University Press.

Avi-Yonah, R. 2019. "The Shaky Case against Wealth Taxation." *American Prospect,* August 28. Retrieved from https://prospect.org/economy/shaky-case-wealth-taxation/.

Axelsen, D. V., and L. Nielsen. 2015. "Sufficiency as Freedom from Duress." *Journal of Political Philosophy* 23(4): 406–426.

Axelsen, D. V., and L. Nielsen. 2016. "Essentially Enough: Elements of a Plausible Account of Sufficientarianism." In *What Is Enough? Sufficiency, Justice and Health,* edited by C. Fourie and A. Rid, 101–118. Oxford: Oxford University Press.

Bach, S., M. Beznoska, and V. Steiner. 2014. "A Wealth Tax on the Rich to Bring Down Public Debt? Revenue and Distributional Effects of a Capital Levy in Germany." *Fiscal Studies* 35(1): 67–89.

Baker, D. 2005. "The Reform of Intellectual Property." *Post-Autistic Economics Review* 32(5): 2–9.

Baker, D. 2006. *The Conservative Nanny State.* Washington, DC: Center for Economic and Policy Research.

Baker, D. 2011. *The End of Loser Liberalism: Making Markets Progressive.* Washington, DC: Center of Economic and Policy Research.

Baker, D. 2016. *Rigged*. Washington, DC: Center for Economic and Policy Research.

Baker, D., and J. Bernstein. 2013. *Getting Back to Full Employment*. Washington, DC: Center for Economic and Policy Research.

Baker, D., J. Bivens, and J. Schieder. 2019. *Reining in CEO Compensation and Curbing the Rise of Inequality*. Washington, DC:

Baker, J. 1987. *Arguing for Equality*. London: Verso.

Baldiga, M., P. Joshi, E. Hardy, and D. Acevedo-Garcia. 2018. "Data-for-Equity Research Brief: Child Care Affordability for Working Parents." Brandeis University, November 1. http://www.diversitydatakids.org/sites/default/files/2020-02/child-care_update.pdf.

Bandura, A. 1997. *Self-Efficacy: The Exercise of Control*. New York: W. H. Freeman.

Banks, N. 2020. "Black Women in the United States and Unpaid Collective Work: Theorizing the Community as a Site of Production." *Review of Black Political Economy* 47(4): 343–362.

Banks, R. R., J. L. Eberhardt, and L. Ross. 2006. "Discrimination and Implicit Bias in a Racially Unequal Society." *California Law Review* 94(4): 1169–1190.

Barker, G. 2015. *Beyond Biofatalism: Human Nature for an Evolving World*. New York: Columbia University Press.

Barry, B. 1975. "Review of Robert Nozick's *Anarchy, State, and Utopia*." *Political Theory* 3(3): 331–336.

Barry, B. 2005. *Why Social Justice Matters*. Cambridge, UK: Polity.

Barry, E., and M. S. Sorensen. 2018. "In Denmark, Harsh New Laws for Immigrant 'Ghettos.'" *New York Times*, July 1. https://www.nytimes.com/2018/07/01/world/europe/denmark-immigrant-ghettos.html.

Bartels, Larry M. 2004. "Partisan Politics and the US Income Distribution." Russell Sage. http://www.russellsage.org/sites/all/files/u4/Bartels_Partisan%20Politics.pdf.

Bartels, Larry M. 2016. *Unequal Democracy*. 2nd ed. Princeton, NJ: Princeton University Press.

Batchelder, L. L. 2009. "What Should Society Expect from Heirs: The Case for a Comprehensive Inheritance Tax. *Tax Law Review* 63: 1.

Batchelder, L. L. 2016. "The 'Silver Spoon' Tax: How to Strengthen Wealth Transfer Taxation." In *Delivering Equitable Growth: Strategies for the Next Administration,* edited by WCEG, 85–96. Washington, DC: Washington Center for Equitable Growth.

Bateson, M., D. Nettle, and G. Roberts. 2006. "Cues of Being Watched Enhance Cooperation in a Real-World Setting." *Biology Letters* 2(3): 412–414.

Batty, D. 2016. "Superyachts and Bragging Rights: Why the Super-rich Love Their 'Floating Homes.'" *The Guardian*, October 9. https://www.theguardian.com/lifeandstyle/2016/oct/09/superyachts-and-bragging-rights-why-the-super-rich-love-their-floating-homes.

BBC. 2018. "Trump: Immigrant Gangs 'Animals, Not People.'" May 17. https://www.bbc.com/news/av/world-us-canada-44148697/trump-immigrant-gangs-animals-not-people.

Bebchuk, L. A., J. M. Fried, and D. I. Walker. 2002. "Managerial Power and Rent Extraction in the Design of Executive Compensation." NBER Working Papers 9068, Cambridge, MA. https://www.nber.org/system/files/working_papers/w9068/w9068.pdf.

Bell, D. A., and A. de-Shalit, A. eds. 2003. *Forms of Justice: Critical Perspectives on David Miller's Political Philosophy*. Lanham, MD: Rowman & Littlefield.

Bénabou, R., and J. Tirole. 2006. "Belief in a Just World and Redistributive Politics." *Quarterly Journal of Economics* 121(2): 699–746.

Benbaji, Y. 2005. "The Doctrine of Sufficiency: A Defence." *Utilitas* 17(3): 310–332.

Benko, J. 2015. "The Radical Humaneness of Norway's Halden Prison." *New York Times*, March 29. https://www.nytimes.com/2015/03/29/magazine/the-radical-humaneness-of-norways-halden-prison.html.

Berg, A., J. D. Ostry, C. G. Tsangarides, and Y. Yakhshilikov. 2018. "Redistribution, Inequality, and Growth: New Evidence." *Journal of Economic Growth* 23(3): 259–305.

Berg, K., and S. Hebous. 2021. "Does a Wealth Tax Improve Equality of Opportunity?" CESifo Working Paper, No. 9174, Center for Economic Studies and ifo Institute (CESifo), Munich. https://www.econstor.eu/bitstream/10419/245355/1/cesifo1_wp9174.pdf.

Bergh, A., and M. Henrekson. 2011. "Government Size and Growth: A Survey and Interpretation of the Evidence." *Journal of Economic Surveys* 25(5): 872–897.

Bertrand, M., and S. Mullainathan. 2004. "Are Emily and Greg More Employable Than Lakisha and Jamal? A Field Experiment on Labor Market Discrimination." *American Economic Review* 94(4): 991–1013.

Bhagwati, J. 1998. "The Capital Myth: The Difference between Trade in Widgets and Dollars." *Foreign Affairs* 77(3): 7–12.

Binder, A. J. 2014. "Why Are Harvard Grads Still Flocking to Wall Street?" *Washington Monthly*, August 21. https://washingtonmonthly.com/2014/08/21/why-are-harvard-grads-still-flocking-to-wall-street/.

Biswas, S., I. Chakraborty, R. Hai. 2017. "Income Inequality, Tax Policy, and Economic Growth." *Economic Journal* 127(601): 688–727.

Bivens, J., and L. Mishel. 2013. "The Pay of Corporate Executives and Financial Professionals as Evidence of Rents in Top 1 Percent Incomes." *Journal of Economic Perspectives* 27(3): 57–78.

Bjørneby, M., S. Markussen, and K. Røed. 2020. "Does the Wealth Tax Kill Jobs." IZA Discussion Papers 13766, Bonn. https://www.econstor.eu/bitstream/10419/227293/1/dp13766.pdf.

Blanchflower, D. G., and R. B. Freeman. 1992. "Unionism in the United States and Other Advanced OECD Countries." *Industrial Relations: A Journal of Economy and Society* 31(1): 56–79.

Blanco, C., J. Grant, N. M. Petry, H. B. Simpson, A. Alegria, S.-M. Liu, and D. Hasin. 2008. "Prevalence and Correlates of Shoplifting in the United States: Results from the National Epidemiologic Survey on Alcohol and Related Conditions (NESARC)." *American Journal of Psychiatry* 165(7): 905–913.

Blasi, J. R., R. B. Freeman, and D. L. Kruse, 2013. *The Citizen's Share.* New Haven, CT: Yale University Press.

Blasi, J., and D. Kruse. 2012. "Broad-Based Worker Ownership and Profit Sharing: Can These Ideas Work in the Entire Economy?" Paper presented at the International Association for the Economics of Participation, New Brunswick, NJ.

Block, Fred. 1977. "The Ruling Class Does Not Rule: Notes on the Marxist Theory of the State." *Socialist Revolution* 33(6): 6–28.

Block, Fred, and Matthew R. Keller. 2009. "Where Do Innovations Come From? Transformations in the US Economy, 1970–2006." *Socio-Economic Review* 7(3): 459–483.

Bloom, N., and J. Van Reenen. 2007. "Measuring and Explaining Management Practices across Firms and Countries." *Quarterly Journal of Economics* 122(4): 1351–1408.

Bloomberg. 2022. "Bloomberg Billionaires Index." Last accessed December 3, 2021. https://www.bloomberg.com/billionaires/profiles/elon-r-musk/.

BLS. 2020. "Union Members Summary." Last accessed November 24, 2022. https://www.bls.gov/news.release/union2.nr0.htm.

Blum, W. 2002. *Rogue State*. London: Zed Books.

Blumenthal, P. M., and J. R. McGinty. 2015. "Housing Policy Levers to Promote Economic Mobility." Washington, DC: Policy Commons. https://policycommons.net/artifacts/632258/housing-policy-levers-to-promote-economic-mobility/1613581/.

Boadway, R., and P. Pestieau. 2018. "The Tenuous Case for an Annual Wealth Tax." Barcelona: IEB Working Papers 2018/01. http://diposit.ub.edu/dspace/bitstream/2445/120226/1/IEB18-01_Boadway%2BPestieau.pdf.

Boorstein, E. 1977. *Allende's Chile*. New York: International Publishers.

Booth, R. 2014. "Inside 'Billionaires Row': London's Rotting, Derelict Mansions Worth £350m." *The Guardian*, January 31. https://www.theguardian.com/society/2014/jan/31/inside-london-billionaires-row-derelict-mansions-hampstead.

Bowles, S., and Y. Park. 2005. "Emulation, Inequality, and Work Hours: Was Thorsten Veblen Right?" *Economic Journal* 115(507): 397–412.

Bowman, S. R. 1996. *The Modern Corporation and American Political Thought*. University Park: Pennsylvania State University Press.

Brighouse, H., and I. Robeyns, eds. 2010. *Measuring Justice: Primary Goods and Capabilities*. Cambridge: Cambridge University Press.

Brown, J. K. 1970. "Economic Organization and the Position of Women among the Iroquois." *Ethnohistory* 17(3/4): 151–167.

Brown, J. R., C. C. Coile, and S. J. Weisbenner. 2010. "The Effect of Inheritance Receipt on Retirement." *Review of Economics and Statistics* 92(2): 425–434.

Brown, W. 2011. "The End of Educated Democracy." *Representations* 116(1): 19–41.

Brownlee, W. E. 2000. "Historical Perspective on U.S. Tax Policy toward the Rich." In *Does Atlas Shrug? The Economic Consequences of Taxing the Rich*, edited by J. Slemrod, 29–73. Cambridge, MA: Harvard University Press.

Brülhart, M., J. Gruber, M. Krapf, and K. Schmidheiny. 2019a. "Behavioral Responses to Wealth Taxes: Evidence from Switzerland." Munich: CESifo Working Paper 7908. https://www.econstor.eu/bitstream/10419/207299/1/cesifo1_wp7908.pdf.

Brülhart, M., J. Gruber, M. Krapf, and K. Schmidheiny. 2019b. "Wealth Taxation: The Swiss Experience." VoxEU, December 23. https://voxeu.org/article/wealth-taxation-swiss-experience.

Buch-Hansen, H., and M. Koch. 2019. "Degrowth through Income and Wealth Caps?" *Ecological Economics* (160): 264–471.

Burgherr, D. 2021. "The Costs of Administering a Wealth Tax." *Fiscal Studies* 42(3–4): 677–697.

Cabrera, L. 2010. *The Practice of Global Citizenship*. New York: Cambridge University Press.

Cacioppo, J. T., R. E. Petty, J. A. Feinstein, and W. B. G. Jarvis. 1996. "Dispositional Differences in Cognitive Motivation: The Life and Times of Individuals Varying in Need for Cognition." *Psychological Bulletin* 119(2): 197–253.

Cagé, J. 2016. *Saving the Media: Capitalism, Crowdfunding, and Democracy*. Cambridge, MA: Harvard University Press.

Calaprice, A. 2011. *The Ultimate Quotable Einstein*. Princeton, NJ: Princeton University Press.

Calnitsky, D., and P. Gonalons-Pons. 2021. "The Impact of an Experimental Guaranteed Income on Crime and Violence." *Social Problems* 68(3): 778–798.

Calton, C. 2018. "Reparations vs. Property Rights." Mises Institute, July 5. https://mises.org/wire/reparations-vs-property-rights.

Cammaerts, B., B. DeCillia, J. Magalhães, and C. Jimenez-Martínez. 2016. "Journalistic Representations of Jeremy Corbyn in the British Press." London: London School of Economics. https://www.lse.ac.uk/media-and-communications/assets/documents/research/projects/corbyn/Cobyn-Report.pdf.

Card, D., and A. B. Krueger. 1993. "Minimum Wages and Employment: A Case Study of the Fast Food Industry in New Jersey and Pennsylvania." NBER Working Papers 4509, Cambridge, MA. https://www.nber.org/system/files/working_papers/w4509/w4509.pdf.

Carens, J. H. 1981. *Equality, Moral Incentives, and the Market: An Essay in Utopian Politico-economic Theory.* Chicago: University of Chicago Press.

Carnes, N. 2012. "Does the Numerical Underrepresentation of the Working Class in Congress Matter?" *Legislative Studies Quarterly* 37(1): 5–34.

Carnes, N., and N. Lupu. 2015. "Rethinking the Comparative Perspective on Class and Representation: Evidence from Latin America." *American Journal of Political Science* 59(1): 1–18.

Carroll, R., D. Holtz-Eakin, M. Rider, and H. S. Rosen. 1998. "Entrepreneurs, Income Taxes, and Investment." NBER Working Papers 6374, Cambridge, MA. https://www.nber.org/system/files/working_papers/w6374/w6374.pdf.

Caruso, G. D. 2016. "Free Will Skepticism and Criminal Behavior: A Public Health-Quarantine Model." *Southwest Philosophy Review* 32(1): 25–48.

Carvalho, B. S. M., and M. G. P. Garcia. 2008. *Ineffective Controls on Capital Inflows under Sophisticated Financial Markets: Brazil in the Nineties.* Chicago: National Bureau of Economic Research, University of Chicago Press.

Cassidy, John. 2019. "Why Elizabeth Warren's Wealth Tax Would Work." *New Yorker,* January 31. https://www.newyorker.com/news/our-columnists/elizabeth-warrens-wealth-tax-is-an-old-idea-and-its-time-has-come.

Cassidy, Jude, and P. R. Shaver, eds. 2008. *Handbook of Attachment.* 2nd ed. New York: Guilford Press.

CBC. 2021. "130 Countries Back OECD Plan to Set Global Minimum Corporate Tax Rate." July 3. https://www.cbc.ca/news/business/oecd-corporate-tax-rate-1.6087464.

Chakrabortty, A. 2016. "I've Found the Key to Britain's Recovery: An Orange Shed in Shanktown." *The Guardian,* March 29. http://www.theguardian.com/commentisfree/2016/mar/29/key-britains-recovery-orange-shed-shanktown-social-enterprise-building-bloqs.

Chamberlain, E. 2020. "Defining the Tax Base: Design Issues." Wealth Tax Commission Evidence Paper 8. https://www.wealthandpolicy.com/wp/EP8_TaxBase.pdf.

Chamberlain, E. 2021. "Who Should Pay a Wealth Tax? Some Design Issues." *Fiscal Studies* 42(3–4): 599–613.

Chamon, M., and M. Garcia. 2016. "Capital Controls in Brazil: Effective?" *Journal of International Money and Finance* 61: 163–187.

Chang, Ha-Joon. 2002. *Kicking Away the Ladder: Development Strategy in Historical Perspective.* London: Anthem.

Chang, Ha-Joon. 2006. *The East Asian Development Experience: The Miracle, the Crisis and the Future.* Penang: Third World Network.

Chang, Ha-Joon. 2007. *Bad Samaritans: The Guilty Secrets of Rich Nations and the Threat to Global Prosperity*. London: Random House Business Books.

Chang, Ha-Joon. 2010. *23 Things They Don't Tell You about Capitalism*. London: Allen Lane.

Chappell, M. 2017. "The False Promise of Homeownership." *Washington Post*, July 20. https://www.washingtonpost.com/news/made-by-history/wp/2017/07/20/the-false-promise-of-homeownership/.

Chetty, R., N. Hendren, P. Kline, and E. Saez. 2014. "Where Is the Land of Opportunity? The Geography of Intergenerational Mobility in the United States." *The Quarterly Journal of Economics* 129(4): 1553–1623.

Chetty, R., N. Hendren, P. Kline, E. Saez, and N. Turner. 2014. "Is the United States Still a Land of Opportunity? Recent Trends in Intergenerational Mobility." *American Economic Review* 104(5): 141–147.

Chetty, R., M. Stepner, S. Abraham, S. Lin, B. Scuderi, N. Turner, A. Bergeron, D. Cutler. 2016. "The Association between Income and Life Expectancy in the United States, 2001–2014." *Journal of the American Medical Association* 315(16): 1750–1766.

Cho, S.-W. S., and J. L. Francis. 2011. "Tax Treatment of Owner Occupied Housing and Wealth Inequality." *Journal of Macroeconomics* 33(1): 42–60.

Christiano, T. 2012. "Money in Politics." In *The Oxford Handbook of Political Philosophy*, edited by D. Estlund, 241–257. Oxford: Oxford University Press.

Christman, J. 1994. *The Myth of Property*. New York: Oxford University Press.

Christophers, B. 2019. "A Tale of Two Inequalities: Housing-Wealth Inequality and Tenure Inequality." *EPA: Economy and Space* 53(3): 1–22.

Ciepley, D. 2013. "Beyond Public and Private: Toward a Political Theory of the Corporation." *American Political Science Review* 107(1): 139–158.

Cingano, F. 2014. "Trends in Income Inequality and Its Impact on Economic Growth." Paris: OECD Social, Employment and Migration Working Papers 163. http://englishb ulletin.adapt.it/wp-content/uploads/2014/12/oecd_9_12_2014.pdf.

Clark, A. E., and A. J. Oswald. 1996. "Satisfaction and Comparison Income." *Journal of Public Economics* 61(3): 359–381.

Clark, J. B. (1899) 1956. *The Distribution of Wealth*. New York: Kelley & Millman.

Clark, J. R., and R. A. Lawson. 2008. "The Impact of Economic Growth, Tax Policy and Economic Freedom on Income Inequality." *The Journal of Private Enterprise* 24(1): 23–31.

Clausing, K. A. 2018. "Does Tax Drive the Headquarters Locations of the World's Biggest Companies?" *Transnational Corporations* 25(2): 37–66.

Clifford, S. 2017. "How Companies Actually Decide What to Pay CEOs." *The Atlantic*, June. https://www.theatlantic.com/business/archive/2017/06/how-companies-decide-ceo-pay/530127/.

Cline, W. R. 2007. *Global Warming and Agriculture*. Washington, DC: Center for Global Development.

Clingingsmith, D., and S. Shane. 2015. "How Individual Income Tax Policy Affects Entrepreneurship." *Fordham Law Review* 84: 2495.

CMHC. 2018. "About Affordable Housing in Canada." Last accessed November 25, 2022. https://www.cmhc-schl.gc.ca/en/developing-and-renovating/develop-new-afforda ble-housing/programs-and-information/about-affordable-housing-in-canada.

Coates, T.-N. 2014. "The Case for Reparations." *The Atlantic*, June.

Cobham, A. 2020. "A UN Tax Convention—Then a U-turn." Tax Justice, September 4. https://taxjustice.net/2020/09/04/a-un-tax-convention-then-a-u-turn/.

Cobham, A. 2021. "Is Today a Turning Point against Corporate Tax Abuse?" Tax Justice, June 4. https://taxjustice.net/2021/06/04/is-today-a-turning-point-against-corporate-tax-abuse/.

Cohen, B. J. 2002. "Capital Controls: Why Do Governments Hesitate?" In *Debating the Global Financial Architecture,* edited by L. E. Armijo, 93–117. New York: State University of New York Press.

Cohen, D. A., P. Gowan, S. Lopez, M. Weeks, M. Paul, T. Silverstein, K. Viselman, C. Weaver, T. Raghuveer, and K. Simowitz. 2019. *A National Homes Guarantee.* Chicago: People's Action.

Cohen, G., J. T. Jalles, P. Loungani, and R. Marto. 2017. "Emissions and Growth: Trends and Cycles in a Globalized World." Washington, DC: IMF Working Paper 191. https://www.elibrary.imf.org/downloadpdf/journals/001/2017/191/article-A001-en.xml.

Cohen, G. A. 1989. "On the Currency of Egalitarian Justice." *Ethics* 99(4): 906–944.

Cohen, G. A. 1995. *Self-Ownership, Freedom, and Equality.* Cambridge: Cambridge University Press.

Cohen, G. A. 2000. *If You're an Egalitarian, How Come You're So Rich?* Cambridge, MA: Harvard Univeristy Press.

Cohen, J., and J. Rogers. 1983. *On Democracy.* Harmondsworth: Penguin Books.

Coletta, A. 2020. "Canada's Coronavirus Performance Hasn't Been Perfect. But It's Done Far Better Than the U.S." *Washington Post,* July 14. https://www.washingtonpost.com/world/the_americas/coronavirus-canada-united-states/2020/07/14/0686330a-c14c-11ea-b4f6-cb39cd8940fb_story.html.

Collins, C. 2019. "Bernie's Right: Three Billionaires Really Do Have More Wealth Than Half of America." Inequality. Last accessed November 25, 2022. https://inequality.org/great-divide/bernie-3-billionaires-more-wealth-half-america/.

Corak, M. 2013. "Income Inequality, Equality of Opportunity, and Intergenerational Mobility." *Journal of Economic Perspectives* 27(3): 79–102.

Correa, R., and U. Lel. 2016. "Say on Pay Laws, Executive Compensation, Pay Slice, and Firm Valuation around the World." *Journal of Financial Economics* 122(3): 500–520.

Crisp, R. 2003. "Equality, Priority, and Compassion." *Ethics* 113(4): 745–763.

Cross, S., Y. Rho, H. Reddy, T. Pepperrell, F. Rodgers, R. Osborne, A. Eni-Oluto, R. Banerjee, S. Wimmer, S. Keestra. 2021. "Who Funded the Research behind the Oxford–AstraZeneca COVID-19 Vaccine?" *BMJ Global Health* 6(12): e007321.

Crotty, J., and G. Epstein. 1996. "In Defense of Capital Controls." *Socialist Register* 32: 118–149.

Dahl, R. 1985. *A Preface to Economic Democracy.* Berkeley: University of California Press.

Dal Bó, E., F. Finan, O. Folke, T. Persson, and J. Rickne. 2018. "Economic Losers and Political Winners: Sweden's Radical Right." Unpublished paper.

Daly, H. E., and J. Farley. 2011. *Ecological Economics.* 2nd ed. Seattle, WA: Island Press.

Daly, S., H. Hughson, and G. Loutzenhiser. 2021. "Valuation for the Purposes of a Wealth Tax." *Fiscal Studies* 42(3–4): 615–650.

Darity, W., and K. Mullen. 2020. "Black Reparations and the Racial Wealth Gap." Brookings, June 15. https://www.brookings.edu/blog/up-front/2020/06/15/black-reparations-and-the-racial-wealth-gap/.

Darnihamedani, P., J. H. Block, J. Hessels, and A. Simonyan. 2018. "Taxes, Start-up Costs, and Innovative Entrepreneurship." *Small Business Economics* 51(2): 355–369.

Datil, A. 2019. "300 Scholars Say It's OK for People to Compare Detention Centers to Concentration Camps." WUSA9, July 3. https://www.wusa9.com/article/news/local/300-scholars-say-its-ok-for-people-to-compare-detention-centers-to-concentration-camps/65-dc7da269-85cb-45fb-a0cf-164d31b21be5.

Davis, A. 2011. *Are Prisons Obsolete?* New York: Seven Stories Press.

Davis, M. 2010. "Who Will Build the Ark?" *New Left Review* 61: 29–46.

Davis, W. 2009. *The Wayfinders*. Toronto: House of Anasi Press.

Deci, E. L., and R. M. Ryan. 2000. "The 'What' and 'Why' of Goal Pursuits: Human Needs and the Self-Determination of Behavior." *Psychological Inquiry* 11(4): 227–268.

De Henau, J. 2015. "Costing a Feminist Plan for a Caring Economy: The Case of Free Universal Childcare in the UK." *Open Discussion Papers in Economics* 79: 1–17.

Deming, D. 2019. "Tuition-Free College Could Cost Less Than You Think." *New York Times*, July 19. https://www.nytimes.com/2019/07/19/business/tuition-free-college.html.

Dennett, D. 2015. *Elbow Room*. 2nd ed. Cambridge, MA: MIT Press.

Desmond, M. 2012. "Eviction and the Reproduction of Urban Poverty." *American Journal of Sociology* 118(1): 88–133.

de Vries, R., S. Gosling, and J. Potter. 2011. "Income Inequality and Personality: Are Less Equal US States Less Agreeable?" *Social Science & Medicine* 72(12): 1978–1985.

Di, Z. X. 2005. "Does Housing Wealth Contribute to or Temper the Widening Wealth Gap in America?" *Housing Policy Debate* 16(2): 281–296.

Di, Z. X., Y. Yang, and X. Liu. 2003. "The Importance of Housing to the Accumulation of Household Net Wealth." Working paper. Cambridge, MA: Joint Center for Housing Studies W03-5. https://www.jchs.harvard.edu/sites/default/files/media/imp/w03-5_di.pdf.

Diamond, P., and E. Saez. 2011. "The Case for a Progressive Tax: From Basic Research to Policy Recommendations." *Journal of Economic Perspectives* 25(4): 165–190.

Dietsch, P. 2015. *Catching Capital: The Ethics of Tax Competition*. New York: Oxford University Press.

Dinan, T. G., R. M. Stilling, C. Stanton, and J. F. Cryan. 2015. "Collective Unconscious: How Gut Microbes Shape Human Behavior." *Journal of Psychiatric Research* 63: 1–9.

Doidge, N. 2010. *The Brain That Changes Itself*. Melbourne: Scribe.

Doris, J. 2002. *Lack of Character: Personality and Moral Behavior*. Cambridge: Cambridge University Press.

Dow, G. 2003. *Governing the Firm: Workers' Control in Theory and Practice*. Cambridge: Cambridge University Press.

Dow, W. H., A. Godøy, C. A. Lowenstein, and M. Reich. 2019. "Can Economic Policies Reduce Deaths of Despair." NBER Working Papers 25787, Cambridge, MA. https://www.nber.org/system/files/working_papers/w25787/w25787.pdf.

Drometer, M., M. Frank, M. H. Pérez, C. Rhode, S. Schworm, and T. Stitteneder. 2018. "Wealth and Inheritance Taxation: An Overview and Country Comparison." *ifo DICE Report* 16(2): 45–54.

Duran-Cabré, J. M., A. Esteller-Moré, and M. Mas-Montserrat. 2019. "Behavioural Responses to the (Re)introduction of Wealth Taxes: Evidence from Spain." Barcelona: IEB Working Paper 2019/04. http://diposit.ub.edu/dspace/bitstream/2445/134066/1/IEB19-04_Duran+Esteller+Mas.pdf.

Durkheim, E. (1893) 1984. *The Division of Labour in Society*. Translated by W. D. Halls. London: Macmillan.

Durst, M. C. 2016. "Self-Help and Altruism: Protecting Developing Countries' Tax Revenues." In *Global Tax Fairness*, edited by T. Pogge and K. Mehta, 316–338. Oxford: Oxford University Press.

Dworkin, R. 1981a. "What Is Equality? Part 1: Equality of Welfare." *Philosophy & Public Affairs* 10(3): 185–246.

Dworkin, R. 1981b. "What Is Equality? Part 2: Equality of Resources." *Philosophy & Public Affairs* 10(4): 283–345.

Dworkin, R. 2000. *Sovereign Virtue: The Theory and Practice of Equality*. Cambridge, MA: Harvard University Press.

Eckert, J.-B., and L. Aebi. 2020. "Wealth Taxation in Switzerland." London: Wealth Tax Commission Background Paper 133. https://www.google.com/url?sa=t&rct=j&q= &esrc=s&source=web&cd=&ved=2ahUKEwjKhojhy8n7AhWmJjQIHd_4D_gQFno ECBUQAw&url=https%3A%2F%2Fwww.wealthandpolicy.com%2Fwp%2FBP133_ Countries_Switzerland.pdf&usg=AOvVaw3p8mukQ5OPFjR0t62LlocB.

Edison, H., and C. Reinhart. 2001. "Stopping Hot Money." *Journal of Development Economics* 66(2): 533–553.

Edwards, C. 2019. "Taxing Wealth and Capital Income." *Cato Institute Tax and Budget Bulletin* (85): 1–15.

Edwards, S. 1999. "How Effective Are Capital Controls?" *Journal of Economic Perspectives* 13(4): 65–84.

Elsässer, L., S. Hense, and A. Schäfer. 2021. "Not Just Money: Unequal Responsiveness in Egalitarian Democracies." *Journal of European Public Policy* 28(12): 1890–1908.

Epstein, G., I. Grabel, and K. S. Jomo. 2003. "Capital Management Techniques in Developing Countries: An Assessment of Experiences from the 1990's and Lessons for the Future." Working paper. Amherst, MA: Political Economy Research Institute 56. https://scholarworks.umass.edu/cgi/viewcontent.cgi?article=1043&context=peri_wo rkingpapers.

Epstein, R. A. 2014. "The Case against Reparations for Slavery." Hoover Institution, May 27. https://www.hoover.org/research/case-against-reparations-slavery.

Equality Trust. 2012. "The Equality Trust Research Digest: Inequality and the 2011 England Riots." August 2. https://www.equalitytrust.org.uk/sites/default/files/riots-2- august-2012.pdf.

Erten, B., A. Korinek, and J. A. Ocampo. 2019. "Capital Controls: Theory and Evidence." NBER Working Papers 26447, Cambridge, MA. https://www.nber.org/system/files/ working_papers/w26447/w26447.pdf.

Esaiasson, P., and S. Holmberg. 1996. *Representation from Above: Members of Parliament and Representative Democracy in Sweden*. Translated by J. Westerlund. Aldershot: Darmouth.

Esping-Andersen, G., ed. 2002. *Why We Need a New Welfare State*. Oxford: Oxford University Press.

Fairbrother, M., and I. W. Martin. 2013. "Does Inequality Erode Social Trust? Results from Multilevel Models of US States and Counties." *Social Science Research* 42(2): 347–360.

Farber, H. S., D. Herbst, I. Kuziemko, and S. Naidu. 2021. "Unions and Inequality over the Twentieth Century: New Evidence from Survey Data." *The Quarterly Journal of Economics* 136(3): 1325–1385.

Feinberg, R. E. 1974. "Dependency and the Defeat of Allende." *Latin American Perspectives* 1(2): 30–43.

Ferreras, I. 2017. *Firms as Political Entities*. Cambridge: Cambridge University Press.

Ferreras, I., T. Malleson, J. Rogers, eds. Forthcoming. *Democratizing the Corporation: The Bicameral Firm and Beyond*. London: Verso.

Fineman, M. A. 2004. *The Autonomy Myth: A Theory of Dependency*. New York: New Press.

Finley, M. I. 1973. *The Ancient Economy*. Berkeley: University of California Press.

Fitzgerald, J. B., J. B. Schor, and A. K. Jorgenson. 2018. "Working Hours and Carbon Dioxide Emissions in the United States, 2007–2013." *Social Forces* 96(4): 1851–1874.

Flavin, P. 2012. "Income Inequality and Policy Representation in the American States." *American Politics Research* 40(1): 29–59.

Fonger, J. 2021. "Corporations Are Spending Millions on Lobbying to Avoid Taxes." Public Citizen, August 11. https://www.citizen.org/news/corporations-are-spending-millions-on-lobbying-to-avoid-taxes/.

Foot, P. 2005. *The Vote*. London: Penguin Books.

Forbes, K. J. 2007. "The Microeconomic Evidence on Capital Controls: No Free Lunch." In *Capital Controls and Capital Flows in Emerging Economies: Policies, Practices and Consequences*, edited by S. Edwards, 171–202. Chicago: University of Chicago Press.

Fortin, P., L. Godbout, and S. St-Cerny. 2012. "Impact of Quebec's Universal Low Fee Childcare Program on Female Labour Force Participation, Domestic Income, and Government Budgets." Sherbrooke: Working Paper of the Research Chair in Taxation and Public Finance. http://cffp.recherche.usherbrooke.ca/wp-content/uploads/2018/12/cr_2012-02_impact_of_quebecs_universal_low_fee.pdf.

Foster, J. B., R. W. McChesney, and R. J. Jonna. 2011. "Monopoly and Competition in Twenty-First Century Capitalism." *Monthly Review* 62(11): 1–39.

Fourie, C., F. Schuppert, and I. Wallimann-Helmer, eds. 2015. *Social Equality*. Oxford: Oxford University Press.

Frank, R. H. 2000. "Progressive Taxation and the Incentive Problem." In *Does Atlas Shrug? The Economic Consequences of Taxing the Rich*, edited by J. B. Slemrod, 490–507. Cambridge, MA: Harvard University Press.

Frankfurt, H. 1971. "Freedom of the Will and the Concept of a Person." *Journal of Philosophy* 68: 5–20.

Frankfurt, H. 1987. "Equality as a Moral Ideal." *Ethics* 98(1): 21–43.

Frankfurt, H. 2016. *On Inequality*. Princeton, NJ: Princeton University Press.

Fremstad, A., M. Paul, and A. Underwood. 2019. "Work Hours and CO_2 Emissions: Evidence from US Households." *Review of Political Economy* 31(1): 42–59.

Frick, W. 2015. "Welfare Makes America More Entreprenurial." *The Atlantic*, March. https://www.theatlantic.com/politics/archive/2015/03/welfare-makes-america-more-entrepreneurial/388598/.

Fried, B. 1995. "Wilt Chamberlain Revisited: Nozick's 'Justice in Transfer' and the Problem of Market-Based Distribution." *Philosophy & Public Affairs* 24(3): 226–245.

Friedman, Milton. (1962) 2002. *Capitalism and Freedom*. Chicago: University of Chicago Press.

Fritzon, G., and J. Lundberg. 2019. "Taxing High Incomes: A Comparison of 41 Countries." Tax Foundation. Last accessed November 25, 2022. https://files.taxfoundation.org/20191022160341/Taxing-High-Income-A-Comparison-of-41-Countries-PDF.pdf.

Fuller, G. W., A. Johnston, and A. Regan. 2020. "Housing Prices and Wealth Inequality in Western Europe." *West European Politics* 43(2): 297–320.

Gailliot, M. T., and R. F. Baumeister. 2007. "The Physiology of Willpower: Linking Blood Glucose to Self-Control." *Personality and Social Psychology Review* 11(4): 303–327.

Gale, W. G., and A. A. Samwick. 2016. "Effects of Income Tax Changes on Economic Growth." Unpublished paper.

Galeano, E. 1973. *Open Veins of Latin America: Five Centuries of the Pillage of a Continent*. Translated by C. Belfrage. London: Monthly Review Press.

Gamage, D. 2015. "The Case for Taxing (All of) Labor Income, Consumption, Capital Income, and Wealth." *Tax Law Review* 68: 355–441.

Gamage, D. 2019. "Five Key Research Findings on Wealth Taxation for the Super Rich." SSRN, July 31. http://dx.doi.org/10.2139/ssrn.3427827.

GAO. 2018. *Discipline Disparities for Black Students, Boys, and Students with Disabilities*. Washington, DC: United States Government Accountability Office.

Gardner, M. 2019. "Amazon in Its Prime: Doubles Profits, Pays $0 in Federal Income Taxes." Institute on Taxation and Economic Policy, February 13. https://itep.org/amazon-in-its-prime-doubles-profits-pays-0-in-federal-income-taxes/.

Gardner, M., and S. Wamhoff. 2021. "55 Corporations Paid $0 in Federal Taxes on 2020 Profits." Institue on Taxation and Economic Policy, April 2. https://itep.org/55-profitable-corporations-zero-corporate-tax/.

Garrison, C. B., and F. Y. Lee. 1992. "Taxation, Aggregate Activity and Economic Growth." *Economic Inquiry* 30(1): 172–176.

Garside, J. 2016. "Inheritance Tax: Why the New Duke of Westminster Will Not Pay Billions." *The Guardian*, August 11. https://www.theguardian.com/money/2016/aug/11/inheritance-tax-why-the-new-duke-of-westminster-will-not-pay-billions.

Gastil, J., and E. O. Wright, eds. 2019. *Legislature by Lot: Transformative Designs for Deliberative Governance*. London: Verso Books.

GATJ, PSI, and TJN. 2021. *The State of Tax Justice 2021*. Ferney-Voltaire: Public Services International and Global Alliance for Tax Justice.

Genschel, P., and P. Schwarz. 2011. "Tax Competition: A Literature Review." *Socio-Economic Review* 9(2): 339–370.

George, H. (1879) 1910. *Progress and Poverty*. London: J. M. Dent.

Gilens, M., and B. I. Page. 2014. "Testing Theories of American Politics: Elites, Interest Groups, and Average Citizens." *Perspectives on Politics* 12(3): 564–581.

Gilmore, S. 2015. "Canada's Race Problem? It's Even Worse Than America's." *Maclean's*, January 22. https://www.macleans.ca/news/canada/out-of-sight-out-of-mind-2/.

Goldmacher, S. 2019. "How David Koch and His Brother Shaped American Politics." *New York Times*, August 23. https://www.nytimes.com/2019/08/23/us/politics/david-koch-republican-politics.html.

Gonalons-Pons, P., and D. Calnitsky. 2021. "Exit, Voice and Loyalty in the Family: Findings from a Basic Income Experiment." *Socio-Economic Review* 20(3): 1395–1423.

Goodhart, M. E. 2018. *Injustice: Political Theory for the Real World*. Oxford: Oxford University Press.

Goolsbee, A. 2000. "What Happens When You Tax the Rich? Evidence from Executive Compensation." *Journal of Political Economy* 108(2): 352–378.

Gordon, C., and R. Eisenbrey. 2012. "As Unions Decline, Inequality Rises." Economic Policy Institute, June 6. https://www.epi.org/publication/unions-decline-inequality-rises/.

Gornick, J. C., and M. K. Meyers, eds. 2009a. *Gender Equality: Transforming Family Divisions of Labor*. London: Verso.

Gornick, J. C., and M. K. Meyers. 2009b. "Institutions That Support Gender Equality in Parenthood and Employment." In *Gender Equality: Transforming Family Divisions of Labour,* edited by J. C. Gornick and M. K. Meyers, 3–66. London: Verso.

Gorton, G., and F. A. Schmid. 2004. "Capital, Labor, and the Firm: A Study of German Codetermination." *Journal of the European Economic Association* 2(5): 863–905.

Govender, S. 2017. "SA Sees Growth in Gated Community Living." *The Times,* December 4. https://www.timeslive.co.za/news/south-africa/2017-12-04-sa-sees-growth-in-gated-community-living/.

Gowan, P., and R. Cooper. 2018. *Social Housing in the United States.* People's Policy Project.

Grapard, U. 1995. "Robinson Crusoe: The Quintessential Economic Man?" *Feminist Economics* 1(1): 33–52.

Gregory, J. 2016. "How Not to Be an Egalitarian: The Politics of Homeownership and Property-Owning Democracy." *International Journal of Housing Policy* 16(3): 337–356.

Guiso, L., H. Herrera, M. Morelli, and T. Sonno. 2017. "Populism: Demand and Supply." Center for Economic Policy Research Discussion Paper 11871. https://www.tcd.ie/Economics/assets/pdf/Seminars/20172018/H.%20Herrera.pdf.

Guiso, L., H. Herrera, M. Morelli, and T. Sonno. 2019. "Global Crises and Populism: The Role of Eurozone Institutions." *Economic Policy* 34(97): 95–139.

Guntermann, E. 2021. "Does Economic Inequality Undermine Political Equality? Testing Two Common Assumptions." *Electoral Studies* 69(102202): 1–11.

Gustavsson, M., and H. Jordahl. 2008. "Inequality and Trust in Sweden: Some Inequalities Are More Harmful Than Others." *Journal of Public Economics* 92(1–2): 348–365.

Hahnel, R. 2002. *The ABC's of Political Economy.* London: Pluto Press.

Hahnel, R. 2011. *Green Economics: Confronting the Ecological Crisis.* Armonk, NY: M. E. Sharpe.

Halikiopoulou, D., and T. Vlandas. 2016. "Risks, Costs and Labour Markets: Explaining Cross-national Patterns of Far Right Party Success in European Parliament Elections." *Journal of Common Market Studies* 54(3): 636–655.

Hanson, E. 2020. "The Residential School System." Indigenous Foundations. Last accessed November 25, 2022. https://indigenousfoundations.arts.ubc.ca/the_residential_school_system/.

Harman, C. 1999. *A People's History of the World.* London: Bookmarks.

Hastings, O. P. 2018. "Less Equal, Less Trusting? Longitudinal and Cross-sectional Effects of Income Inequality on Trust in US States, 1973–2012." *Social Science Research* 74: 77–95.

Hayden, A. 1999. *Sharing the Work, Sparing the Planet.* Toronto: Between the Lines.

Hearne, R. 2017. "A Home or a Wealth Generator? Inequality, Financialisation and the Irish Housing Crisis." In *Cherishing All Equally,* edited by J. Wickham, 61–94. Dublin: TASC.

Hegewisch, A. 2009. *Flexible Working Policies: A Comparative Review.* Manchester: Equality and Human Rights Commission.

Hegewisch, A., and E. Williams-Baron. 2018. "The Gender Wage Gap: 2017 Earnings Differences by Race and Ethnicity." Institute for Women's Policy Research, September. https://iwpr.org/wp-content/uploads/2020/08/C473.pdf.

Hemel, D. 2019. "Elizabeth Warren's Wealth Tax on the Super-Rich Is the Wrong Solution to the Right Problem." *Time,* January 30. https://time.com/5516903/elizabeth-warren-wealth-tax-income-assets/.

Henrekson, M. 2017. "Taxation of Swedish Firm Owners: The Great Reversal from the 1970s to the 2010s." *Nordic Tax Journal* 2017(1): 26–46.

Henrekson, M., and D. Waldenström. 2016. "Inheritance Taxation in Sweden, 1885–2004: The Role of Ideology, Family Firms, and Tax Avoidance." *Economic History Review* 69(4): 1228–1254.

Henry, J. S. 2016. "Let's Tax Anonymous Wealth." In *Global Tax Fairness*, edited by T. Pogge and K. Mehta, 31–95. Oxford: Oxford University Press.

Herlitz, A. 2018. "The Indispensability of Sufficientarianism." *Critical Review of International Social and Political Philosophy* 22(7): 929–942.

Herman, E. S., and N. Chomsky. 1988. *Manufacturing Consent: The Political Economy of the Mass Media*. New York: Pantheon Books.

Hill, R., C. Lakner, D. Mahler, A. Narayan, and N. Yonzan. 2021. "Poverty, Median Incomes, and Inequality in 2021: A Diverging Recovery." Washington, DC: World Bank Report. https://www.google.com/url?sa=t&rct=j&q=&esrc=s&source=web&cd=&ved=2ahUKEwi31Nn86cn7AhXyHTQIHbw2Bz8QFnoECBMQAQ&url=https%3A%2F%2Fdocuments1.worldbank.org%2Fcurated%2Fen%2F936001635880885713%2Fpdf%2FPoverty-Median-Incomes-and-Inequality-in-2021-A-Diverging-Recovery.pdf&usg=AOvVaw2aVXUbwQtHi5_QuicOX-cu.

Hill, T. D., and A. Jorgenson. 2018. "Bring Out Your Dead! A Study of Income Inequality and Life Expectancy in the United States, 2000–2010." *Health & Place* 49: 1–6.

Hirst, S., and L. Bebchuk. 2019. "The Specter of the Giant Three." *Boston University Law Review* 99(3): 721–741.

Hobbes, T. (1651) 2002. *Leviathan*. Peterborough: Broadview Press.

Hobsbawm, E. 1987. *The Age of Empire, 1875–1914* London: Weidenfeld and Nicolson.

Hochguertel, S., and H. Ohlsson. 2012. "Who Is at the Top? Wealth Mobility over the Life Cycle." Uppsala: Uppsala Center for Fiscal Studies, Working Paper 2012/1. https://www.diva-portal.org/smash/get/diva2:480739/FULLTEXT01.pdf.

Hochschild, A. 2003. *The Second Shift*. New York: Penguin Books.

Hochschild, A. 2016. *Strangers in Their Own Land*. New York: New Press.

Holtz-Eakin, D., D. Joulfaian, and H. S. Rosen. 1993. "The Carnegie Conjecture: Some Empirical Evidence." *Quarterly Journal of Economics* 108(2): 413–435.

Hörisch, F. 2012. "The Macro-economic Effect of Codetermination on Income Equality." Working paper. Mannheim: Mannheimer Zentrum für Europ ische Sozialforschung 147. https://core.ac.uk/download/pdf/71741950.pdf.

Hresko, T. 2006. "In the Cellars of the Hollow Men: Use of Solitary Confinement in US Prisons and Its Implications under International Laws against Torture." *Pace International Law Review* 18: 1.

Hsieh, C.-C., and M. D. Pugh. 1993. "Poverty, Income Inequality, and Violent Crime: A Meta-analysis of Recent Aggregate Data Studies." *Criminal Justice Review* 18(2): 182–202.

Hungerford, T. L. 2012. *Taxes and the Economy: An Economic Analysis of the Top Tax Rates since 1945 (Updated)*. Washington, DC: Congressional Research Service.

Hurst, E., and A. Lusardi. 2004. "Liquidity Constraints, Household Wealth, and Entrepreneurship." *Journal of Political Economy* 112(2): 319–347.

Huseby, R. 2010. "Sufficiency: Restated and Defended." *Journal of Political Philosophy* 18(2): 178–197.

IMF. 2018. "Denmark: Selected Issues." *IMF Country Report* 18(178): 1–75.

IPCC. 2018a. "Global Warming of 1.5 °C: Special Report." Last accessed November 25, 2022. https://www.ipcc.ch/sr15/.

IPCC. 2018b. "Summary for Policymakers." February. https://www.ipcc.ch/site/assets/uploads/2018/02/ipcc_wg3_ar5_summary-for-policymakers.pdf.

Isen, A. M., and P. F. Levin. 1972. "Effect of Feeling Good on Helping: Cookies and Kindness." *Journal of Personality and Social Psychology* 21(3): 384–388.

Ishi, H. 1980. "Effects of Taxation on the Distribution of Income and Wealth in Japan." *Hitotsubashi Journal of Economics* 21(1): 27–47.

Islam, F. 2021. "G7: Rich Nations Back Deal to Tax Multinationals." BBC, June 5. https://www.bbc.com/news/world-57368247.

ITEP. 2017. "Fact Sheet: Apple and Tax Avoidance." Institute on Taxation and Economic Policy, November 5. https://itep.org/fact-sheet-apple-and-tax-avoidance/.

ITEP. 2020. "Who Pays Taxes in America in 2020?" Institute on Taxation and Economic Policy, July 14. https://itep.org/who-pays-taxes-in-america-in-2020/.

Jackson, T. 2009. *Prosperity without Growth: Economics for a Finite Planet*. London: Earthscan.

Jäger, S., S. Noy, and B. Schoefer. 2021. "What Does Codetermination Do?" *Industrial and Labor Relations Review* 75(4): 857–890.

Jakobsen, K., K. Jakobsen, H. Kleven, and G. Zucman. 2020. "Wealth Taxation and Wealth Accumulation: Theory and Evidence from Denmark." *Quarterly Journal of Economics* 135(1): 329–388.

Johannesen, N., P. Langetieg, D. Reck, M. Risch, and J. Slemrod. 2018. "Taxing Hidden Wealth: The Consequences of US Enforcement Initiatives on Evasive Foreign Accounts." NBER Working Papers 24366, Cambridge, MA. https://www.nber.org/system/files/working_papers/w24366/w24366.pdf.

Johnsen, D., and W. Dellinger. 2018. "The Constitutionality of a National Wealth Tax." *Indiana Law Journal* 93(1): 111–138.

Jorgenson, A., and R. Birkholz. 2010. "Assessing the Causes of Anthropogenic Methane Emissions in Comparative Perspective, 1990–2005." *Ecological Economics* 69(12): 2634–2643.

Jorgenson, A., and B. Clark. 2012. "Are the Economy and the Environment Decoupling? A Comparative International study, 1960–2005." *American Journal of Sociology* 118(1): 1–44.

Jorgenson, A., J. Schor, and X. Huang. 2017. "Income Inequality and Carbon Emissions in the United States: A State-Level Analysis, 1997–2012." *Ecological Economics* 134: 40–48.

Jorgenson, D. W., M. S. Ho, and J. D. Samuels. 2014. "Long-Term Estimates of US Productivity and Growth." Unpublished paper.

Joseph, R. 2018. "Canadians Overestimate Number of Female CEOs in 'Peril of Perception': Ipsos Poll." Global News, March 8. https://globalnews.ca/news/4069615/canadians-number-of-female-ceos-poll/.

Kahneman, D. 2011. *Thinking, Fast and Slow*. Toronto: Doubleday.

Kamin, D. 2015. "How to Tax the Rich." *Tax Notes* 146(1): 119–129.

Kaminsky, G., and C. Reinhart. 1999. "The Twin Crises: The Causes of Banking and Balance-of-Payments Problems." *American Economic Review* 89(3): 473–500.

Kanschik, P. 2015. "Why Sufficientarianism Is Not Indifferent to Taxation." *Kriterion* 29(2): 81–102.

Kapeller, J., S. Leitch, and R. Wildauer. 2021. "A European Wealth Tax for a Fair and Green Recovery." Linz: ICAE Working Paper Series 129. https://www.econstor.eu/bitstream/10419/246862/1/1777393078.pdf.

Kaplan, E., and D. Rodrik. 2002. "Did the Malaysian Capital Controls Work?" In *Preventing Currency Crises in Emerging Markets*, edited by S. Edwards and J. Frankel, 393–431. Chicago: University of Chicago Press.

Kaplan, S. N. 2012. "Executive Compensation and Corporate Governance in the U.S.: Perceptionis, Facts and Challenges." NBER Working Papers 18395, Cambridge, MA. https://www.nber.org/system/files/working_papers/w18395/w18395.pdf.

Katznelson, I. 2005. *When Affirmative Action Was White: An Untold History of Racial Inequality in Twentieth-Century America*. New York: W. W. Norton.

Kearney, M. S., and P. B. Levine. 2014. "Income Inequality, Social Mobility, and the Decision to Drop Out of High School." Working paper. Cambridge, MA: National Bureau of Economic Research 20195. https://www.nber.org/system/files/working_pap ers/w20195/w20195.pdf.

Kenneth, B., and M. P. Clark. 1947. "Racial Identification and Preference in Negro Children." In *Readings in Social Psychology*, edited by E. L. Hartley, 551–560. New York: Holt, Rinehart, and Winston.

Kenworthy, L. 2016. "Is Income Inequality Harmful?" The Good Society. Last accessed November 26, 2022. https://lanekenworthy.net/is-income-inequality-harmful/#fnref-8676-115.

Kenworthy, L. 2020. *Social Democratic Capitalism*. New York: Oxford University Press.

Kenworthy, L. 2022. *Would Democratic Socialism Be Better?* New York: Oxford University Press.

Kershnar, S. 2005. "Giving Capitalists Their Due." *Economics and Philosophy* 21(1): 65–87.

Khimm, S. 2011. "Who Are the 1 Percent?" *Washington Post*, October 6. https://www.was hingtonpost.com/blogs/ezra-klein/post/who-are-the-1-percenters/2011/10/06/gIQA n4JDQL_blog.html.

Kimmerer, R. W. 2013. *Braiding Sweetgrass*. Minneapolis, MN: Milkweed Editions.

Kingsley, P. 2016. "Migration between Poor Countries Rising Faster Than to Rich Ones—Study." *The Guardian*, April 20. https://www.theguardian.com/world/2016/apr/20/migration-between-poor-countries-rising-faster-than-to-rich-ones-study.

Kittay, E. 1999. *Love's Labor*. New York: Routledge.

Klein, N. 2014. *This Changes Everything: Capitalism vs. the Climate*. Toronto: Alfred A. Knopf Canada.

Kleinbard, E. D. 2016. "Stateless Income and Its Remedies." In *Global Tax Fairness*, edited by T. Pogge and K. Mehta, 129–152. Oxford: Oxford University Press.

Kleven, H. J. 2014. "How Can Scandinavians Tax So Much?" *Journal of Economic Perspectives* 28(4): 77–98.

Kleven, H. J., M. B. Knudsen, C. T. Kreiner, S. Pedersen, and E. Saez. 2011. "Unwilling or Unable to Cheat? Evidence from a Tax Audit Experiment in Denmark." *Econometrica* 79(3): 651–692.

Kleven, H. J., C. T. Kreiner, and E. Saez. 2016. "Why Can Modern Governments Tax So Much? An Agency Model of Firms as Fiscal Intermediaries." *Economica* 83(330): 219–246.

Kleven, H. J., C. Landais, and E. Saez. 2013. "Taxation and International Migration of Superstars: Evidence from the European Football Market." *American Economic Review* 103(5): 1892–1924.

Kleven, H. J., C. Landais, E. Saez, and E. Schultz. 2014. "Migration and Wage Effects of Taxing Top Earners: Evidence from the Foreigners' Tax Scheme in Denmark." *Quarterly Journal of Economics* 129(1): 333–378.

Kleven, H. J., and E. A. Schultz. 2014. "Estimating Taxable Income Responses Using Danish Tax Reforms." *American Economic Journal: Economic Policy* 6(4): 271–301.

Knight, K. W., E. A. Rosa, and J. B. Schor. 2013. "Could Working Less Reduce Pressures on the Environment? A Cross-national Panel Analysis of OECD Countries, 1970–2007." *Global Environmental Change* 23(4): 691–700.

Knight, K. W., and J. B. Schor. 2014. "Economic Growth and Climate Change: A Cross-national Analysis of Territorial and Consumption-Based Carbon Emissions in High-Income Countries." *Sustainability* 6(6): 3722–3731.

Knight, K. W., J. B. Schor, and A. K. Jorgenson. 2017. "Wealth Inequality and Carbon Emissions in High-Income Countries." *Social Currents* 4(5): 403–412.

Knobel, A. 2019a. *Beneficial Ownership Verification: Ensuring the Truthfulness and Accuracy of Registered Ownership Information.* Buckinghamshire: Tax Justice Network.

Knobel, A. 2019b. "Global Asset Registries: A Game Changer for the Fight against Inequality and Illicit Financial Flows?" Tax Justice, September 17. https://taxjustice. net/2019/09/17/global-asset-registries-a-game-changer-for-the-fight-against-inequal ity-and-illicit-financial-flows/.

Koch, A., C. Brierley, M. M. Maslin, and S. L. Lewis. 2019. "Earth System Impacts of the European Arrival and Great Dying in the Americas after 1492." *Quaternary Science Reviews* 207: 13–36.

Koeniger, W., M. Leonardi, and L. Nunziata. 2007. "Labor Market Institutions and Wage Inequality." *ILR Review* 60(3): 340–356.

Kolata, G. 2021. "Kati Kariko Helped Shield the World from the Coronavirus." *New York Times,* April 8. https://www.nytimes.com/2021/04/08/health/coronavirus-mrna-kar iko.html.

Kopczuk, W. 2013. "Taxation of Intergenerational Transfers and Wealth." In *Handbook of Public Economics,* edited by A. J. Auerbach, R. Chetty, M. Feldstein, and E. Saez, vol. 5, 329–390. Amsterdam: Elsevier.

Kose, M. A., E. Prasad, K. Rogoff, and S.-J. Wei. 2009. "Financial Globalization: A Reappraisal." *IMF Staff Papers* 56(1): 8–62.

Kraus, L., E. Lauer, R. Coleman, and A. Houtenville. 2018. *2017 Disability Statistics Annual Report.* Durham, NH: University of New Hampshire.

Kraus, M. W., P. K. Piff, R. Mendoza-Denton, M. L. Rheinschmidt, and D. Keltner. 2012. "Social Class, Solipsism, and Contextualism: How the Rich Are Different from the Poor." *Psychological Review* 119(3): 546.

Krieger, T., and D. Meierrieks. 2019. "Income Inequality, Redistribution and Domestic Terrorism." *World Development* 116: 125–136.

Kristiansen, K., S. Vehmas, and T. Shakespeare, eds. 2009. *Arguing about Disability: Philosophical Perspectives.* London: Routledge.

Krugman, Paul. 1998. "Open Letter to Mr. Mahathir." *Fortune,* September 28.

Krugman, Paul. 2009. *The Return of Depression Economics and the Crisis of 2008.* New York: W. W. Norton.

Kruse, D., R. Freeman, and J. Blasi, eds. 2010. *Shared Capitalism at Work: Employee Ownership, Profit and Gain Sharing, and Broad-Based Stock Options.* Chicago: University of Chicago Press.

Kuznets, S. 1971. *Economic Growth of Nations: Total Output and Production Structure*. Cambridge, MA: Harvard University Press.

Kymlicka, W. 1990. *Contemporary Political Philosophy: An Introduction*. Oxford: Clarendon Press.

Kymlicka, W. (1990) 2000. "Property-Rights and the Self-Ownership Argument." In *Left-Libertarianism and Its Critics: The Contemporary Debate*, edited by P. Vallentyne and H. Steiner, 295–321. Houndmills: Palgrave.

LaJeunesse, R. 2009. *Work Time Regulation as a Sustainable Full Employment Strategy: The Social Effort Bargain*. London: Routledge.

Lakhani, N. 2022. "Starbucks Fires Workers Involved in Union Push as US Movement Gains Momentum." *The Guardian*, February 9. https://www.theguardian.com/business/2022/feb/09/starbucks-union-memphis-workers-fired-us-movement.

Lammers, J., D. A. Stapel, and A. D. Galinsky. 2010. "Power Increases Hypocrisy: Moralizing in Reasoning, Immorality in Behavior." *Psychological Science* 21(5): 737–744.

Lammers, J., J. I. Stoker, J. Jordan, M. Pollmann, and D. A. Stapel. 2011. "Power Increases Infidelity among Men and Women." *Psychological Science* 22(9): 1191–1197.

Lamont, J. 1995. "Problems for Effort-Based Distribution Principles." *Journal of Applied Philosophy* 12(3): 215–229.

Lancee, B., and H. G. Van de Werfhorst. 2012. "Income Inequality and Participation: A Comparison of 24 European Countries." *Social Science Research* 41(5): 1166–1178.

Lartey, J. 2019. "'It's Totally Unfair': Chicago, Where the Rich Live 30 Years Longer Than the Poor." *The Guardian*, June 23. https://www.theguardian.com/us-news/2019/jun/23/chicago-latest-news-life-expectancy-rich-poor-inequality.

Layte, R. 2012. "The Association between Income Inequality and Mental Health: Testing Status Anxiety, Social Capital, and Neo-materialist Explanations." *European Sociological Review* 28(4): 498–511.

Le, A. T. 1999. "Empirical Studies of Self-Employment." *Journal of Economic Surveys* 13(4): 381–416.

Leiserson, G. 2020. "Taxing Wealth." In *Tackling the Tax Code: Efficient and Equitable Ways to Raise Revenue*, edited by J. Shambaugh and R. Nunn, 89–148. Washington, DC: The Hamilton Project.

Levy, N. 2011. *Hard Luck: How Luck Undermines Free Will and Moral Responsibility*. Oxford: Oxford University Press.

Lewis, P., and T. Silverstone. 2016. "Trump Campaign Chair in Ohio Resigns Over 'No Racism before Obama' Remarks." *The Guardian*, September 22. https://www.theguardian.com/us-news/2016/sep/22/trump-campaign-chair-kathy-miller-resigns-ohio-racism-obama.

Lindblom, C. 1982. "The Market as Prison." *Journal of Politics* 44(2): 324–336.

Lindeman, T. 2021. "Canada: Remains of 215 Children Found at Indigenous Residential School Site." *The Guardian*, May 28. https://www.theguardian.com/world/2021/may/28/canada-remains-indigenous-children-mass-graves.

Lippert-Rasmussen, K. 2015. *Luck Egalitarianism*. London: Bloomsbury.

Lipsitz, G. 1998. *The Possessive Investment in Whiteness*. Philadelphia, PA: Temple University Press.

Locke, J. (1689) 1980. *Second Treatise of Government*. Indianapolis, IN: Hackett.

Lombardo, G., and F. Ravenna. 2012. "The Size of the Tradable and Non-tradable Sectors: Evidence from Input-Output Tables for 25 Countries." *Economics Letters* 116: 558–561.

Loutzenhiser, G., and E. Mann. 2021. "Liquidity Issues: Solutions for the Asset Rich, Cash Poor." *Fiscal Studies* 42(3–4): 651–675.

Lucas, R. E. 2004. "The Industrial Revolution: Past and Future. 2003 Annual Report Essay." Federal Reserve Bank of Minneapolis, May 1. https://www.minneapolisfed.org/publications/the-region/the-industrial-revolution-past-and-future.

Luhby, T. 2014. "America's Middle Class: Poorer Than You Think." CNN, June 11. http://money.cnn.com/2014/06/11/news/economy/middle-class-wealth/index.html.

Lupu, N., and Z. Warner. 2022. "Affluence and Congruence: Unequal Representation around the World." *Journal of Politics* 84(1): 276–290.

Lutz, A. 2012. "These 6 Corporations Control 90% of the Media in America." *Business Insider*, June 14. https://www.businessinsider.com/these-6-corporations-control-90-of-the-media-in-america-2012-6?IR=T.

Ma, G., and R. McCauley. 2008. "Efficacy of China's Capital Controls: Evidence from Price and Flow Data." *Pacific Economic Review* 13(1): 104–123.

MacFarquhar, L. 2015. *Strangers Drowning*. New York: Penguin Press.

Mackin, C. Forthcoming. "Ferreras and the Economic Democracy Debate." In *Democratizing the Corporation,* edited by I. Ferreras, T. Malleson, and J. Rogers. London: Verso.

Maddison, A. 2007. *The World Economy: A Millennial Perspective*. Paris: OECD Publishing.

Madrigal, A. C. 2018. "Against Big Philanthropy." *The Atlantic*, June. https://www.theatlantic.com/technology/archive/2018/06/against-philanthropy/563834/.

Magud, N., and C. Reinhart. 2006. "Capital Controls: An Evaluation." NBER Working Papers 11973, Cambridge, MA. http://www.nber.org/papers/w11973.

Malleson, T. (2013). What Does Mondragon Teach Us About Workplace Democracy? Sharing Ownership, Profits, and Decision-Making in the 21st Century (Advances in the Economic Analysis of Participatory & Labor-Managed Firms), 14, 127–157.

Malleson, T. 2014a. *After Occupy: Economic Democracy for the 21st Century*. New York: Oxford University Press.

Malleson, T. 2014b. "Rawls, Property-Owning Democracy, and Democratic Socialism." *Journal of Social Philosophy* 45(2): 228–251.

Malleson, T. 2016. *Fired Up about Capitalism*. Toronto: Between the Lines.

Malleson, T. 2018. "Should Democracy Work through Elections or Sortition?" *Politics & Society* 46(3): 401–417.

Malleson, T. 2019. "To Each according to Their Effort? On the Ethical Significance of Hard Work." *Constellations* 26(2): 257–267.

Malleson, T. 2022. "Good Life Egalitarianism." *Philosophy & Social Criticism* 48(1): 14–39.

Malleson, T., and D. Calnitsky. 2021. "Which Way Forward for Economic Security: Basic Income or Public Services?" *Basic Income Studies*: 1–43.

Mani, A., S. Mullainathan, E. Shafir, and J. Zhao. 2013. "Poverty Impedes Cognitive Function." *Science* 341(6149): 976–980.

Manin, B. 1997. *The Principles of Representative Government*. Cambridge: Cambridge University Press.

Manjoo, F. 2020. "Even in a Pandemic, the Billionaires Are Winning." *New York Times*, November 25. https://www.nytimes.com/2020/11/25/opinion/coronavirus-billionaires.html?smid=em-share.

Mankiw, N. G. 2013. "Defending the One Percent." *Journal of Economic Perspectives* 27(3): 21–34.

Manuel, A., and R. M. Derrickson. 2015. *Unsettling Canada: A National Wake-up Call.* Toronto: Between the Lines.

Marçal, K. 2015. *Who Cooked Adam Smith's Dinner?* London: Portobello Books.

Martin, P., and D. Costa. 2017. "Farmworker Wages in California: Large Gap between Full-Time Equivalent and Actual Earnings." Economic Policy Institute, March 21. https://www.epi.org/blog/farmworker-wages-in-california-large-gap-between-full-time-equivalent-and-actual-earnings/.

Martinez, R. 2016. *Creating Freedom.* Edinburgh: Canongate.

Marx, K. (1867) 1933. *Capital.* Translated by E. A. C. Paul. London: Dent.

Maslow, A. H. 1943. "A Theory of Human Motivation." *Psychological Review* 50(4): 370.

Mayer, E. A. 2011. "Gut Feelings: The Emerging Biology of Gut-Brain Communication." *Nature Reviews Neuroscience* 12(8): 453–466.

Maynard, R. 2018. *Policing Black Lives.* Winnipeg: Fernwood.

Mazor, J. 2019. "Income Redistribution, Body-Part Redistribution, and Respect for the Separateness of Persons." *Journal of Ethics and Social Philosophy* 16(3): 192–228.

Mazzucato, M. 2013. *The Entreprenurial State.* London: Anthem Press.

McCabe, B. J. 2016. *No Place Like Home: Wealth, Community, and the Politics of Homeownership.* Oxford: Oxford University Press.

McGaughey, E. 2016. "The Codetermination Bargains: The History of German Corporate and Labor Law." *Columbia Journal of European Law* 23(1): 135–176.

McGaughey, E. 2017. "A Twelve Point Plan for Labour and a Manifesto for Labour Law." *Industrial Law Journal* 46(1): 169–184.

McIntosh, E. 2020. "What We Mean When We Say Indigenous Land Is 'Unceded.'" *National Observer*, January 24. https://www.nationalobserver.com/2020/01/24/analysis/what-we-mean-when-we-say-indigenous-land-unceded.

McKibben, B. 2007. *Deep Economy.* New York: Times Books.

Meghir, C., and D. Phillips. 2008. "Labour Supply and Taxation." London: IFS Working Papers 08(04). https://www.econstor.eu/bitstream/10419/47455/1/571756840.pdf

Mendoza, E. G., G. M. Milesi-Ferretti, and P. Asea. 1997. "On the Ineffectiveness of Tax Policy in Altering Long-Run Growth: Harberger's Superneutrality Conjecture." *Journal of Public Economics* 66(1): 99–126.

Milanovic, B. 2008. "Where in the World Are You? Assessing the Importance of Circumstance and Effort in a World of Different Mean Country Incomes and (Almost) No Migration." Washington: The World Bank Policy Research Working Paper 4493. https://openknowledge.worldbank.org/bitstream/handle/10986/6391/wps4493.pdf?sequence=1&isAllowed=y

Milanovic, B. 2011. *The Haves and the Have-Nots.* New York: Basic Books.

Milanovic, B. 2012. "Global Inequality: From Class to Location, from Proletarians to Migrants." *Global Policy* 3(2): 125–134.

Milanovic, B. 2016. *Global Inequality.* Cambridge, MA: Belknap Press.

Milgram, S. 1963. "Behavioral Study of Obedience." *Journal of Abnormal and Social Psychology* 67(4): 371–378.

Miller, D. 1989. *Market, State, and Community: Theoretical Foundations of Market Socialism.* Oxford: Clarendon Press.

Miller, D. 1999. *Principles of Social Justice.* Cambridge, MA: Harvard University Press.

Miller, D. 2000. *Citizenship and National Identity.* Cambridge, UK: Polity Press.

Miller, D. 2004. "The Concept of Desert." In *Social Justice,* edited by M. Clayton and A. Williams, 186–200. Malden, MA: Blackwell.

Miller, D. 2007. *National Responsibility and Global Justice*. Oxford: Oxford University Press.

Miller, D. 2014. "Our Unfinished Debate about Market Socialism." *Politics, Philosophy & Economics* 13(2): 119–139.

Miller, W. R., and M. E. Seligman. 1975. "Depression and Learned Helplessness in Man." *Journal of Abnormal Psychology* 84(3): 228–238.

Mills, C. W. 2013. "Retrieving Rawls for Racial Justice? A Critique of Tommie Shelby." *Critical Philosophy of Race* 1(1): 1–27.

Milman, O. 2015. "Rate of Environmental Degradation Puts Life on Earth at Risk, Say Scientists." *The Guardian*, January 15. https://www.theguardian.com/environment/2015/jan/15/rate-of-environmental-degradation-puts-life-on-earth-at-risk-say-scientists.

Milne, H. 1986. "Desert, Effort and Equality." *Journal of Applied Philosophy* 3(2): 235–243.

Mirowski, P., and D. Plehwe, eds. 2009. *The Road from Mont Pèlerin: The Making of the Neoliberal Thought Collective*. Cambridge, MA: Harvard University Press.

Mishel, L., and J. Kandra. 2021. "CEO Pay Has Skyrocketed 1,322% since 1978." Economic Policy Institute, August 10. https://www.epi.org/publication/ceo-pay-in-2020/.

Mishel, L., and N. Sabadish. 2013. "CEO Pay in 2012 Was Extraordinarily High Relative to Typical Workers and Other High Earners." Economic Policy Institute, June 26. https://www.epi.org/publication/ceo-pay-2012-extraordinarily-high/

Mitchell, P. R., and J. Schoeffel, eds. 2002. *Understanding Power: The Indispensable Chomsky*. New York: New Press.

Moffitt, R. A., and M. O. Wilhelm. 2000. "Taxation and the Labor Supply Decisions of the Affluent." In *Does Atlas Shrug? The Economic Consequences of Taxing the Rich*, edited by J. B. Slemrod, 193–234. Cambridge, MA: Harvard University Press.

Moffitt, T. E., L. Arseneault, D. Belsky, N. Dickson, R. J. Hancox, H. Harrington, R. Houts, R. Poulton, B. Roberts, S. Ross, M. Sears, W. Thomson, and A. Caspi. 2011. "A Gradient of Childhood Self-Control Predicts Health, Wealth, and Public Safety." *Proceedings of the National Academy of Sciences* 108(7): 2693–2698.

Mokyr, J. 2017. *A Culture of Growth: The Origins of the Modern Economy*. Princeton, NJ: Princeton University Press.

Molly, V., E. Laveren, and M. Deloof. 2010. "Family Business Succession and Its Impact on Financial Structure and Performance." *Family Business Review* 23(2): 131–147.

Monbiot, G. 2006. *Heat*. Toronto: Doubleday Canada.

Moore, A. 2017. "America's Financial Divide: The Racial Breakdown of US Wealth in Black and White." *Huffington Post*, December 6. https://www.huffpost.com/entry/americas-financial-divide_b_7013330.

Moretti, E., and D. J. Wilson. 2017. "The Effect of State Taxes on the Geographical Location of Top Earners: Evidence from Star Scientists." *American Economic Review* 107(7): 1858–1903.

Moriarty, J. 2003. "Against the Asymmetry of Desert." *Nous* 37(3): 518–536.

Morray, J. P. 1997. *Grand Disillusion: Francois Mitterrand and the French Left*. Westport, CT: Greenwood.

Moyser, M. 2017. *Women and Paid Work*. Ottawa: Statistics Canada.

Murphy, L., and T. Nagel. 2002. *The Myth of Ownership: Taxes and Justice*. New York: Oxford University Press.

Murphy, R. 2016. "Country-by-Country Reporting." In *Global Tax Fairness*, edited by T. Pogge and K. Mehta, 96–112. Oxford: Oxford University Press.

Narveson, J. 2001. *The Libertarian Idea*. Peterborough: Broadview Press.

Narveson, J. 2010. "Property and Rights." *Social Philosophy & Policy* 27(1): 101–134.

Navia, P., and R. Osorio. 2017. "'Make the Economy Scream'? Economic, Ideological and Social Determinants of Support for Salvador Allende in Chile, 1970–3." *Journal of Latin American Studies* 49(4): 771–797.

Neate, R. 2018. "Number of Billionaires Worldwide Surged to 2,754 in 2017." *The Guardian*, May 15. https://www.theguardian.com/business/2018/may/15/number-of-billionaires-worldwide-wealth-x-census.

Nedelsky, J., and T. Malleson. Forthcoming. *Part-Time for All: A Care Manifesto*. New York: Oxford University Press.

Ngamaba, K. H., M. Panagioti, and C. J. Armitage. 2018. "Income Inequality and Subjective Well-being: A Systematic Review and Meta-analysis." *Quality of Life Research* 27(3): 577–596.

Nielsen, L. 2017. "Shielding Sufficientarianism from the Shift." *Law, Ethics and Philosophy* 142–153.

Niyette, A. E. 2011. "Cross-national Predictors of Crime: A Meta-analysis." *Homicide Studies* 15(2): 103–131.

Noked, N. 2018. "Tax Evasion and Incomplete Tax Transparency." *Laws* 7(3): 31.

Nosek, B. A., F. L. Smyth, J. J. Hansen, T. Devos, N. M. Lindner, K. A. Ranganath, C. T. Smith, K. R. Olson, D. Chugh, A. G. Greenwald, and M. R. Banaji. 2007. "Pervasiveness and Correlates of Implicit Attitudes and Stereotypes." *European Review of Social Psychology* 18(1): 36–88.

Nove, A. 1991. *The Economics of Feasible Socialism*. 2nd ed. London: Harper Collins.

Novokmet, F., T. Piketty, and G. Zucman. 2018. "From Soviets to Oligarchs: Inequality and Property in Russia 1905–2016." *Journal of Economic Inequality* 16(2): 189–223.

Nozick, R. 1974. *Anarchy, State, and Utopia*. New York: Basic Books.

Nutt, D., L. A. King, W. Saulsbury, and C. Blakemore. 2007. "Development of a Rational Scale to Assess the Harm of Drugs of Potential Misuse. *The Lancet* 369(9566): 1047–1053.

O'Neill, M., and T. Williamson, eds. 2012. *Property-Owning Democracy: Rawls and Beyond*. Chichester: Wiley-Blackwell.

O'Reilly, P., K. P. Ramirez, and M. A. Stemmer. 2019. "Exchange of Information and Bank Deposits in International Financial Centres." Paris: OECD Taxation Working Papers 46. https://www.sipotra.it/wp-content/uploads/2019/12/Exchange-of-information-and-bank-deposits-in-international-financial-centres.pdf.

Oatley, T. 1999. "How Constraining Is Capital Mobility? The Partisan Hypothesis in an Open Economy." *American Journal of Political Science* 43(4): 1003–1027.

Obadić, A., N. Šimurina, and R. J. Sonora. 2014. "The Effects of Tax Policy and Labour Market Institutions on Income Inequality." *Proceedings of Rijeka Faculty of Economics, Journal of Economics and Business* 32(1): 121–140.

OECD. 2011. "Average of total exports and imports as a percentage of GDP, 2000, 2008 and 2009." In *OECD Science, Technology and Industry Scoreboard 2011* edited by OECD, 176–177. Paris: OECD.

OECD. 2018a. *The Role and Design of Net Wealth Taxes in the OECD*. Paris: Organisation for Economic Co-Operation and Development.

OECD. 2018b. "Tax Revenue." Last accessed November 26, 2022. https://data.oecd.org/tax/tax-revenue.htm.

OECD. 2019a. "Adult Education Level." Last accessed November 26, 2022. https://data.oecd.org/eduatt/adult-education-level.htm#indicator-chart.

OECD. 2019b. "Trade Union Density." Last accessed November 26, 2022. https://stats.oecd.org/Index.aspx?DataSetCode=TUD.

OECD. 2020a. "General Government Spending." Last accessed November 26, 2022. https://data.oecd.org/gga/general-government-spending.htm#indicator-chart.

OECD. 2020b. "Level of GDP per Capita and Productivity." Last accessed November 26, 2022. https://stats.oecd.org/index.aspx?DataSetCode=PDB_LV.

OECD. 2020c. "Public Spending on Education." Last accessed November 26, 2022. https://data.oecd.org/eduresource/public-spending-on-education.htm.

OECD. 2020d. "Tax Revenue." Last accessed November 26, 2022. https://data.oecd.org/tax/tax-revenue.htm.

Olds, Gareth. 2016. "Food Stamp Entrepreneurs." *Harvard Business School Working Papers* 16(143): 1–37.

Olsaretti, S., ed. 2003. *Desert and Justice*. Oxford: Oxford University Press.

Olsaretti, S. 2004. *Liberty, Desert and the Market*. Cambridge: Cambridge University Press.

Omojuwa, J. J. 2012. "Ghana: How the NPP Free Educaiton Policy Adds Up." African Liberty, March 13. https://www.africanliberty.org/2012/03/13/ghana-how-the-npp-free-education-policy-adds-up/.

OpenSecrets. 2018. "Personal Finances." Last accessed November 26, 2022. https://www.opensecrets.org/personal-finances.

OpenSecrets. 2022. "Business-Labor-Ideology Split in PAC and Individual Donations to Candidates, Parties, Super PACs and Outside Spending Groups." Last accessed November 26, 2022. https://www.opensecrets.org/elections-overview/business-labor-ideology-split.

OSAC. 2012. " 'Lightning Kidnappings' in Sao Paulo and Rio de Janeiro." July. http://www.afimac-us.com/bulletin/wp-content/uploads/2012/07/Sao-Paulo-Kidnappings.pdf.

Ostry, J., A. Ghosh, K. Habermeier, M. Chamon, M. Qureshi, and D. Reinhardt. 2010. "Capital Inflows: The Role of Controls." IMF Staff Position Note. https://www.google.com/url?sa=t&rct=j&q=&esrc=s&source=web&cd=&ved=2ahUKEwjht_Xovsz7AhX opIkEHQDVCt8QFnoECBwQAQ&url=https%3A%2F%2Fwww.imf.org%2Fexter nal%2Fpubs%2Fft%2Fspn%2F2010%2Fspn1004.pdf&usg=AOvVaw3PBGu4PJfHK YXXmLioyODK.

Otsuka, M. 2003. *Libertarianism without Inequality*. Oxford: Clarendon Press.

Oxfam. 2015. *Extreme Carbon Inequality*. Nairobi: Oxfam.

Oxfam. 2017. "An Economy for the 99%." Last accessed November 26, 2022. https://oxfamilibrary.openrepository.com/bitstream/handle/10546/620170/bp-economy-for-99-percent-160117-en.pdf;jsessionid=33258DA0F99CF9EE3DAE8B4BBAF14 EE1?sequence=1.

Oxfam. 2020. *Confronting Carbon Inequality*. Nairobi: Oxfam.

Oxfam. 2022. *Inequality Kills*. Nairobi: Oxfam.

Padovano, F., and E. Galli. 2001. "Tax Rates and Economic Growth in the OECD Countries." *Economic Inquiry* 39(1): 44–57.

Painter, N. 2010. *The History of White People*. New York: W. W. Norton.

Papadimitriou, D. B., M. Nikiforos, and G. Zezza. 2019. "Can Redistribution Help Build a More Stable Economy?" *Real-World Economics Teview* (88): 1–22.

Parfit, D. 2000. "Equality or Priority?" In *The Ideal of Equality*, edited by M. Clayton and A. Williams, 81–125. New York: Palgrave Macmillan.

Parker, D. 2005. "Chàvez and the Search for an Alternative to Neoliberalism." *Latin American Perspectives* 32(141): 39–50.

Parkin, Z. 2021. "A Year the Tide Turned in the Fight for Tax Justice." Tax Justice, December 20. https://taxjustice.net/2021/12/20/a-year-the-tide-turned-in-the-fight-for-tax-justice/.

Paskov, M., and C. Dewilde. 2012. "Income Inequality and Solidarity in Europe." Research in Social Stratification and Mobility 30(4): 415–432.

Pasternak, S., and H. King. 2019. Land Back. Toronto: Yellowhead Institute.

Patel, V., J. K. Burns, M. Dhingra, L. Tarver, B. A. Kohrt, and C. Lund. 2018. "Income Inequality and Depression: A Systematic Review and Meta-analysis of the Association and a Scoping Review of Mechanisms." World Psychiatry 17(1): 76–89.

Patriquin, L. 2015. Economic Equality and Direct Democracy in Ancient Athens. New York, NY: Palgrave Macmillan.

Paul, M., W. Darity Jr., and D. Hamilton. 2018. The Federal Job Guarantee: A Policy to Achieve Permanent Full Employment. Washington, DC: Center on Budget and Policy Priorities.

PBO. 2018. Costing a National Guaranteed Basic Income Using the Ontario Basic Income Model. Ottawa: Office of the Parliamentary Budget Officer.

Pen, Jan. 1971. Income Distribution. Translated by T. S. Preston. New York: Praeger.

Pereboom, D. 2014. Free Will, Agency, and Meaning in Life. Oxford: Oxford University Press.

Pérez-González, F. 2006. "Inherited Control and Firm Performance." American Economic Review 96(5): 1559–1588.

Perret, S. 2021. "Why Were Most Wealth Taxes Abandoned and Is This Time Different?" Fiscal Studies 42(3–4): 539–563.

Phillips, B. 2015. "I Was One of the London Rioters. In 2011 We Didn't Know How to Express Our Anger." The Guardian, March 11. https://www.theguardian.com/commentisfree/2015/mar/11/london-rioters-2011-anger-inequality-distrust-police.

Pierotti, R. 2010. Indigenous Knowledge, Ecology, and Evolutionary Biology. New York: Routledge.

Piff, P. K. 2014. "Wealth and the Inflated Self: Class, Entitlement, and Narcissism." Personality and Social Psychology Bulletin 40(1): 34–43.

Piff, P. K., M. W. Kraus, S. Côté, B. H. Cheng, and D. Keltner. 2010. "Having Less, Giving More: The Influence of Social Class on Prosocial Behavior." Journal of Personality and Social Psychology 99(5): 771.

Piff, P. K., D. M. Stancato, S. Côté, R. Mendoza-Denton, and D. Keltner. 2012. "Higher Social Class Predicts Increased Unethical Behavior." Proceedings of the National Academy of Sciences 109(11): 4086–4091.

Piketty, T. 2014. Capital in the Twenty-First Century. Translated by A. Goldhammer. Cambridge, MA: Belknap Press.

Piketty, T. 2020. Capital and Ideology. Cambridge, MA: Belknap Press of Harvard University Press.

Piketty, T. 2022. "The Western Elite Is Preventing Us from Going After the Assets of Russia's Hyper-rich." The Guardian, March 16. https://www.theguardian.com/commentisfree/2022/mar/16/russia-rich-wealthy-western-elites-thomas-piketty.

Piketty, T., and L. Chancel. 2015. Carbon and Inequality: From Kyoto to Paris. Paris: Paris School of Economics.

Piketty, T., E. Saez. 2007. "How Progressive Is the US Federal Tax System? A Historical and International Perspective." Journal of Economic Perspectives 21(1): 3–24.

Piketty, T., and Saez, E. 2013. "Optimal Labor Income Taxation. In *Handbook of Public Economics* edited by A. J. Auerbach, R. Chetty, M. Feldstein, and E. Saez, vol. 5, 391–474. Amsterdam: Elsevier.

Piketty, T., E. Saez, and S. Stantcheva. 2014. "Optimal Taxation of Top Labor Incomes: A Tale of Three Elasticities." *American Economic Journal: Economic Policy* 6(1): 230–271.

Piketty, T., E. Saez, and G. Zucman. 2013. "Rethinking Capital and Wealth Taxation." Piketty Files. Last accessed November 26, 2022. http://www.piketty.pse.ens.fr/files/Pik ettySaez2013RKT.pdf.

Piketty, T., E. Saez, and G. Zucman. 2018. "Distributional National Accounts: Methods and Estimates for the United States." *Quarterly Journal of Economics* 133(2): 553–609.

Pischke, J.-S., K. F. Hallock, and J. DiNardo. 2000. "Unions and the Labor Market for Managers." *IZA Discussion Papers* 150: 1–54.

Pistor, K. 2019. *The Code of Capital*. Princeton, NJ: Princeton University Press.

Pizzigati, S. 2004. *Greed and Good: Understanding and Overcoming the Inequality That Limits Our Lives*. New York: Apex Press.

Pizzigati, S. 2018. *The Case for a Maximum Wage*. Cambridge, UK: Polity Press.

PK. 2020. "Average, Median, Top 1%, and All United States Net Worth Percentiles." DQYDJ. Last accessed November 26, 2022. https://dqydj.com/average-median-top-net-worth-percentiles/.

Pogge, T., and K. Mehta, eds. 2016. *Global Tax Fairness*. Oxford: Oxford University Press.

Polanyi, K. (1944) 2001. *The Great Transformation*. Boston: Beacon Press.

Policardo, L., E. J. S. Carrera, and W. A. Risso. 2019. "Causality between Income Inequality and Corruption in OECD Countries. *World Development Perspectives* 14: 100102.

Ponsford, D. 2021. "Four Men Own Britain's News Media. Is That a Problem for Democracy?" *New Statesman*, February. https://www.newstatesman.com/2021/02/four-men-own-britain-s-news-media-problem-democracy.

Pontusson, J. 2005. *Inequality and Prosperity: Social Europe vs. Liberal America*. Ithaca, NY: Cornell University Press.

Pontusson, J. 2011. "Once Again a Model: Nordic Social Democracy in a Globalized World." In *What's Left of the Left: Democrats and Social Democrats in Challenging Times*, edited by J. Cronin, G. Ross, and J. Shoch, 89–115. Durham, NC: Duke University Press.

Pontusson, J. 2013. "Unionization, Inequality and Redistribution." *British Journal of Industrial Relations* 51(4): 797–825.

Porter, B. 2010. "World Bank Says Asia May Need Capital Controls to Curb Bubbles." Bloomberg, November 8. http://www.bloomberg.com/news/2010-11-08/world-bank-says-asia-may-need-capital-controls-to-curb-fed-created-bubbles.html.

Portes, J., H. Reed, and A. Percy. 2017. *Social Prosperity for the Future: A Proposal for Universal Basic Services*. London: Institute for Global Prosperity.

Prasad, E. S., R. G. Rajan, and A. Subramanian. 2007. "Foreign Capital and Economic Growth." NBER Working Papers 13619, Cambridge, MA. https://www.nber.org/sys tem/files/working_papers/w13619/w13619.pdf.

Prasad, E. S., K. Rogoff, S.-J. Wei, and M. A. Kose. 2003. *Effects of Financial Globalization on Developing Countries: Some Empirical Evidence*. Vol. 220. Washington, DC: International Monetary Fund.

Pruitt, S. 2020. "Broken Treaties with Native American Tribes: Timeline." History, November 10. https://www.history.com/news/native-american-broken-treaties.

Prushinskaya, O. 2020. "Worker Co-ops Show Significant Growth in Latest Survey Data." *Fifty by Fifty*, February. https://www.fiftybyfifty.org/2020/02/worker-co-ops-show-significant-growth-in-latest-survey-data/.

Punwasi, S. 2022. "Canadian Cities Have Seen Up to 90% of New Real Estate Supply Scooped by Investors." Better Dwelling, January 14. https://betterdwelling.com/canadian-cities-have-seen-up-to-90-of-new-real-estate-supply-scooped-by-investors/.

Putnam, R. D., R. Leonardi, and R. Y. Nanetti. 1993. *Making Democracy Work: Civic Traditions in Modern Italy*. Princeton, NJ: Princeton University Press.

Quigley, T. J., C. Crossland, and R. J. Campbell. 2017. "Shareholder Perceptions of the Changing Impact of CEOs: Market Reactions to Unexpected CEO Deaths, 1950–2009." *Strategic Management Journal* 38(4): 939–949.

Raghavan, P. 2017. "Income of Uttar Pradesh Farmers Are Among the Lowest in the Country." *Times of India*, April 8. https://blogs.timesofindia.indiatimes.com/minorityview/income-of-uttar-pradesh-farmers-are-among-the-lowest-in-the-country/.

Ramsay, M. 2005. "A Modest Proposal: The Case for a Maximum Wage." *Contemporary Politics* 11(4): 201–216.

Rawls, J. 1971. *A Theory of Justice*. Cambridge, MA: Harvard University Press.

Rawls, J. 2001. *Justice as Fairness: A Restatement*. Cambridge, MA: Harvard University Press.

Rawls, J., and P. V. Parijs. 2003. "Three Letters on the Law of Peoples and the European Union." In "Autour de Rawls." Special issue of *Revue de philosophie économique* 7: 7–20. http://www.uclouvain.be/cps/ucl/doc/etes/documents/RawlsVanParijs1.Rev.phil.Econ.pdf.

RCMP. 2014. "Missing and Murdered Aboriginal Women: A National Operational Overview." Ottawa: Royal Canadian Mounted Police.

Reich, Rob. 2018. *Just Giving: Why Philanthropy Is Failing Democracy and How It Can Do Better*. Princeton, NJ: Princeton University Press.

Reich, Robert. 2015. *Saving Capitalism*. New York: Alfred A. Knopf.

Reich, Robert. 2019. "Trump Is the Natural Consequence of Our Anti-democracy Decade." *The Guardian*, December 8. https://www.theguardian.com/commentisfree/2019/dec/08/donald-trump-citizens-united-anti-democracy-decade.

Reinhart, C. M., and K. S. Rogoff. 2009. *This Time Is Different: Eight Centuries of Financial Folly*. Princeton, NJ: Princeton University Press.

Riddell, C. 2004. "Union Certification Success under Voting versus Card-Check Procedures: Evidence from British Columbia, 1978–1998." *ILR Review* 57(4): 493–517.

Rigby, E., and G. C. Wright. 2013. "Political Parties and the Representation of the Poor." *American Journal of Political Science* 57(3): 552–565.

Ring, M. A. K. 2021. "Wealth Taxation and Household Saving: Evidence from Assessment Discontinuities in Norway." *Working Paper* 1–84. https://mariusring.github.io/web/Ring_wealth_tax.pdf.

Ritchie, H., and M. Roser. 2020. "CO_2 Emissions." Our World in Data. Last accessed November 26, 2022. https://ourworldindata.org/co2-emissions.

Roberton, T., M. Daffern, and R. S. Bucks. 2014. "Maladaptive Emotion Regulation and Aggression in Adult Offenders." *Psychology, Crime & Law* 20(10): 933–954.

Robeyns, I. 2017. "Having Too Much." *NOMOS: American Society for Political and Legal Philosophy* 58: 1–44.

Robeyns, I. 2022. "Why Limitarianism?" *Journal of Political Philosophy* 30(2): 249–270.

Rodrik, D. 1998. "Who Needs Capital-Account Convertibility?" Working Paper. Cambridge, MA: Harvard University. https://policydialogue.org/files/publications/papers/Capital_Accnt_Convertability.pdf.

Roemer, J. 1988. *Free to Lose*. Cambridge, MA: Harvard University Press.

Roemer, J. 1993. "A Pragmatic Theory of Responsibility for the Egalitarian Planner." *Philosophy & Public Affairs* 22(2): 146–166.

Roemer, J. 1998. *Equality of Opportunity*. Cambridge, MA: Harvard University Press.

Roemer, J. 2003. "Defending Equality of Opportunity." *The Monist* 86(2): 261–282.

Roemer, J. 2020. "What Is Socialism Today? Conceptions of a Cooperative Economy." New Haven, CT: Cowles Foundation Discussion Paper 2220. https://www.google.com/url?sa=t&rct=j&q=&esrc=s&source=web&cd=&cad=rja&uact=8&ved=2ahUKEwixiMncx8z7AhWykYkEHeUFB7IQFnoECA0QAQ&url=https%3A%2F%2Fcowles.yale.edu%2Fsites%2Fdefault%2Ffiles%2Fd2220.pdf&usg=AOvVaw3CsNxfcM7bpLkORHLQsWnw.

Rognlie, M. 2016. "Deciphering the Fall and Rise in the Net Capital Share: Accumulation or Scarcity?" *Brookings Papers on Economic Activity* 2015(1): 1–69.

Roosevelt, F. D. 1936. "Speech before the 1936 Democratic National Convention: A Rendezvous with Destiny." L. Patrick Huges Website. Last accessed November 26, 2022. http://www.austincc.edu/lpatrick/his2341/fdr36acceptancespeech.htm.

Rose, S. J., and H. I. Hartmann. 2018. *Still a Man's Labor Market*. Wasington, DC: Institute for Women's Policy Research.

Rosenfeld, J., and M. Kleykamp. 2012. "Organized Labor and Racial Wage Inequality in the United States." *American Journal of Sociology* 117(5): 1460–1502.

Rosset, J. 2013. "Are the Policy Preferences of Relatively Poor Citizens Under-represented in the Swiss Parliament?" *The Journal of Legislative Studies* 19(4): 490–504.

Rothbard, M. 1982. *The Ethics of Liberty*. Atlantic Highlands, NJ: Humanities Press.

Rothschild, J., and J. A. Whitt. 1986. *The Cooperative Workplace*. Cambridge: Cambridge University Press.

Rufrancos, H., M. Power, K. E. Pickett, and R. Wilkinson. 2013. "Income Inequality and Crime: A Review and Explanation of the Time-Series Evidence." *Sociology and Criminology* 1(1): 1–9.

Russell, B. 1923. *A Free Man's Worship*. Portland, ME: T. B. Mosher.

Saborowski, C., S. Sanya, H. Weisfeld, and J. Yepez. 2014. "Effectiveness of Capital Outflow Restrictions." *IMF Working Paper* 14(8): 1–34.

Sachs, J. 2005. *The End of Poverty*. New York: Penguin Books.

Sadurski, W. 1985. *Giving Desert Its Due: Social Justice and Legal Theory*. Dordrecht: D. Reidel.

Saez, E., J. Slemrod, and S. H. Giertz. 2012. "The Elasticity of Taxable Income with Respect to Marginal Tax Rates: A Critical Review." *Journal of Economic Literature* 50(1): 3–50.

Saez, E., and G. Zucman. 2019a. "Comparison of the Warren and Sanders Wealth Tax Proposals (September 22, 2019)." Gabriel Zucman Webpage, September 22. http://gabriel-zucman.eu/files/saez-zucman-wealthtax-sanders-online.pdf.

Saez, E., and G. Zucman. 2019b. "How Would a Progressive Wealth Tax Work? Evidence from the Economics Literature." Unpublished paper.

Saez, E., and G. Zucman. 2019c. "Letter to Senator Warren (January 19, 2019)." Gabriel Zucman Webpage, January 19. https://gabriel-zucman.eu/files/saez-zucman-wealthtax-warren.pdf.

Saez, E., and G. Zucman. 2019d. "Response to Summers and Sarin, 'A Wealth Tax Presents a Revenue Estimation Puzzle.'" *Washington Post*, April 4. https://gabriel-zucman.eu/files/saez-zucman-responseto-summers-sarin.pdf.

Saez, E., and G. Zucman. 2019e. *The Triumph of Injustice*. New York: W. W. Norton.

Sahlins, M. 2005. "The Original Affluent Society." In *Culture in Practice: Selected Essays*, edited by M. Sahlins, 95–138. New York: Zone Books.

Sandel, M. 2020. *The Tyranny of Merit*. New York: Farrar, Straus and Giroux.

Sanders, B. 2019. "Tax on Extreme Wealth." Friends of Bernie Sanders. Last accessed November 26, 2022. https://berniesanders.com/issues/tax-extreme-wealth.

Sarin, N. 2021. "The Case for a Robust Attack on the Tax Gap." U.S. Department of the Treasury, September 7. https://home.treasury.gov/news/featured-stories/the-case-for-a-robust-attack-on-the-tax-gap.

Sarin, N., and L. Summers. 2019. "A Broader Tax Base That Closes Loopholes Would Raise More Money Than Plans by Ocasio-Cortez and Warren." *Boston Globe*, March 28. https://www.bostonglobe.com/opinion/2019/03/28/broader-tax-base-that-closes-loopholes-would-raise-more-money-than-plans-ocasio-cortez-and-warren/Bv16zhT AkuEx08SiNrjx9J/story.html.

Saunt, C. 2021. "The Invasion of America." Aeon, January 7. https://aeon.co/essays/how-were-1-5-billion-acres-of-land-so-rapidly-stolen.

SBECouncil. 2018. "Facts and Data on Small Business and Entrepreneurship." Small Business & Entreprenurship Council. Last accessed November 26, 2022. https://sbe council.org/about-us/facts-and-data/.

Scanlon, K., C. Whitehead, and M. F. Arrigoitia, eds. 2014. *Social Housing in Europe*. Chichester: Wiley Blackwell.

Scheffler, S. 2003. "What Is Egalitarianism?" *Philosophy & Public Affairs* 31(1): 5–39.

Scheffler, S. 2005. "Choice, Circumstance, and the Value of Equality." *Politics, Philosophy & Economics* 4(1): 5–28.

Scheidel, W. 2017. *The Great Leveler: Violence and the History of Inequality from the Stone Age to the Twenty-First Century*. Princeton, NJ: Princeton University Press.

Scheidel, W., and S. J. Friesen. 2009. "The Size of the Economy and the Distribution of Income in the Roman Empire." *Journal of Roman Studies* 99: 61–91.

Scheuer, F., and J. Slemrod. 2021. "Taxing Our Wealth." *Journal of Economic Perspectives* 35(1): 207–230.

Scheve, K., and D. Stasavage. 2016. *Taxing the Rich: A History of Fiscal Fairness in the United States and Europe*. Princeton, NJ: Princeton University Press.

Schmitt, J. 2013. *Why Does the Minimum Wage Have No Discernible Effect on Employment?* Washington, DC: Center for Economic and Policy Research.

Schor, J. B. 2010. *Plenitude*. New York: Penguin Press.

Schulte, B. 2014. *Overwhelmed*. New York: Sarah Crichton Books.

Schweickart, D. 2011. *After Capitalism*. 2nd ed. Lanham, MD: Rowman & Littlefield.

Scott, J. C. 2017. *Against the Grain*. New Haven, CT: Yale University Press.

Seim, D. 2017. "Behavioral Responses to Wealth Taxes: Evidence from Sweden." *American Economic Journal: Economic Policy* 9(4): 395–421.

Sen, A. 1982. "Just Deserts." The New York Review, March 4. https://www.nybooks.com/articles/1982/03/04/just-deserts/.

Sen, A. 1992. *Inequality Reexamined*. Cambrdige Harvard University Press.

Sen, A. 2009. *The Idea of Justice*. London: Allen Lane.

Shakow, D. J. 2016. "A Wealth Tax: Taxing the Estates of the Living." *Boston College Law Review* 57: 947–978.

Shaxson, N. 2011. *Treasure Islands: Tax Havens and the Men Who Stole the World.* London: Bodley Head.

Shaxson, N. 2018. "How to Crack Down on Tax Havens: Start with the Banks." *Foreign Affairs* 97: 94–107.

Shaxson, N., and J. Christensen. 2016. "Tax Competitiveness—A Dangerous Obsession." In *Global Tax Fairness,* edited by T. Pogge and K. Mehta, 265–297. Oxford: Oxford University Press.

Sher, G. 1987. *Desert.* Princeton, NJ: Princeton University Press.

Sher, G. 2003. "Effort and Imagination." In *Desert and Justice,* edited by S. Olsaretti, 205–217. Oxford: Oxford University Press.

Shields, L. 2012. "The Prospects for Sufficientarianism." *Utilitas* 24(1): 101–117.

Shields, L. 2020. "Sufficientarianism." *Philosophy Compass* 15(11): 1–10.

Shrubsole, G. 2019. *Who Owns England? How We Lost Our Green and Pleasant Land and How to Take It Back.* London: William Collins.

Siddiqi, A., I. Kawachi, L. Berkman, C. Hertzman, and S. Subramanian. 2012. "Education Determines a Nation's Health, but What Determines Educational Outcomes? A Cross-national Comparative Analysis." *Journal of Public Health Policy* 33(1): 1–15.

Sidgwick, H. (1907) 1999. "Justice as Desert." In *What Do We Deserve? A Reader on Justice and Desert,* edited by L. P. Pojman and O. McLeod, 47–55. Oxford: Oxford University Press.

Simmons, A. J. 2010. "Ideal and Nonideal Theory." *Philosophy & Public Affairs* 38(1): 5–36.

Simon, H. A. 2000. "Public Administration in Today's World of Organizations and Markets." *PS: Political Science and Politics* 33(4): 749–756.

Singer, D. 1988. *Is Socialism Doomed? The Meaning of Mitterrand.* New York: Oxford University Press.

SkyNews. 2016. "New Duke of Westminster 'Owns Half of London.'" https://news.sky.com/story/new-duke-of-westminster-owns-half-of-london-10530530.

Slaughter, A.-M. 2012. "Why Women Still Can't Have It All." *The Atlantic* 310(1): 84–102.

Slemrod, J. B., ed. 2000. *Does Atlas Shrug? The Economic Consequences of Taxing the Rich.* Cambridge, MA: Harvard University Press.

Slemrod, J. 2001. "A General Model of the Behavioral Response to Taxation." *International Tax and Public Finance* 8(2): 119–128.

Slemrod, J. 2007. "Cheating Ourselves: The Economics of Tax Evasion." *Journal of Economic Perspectives* 21(1): 25–48.

Smith, S. 2017. "Why People Are Rich and Poor: Republicans and Democrats Have Very Different Views." Pew Research, May 2. https://www.pewresearch.org/fact-tank/2017/05/02/why-people-are-rich-and-poor-republicans-and-democrats-have-very-different-views/.

Sniderman, A. S. 2013. "The Man Wrongly Attributed with Uttering 'Kill the Indian in the Child.'" *Maclean's,* November 8. https://www.macleans.ca/culture/books/conversations-with-a-dead-man-the-legacy-of-duncan-campbell-scott/.

Solow, R. M. 1957. "Technical Change and the Aggregate Production Function." *Review of Economics and Statistics* 39(3): 312–320.

Solt, F. 2008. "Economic Inequality and Democratic Political Engagement." *American Journal of Political Science* 52(1): 48–60.

Spencer, C. M., M. Mendez, and S. M. Stith. 2019. "The Role of Income Inequality on Factors Associated with Male Physical Intimate Partner Violence Perpetration: A Meta-analysis." *Aggression and Violent Behavior* 48: 116–123.

Spinner-Halev, J. 2017. "Liberalism, Markets, and Responsibility." *Journal of Politics* 79(4): 1329–1341.

SPLC. 2019. "Hate Groups Reach Record High." February 19. https://www.splcenter.org/news/2019/02/19/hate-groups-reach-record-high.

Standing, G. 2002. *Beyond the New Paternalism: Basic Security as Equality.* London: Verso.

Standing, G. 2011. *The Precariat.* London: Bloomsbury Academic.

Statista. 2020. "Total Financial Assets Value as a Part of Individual Wealth across India from FY 2015 to FY 2019." Last accessed November 28, 2022. https://www.statista.com/statistics/723464/india-total-financial-assets-in-individual-wealth/.

StatisticsCanada. 2012. "Education Indicators in Canada: An International Perspective." Ottawa: Statistics Canada. http://cmec.ca/Publications/Lists/Publications/Attachments/286/Education-Indicators-Canada-International-Perspective-2012.pdf.

Stebbins, S., and E. Comen. 2020. "How Much Do You Need to Make to Be in the Top 1% in Every State? Here's the List." *USA Today,* July 1. https://www.usatoday.com/story/money/2020/07/01/how-much-you-need-to-make-to-be-in-the-1-in-every-state/112002276/.

Stellar, J. E., V. M. Manzo, M. W. Kraus, and D. Keltner. 2012. "Class and Compassion: Socioeconomic Factors Predict Responses to Suffering." *Emotion* 12(3): 449.

Stenkula, M., D. Johansson, and G. Du Rietz. 2014. "Marginal Taxation on Labour Income in Sweden from 1862 to 2010." *Scandinavian Economic History Review* 62(2): 163–187.

Stephany, F. 2017. "Who Are Your Joneses? Socio-specific Income Inequality and Trust." *Social Indicators Research* 134(3): 877–898.

Stern, K. 2013. "Why the Rich Don't Give to Charity." *The Atlantic,* April. https://www.theatlantic.com/magazine/archive/2013/04/why-the-rich-dont-give/309254/.

Stiglitz, J. 1996. "Some Lessons from the East Asian Miracle." *World Bank Research Observer* 11(2): 151–177.

Stiglitz, J. 2002. *Globalization and Its Discontents.* London: Penguin.

Stiglitz, J. 2007. "Prizes, Not Patents." *Post-Autistic Economics Review* 42: 46–47.

Stiglitz, J. 2012. *The Price of Inequality.* New York: W. W. Norton.

Stiglitz, J. 2016. "Inequality and Economic Growth." In *Rethinking Capitalism,* edited by M. Jacobs and M. Mazzucato, 135–155. Chichester: John Wiley & Sons.

Stiglitz, J. 2019. *People, Power, and Profits: Progressive Capitalism for an Age of Discontent.* London: Allen Lane.

Stiglitz, J., A. Sen, and J.-P. Fitoussi. 2009. *Report by the Commission on the Measurement of Economic Performance and Social Progress.* Paris: Commission on the Measurement of Economic Performance and Social Progress.

Stokey, N. L., and S. Rebelo. 1995. "Growth Effects of Flat-Rate Taxes." *Journal of Political Economy* 103(3): 519–550.

Strand, P. J., and N. A. Mirkay. 2020. "Racialized Tax Inequity: Wealth, Racism, and the US System of Taxation." *Northwestern Journal of Law and Social Policy* 15(3): 265–304.

Summers, L. H., and N. Sarin. 2019. "A 'Wealth Tax' Presents a Revenue Estimation Puzzle." *Washington Post,* April 4. https://www.washingtonpost.com/opinions/2019/04/04/wealth-tax-presents-revenue-estimation-puzzle/.

Swank, D., and H.-G. Betz. 2003. "Globalization, the Welfare State and Right-Wing Populism in Western Europe." *Socio-Economic Review* 1(2): 215–245.

Sweeney, P. 2015. *Tackling Tax Evasion, Avoidance and Tax Havens*. Brussels: European Trade Union Institute.

Tanzi, V. 2016. "Lakes, Oceans, and Taxes: Why the World Needs a World Tax Authority." In *Global Tax Fairness*, edited by T. Pogge and K. Mehta, 251–264. Oxofrd: Oxford University Press.

Tartar, A. 2017. "How the Populist Right Is Redrawing the Map of Europe." Bloomberg. https://www.bloomberg.com/graphics/2017-europe-populist-right/.

Tawney, R. H. 1952. *Equality*. 4th ed. London: George Allen & Unwin.

Tay, L., and E. Diener. 2011. "Needs and Subjective Well-being around the World." *Journal of Personality and Social Psychology* 101(2): 354.

Taylor, C. 1989. *Sources of the Self: The Making of the Modern Identity*. Cambridge: Cambridge University Press.

Taylor, K.-Y. 2018. "How Real Estate Segregated America." *Dissent* 65(4): 23–32.

Thomas, L. 2021. "Walmart Hikes Hourly Pay by $1 for More Than 550,000 Workers ahead of the Holidays." CNBC, September 2. https://www.cnbc.com/2021/09/02/walmart-hikes-hourly-pay-by-1-for-over-550000-workers.html.

Tilly, C. 1985. "War-Making and State-Making as Organized Crime." In *Bringing the State Back In*, edited by P. Evans, D. Rueschemeyer, and T. Skocpol, 169–191. Cambridge: Cambridge University Press.

Timmer, D. 2021. "Justice, Thresholds, and the Three Claims of Sufficientarianism." *Journal of Political Philosophy* 30(3): 298–323.

TJN. 2020. "Country by Country Reporting." Tax Justice Network, November 14. https://taxjustice.net/topics/country-by-country-reporting/.

TJN. 2022. "10 Measures to Expose Sanctioned Russian oligarchs' Hidden Assets." Tax Justice Network, March 3. https://taxjustice.net/press/10-measures-to-expose-sanctioned-russian-oligarchs-hidden-assets/.

TRC. 2015. *A Knock on the Door: The Essential History of Residential Schools from the Truth and Reconciliation Commission of Canada*. Winnipeg: University of Manitoba Press.

Tronto, J. C. 2013. *Caring Democracy: Markets, Equality, and Justice*. New York: New York University Press.

Troup, E., J. Barnett, and K. Bullock. 2020. "The Administration of a Wealth Tax" London: Wealth Tax Commission Evidence Paper 11. https://www.wealthandpolicy.com/wp/EP11_Administration.pdf.

Ura, J. D., and C. R. Ellis. 2008. "Income, Preferences, and the Dynamics of Policy Responsiveness." *PS: Political Science & Politics* 41(4): 785–794.

Urban Institute. 2017. "Nine Charts about Wealth Inequality in America (Updated)." Urban Institute, October 5. https://apps.urban.org/features/wealth-inequality-charts/.

US Census. 2018a. "Health Insurance Coverage in the United States: 2017." United States Census Bureau, September 12. https://www.census.gov/library/publications/2018/demo/p60-264.html.

US Census. 2018b. *PINC-01. Selected Characteristics of People 15 Years Old and Over by Total Money Income in 2018, Work Experience in 2018, Race, Hispanic Origin, and Sex*. Washington, DC: United States Census Bureau.

US Census. 2020. "Income and Poverty in the United States: 2019." United States Census Bureau, September 15. https://www.census.gov/library/publications/2020/demo/p60-270.html.

US Census. 2021a. "Table A-6. Earnings Summary Measures by Selected Characteristics: 2019 and 2020." United States Census Bureau. Last accessed November 28, 2022. https://www.census.gov/data/tables/2021/demo/income-poverty/p60-273.html.

US Census. 2021b. "Table P-7. Region—All People (Both Sexes Combined) by Median and Mean Income: 1974 to 2020." Last accessed November 28, 2022. https://www.census.gov/data/tables/time-series/demo/income-poverty/historical-income-people.html.

US Department of Housing and Urban Development. 2018. "The 2018 Annual Homeless Assessment Report (AHAR) to Congress." Last accessed November 28, 2022. https://files.hudexchange.info/resources/documents/2018-AHAR-Part-1.pdf.

Uslaner, E. M. 2008. Corruption, Inequality, and the Rule of Law. New York: Cambridge University Press.

Uslaner, E. M., and M. Brown. 2005. "Inequality, Trust, and Civic Engagement." American Politics Research 33(6): 868–894.

USSC. 2019a. "Quick Facts: Marijuana Trafficking Offences." Last accessed November 28, 2022. https://www.ussc.gov/sites/default/files/pdf/research-and-publications/quick-facts/Marijuana_FY18.pdf.

USSC. 2019b. "Quick Facts: Robbery Offences." Last accessed November 28, 2022. https://www.ussc.gov/sites/default/files/pdf/research-and-publications/quick-facts/Robbery_FY18.pdf.

USSC. 2019c. "Quick Facts: Tax Fraud Offences." Last accessed November 28, 2022. https://www.ussc.gov/sites/default/files/pdf/research-and-publications/quick-facts/Tax_Fraud_FY18.pdf.

Valdés-Prieto, S., and M. Soto. 1998. "The Effectiveness of Capital Controls: Theory and Evidence from Chile." Empirica 25(2): 133–164.

Van Parijs, P. 1995. Real Freedom for All. Oxford: Clarendon Press.

Varnum, M. E., C. Blais, R. S. Hampton, and G. A. Brewer. 2015. "Social Class Affects Neural Empathic Responses." Culture and Brain 3(2): 122–130.

Vartia, L. 2008. "How Do Taxes Affect Investment and Productivity? An Industry-Level Analysis of OECD Countries." Paris: OECD Economic Department Working Papers 656. https://www.oecd-ilibrary.org/content/paper/230022721067.

Veblen, T. (1918) 2007. The Theory of the Leisure Class. Oxford: Oxford University Press.

Vermeylen, G., G. Ziniel, J. Hurley, K. Jurczak, and M. Lyly-Yrjänäinen. 2008. Women at Work: Paths to Equality. Dublin: European Foundation for the Improvement of Living and Working Conditions.

Villalonga, B., and R. Amit. 2006. "How Do Family Ownership, Control and Management Affect Firm Value?" Journal of Financial Economics 80(2): 385–417.

Visser, J. 2002. "The First Part-Time Economy in the World: A Model to Be Followed?" Journal of European Social Policy 12(1): 23–42.

Vitale, A. 2018. The End of Policing. Verso: London.

Vitols, S. 2021. "Board Level Employee Representation and Tax Avoidance in Europe." Accounting, Economics, and Law: A Convivium 2021: 1–22.

Vlandas, T., and D. Halikiopoulou. 2019. "Does Unemployment Matter? Economic Insecurity, Labour Market Policies and the Far-Right Vote in Europe." European Political Science 18(3): 421–438.

Voigt, K. 2007. "The Harshness Objection: Is Luck Egalitarianism Too Harsh on the Victims of Option Luck?" Ethical Theory and Moral Practice 10(4): 389–407.

Volacu, A., and A. C. Dumitru. 2019. "Assessing Non-intrinsic Limitarianism." *Philosophia* 47(1): 249–264.

Waldron, J. 2020. "Property and Ownership." Stanford Encyclopedia of Philosophy, March 21. https://plato.stanford.edu/archives/sum2020/entries/property/.

Walker, H. 2021. "Wealthiest Americans' Tax Avoidance—The Shock Report's Most Striking Details." *The Guardian*, June 10. https://www.theguardian.com/inequality/2021/jun/10/wealthiest-americans-tax-report-details.

Waller, B. 2011. *Against Moral Responsibility.* Cambridge, MA: MIT Press.

Waller, B. 2018. *The Injustice of Punishment.* New York: Routledge.

Waller, B. 2020. *Free Will, Moral Responsibility, and the Desire to Be a God.* Lanham, MD: Lexington Books.

Wang, L., and J. K. Murnighan. 2014. "Money, Emotions, and Ethics across Individuals and Countries." *Journal of Business Ethics* 125(1): 163–176.

Weber, Max. (1904) 2003. *The Protestant Ethic and the Spirit of Capitalism.* Translated by Talcott Parsons. Mineola, NY: Dover.

WEF. 2018. *The Global Gender Gap Report.* Geneva: World Economic Forum.

Weisbrot, M., R. Ray, L. Sandoval. 2009. *The Chavez Administration at 10 Years: The Economy and Social Indicators.* Washington, DC: Center for Economic and Policy Research.

Westin, R. A. 2013. "Tax Exiles: A Comparative Study (Part 1)." *Journal of International Taxation* 24(3): 22–33.

Wheeler, S. C. 1980. "Natural Property Rights as Body Rights." *Nous* 14(2): 171–193.

White, P. R. 2019. "Grounds for Being Fired for Just Cause." Employment Law 101. Last accessed November 28, 2022. https://employmentlaw101.ca/termination-for-cause/grounds-for-being-fired-for-just-cause/.

WHO. 2018. "A Child under 15 Dies Every 5 Seconds around the World." World Health Organization, September 18. https://www.who.int/news/item/18-09-2018-a-child-under-15-dies-every-5-seconds-around-the-world-.

Whyte, W. F., and K. K. Whyte. 1988. *Making Mondragon: The Growth and Dynamics of the Worker Cooperative Complex.* Ithaca, NY: ILR Press.

Widerquist, K. 2010. "Lockean Theories of Property: Justifications for Unilateral Appropriation." *Public Reason* 2(1): 3–26.

Widerquist, K. 2013. "What (If Anything) Can We Learn from the Negative Income Tax Experiments?" In *Basic Income: An Anthology of Contemporary Research,* edited by K. Widerquist, J. A. Noguera, Y. Vanderborght, and J. D. Wispelaere, 216–239. Chichester: Wiley Blackwell.

Widerquist, K. 2017. "The Cost of Basic Income: Back-of-the-Envelope Calculations." *Basic Income Studies* 12(2): 107–118.

Widfeldt, A. 2018. *The Growth of the Radical Right in Nordic Countries.* Washinton, DC: Migration Policy Institute.

Wilkinson, R. 2011. "How Economic Inequality Harms Society." TED Talks. Last accessed November 28, 2022. https://www.ted.com/talks/richard_wilkinson_how_economic_inequality_harms_societies?language=en

Wilkinson, Richard, and Kate E. Pickett. 2006. "Income Inequality and Population Health: A Review and Explanation of the Evidence." *Social Science & Medicine* 62(7): 1768–1784.

Wilkinson, Richard, and Kate Pickett. 2010. *The Spirit Level: Why Equality Is Better for Everyone.* London: Penguin Books.

Wilkinson, Richard, and Kate Pickett. 2018. *The Inner Level*. London: Penguin.

Williams, Z. 2015. "Katie Hopkins Calling Migrants Vermin Recalls the Darkest Events of History." *The Guardian*, April 19. https://www.theguardian.com/commentisfree/2015/apr/19/katie-hopkins-migrants-vermin-darkest-history-drownings.

Winseck, D. 2015. "Canadian Newspaper Editorial Election Endorsements: Elite and Out of Sync." Policy Options, November 3. https://policyoptions.irpp.org/2015/11/03/canadian-newspaper-editorial-endorsements-in-the-2015-federal-election-elite-and-out-of-sync/.

Winters, J. A. 2017. "Wealth Defense and the Complicity of Liberal Democracy." *NOMOS: American Society for Political and Legal Philosophy* 58: 158–225.

Wittgenstein, L. (1921) 2014. *Tractatus Logico-philosophicus* Peterborough: Broadview Press.

Wolff, E. 2010. "Recent Trends in Household Wealth in the United States: Rising Debt and the Middle-Class Squeeze—An Update to 2007." Annandale-on-Hudson, NY: Levy Economics Institute Working Paper Collection 589. https://www.econstor.eu/bitstream/10419/57025/1/621628832.pdf.

World Bank. 2015. "Overview." The World Bank. Last accessed November 28, 2022. http://www.worldbank.org/en/topic/poverty/overview.

World Bank. 2017. "GINI Index (World Bank Estimate)." The World Bank. Last accessed November 28, 2022. https://data.worldbank.org/indicator/SI.POV.GINI/.

World Bank. 2018. "Nearly Half the World Lives on Less than \$5.50 a Day." October 17. https://www.worldbank.org/en/news/press-release/2018/10/17/nearly-half-the-world-lives-on-less-than-550-a-day.

World Bank. 2020. "Poverty: Overview." The World Bank. Last accessed November 28, 2022. https://www.worldbank.org/en/topic/poverty/overview.

Wright, E. O. 2010. *Envisioning Real Utopias*. London: Verso.

Wrigley, E. A. 2010. *Energy and the English Industrial Revolution*. Cambridge: Cambridge University Press.

Wudrick, A. 2019. "Should There Be a Wealth Tax on the Very Rich?" *The Star*, September 24. https://www.thestar.com/opinion/contributors/thebigdebate/2019/09/24/should-there-be-a-wealth-tax-on-the-very-rich.html.

Yeyati, E., S. Schmukler, and N. Van Horen. 2008. "Crises, Capital Controls, and Financial Integration." Washington, DC: World Bank Policy Research Working Papers 4770. http://papers.ssrn.com/sol3/papers.cfm?abstract_id=1297809.

Young, C., and C. Varner. 2011. "Millionaire Migration and State Taxation of Top Incomes: Evidence from a Natural Experiment." *National Tax Journal* 64(2): 255–284.

Zamagni, S., and V. Zamagni. 2010. *Cooperative Enterprise: Facing the Challenges of Globalization*. Cheltenham: Edward Elgar.

Zehr, H. 2015. *Changing Lenses: Restorative Justice for Our Times*. Harrisonburg, VA: Herald Press.

Zinn, H. 1996. *A People's History of the United States*. 2nd ed. New York: Longman.

Zinn, H. 1999. *Marx in Soho: A Play on History*. Boston: South End Press.

Zoutman, F. T. 2018. "The Elasticity of Taxable Wealth: Evidence from the Netherlands." *Working Paper* 1–24. Bergen: Norwegian School of Economics. https://nta.confex.com/nta/2019/mediafile/ExtendedAbstract/Paper2418/Zoutman%20%282018%29%20Wealth%20tax%20Netherlands.pdf.

Zucman, G. 2015. *The Hidden Wealth of Nations: The Scourge of Tax Havens*. Chicago: University of Chicago Press.

Index

*For the benefit of digital users, indexed terms that span two pages (e.g., 52–53) may, on
occasion, appear on only one of those pages.*

Figures are indicated by *f* following the page number